Price Guide to

# Oriental
## Antiques

Second
Edition

Sandra Andacht, Nancy Garthe and Robert Mascarelli

Cover Design: Heather Miller
Layout: Group One Graphics

Copyright © 1984
Sandra Andacht, Nancy Garthe, Robert Mascarelli

ISBN 0-87069-382-4
Library of Congress
Catalog Card Number 79-65308

*10  9  8  7  6  5  4  3  2  1*

For those who must know and be sure of what they're buying, or selling.

THE ORIENTALIA JOURNAL is a comprehensive guide for collectors and dealers.

Bi-monthly you'll receive a journal filled with special features and illustrations on such topics as cloisonné, prints, porcelain, pottery, rugs, and all other aspects of orientalia, including influence products from all over the world. A question and answer column provides you with active reader responses.

**THE ORIENTALIA JOURNAL published 6 times per year costs $12/1 yr., $22/2 yrs. (U.S. and Canada), foreign rate $21 per year (payable in US funds). A check or money order to be sent to THE ORIENTALIA JOURNAL, POB 94P, Little Neck, New York 11363.**

Published by

Wallace-Homestead Book Company
One Corporate Place
1501 Forty-second Street
West Des Moines, Iowa 50265

# Contents

# Acknowledgments

No undertaking of this magnitude could have been accomplished without the help of many. The authors wish to express their admiration and gratitude to those whose input helped to produce this publication, the first in its field.

The photography of many items pictured herein is due to the expertise of Daniel Stone, Bill Garthe, and co-author Nancy Garthe. Carl Andacht is responsible for the Chinese and Japanese motifs line art and layout. The coordination of Chinese ceramics was accomplished by Gloria Mascarelli, and Sato Hideo was again generous with his time in translating many Japanese marks.

A special thanks is extended to Joe Franklin and WOR-TV, New York, and to Christie's, New York, Christie's, London, and Christie's East, New York, for their courtesy and cooperation in providing information and photographs.

The authors also wish to express sincere appreciation for the courtesies extended by the following: Leon Andors (Ancraft), New York; The Antique Trader Weekly; Tom and Lynn Austern, E. Meadow, N.Y.; Ed Babka; William Doyle Galleries; E & E Collectibles & Antiques; Diane Finegold (Finegold Marketing), New York; Chase Gilmore Art Galleries; The Hamilton Collection; Dorothy Hammond; Kyle Husfloen; I Ching Antique Gallery; Interiors Unlimited, Goodlettsville, Tenn.; Jade Butterfly; Jean Keats (Compliments Oriental Antiques), Pt. Wash., N.Y.; Kelly's Worldwide Antiques, Alexandria, Va.; Jerry King, Tyler, Tex.; Dr. Michael Krassner; Bob Law; Maine Antiques Digest; David Migden (Old Horizons), New York; Kathleen Norton, Norton's Objet's d' Art; Sam Pennington; Phillips; Gardner Pond; Recollection Gallery, Brighton, Mich.; Renee's Antique Shoppe, Winthrop, Mass.; A. Christian Revi, Cumberland, Md.; Ron Roberts, Tulsa, Okla.; The Rosett Collection, Forest Hills, N.Y.; Sign of the Crane; Florence Simon; Alan and Ina Sims (Ming and Ching Antiques), Hauppauge, N.Y.; Lita Solis-Cohen; Sotheby Parke Bernet, Inc.; Jabe Tarter; TK Oriental Antiques of Williamsburg; Zora's Antiques; and those collectors who allowed us to photograph items in their collections but who wish to remain anonymous.

Orientalia — for your support, your suggestions, and your patronage. We have designed this book with you in mind, and in future editions we shall strive to enlarge, improve, and reassess the various categories according to your needs.

# Introduction

This publication is the result of a collaboration among three authors, expert in their respective fields. In the increasingly important field of Oriental Art, it was felt that a specialized guide such as this would be of value to many.

All of the items within this volume are not "antique" by the strict definition. We have tried to provide a cross section of the available Oriental antiques market, thereby including objects selling for thousands, as well as those within the budget of all. This price guide reflects offerings currently available and the price ranges for which they sell. We have tried to maintain a geographical cross section in the prices herein. Unless otherwise noted, all entries are in perfect condition (relatively speaking, of course, as an encrusted bronze vase over 2,000 years old cannot be considered "imperfect"). Where items have been sold in "as is" condition, and where such information has been made known to us, it is so stated in the description.

Some descriptions may be erroneous, but since the authors did not have the opportunity to personally examine each of the many items listed, descriptions from dealers and auction houses have been incorporated, some of which may be incorrect. Also, because terminology is subjective, what may be a "bowl" to one may be a "dish" to another, or a "plate" may be termed a "charger" (which technically should be dished). Through diligence, dedication, and devotion, the authors have attempted to unravel these complexities, but some remnants must remain.

Unlike other similar publications, which incorporate terms that are in common usage by dealers (often erroneous or unreliable), the nomenclature and terminology used in this price guide are proper and authentic.

There will be some categories that our readers may desire to be included that do not appear in this volume. We encourage your input so that such additions may be considered for future editions. We strive to make this a valuable reference for your library.

**NOTE: All illustrations which are asterisked (\*) are items which were sold at Christie's in New York City, and the value listed for each of these is the price realized at auction.**

# Oriental Antiques
# From A to Z

*Abumi (pair) silver inlay*

## Abumi
*(Japanese)*

Abumi (stirrups) were generally made of iron and at times were adorned with various forms of decorations. Some forms of abumi provided comfort for the foot by having a raised heel and cover for the front of the foot. Others were curved in the front. Abumi are among the many varied antique items which form part of the overall armor equipment.

Abumi (single), Yoshiro-zogan, 16th century, pierced neck panel and overall stylized foliage scrolls . . . . . . . . . . . . . . . . . . . . . . . . . . . . . . . . . . . . . . . $450-650

Abumi (pair), 18th century, silver inlaid with motif of insects. (Illus.) . . . . . . . . . . . . . . . . . . . . . . . . . . . . . . . . . . . . . . . . . . . . . . . . . . . . . . . . . . $800-1,100

Abumi (pair), silver inlaid, early 19th century . . . . . . . . . . . . . . . . . . . . . . . . . . . . $1,000-1,500

Abumi (pair), silver and Yoshiro-zogan, stylized scrolling foliage in silver with red lacquer lining, 17th century . . . . . . . . . . . . . . . . . . . . . $2,250-3,700

*Annamese jarlet, 3" h., 14/16th century*

Annam produced ancient earthenware which resembles the Sawankhalok and Sukhothai wares of Thailand. Many of the wares from the 9th to 16th century were influenced by Chinese ceramics. Blue and white wares were produced for export in the 17th century.

## Annamese Ware
*(Vietnamese)*

Bottle, 9" h., 14/15th century, pear-shaped, decorated in iron red with two phoenixes in flight ............................................. $600-800

Bowl, 5" dia., polychrome decoration, interior with an unglazed ring around a floral medallion in underglaze blue, exterior with a simple band of peonies and leaves in red and green enamels; some ground down rim chips, small crack ....................... $500-700

Bowl, 5½"h., 14/16th century, painted in underglaze black with a band of calligraphy, covered in a crackled, grayish white glaze ......................................................... $400-600

Bowl, 7½" dia., 14/16th century, blue and white decoration, interior with waves, exterior covered with a pale gray glaze ..................... $100-175

Bowl, 8" dia., blue and white decoration, inside with a scroll border surrounding a flower spray, exterior with a flower scroll banded by gray lines, beige glaze with a brown wash at the base ............................................................. $600-800

Box, 3" dia., 14/15th century, polychrome decoration, with lobed sides, the eight panels with plant and scroll designs in underglaze blue and red enamels highlighted with green; some wear to the enamel ................................................. $600-800

Box, 3" dia., 14/16th century, blue and white decoration with a scene of a hut in landscape setting ....................................... $200-250

Dish, 5½" dia., polychrome decoration, with floral medallion in center and peony blossom border in iron red and bright green enamels ............................................................. $400-600

Dish, 7" dia., polychrome decoration, with scroll and medin center, the border with blossoms, painted in iron red and green enamels ............................................................. $700-900

Jarlet, 3" h., 14th/16th century, dark brown glaze ending above unglazed foot rim. (Illus.) ............................................. $60-80

## Apparel
*(Indian)*

Sari, pale blue silk gauze woven with fruiting vines in silver and pink, borders woven with flowers and medallions . . . . . . . . . . . . . . . . . . . . . . . . . $85-140

Sari, cerise silk gauze, woven with boughs and blossoms in silver and chartreuse with gold threads in the border and around floral sprays . . . . . . . . . . . . . . . . . . . . . . . . . . . . . . . . . . . . . . $110-160

## Arita
*(Japanese)*

When Japan established open trade with the West (from approximately 1858 on), the Arita kiln produced Nagasaki wares (made specifically for Western export). Among the objects produced were flower vases with wide flaring mouths decorated in Imari colors. Some of these wares were also embellished with lacquer. The kilns associated with Arita are Uchiyama, Sotoyama, and Osotoyama.

### Blue and White

Bottle, 9" h., with underglaze blue spray of flowers . . . . . . . . . . . . . . . . . . . . . . . . $125-145

Bottle, 10" h., underglaze blue landscape motif . . . . . . . . . . . . . . . . . . . . . . . . . . . . $80-105

Bottle, 11½" h., late Edo period, underglaze blue motifs . . . . . . . . . . . . . . . . . . $320-385

Bowl, 9" dia., exterior with pine and bamboo . . . . . . . . . . . . . . . . . . . . . . . . . . . . . . $500-650

Bowl, 11½" h., late 19th century, molded in relief with two panels of ladies holding fans . . . . . . . . . . . . . . . . . . . . . . . . . . . . . . . . . . . . . . . . . $300-400

Charger, 15⅝" dia., late 17th century, raised foot ring, motifs of roundels of birds within a garden, within floral panels separated by geometric dividers . . . . . . . . . . . . . . . . . . . . . . . . . . . . . . . . . . . $950-1,200

Dish, 8¼" dia., 18th century, six-pointed reserves of flowers within floral panels . . . . . . . . . . . . . . . . . . . . . . . . . . . . . . . . . . . . . . . . . . . . . $300-400

Ewer, 8¼" h., motifs of pine and bamboo . . . . . . . . . . . . . . . . . . . . . . . . . . . . . . . . $250-325

Jar, 24" h., 18th century, knob finial, pine, plum, bamboo (three friends) . . . . . . . . . . . . . . . . . . . . . . . . . . . . . . . . . . . . . . . . . . . . . . $1,200-1,600

### Polychrome

Bowl and cover (pair), 4¼" dia., dragons and clouds on the exterior (Imari palette) . . . . . . . . . . . . . . . . . . . . . . . . . . . . . . . . . . . . . . . . . . $90-125

Bowl (pair), 5¼" dia., lotus shape, underglaze blue, red, and gold . . . . . . . . . . . . . . . . . . . . . . . . . . . . . . . . . . . . . . . . . . . . . . . . . . . . . . . $145-180

Charger, 18" dia., 19th century. (Illus.) . . . . . . . . . . . . . . . . . . . . . . . . . . . . $2,400-3,000

Incense burner, cat form. (Illus. here and in Color Section) . . . . . . . . . . . $1,200-1,500

Sake bottle, 7" h., 19th century, flowers and insects . . . . . . . . . . . . . . . . . . . . . $400-500

Vase, 10½" h., slender neck, underglaze blue, turquoise, red, black, and gold with two figures in a garden setting . . . . . . . . . . . . . . . . . . . . $300-400

*Arita charger, 19th century, polychrome. Courtesy A. Christian Revi*

*Arita censer, cat form*

**Terminology:**

**Yoroi (Do Yoroi)** — the general term for the suit of armor.
**Kabuto** — helmet.
**Abumi** — stirrups (see Abumi).
**Kardate** — thigh protection.
**Suneate** — shin guards.
**Sode-juriashi** — an identification badge worn on the sode.
**Sode** — sleeves which protect the shoulder and arms.
**Youoi Hitsu** — the container for arms (arrows, polearms, firearms, etc.).

# Armor
## *(Japanese)*

Kabuto (helmet), 19th century, 12 plates, inlaid in silver and gold nunome zogan with stars and clouds, applied with mokko form mon . . . . . . . . . . . . . . . . . . . . . . . . . . . . . . . . . . $900-1,300

Yoroi (suit of armor), 19th century, 62 plates with standing ridges and lacquered black, complete with a bow and arrows, a haidate, a pair of sanmai-zutsu suneate, a yodarekake, an uba-hoko mempo . . . . . . . . . . . . . . . . . . . . . . . . . . . . . . . . . . . . $8,000-12,000

Yoroi (suit of armor), 62 plates, 18th century, iron tehenhanamono on a uchiwa plate, mabisashi with shakudo trim, shakudo tomo-e mon, five lame roiro shikoro laced deep blue, mempo engraved with wheels, yukinoshita-do with shakudo mounts, roiro kusazuri laced deep blue, shino-gote with shakudo tomo-e mon, mogami-sode with shakudo mounts laced deep blue . . . . . . . . . . . . . . . . . . . . . . . . . . . . . . . . . . . $6,000-9,000

# Armorial Porcelain
## *(Chinese)*

Armorial porcelain was copiously produced in China in the 18th century to satisfy Western tastes and designs. It was a "made to order" export porcelain that bore incorporated designs of crests, coats of arms, individual monograms, etc. The illustrations for decoration were carried to China by the traders, who then carried the completed orders back to their clients. The United States began open trade with the port of Canton in the 19th century and amorial porcelains then began to appear on the American scene.

(See: Chinese Export)

# Azalea Pattern
## *(Japanese)*

The Azalea patterned dinnerwares are closely associated with the Noritake Company. However, many other backstamps have been found on dinnerware in this pattern. Among the backstamps associated with Azalea are Green M in Wreath Nippon, Blue Maple Leaf Nippon, Rising Sun Nippon, Red M in Wreath Noritake Japan, Green M in Wreath Noritake Japan. Backstamps are not listed for items described below. Regardless of whether a particular piece dates from the Nippon era or the post-Nippon era, values are the same. One can mix and match pieces with various markings when completing an entire dinner service. Values are given for pieces in perfect condition.

Basket, 4¼" 1. . . . . . . . . . . . . . . . . . . . . . . . . . . . . . . . . . . . . . . . . . . . . . . . . . . . . $90-105

Bonbon dish, 6¼" . . . . . . . . . . . . . . . . . . . . . . . . . . . . . . . . . . . . . . . . . . . . . . . . . $40-50

Bowl, 9½" . . . . . . . . . . . . . . . . . . . . . . . . . . . . . . . . . . . . . . . . . . . . . . . . . . . . $25-32.50

Bowl, 11½" . . . . . . . . . . . . . . . . . . . . . . . . . . . . . . . . . . . . . . . . . . . . . . . . . . . . $30-35

Bowl (shell contour) . . . . . . . . . . . . . . . . . . . . . . . . . . . . . . . . . . . . . . . . . . . . $150-170

Butter . . . . . . . . . . . . . . . . . . . . . . . . . . . . . . . . . . . . . . . . . . . . . . . . . . . . . . $20-27.50

Butter tub (with liner) . . . . . . . . . . . . . . . . . . . . . . . . . . . . . . . . . . . . . . . . . . . . $40-55

Cake plate . . . . . . . . . . . . . . . . . . . . . . . . . . . . . . . . . . . . . . . . . . . . . . . . . . $18-22.50

Candy (covered) . . . . . . . . . . . . . . . . . . . . . . . . . . . . . . . . . . . . . . . . . . . . . . $275-320

Celery dish, 12½" . . . . . . . . . . . . . . . . . . . . . . . . . . . . . . . . . . . . . . . . . . . . . . $50-65

Cheese dish (slant lid) . . . . . . . . . . . . . . . . . . . . . . . . . . . . . . . . . . . . . . . . . $52-57.50

Child's set . . . . . . . . . . . . . . . . . . . . . . . . . . . . . . . . . . . . . . . . . . . . . . . . . . $320-350

Coffeepot (demitasse) . . . . . . . . . . . . . . . . . . . . . . . . . . . . . . . . . . . . . . . . . . $400-450

Compote, 2¼"h. . . . . . . . . . . . . . . . . . . . . . . . . . . . . . . . . . . . . . . . . . . . . . . . $45-55

Condiment set . . . . . . . . . . . . . . . . . . . . . . . . . . . . . . . . . . . . . . . . . . . . . . $27.50-33

Cruet with stopper . . . . . . . . . . . . . . . . . . . . . . . . . . . . . . . . . . . . . . . . . . . . $155-170

Cup and saucer . . . . . . . . . . . . . . . . . . . . . . . . . . . . . . . . . . . . . . . . . . . . . . . . $10-12

Dinner plate, 9¾" dia. . . . . . . . . . . . . . . . . . . . . . . . . . . . . . . . . . . . . . . . . . . . $15-20

Egg cup . . . . . . . . . . . . . . . . . . . . . . . . . . . . . . . . . . . . . . . . . . . . . . . . . . . $33-41.50

Fruit saucer . . . . . . . . . . . . . . . . . . . . . . . . . . . . . . . . . . . . . . . . . . . . . . . . . . . . $5-8

Grapefruit dish . . . . . . . . . . . . . . . . . . . . . . . . . . . . . . . . . . . . . . . . . . . . . . . . $57-62

Gravy with attached underplate . . . . . . . . . . . . . . . . . . . . . . . . . . . . . . . . . . . $35-38.50

Jam jar (covered) with underplate . . . . . . . . . . . . . . . . . . . . . . . . . . . . . . . . . . $70-90

Lemon plate . . . . . . . . . . . . . . . . . . . . . . . . . . . . . . . . . . . . . . . . . . . . . . . . . . $15-17

Mayonnaise set (3 pcs.) . . . . . . . . . . . . . . . . . . . . . . . . . . . . . . . . . . . . . . . . . . $25-35

Milk pitcher . . . . . . . . . . . . . . . . . . . . . . . . . . . . . . . . . . . . . . . . . . . . . . . . . $125-130

Nut dish (footed) . . . . . . . . . . . . . . . . . . . . . . . . . . . . . . . . . . . . . . . . . . . . . $18-23.50

Pickle dish . . . . . . . . . . . . . . . . . . . . . . . . . . . . . . . . . . . . . . . . . . . . . . . . . . $23.50-31

Platter, 12" . . . . . . . . . . . . . . . . . . . . . . . . . . . . . . . . . . . . . . . . . . . . . . . . . . . $90-105

Platter, 14" . . . . . . . . . . . . . . . . . . . . . . . . . . . . . . . . . . . . . . . . . . . . . . . . . . . $27-33

Platter, 16" . . . . . . . . . . . . . . . . . . . . . . . . . . . . . . . . . . . . . . . . . . . . . . . . . . $300-325

Relish dish (four sections) . . . . . . . . . . . . . . . . . . . . . . . . . . . . . . . . . . . . . . . . $90-105

Salad plate, 7½" . . . . . . . . . . . . . . . . . . . . . . . . . . . . . . . . . . . . . . . . . . . . . . . . $7-9

Salt and pepper, 3"h. . . . . . . . . . . . . . . . . . . . . . . . . . . . . . . . . . . . . . . . . . . . . $15-18

Saucedish, 5¼" . . . . . . . . . . . . . . . . . . . . . . . . . . . . . . . . . . . . . . . . . . . . . . . . . . $7-9

Spoonholder . . . . . . . . . . . . . . . . . . . . . . . . . . . . . . . . . . . . . . . . . . . . . . . . . $47.50-53

Sugar (covered) and creamer . . . . . . . . . . . . . . . . . . . . . . . . . . . . . . . . . . . . $22.50-28

Sugar (open) and creamer . . . . . . . . . . . . . . . . . . . . . . . . . . . . . . . . . . . . . . . . $70-75

Sugar shaker . . . . . . . . . . . . . . . . . . . . . . . . . . . . . . . . . . . . . . . . . . . . . . . . $45-52.50

Syrup pitcher and underplate . . . . . . . . . . . . . . . . . . . . . . . . . . . . . . . . . . . . . . $52-58

Teapot, 4¼"h. . . . . . . . . . . . . . . . . . . . . . . . . . . . . . . . . . . . . . . . . . . . . . . . . . $60-70

Tea tile . . . . . . . . . . . . . . . . . . . . . . . . . . . . . . . . . . . . . . . . . . . . . . . . . . . . $35-47.50

Toothpick holder . . . . . . . . . . . . . . . . . . . . . . . . . . . . . . . . . . . . . . . . . . . . . . $90-125

Vase . . . . . . . . . . . . . . . . . . . . . . . . . . . . . . . . . . . . . . . . . . . . . . . . . . . . . . . $300-325

Vegetable, 8" . . . . . . . . . . . . . . . . . . . . . . . . . . . . . . . . . . . . . . . . . . . . . . . . . . $30-36

Vegetable, oval, 10½" . . . . . . . . . . . . . . . . . . . . . . . . . . . . . . . . . . . . . . . . . . . . $28-33

Banko was one of two names (the other being Fuyeki) used by Numanomi Gozayemon, a Japanese merchant and amateur potter, working in Ise province during the late 18th century up to his death in 1830. It is the Banko wares associated with his predecessors, including Mori Yesetsu, which are of most interest to dealers and collectors. Banko wares come in many varieties, including gray, tapestry, marbleized, white, brown, tree bark (mokume), etc. Most Banko wares are thin and translucent and are often mistaken for porcelain even though they are pottery wares. Banko wares generally have unglazed exteriors, glazed interiors, and often have movable parts such as pivotable knobs. Motifs can be enameled, applied in relief, molded in relief, incised and/or impressed, used singularly or in combination. Banko wares have just been rediscovered by the collecting community and prices are rising steadily and rapidly.

# Banko
## (Japanese)

*Banko elephant stein (left), 5" h.; Banko humidor in Daruma form (right)*

| | |
|---|---|
| Bowl, grayware, polychrome, butterflies. (See Color Section) | $600-850 |
| Figures, 7" w., monkeys. (Illus.) | $300-350 |
| Humidor, 6" h., Daruma. (Illus.) | $400-500 |
| Humidor, seven gods of good luck | $400-500 |
| Incense burners, 12" h. (See Color Section) | $1,800-2,500 |
| Kogo, early 19th century. (See Color Section) | $600-800 |
| Nodder, 5½" h. (Illus.) | $400-500 |
| Stein, green, yellow, and gray. (Illus.) | $200-300 |
| Teapot, c. 1890 (grayware), in form of Mt. Fuji with snow-capped peak | $145-160 |
| Teapot, c. 1890 (tapestry ware), with pivotable finial | $285-325 |
| Teapot, c. 1930 (grayware), elephant figural with mahoot | $120-140 |
| Teapot, 20th century, grapefruit form | $250-350 |
| Teapot (grayware), molded with the seven gods of good luck | $350-375 |
| Vase, 7" h., wasps and nests. (Illus.) | $300-450 |
| Vase, 7¼" h., crane motif. (See Color Section) | $1,500-1,900 |
| Vase, 8" h., double gourd. (Illus.) | $200-300 |
| Vase, c. 1865 (brownware), signed Fuyeki, with motif of falcon and plum blossoms in colors and gilt | $450-550 |
| Vases, 8" h. (marbleized), gray glaze with applied lotus blossoms in colors and gilt. (Illus.) | $400-455 |
| Wine pot, late 18th century. (See Color Section) | $1,200-1,500 |

*Banko vase, art nouveau, marbleized, late 19th century*

*Banko monkey group, c. 1913*

*Banko double gourd vase (left); Banko bottle form vase with wasps and nests (right)*

*Banko humidor (left) with seven gods of good luck in relief; Banko nodder of Fukujurojin, 5½" h.*

11

## Baskets

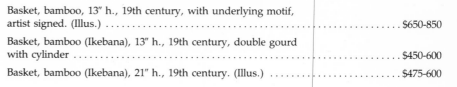

Basket, bamboo, 13" h., 19th century, with underlying motif, artist signed. (Illus.) . . . . . . . . . . . . . . . . . . . . . . . . . . . . . . . . . . . . . . . . $650-850

Basket, bamboo (Ikebana), 13" h., 19th century, double gourd with cylinder . . . . . . . . . . . . . . . . . . . . . . . . . . . . . . . . . . . . . . . . . . . . . . . $450-600

Basket, bamboo (Ikebana), 21" h., 19th century. (Illus.) . . . . . . . . . . . . . . . . $475-600

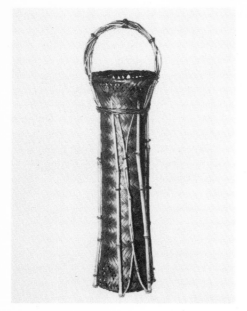

*Basket, 21" h., 19th century. Courtesy collection of Jean Keats*

*Basket with underlying motif, 13" h. Courtesy collection of Jean Keats*

## Bizen Wares
### (Japanese)
### (Also known as Imbe Wares)

*Bizen tiger. Courtesy collection of Jean Keats*

The unglazed Bizen (Imbe) stonewares were produced in an area near Imbe in Bizen province (modern prefecture — Okayama), Japan. The earliest pieces date from the Kakamura period and these early wares were usually in the form of storage vessels.

The three basic types of Bizen wares are:

**Ao** — Bizen wares made from green clay.

**Hidasuki** — Bizen wares which were wrapped in damp straw and then fired. During the firing process, the straw produced red streaks (or blotches) on the body. Such wares are highly prized.

**Bizen or Imbe wares** — a stoneware, unglazed, having a deep red/brown color, resembling bronze. From the Edo period on, many forms were developed and among the most popular are figures, animals, incense burners, and other ornamental objects.

Cat, 7" w., 19th century, reclining . . . . . . . . . . . . . . . . . . . . . . . . . . . . . . . . . . $700-900

Chaire, Edo period, double gourd, ivory cover . . . . . . . . . . . . . . . . . . . . . . . . $200-400

Pourer (cup form), 3½" h., 18th century cover having loop finial, gray/buff glaze . . . . . . . . . . . . . . . . . . . . . . . . . . . . . . . . . . . . . . . . . . $1,200-1,500

Storage jar, 13" h., 19th century, baluster form . . . . . . . . . . . . . . . . . . . . . . . $350-450

Storage jar, 13" h., 19th century, dark brown, baluster form . . . . . . . . . . . . . . . $225-300

Tiger, 19th century. (Illus.) . . . . . . . . . . . . . . . . . . . . . . . . . . . . . . . . . . . . . . . $600-900

## Blanc de Chine
### (Chinese)

Blanc de chine porcelain was first made at the Tê-hua kilns in the province of Fukien during the Ming Dynasty. This pliable molding porcelain was excellent for modeling figures. The color of the clay was generally a creamy white although it can tend to other shades of white. The clear glaze is brilliant and smooth. Blanc de chine is still being produced. Of all the figures produced in this porcelain the Kuan Yin was and still is the most popular.

*Blanc de chine figure group, Empress and attendants, 19th century*

Bowl, 8" dia., 18th century, with rounded sides, relief-molded with decoration of prunus branches . . . . . . . . . . . . . . . . . . . . . . . . . . . . . . . . . . . . . . . $400-500

Censer, 3½" dia., 17th century, decorated with lion masks at either side, creamy white glaze . . . . . . . . . . . . . . . . . . . . . . . . . . . . . . . . . . . . . . . . . $400-600

Censer, 6" h., K'ang Hsi period (commemorative six-character mark of Hsüan Tê). Raised on high feet with two lion head masks, with bluish white glaze . . . . . . . . . . . . . . . . . . . . . . . . . . . . . . . . . . . $900-1,300

Cup, 4¼" h., 18th century, octagonal form, flared shape, relief-molded with a floral spray of prunus blossoms . . . . . . . . . . . . . . . . . . . . . . . $200-300

Figure, Pu Tai, 5⅝" h., 18th century, grayish glaze with brown flecks . . . . . . . . . . . . . . . . . . . . . . . . . . . . . . . . . . . . . . . . . . . . . . . . . $600-800

Figure, Kuan Yin, 7½" h., K'ang Hsi period (unmarked), posed in a seated position with legs folded, robes draping over base, base impressed with the Ho family potter's mark, white glaze with pale bluish tint . . . . . . . . . . . . . . . . . . . . . . . . . . . . . . $2,000-2,500

*Figure, 8¼" h., Kuan Yin, 18th century, the Goddess in a seated position on a recumbent elephant, holding an upturned flask and wearing jeweled pendants. (Illus.) . . . . . . . . . . . . . . . . . . . . . $1,400

Figure, Chen Wu, 8½" h., 18th century, shown on a rocky throne with snake and tortoise underfoot, creamy-toned glaze . . . . . . . . . . . . . . . . . . . . . . . . . . . . . . . . . . . . . . . . . . . . . . . . . . . $600-700

Figure, Kuan Yin, 9" h., 18th century, seated with a scroll in her left hand, hair coiled on her head, and legs folded beneath robe, with an impressed, four-character mark on the back "yü pújên ch'i" (meaning, "[virtue] extends to all [even] fishermen"), covered with a grayish white glaze . . . . . . . . . . . . . . . . . . $1,500-2,000

Figure, Lohan, 9½" h., posed seated on rockwork base with his head turned to right, holding small bottle in left hand, partially draped in robe from the waist down, glazed in creamy white with green tint . . . . . . . . . . . . . . . . . . . . . . . . . . . . . . . . . . $1,900-2,200

*Blanc de chine figure group, Kuan Yin with children, 18th century*

Figure, Kuan Yin, 10" h., 18th century, seated on rockwork holding small boy on her lap . . . . . . . . . . . . . . . . . . . . . . . . . . . . . . . . . . . . . . $700-900

Figure, Kuan Yin, 12½" h., 18th century, seated on a high pierced rockwork base, wearing long robes, a jeweled necklace; child holding a lotus spray on her right knee, covered in a pale ivory glaze . . . . . . . . . . . . . . . . . . . . . . . . . . . . . . . . . . $1,600-1,800

Figure, 13½" h., Kuan Yin, 18th century, hollow-based figure of the Goddess holding a child with two children as attendants, off white tinted glaze. (Illus.) . . . . . . . . . . . . . . . . . . . . . . . . . $2,000-2,500

*Figure, 14½" h., Kuan Yin, the knotted hair figure depicted holding a scroll and wearing long robes, standing on a carved wave and scroll base. (Illus.) . . . . . . . . . . . . . . . . . . . . . . . . . . . . . $500

Figure, Kuan Yin, 15" h., 19th century, depicted standing on lotus base with her hands folded in sleeves of robe . . . . . . . . . . . . . . . . . . $125-175

*Figure, 18" h., Kuan Yin, 17th century, the standing figure holding a scroll in her crossed hands, wearing a cowl over her high knotted hair and standing on a domed wave scroll base. (Illus.) . . . . . . . . . . . . . . . . . . . . . . . . . . . . . . . . . . . . . . . . . . . . . . . $650

Figure, Kuan Yin, 19" h., 19th century, depicted standing on a wave base holding a straw basket with a fish, covered in crackled, milky white glaze . . . . . . . . . . . . . . . . . . . . . . . . . . . . . . . . . . $350-500

Figure group, 6" h., European governor and his family, 18th century, two of the figures seated at a table drinking tea, flanked by two standing children, with a monkey, a dog and a jardiniere, all on a low mound base . . . . . . . . . . . . . . . . . . . . . . . . . . . . $2,000-2,500

(L. to R.) *Blanc de chine figure, Kuan Yin, 14¼" h., 18th century. *Blanc de chine figure, Kuan Yin, 18" h., 17th century. *Blanc de chine figure, Kuan Yin seated on elephant, 18th century

Figure group, 11½" h. x 12" l., Empress and her attendants, 19th century, the figures arranged in a floating barge, fine incised decoration under the greenish tinted glaze. (Illus.) .................. $2,500-3,000

Figure group, 12" h., late 19th century, woman and child seated on rockwork under pine tree ................................... $200-250

Figures, cats, 6" h., 18th century, dangling pendants from necks, creamy white glaze ......................................... $2,000-2,500

Jars (pair), 5" h., 18th century, molded in relief with prunus branches between bands of studs and molded masks, the covers with double peach finials ....................................... $1,000-1,200

Libation cup, 3¼" h., 18th century, molded animals and foliage, milky white glaze; chipped on base ........................ $300-350

Tea bowl, 4" dia., K'ang Hsi period (unmarked), octagonal shape, relief-molded equestrian figure, creamy white glaze ......... $350-450

Vase, 5" h., K'ang Hsi period (unmarked), pear shaped with a dragon in relief coiling around base, brilliant milky white glaze ............................................................... $1,000-1,400

Vase, 13" h., K'ang Hsi period (unmarked), incised foliage and molded lion's head masks at the sides; repaired with gold lacquer on lip and side .......................................... $700-900

Vase, 13½" h., 18th century, undecorated except for molded lion's head and ring masks at shoulders, milky white glaze ......... $1,400-1,800

Vase, 17" h., 17th century, beaker form, faintly incised with peony scroll in center ............................................. $700-900

## Blue and White Wares
### (Chinese)

Blue-and-white Chinese brush rest, 5" h., K'ang Hsi

The earliest blue and white ware as we know it today originated in the 14th century. It was not until the 15th century that blue and white began to bear reign marks. Early wares had colors that ranged from dull gray to purplish blue to ultramarine. The decoration was applied in bold, freeflowing splashes which had a "heaped and piled" uneven surface caused by thick black concentrations which sank into the glaze. The greenish blue glaze had an uneven, textured, orange peel surface. Sometimes black dots appeared at the outlines of the decoration. (All these characteristics were imitated in the 18th century copies of these early pieces.) Since the cobalt used to produce early blue and white was of poor quality, a demand for the richer pigments was created. Mohammedan blue was imported from Persia. (It was not until the 17th century that the Chinese succeeded in refining their native cobalt to a color close in quality to that of imported pigments.) The 15th century was one of outstanding blue and white production. The technique of painting in bold strokes gave way to one of painting careful outlines which were then filled in with wash. By the end of the century the "heaped and piled" effect had disappeared. A quantity of "Mohammedan wares," blue and white bearing Arabic inscriptions appeared during the reign of Chêng Tê(1506-1521). The Chia Ching reign (1522-1566) was famous for its brilliant purplish blue. The Wan Li (1573-1619) blue and white followed much of the style of Chia Ching but the decoration also included a new silvery blue. The output of Chinese potters at this time was enormous in efforts to meet the growing export demands. "Kraak" porcelains appeared as a style at the start of the 17th century and thereafter became a prototype for ware produced at Delft and other ceramic centers of Europe. The transitional period of the 17th century introduced new styles of painting which concentrated on scenes of nature influenced by European tastes. The shape of some porcelains became more Western and the scheme of using flowers to separate landscape panels revealed a decidedly European influence. The blue and white of this period has been described as "violets in milk." The blue and white of the reign of K'ang Hsi (1662-1722) reached the heights of technical excellence. The porcelain was a fine textured pure white which was glazed with a blue or greenish tint. During the reign of Yung Chêng (1723-1735) copies of blue and white wares of Hsüan Tê, Hua, and Chia Ching were ordered by the Imperial court. The blue and white export market still flourished and goods could be made to order for the European market. A new trend started to develop, however, during this time. The Chinese began to adopt the use of European colors in their wares. The demand for these decorated wares began to replace that of blue and white. From the Ch'ien Lung period onward through the 19th century the quality of blue and white ware declined. In the last period of the dynasties (the reign of Kuang Hsu 1875-1908) copies of earlier wares were produced, a practice that continued into the thirties and forties. (See: Canton Blue and White; Chinese export; Fitzhugh Pattern; K'ang Hsi; Kraak; Made in China; Ming Dynasty; Nanking Blue and White; Nineteenth Century; Swatow, Transitional period)

*Blue-and-white Chinese dish, 8¼" dia., with bird and floral motif, K'ang Hsi*

Bowl, 6" dia., Ming Dynasty, provincial ware, with freely painted designs of flowers around a central floral medallion, the exterior decorated with flowers ........................................... $300-400

Bowl, 7" dia., Ch'ien Lung seal mark and period, rounded sides and lipped rim, decorated with penciled lotus scroll design on exterior ..................................................... $300-400

Bowl, 8" dia., Ch'ien lung mark and period, with overall design of dragons and cloud scrolls ..................................... $1,200-1,400

Bowl, 8" dia., transitional period, the exterior with two flying kylins, the interior with a kylin within a medallion ....................... $1,000-1,200

Bowl, 10" dia., Ming Dynasty, dated 1572 around the exterior rim, decorated in a washy blue with two winged carp and dragons in pursuit of flaming pearls, with inscription giving the date and name of the maker and offering the "water bowl" as a donation in hopes that his family will be blessed with prosperity and good fortune ...................................... $10,000-12,000

Box, 6" dia., 19th century, the cover decorated with dragons in pursuit of flaming pearls ............................................. $250-350

Box, 10" l., Ming Dynasty, Wan Li six-character mark, rectangular form with domed cover, the pierced box painted with a cartouche of Buddhist emblems and dragons in pursuit of flaming pearls, painted in silvery blue (cover damaged) ............................................................ $4,000-5,000

Brush pot, 8" dia., 18th century, continuous scene of children playing in a courtyard ............................................... $600-800

Brush rest, 5" h. x 5¼" l., K'ang Hsi period, one side depicting relief molded mountains and a bridge, the reverse with relief waves and a flying dragon, with a key fret pattern around the top of the circular plaque. (Illus.) ............................. $400-600

Censer, 10" h., 18th century, supported on tripod legs, decorated with two dragons chasing flaming pearl ........................... $600-800

Dish, 5½" dia., Wan Li period (unmarked), scene of lake with boats, a temple with pine trees in the distance, the underside decorated with floral sprigs and emblems ....................... $300-350

Dish, 7¼" dia., Kuang Hsü mark and period, decorated with a center medallion of lotus scrolls, with a lotus head border, the underside with a lotus scroll band ....................................... $700-900

*Blue-and-white Chinese dish, 15½" dia., floral decoration, K'ang Hsi*

*Blue-and-white Chinese jar, 10¾" h., lotus and scroll motif, Ch'ien Lung*

Dish, 8" dia., Yung Chêng six-character mark and period, interior and exterior design of peaches, fungus, and a bat, executed in an imitative "heaped and piled" effect of the Ming period ...................................... $1,200-1,500

Dish, 8¼" dia., K'ang Hsi period, signed with the symbol of a tripod vase within double concentric circles, with iron oxide visible on the unglazed foot rim. (Illus. here and in Color Section) ................................................. $400-500

Dish, 9" dia., 18th century, decorated with a central medallion of a phoenix bird flying among lotus blossoms surrounded by a double circle .......................... $200-300

Dish, 10" dia., Ming, early 16th century, spontaneously painted in a deep underglaze blue with a kylin in the center, scrolling vines on the border ............................ $1,200-1,400

Dish, 15½" dia., K'ang Hsi period, the motif consisting of numerous varieties of flowers and leafy stems radiating from a central stylized floral design, signed with the symbol of a "fungus" within double concentric circles on the base. (Illus.) ... $1,400-1,600

Dish, 18" dia., K'ang Hsi period (unmarked), with center decoration of children at play, the border of lotus blossoms .... $1,500-1,800

Dish, 20" dia., K'ang Hsi period (unmarked), decorated with vivid blue in pattern of flowers surrounding central circular medallion of radiating curved lines; lip band containing a leaf pattern interspersed with eight fleurettes .................... $2,000-2,500

Dish, 22" dia., K'ang Hsi period, vivid blue central medallion surrounded by smaller medallions containing flowers, the underside decorated with leafy scrolls ...................... $1,800-2,200

Ewer, 8½" h., K'ang Hsi period, double gourd shape, each bulb decorated with panels of flowers .......................... $1,200-1,400

Fish bowl, 22½" h., K'ang Hsi period, the exterior with peony blossoms, scrolling stems and leafy tendrils ............. $3,000-4,000

Garden seat, 17½" h., early 20th century, hexagonal, with waves and dragons bordered by ju-i bands, the top similarly decorated and having a pierced cash symbol .................. $400-500

Ginger jar, 10" h., Ch'ien Lung period, with bright blue designs of kylins on rocky cliffs ............................ $1,000-1,200

Ginger jar, 10½" h., K'ang Hsi period (unmarked), decorated with the "cracked ice" pattern with two reserves of the "hundred antiques," the lid a 19th century replacement ...... $800-1,000

Ginger jar, 18" h., 19th century, overall design of lotus blossoms and scrolling vines in inky blue tones, matching cover, wood stand .................................... $350-450

*Jar, 10¾" h., Ch'ien Lung period, with lotus and scroll decor, baluster form with spreading foot. (Illus.) .................. $1,650

Jar, 16" h., 18th century, baluster form decorated with large peony blossoms and foliage .............................. $600-800

Jardiniere, 14" h., late 19th century, heavily potted with straight, flared sides, decorated with foo dogs playing with ribboned balls in clouds, wide ju-i lappet border at top and at the base, scroll design at the rim .......................... $800-900

Jarlet, 3" h., Yuan Dynasty, with deep inky blue scrolling blossoms below a key fret border at the shoulder; a pair of loop handles at the neck .................................. $800-1,000

Pillow, 13" l., 18th century, both sides with a center medallion showing a foo dog chasing a ball surrounded by puffy clouds; rest of motif with depictions of fruit-bearing branches, with Chinese characters on either end ................ $600-650

Pouring bowl, 6" dia., Yuan Dynasty, spouted bowl with interior and exterior design of lotus, chrysanthemums, and scroll in center; base and rim unglazed; fine blue color ....... $2,500-3,500

Punch bowl, 13″ dia., K'ang Hsi period (unmarked), deep
rounded sides, exterior decorated with insects, birds among
flowering plants; interior with birds, flowers reserved on a
diaper band with barbed, lobed rim ............................................. $1,800-2,200

Stem cup, 4″ h., Ming Dynasty, with floral sprigs, set on
short foot ...................................................................................... $600-900

Temple garniture, 6½″ h., 19th century, composed of
four-legged censer, two candlesticks, two beakers, all
decorated in dark blue with lotus and peony scrolls ....................... $700-1,000

Vase, 7″ h., K'ang Hsi period (unmarked), decorated with
good luck emblems and "hundred antiques" ................................... $700-900

Vase, 7″ h., Ming Dynasty, pear shape, with tall, slender
neck flaring at the rim, one side showing the figure of a sage
in a sparse landscape, the reverse showing flowers ....................... $1,000-1,200

Vase, 7½″ h., K'ang Hsi period (unmarked), beaker form
with floral motif on bulbous center, ascending and
descending large leaf tips ............................................................. $500-700

Vase, 9″ h., Ch'ien Lung, unusual form, with exaggerated
shoulders, large stylized ju-i motif at the base and shoulder,
and a center motif of four phoenixes in flight separated by
four floral and scroll patterns. (See Color Section) ...................... $1,000-1,200

Vase, 9″ h., 19th century, quintal form with lobed body and
petal form mouth, decorated with panels of ladies on a
terrace, separated by lotus scroll designs .................................... $400-500

Vase, 9½″ h., K'ang Hsi period (mark of artemisia leaf in
underglaze blue), mei ping form, with continuous decoration
of ancient men and boys in garden ............................................... $800-1,000

Vase, 11″ h., K'ang Hsi mark and period, baluster form,
depicting a kylin within clouds ..................................................... $900-1,200

Vase (with lid), 11¼″ h., K'ang Hsi period, with molded
reserves in swirls around the body containing floral designs,
a key fret design at the neck. (See Color Section) ........................ $900-1,200

Vase, 12″ h., K'ang Hsi, bulbous form with garlic top, rich,
vivid blue decoration, pitting in glaze. (See Color Section) .......... $1,500-1,700

Vase, 15″ h., 18th century, scene of boats on river, mountains
in background, covered with crackle glaze stained brown ............. $800-1,000

Vase, 17½″ h., K'ang Hsi period (double circles in underglaze
blue on base), decorated with prunus blossoms reserved on a
cracked ice ground ...................................................................... $1,800-2,000

Vase, 18″ h., 19th century, yen yen shape, decorated with
prunus blossoms on cracked ice ground ....................................... $600-700

Vase, 18″ h., 19th century, commemorative Ch'ien Lung
mark, intricate borders and central motif of dragons and
flowers. (Illus.) .......................................................................... $800-1,000

Vase, 18″ h., 18th century, baluster form with ringed neck,
decorated with floral and foliate scrolls, with two large
reserves of birds on flowering branches, with eight small
reserves of repeated floral pattern .............................................. $700-900

Vase, 18″ h., K'ang Hsi period (unmarked), yen yen shape,
decorated with figures of fishermen and scholars at lakeside
with mountains in distance .......................................................... $1,400-1,600

Vase, 18″ h., K'ang Hsi period (unmarked), beaker form,
decorated with soldiers at top of trumpet neck, with children
in a garden in the midsection, rockwork at bottom ........................ $1,400-1,800

Vase, 18″ h., Ch'ien Lung period, mei ping form painted in a
Ming style with free-flowing flowers and vines ............................ $2,500-3,000

Vase (with lid), 24″ h., 18th century, overall floral pattern, foo
dog knop on lid. (Illus.) .............................................................. $1,400-1,600

*Blue-and-white Chinese vase, 18″ h., 19th
century*

*Blue-and-white Chinese vase with lid, 24″ h.,
18th century*

Vases (pair), 10" h., 19th century, flattened body with double lizard handles, one side with two frolicking deer, the other with a river and mountain scene, with flower and scroll borders, key fret on outer vase rim. (Illus., 19th Century) . . . . . . . . . . . . . . . . . . . . . . $500-700

Water vessel, 8¼" h., K'ang Hsi period, the rounded body decorated with two bands of lotus scrolls, surmounted by a dragon handle and flanked by upright tabs . . . . . . . . . . . . . . . . . . . . . . . . . . . $800-1,000

## Brass
### (Chinese)

Box, cricket, 5⅞" x 5" x 4¾" h., c. 1920, rounded corners, handle, engraved floral-leaf design on pierced lid . . . . . . . . . . . . . . . . . . . . . $50-65

Candlesticks, pair, solid brass, with allover embossed designs, four corner figural masks on each base, embossed bobeches. . . . . . . . . . . . . . . . . . . . . . . . . . . . . . . . . . . . . . . . . . . . . . . . . . . . $175-300

Figural group, 7½" h., standing dignitary with a boy at his side . . . . . . . . . . . . . . . . . . . . . . . . . . . . . . . . . . . . . . . . . . . . . . . . . . . . . . . . . $66-130

Figure, standing, of Choulao holding a staff and a peach . . . . . . . . . . . . . . . $66-130

Incense burner, 7¾" h., square tapering form on four hoof feet, with design of two bands of fuyi; pierced cover depicting Buddhistic lion with brocade ball . . . . . . . . . . . . . . . . . . . . $66-130

Lantern, 10" h., 19th century, oviform shaped, pierced with four barred apertures (one hinged for placement of candle); bamboo finial for carrying (dented) . . . . . . . . . . . . . . . . . . . . . . . . . . . . $80-130

Rice bowl set, late 18th/early 19th century, large bowl with eight matching smaller bowls, eight 10" plates, and small compote . . . . . . . . . . . . . . . . . . . . . . . . . . . . . . . . . . . . . . . . . . . . . . . . . . . $400-550

Tray, 36" dia., Shou character central design with border of birds and animals, all chased and incised; geometric and floral bands, scalloped rim, folding wood stand . . . . . . . . . . . . . . . . . $200-330

Vases, pair, 8" h., squared shape, archaic characters on the bases, with four pierced flanges, flying cranes among branches and pairs of trigrams (one flange missing) . . . . . . . . . . . . . . . $66-106

## Brass
### (Indian)

Figure, 4⅝" h., 15th/16th century, seated figure of Trithankara in dhyanasana position on base surrounded by elaborate prabha; his hands are in dhyana hasta; silver highlights . . . . . . . . . . . . . . . . . . . . . . . . . . . . . . . . . . . . . . . . . . . . . . . . $100-300

Figure, 5⅞" h., South Indian, 16th/17th century, seated figure of Mahakali on a single lotus throne holding various attributes . . . . . . . . . . . . . . . . . . . . . . . . . . . . . . . . . . . . . . . . . . . . . . . . . . . $150-450

Figure, 8" h., standing figure of Ganesha, trunk feeding from an outstretched hand, with attributes held in other three arms . . . . . . . . . . . . . . . . . . . . . . . . . . . . . . . . . . . . . . . . . . . . . . . . . . . . . $80-120

Figure, seated, of Gautma Buddha, with a string robe, on lion's throne behind which is circular halo . . . . . . . . . . . . . . . . . . . . . . . . $65-105

Plaque, 9¼" h., South Indian, c. 17th century, depicts Vishnu standing on plain base, with attendants and holding various attributes . . . . . . . . . . . . . . . . . . . . . . . . . . . . . . . . . . . . . . . . . . . . . . . $450-625

## Brass
### (Japanese)

Brush holder, 19th century, cylindrical, with small ink holder attached (form of a tonkotsu), decorated with molded stylized vines and a mon, unsigned . . . . . . . . . . . . . . . . . . . . . . . . . . . . $75-165

Figural group, 15½" h., 19th century, lean male figure standing on rockwork, with large bullfrog at his feet (some holes) . . . . . . . . . . . . . . . . . . . . . . . . . . . . . . . . . . . . . . . . . . . . . . . . . . $270-535

Figure, 7½" h., standing figure of actor on oval, four-footed base (which has impressed characters mark), wearing an elaborate warrior's gown, his left arm raised over his head, right arm lowered by his side (spear and sword missing) . . . . . . . . . . . . . . . . . . . . . . $65-130

Koros, pair, 8¾" h., tripod form, each cast with shaped
panels depicting sparrows among peonies; oviform bodies
standing on three animal mask feet; animal head handles on
the shoulders; karashishi finials on the covers . . . . . . . . . . . . . . . . . . . . . . . . . . . . . $65-105

Ojime, with tiny fly atop an opening lotus pod, unsigned . . . . . . . . . . . . . . . . . . . $175-210

Ojime, with squatting frog atop a closed lotus leaf, unsigned . . . . . . . . . . . . . . . . $60-75

Ojime, rectangular shape with overall filigree, unsigned . . . . . . . . . . . . . . . . . . . . . $60-75

Tsuba, 3¼" dia., third quarter, 19th century, rectangular,
with rounded corners; a figure of Daruma, hosho and scarf
applied in gold inlay; reverse has waterfall design incised,
signed Akichika (by Oishi Akichika) . . . . . . . . . . . . . . . . . . . . . . . . . . . . . . . . . . . . . $500-650

Vases, pair, 11" h., late 19th century, baluster shape raised on
shaped feet, flaring mouths decorated with silver-inlaid
roundels of birds and flowers . . . . . . . . . . . . . . . . . . . . . . . . . . . . . . . . . . . . . . . . . . . $200-333

Bowl, 6⅝" dia., 13th century, deep bowl raised on a thin ring
foot and set with a plain cover . . . . . . . . . . . . . . . . . . . . . . . . . . . . . . . . . . . . . . . . . . $200-333

## Brass
### (Korean)

Figural groups, pair, 8½" h., each portraying Shakti in
yab-yum, standing on a coiled naga and a dwarf, embracing
Hanuman and Garuda, on lotus bases, the arms holding
attributes . . . . . . . . . . . . . . . . . . . . . . . . . . . . . . . . . . . . . . . . . . . . . . . . . . . . . . . . . . . . $105-158

## Brass
### (Nepalese)

Figure, 9" h., Garuda standing on a four-footed square base
with hands raised in prayer and head framed by flames . . . . . . . . . . . . . . . . . . . . . $50-80

Figure, 9½" h., Bhairava with many heads, embracing Shakti
on lotus base, holding many attributes in his hands . . . . . . . . . . . . . . . . . . . . . . . . . $50-80

Figure, 15¾" h., Suryea seated on double lotus base, hands
in vitarka mudra, with two lotuses entwined around the
arms . . . . . . . . . . . . . . . . . . . . . . . . . . . . . . . . . . . . . . . . . . . . . . . . . . . . . . . . . . . . . . . . . $200-265

Figure, 24½" h., Aryalokitesvara standing on double lotus
base, with many arms and heads, holding bow and arrow,
ring, lotus blossom, and other attributes . . . . . . . . . . . . . . . . . . . . . . . . . . . . . . . . . . $265-530

Figures, pair, 8" h., mythical animals standing with long
bushy tails and raised heads; green glass circles applied on
the bodies . . . . . . . . . . . . . . . . . . . . . . . . . . . . . . . . . . . . . . . . . . . . . . . . . . . . . . . . . . . . . $50-75

Figures, pair, 33½" h., each of Padmapani standing on
double lotus base, hands in vitarka and varada mudras,
elaborately piled hair, and flower sprays on right sides . . . . . . . . . . . . . . . . . . . . . . $500-800

Figures, pair, 5½" h., crouching mythical animals with
scrolling tails, spiked manes, and coiled whiskers . . . . . . . . . . . . . . . . . . . . . . . . . . . $30-70

## Brass
### (Thai)

Vessel, 6" h., globular shape, cast with foliate band below
flared lip, band of ovals with seated Buddha separated by
pendant stiff leaves on neck; same design repeated on body,
but with upright stiff leaves, very heavy . . . . . . . . . . . . . . . . . . . . . . . . . . . . . . . . . . . $250-300

## Brass
### (Tibetan)

# Bronze
## (Burmese)

*Burmese bronze Buddha, 25¾" h.*

Figural group, 10½" h., standing woman holding child (detachable), wearing loose gown, on a hardstone stand ........................ $130-265

Figural group, 11½" h., 18th/19th century, seated Jambupati Buddha in dhyanasana, hands in dhyana and bhumisparsa mudras, wearing several ropes of necklaces, with elaborate headdress on high usnisa; accompanied by two kneeling followers praying atop lotus flowers, on stepped base ........................ $665-900

Figure, 9¼" h., seated figure of Buddha, the hands in abhaya and dhyana mudras, wearing a deeply folded robe which pools to the triangular base ........................ $130-200

Figure, 9½" h., head of Buddha with high eyebrows, tightly curled plain headdress, large ears and traces of a smile. Wood base ........................ $200-330

Figure, 9¾" h., 19th century, gilt, seated Buddha on double lotus base, hands in dhyana and bhumisparsa mudras, pendant ears, and high coiled usnisa. Gilt worn ........................ $400-530

Figure, 11" h., seated Buddha, in dhyana and bhumisparsa, eyes inlaid with glass, stylized garment folds, on tiered triangular base ........................ $200-330

Figure, 17½" h., 18th/19th century, seated Buddha (Shakyamuni) in dhyanasana with hands in dhyana and bhumisparsa mudras, high arched eyebrows, long pendant ears, and tight curls in a tall usnisa, on a high stepped base ........................ $750-1,000

Figure, 20" h., seated Buddha, in dhyanasana, hands in dhyana and bhumisparsa mudras, pendant ears, tightly coiled hair, loose robes ........................ $325-500

Figure, 25¾" h., 19th century, seated Buddha, hands in dhyana and bhumisparsa, long pendant ears, tightly curled hair with spiked usnisa, on double lotus base. (Illus.) ........................ $1,000-1,300

Figures, pair, 10½" h., crouching foo lions, each with foliate patterned collar, open mouth, pointed ears, and clusters of fur falling to shoulders from top of head ........................ $180-250

# Bronze
## (Cambodian)

Figural group, 5" h., 11th/12th century, four-armed Vishnu standing on shoulders of the bird-headed Garuda, who has his arm-wings extended, wood base ........................ $2,000-3,000

Figure, 4¾" h., Khmer, 11th/12th century, dancing Apsara wearing short skirt, diadem, and elaborate jewelry, dancing on one foot with hands in vitarka mudra, wood base ........................ $2,000-3,100

Figure, 5½" h., Khmer, 12th/14th century, standing figure of Vishnu holding small attributes in his four arms, wood base, some restoration ........................ $125-425

Figure, 5¾" h., Khmer, 10th/12th century, seated Buddha subduing Mara, in dhyanasana with hands in dhyana mudra, holding a patra atop Naga's coils, with the flaring hoods forming a nimbus behind, wood base ........................ $2,100-3,500

Figure, 5¾" h., Khmer, 12th/14th century, standing figure of Vishnu wearing short skirt and elaborate jewelry, holding two attributes aloft in his four arms, with flaring diadem. Traces of gilding, wood base ........................ $400-665

Figure, 6⅛" h., Khmer, c. 8th century, seated gilt Buddha, in dhyanasana with hands in dhyana mudra, holding attributes and adorned with Bodhisattva jewelry, traces of gilding, wood base ........................ $550-1,100

Figure, 6¼" h., Khmer, probably 12th century, dancing female deity, balanced on left leg and holding four attributes in flailing arms, ribbed skirt rising high in the rear with a fan ornament in relief, straight hair band and cone usnisa, wood block base ........................ $660-1,000

Figure, 6⅜" h., Khmer, probably 13th century, seated Buddha subduing Mara, in dhyanasana and in dhyana mudra, atop coils of Naga, the multiple hooded heads fanned out behind him, wood base . . . . . . . . . . . . . . . . . . . . . . . . . . . . . . . . . . . . . . $1,450-1,800

Figure, 8¼" h., Khmer, 12th/14th century, same as above . . . . . . . . . . . . . . . . . . . $1,400-1,700

Figure, 11¼" h., Khmer, 11th/13th century, standing Buddha dressed in flowing formal robes with hands raised in abhaya mudra; a flared diadem above the serene face with pendant ears, traces of gilding, stone base . . . . . . . . . . . . . . . . . . . . . . . . . . . . . . . . . . . . $3,000-4,800

Figure, 13¼" h., 19th century, standing Buddha wearing a belted skirt and cape flowing from elbows, his hair elaborately piled, some green patination, wood stand . . . . . . . . . . . . . . . . . . . . . . . . $650-925

Figure, 20½" h., Khmer style, four-armed deity holding attributes, wearing necklace, elaborate cloth around torso, and elaborate diadem rising to high usnisa above the pendant ears . . . . . . . . . . . . . . . . . . . . . . . . . . . . . . . . . . . . . . . . . . . . . . . . . . . . $250-375

Figure, 18th century, seated gilt Buddha in dhyanasana on stepped lotus pedestal, both hands in dhyana mudra, dressed in simple robes, some flaking to gilding, some red painted decoration . . . . . . . . . . . . . . . . . . . . . . . . . . . . . . . . . . . . . . . . . . . . . $200-330

Ax head, 5¾"l., probably Shang Dynasty, curved cutting edge pierced in center with circular aperture, rectangular openings on either side of plain rectangular nei, some green patination on the dark brown bronze . . . . . . . . . . . . . . . . . . . . . . . . . . . . . . . . . . $90-160

Beaker, ritual, 8¾"h., Shang Dynasty, plain flared trumpet neck, body with two t'ao t'ieh masks divided by a shallow flange, with raised bands above and below and pierced apertures above the foot, and four panels of descending dragons, with spirals and quills flanking each; dark, silvery gray, smooth patina . . . . . . . . . . . . . . . . . . . . . . . . . . . . . . . . . . . . . $8,000-10,000

Bell, archaic, 7¼" h., Chou Dynasty, flat-topped conical oval section, carved with t'ao t'ieh masks below bands of studs on the sides; surmounted by a high bracket handle on the top, worn surface . . . . . . . . . . . . . . . . . . . . . . . . . . . . . . . . . . . . . . . . . . . . . . . . $400-650

Belt hook, 6¼"l. Chou Dynasty, Ch'ih lung terminal on spatulate-shaped shaft, with a circular boss set into a square plateau on the underside . . . . . . . . . . . . . . . . . . . . . . . . . . . . . . . . . . . . . . $475-700

Bowl, 6½" dia., 19th century, five-lobed, each with a dragon or phoenix roundel in relief below key pattern, on four legs, with three-character cast mark . . . . . . . . . . . . . . . . . . . . . . . . . . . . . . . . . . $100-200

Bowl, 8½" dia., Han Dynasty, shallow, with a lipped rim and flat foot support, heavy malachite encrustation, blackish patina, wood stand . . . . . . . . . . . . . . . . . . . . . . . . . . . . . . . . . . . . . . . . $675-800

Censer, 5½" h., eastern Han Dynasty, hinged cover cast with stylized mountain peaks pierced with vents and topped with bird shaped finial; stepped pedestal with animals and mountains motif, lightly encrusted green patina (shading to bright green on interior with patches of blue) . . . . . . . . . . . . . . . . . . $2,700-3,600

Censer, 7¼" dia., 17th/18th century, squat, globular form, with lion mask handles on the shoulders, supported on slightly flared foot ring base, Hsuan Te mark cast on base in Hsing shu script . . . . . . . . . . . . . . . . . . . . . . . . . . . . . . . . . . . . . . . . . $300-435

Dagger, archaic, 9" l., Shang/early western Chou Dynasty, archaic motifs deeply cast on either side of the handle, with triangular shape blade pierced with two apertures, extensively corroded and encrusted surface . . . . . . . . . . . . . . . . . . . . . $400-500

Drum, funerary, 27" dia., 18½" h., central star medallion on top with four stylized frogs within concentric bands; cylindrical body with small elephant design along one of the chased flanges; double loop handles on either side . . . . . . . . . . . . . . . . . . $650-900

# Bronze
## (Chinese)

*Chinese bronze figure, 12½" h.*

*Chinese bronze vessel, 6¼" h.*

Figure, 2¼" h., early Ming, late 14th century (dated 1396), seated gilt Buddha in pose of meditation, left hand upturned in lap; lightly punched rings indicating tightly curled hair, loosely draped robe, on a lotus throne placed on tiered plinth resting on six small feet inscribed on five of the six facets of the plinth corresponding to A.D. 1396; gilt worn, wood stand ............... $950-1,400

Figure, 2 1/5" h., Han Dynasty, gilt standing figure of horse with curving legs, arched head; malachite encrustations and extensive gilding remaining ......................................... $1,500-2,400

Figure, 2½" l., Ming Dynasty, crouching figure of Ch'i-lin, head held up, one horn bushy tail, and alert expression. Surface worn, with golden olive color, wood stand ........................... $625-900

Figure, 3⅜" h., Tang Dynasty, gilt Bodhisattva holding an alms bowl, with three seated deities, on a four-legged square base, traces of gilding and green encrustation on dark patina ... ................. $250-385

Figure, 4" h., Ming Dynasty, Buddhist acolyte holding a vessel in his hands and wearing long flowing robes, with two knots in his hair ............................................... $260-400

Figure, 7" h., possibly Sung Dynasty, seated Buddhist figure wearing long robes, knotted hair and pierced diadem, with legs crossed and right hand in devotional pose. Irregular patches of red and gilt lacquer remaining on the surface, wood stand ....................................................... $530-800

Figure, 8" h., Ming Dynasty, seated Tantric Buddha in dhyanasana, holding various attributes in his 18 arms, gilding highlighting flesh details, wood stand ........................... $1,000-1,300

Figure, 8¾" h. seated P'u T'ai on a brocade cushion, wearing a loose-fitting robe with floral border, his left arm resting on a sack; traces of gilt on the brown patina and lacquer on face and back ....................................................... $400-665

Figure, 12½" h., probably 17th century, seated Lohan in dhyanasana, both hands in vitarka mudra, either arm with flower branch entwined around it, high jeweled diadem, on a double lotus base. Traces of gilt and red pigment remaining, minor damage. (Illus.) ........................... $600-875

Figures, pair, 7¼" h., standing mythical animals, each with bushy tail and upon rectangular base with foliage band. One animal has a single horn. Some gilt traces remaining .......................... $130-260

Figures, pair, 14½" h., Ming Dynasty or later, heads of Buddha, each with hair arranged in large curls and faces with serene expressions, cylindrical wood bases ........................... $500-800

Incense burner, 3¾" sq., late 19th century, stylized t'ao t'ieh masks on key-scroll ground of lobed body, standing on four feet, with animal head loop handles on the short neck .......................... $65-105

Incense burner, 4½" dia., Ming Dynasty, Xuande six-character mark impressed on base. Pear-shaped body, slightly flared neck, with mythical animal head handles on either side ........................................................ $200-330

Incense burner, 10½" h., tripod burner and cover, Ting body on three long, cylindrical legs decorated with three stylized t'ao t'ieh between vertical flanges, the cover pierced and surmounted with Buddhistic lion and brocade ball ........................... $105-200

*Chinese bronze mirror, 10½" dia.*

Mirror, 3⅛" dia., Ming Dynasty or earlier, central boss between two vertical rows of calligraphy on plain surface, fitted box ...................................................... $130-200

Mirror, 3⅜" dia., 2nd century B.C., archaic, the main field with flame motifs connected with lozenges by an incised meandering line; a central grooved loop with two incised characters on either side surrounded by two plain concentric circles; a sharp edge on the concave rim. Gray patina lightly encrusted, the reverse with patches of bright green on the silvery color, crack ............................................... $370-500

Mirror, 6¾" dia., Sung Dynasty, barbed, with concave main
field in relief with two birds, floral motifs between them;
central knop surrounded by bands of rounded bosses, with
scrolling floral border within raised, smooth barbed rim,
patches of rust on the light green patina ........................ $600-950

*Mirror, 10½" dia., Tang Dynasty, lobed circular plate cast in
rich, low relief with two long-tailed parrots, branches of
exotic fruits in their beaks, the mirror plate heavily encrusted.
(Illus.) .................................................... $4,400

Spearhead, 7¾" l., early Shang Dynasty, two projecting
triangular loops set into the hollow faceted socket,
leaf-shaped blade with smaller leaf-shaped panels on either
side, brownish-green patina ................................. $400-665

Vase, 12½" h., late 19th century, archaic style, with bands of
t'ao t'ieh masks on a lei wen ground above hanging leaf
darts on the ovoid body and concave neck, loose rings hung
from lug handles beneath masks on the sides ................. $175-300

Vase, 14" h., 19th century, archaic form with shallow broken
flanges dividing bands of t'ao t'ieh masks, a bud finial on the
cover. Suspended from a chain and bar handle attached to
wood frame ................................................ $300-435

Vessel, 4¼" h., Shang Dynasty, Li ting shape, plain,
three-lobed, on tripod legs; two small handles set into rim,
traces of blue encrustation on smooth, light green patina ... $2,900-3,100

Vessel, 5¼" h., Han Dynasty, Hu shape, with round-sided
square section, two loose ring, animal mask handles,
malachite encrustation .................................... $1,200-2,100

*Vessel, 6¼" h., 17th century, archaistic, in shape of Hu,
globular body, tall neck with three horizontal ribs and two
dragon-mask loose-ring handles, Hsuan Te six-character mark
on base, irregular gold splashes on surface, wood stand.
(Illus.) .................................................... $1,550

Vessel, 6¾" h. Ming Dynasty, Fu form cast in relief with
curling waves, a band of cicadas inlaid on the flared
rectangular lip, t'ao t'ieh mask decorations on the splayed
foot, with dragon-head spout and handle inlaid with silver
whorl pattern. Details in gilt. Bronze cover .............. $1,100-1,365

Vessel, 8" h., early western Chou Dynasty, Ting shape with
rope twist loop handles set into the everted rim, tripod legs,
a design of dissolved t'ao t'ieh masks in a band on the wide
bowl. Mottled green and brown surface with dark blue
traces; bright green encrustation on interior, two legs
repaired ................................................. $1,650-3,200

Vessel, 8¾" h., Shang Dynasty, archaic Ku, central bulb
decorated with two t'ao t'ieh masks separated by shallow
flange, four dragons cast on the base, each area enclosed by
rows of embossed circles, patches of azurite on the green
patina, relief pictogram on base ......................... $8,000-9,500

Vessel, 12⅝" h., Shang Dynasty, Ku form with tall trumpet
neck above a design of snakes in four panels, central area
and foot decorated with t'ao t'ieh masks on lei wen ground,
four kuei dragons above masks on foot; plain cylindrical foot
rim, some malachite encrustation and cuprite patches on the
smooth green patina, wood stand ...................... $55,000-60,000

Vessel, 14⁷⁄₁₆" h., Han Dynasty, Hu form, with three ribs
divided by two monster-mask loose-ring handles on the
shoulder of the pear-shaped body; some encrustation on the
surface .................................................. $4,000-5,500

Altar, 74" h., 18th/19th century, standing figure of Shiva with
battle-ax and trisula, naga wreath, and pierced fire mandorla
behind him, on rectangular tiered base ................... $200-330

**Bronze**
*(Indian)*

Figural group, 6⅜" h., 16th/17th century, seated figure of Ganesha on double lotus throne raised on simple dais, Devi on his lap, elaborate prabha surrounding the pair ............... $1,400-1,800

Figure, 5¼" h., early 19th century, standing figure of Vishnu, holding attributes in his eight arms and a dwarf by the hair lock, Nandi the bull beneath his right foot ............... $105-160

Figure, 9½" h. (East Indian), standing figure of Shiva, arms raised in vitarka mudra, wearing high headdress, on a jeweled-lappet circular base ............... $90-117

Figure, 19¾" h., c. 17th century, standing figure of Rama, wearing short skirt, on a double conical base elevated from a low pedestal ............... $1,050-2,300

Figures, pair, 12¾" h., seated figures of Garuda, each with left hand on hip and right arm raised, well defined head and shoulder wings, on flaring base ............... $266-530

Figures, pair, 14¾" h., seated figures of Gautama Buddha, each seated on throne, hands raised in prayer, wearing sheer string fold attire, with frieze depicting lions and deer aside seated figure ............... $266-400

Lamp, oil, 12" h., 19th century, standing curvaceous female shape, depicted as holding three receptacles in her outstretched hands, standing on tiered circular base, traces of gilding ............... $200-265

Lamp, oil, 14" h., standing female shape holding large oil container in outstretched arms, upon her right shoulder a bird, on squarish base ............... $130-200

Toy, 11" h., rider on camel supported by wheels with geometric and foliate motifs ............... $75-140

Toy, 12" h., elephant with man atop, supported by wheels with geometric and foliate motifs ............... $75-140

# Bronze
## (Japanese)

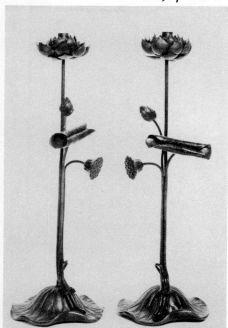

*Japanese bronze pair of candlesticks, 21 5/6" h.

Bottle, 12¼" h., Meiji period, elongated shape with two dried salmon, one in a woven straw wrapper, molded design; small foot ............... $175-300

Box, 8¾" x 8", late 19th century, covered, rectangular, silver-lined interior with small dents. Cover decorated in gold, bronze takazogan, copper, and sukibori, showing a paddy field with farmers planting rice, a mountain in the distance and trees. Signed Kaneyasu Masatoshi tsukuru ............... $5,200-6,500

*Candlesticks, pair, 21⅞" h., with lotus buds at top, seedpods and curled leaves adorning the sticks, lotus leaf shaped bases, signed Joeki IX. (Illus.) ............... $1,450

Dish, 6⁵⁄₁₆" dia., late 19th century, circular, with scalloped rim, design of wasps among wild vine and grape branches in iro-e takazogan, signed Hitachi no kuni Mito ju Hagiya Katsuyasu and kao ............... $4,100-6,000

Figural group, 10" w., 19th century, two rabbits gamboling on rocky terrace, with small thatched hut in background, on a rocky outcrop ............... $265-530

*Figural group, 21⅞" h., late 19th/early 20th century, standing figures of a farmer and wife; she with basket at her side and he working with a hoe and wearing plain kimono. Dull sheen on the bronze, irregularly carved wood base. (Illus.) ............... $4,200

*Figure, 7¼" h., late 19th century, seated figure of a monkey examining its hands and wearing a short garment with flower scroll design; finely detailed fur, some damage. (Illus.) ............... $800

Figure, 9½" h., probably Muromachi period, standing figure of Myo-o holding a single vajra aloft and wearing a tiger skin, wood base ............... $250-600

Figure, 10¼" h., 19th century, eagle perched on rockwork base, wings outstretched and claws grasping the crest, gilded highlights in eyes and beak . . . . . . . . . . . . . . . . . . . . . . . . . . . . . . . $225-500

Figure, 10½" h., late 19th century, standing figure of Sarumawashi, the monkey perched on a backpack of an old man, and receiving a peach from the elder, base missing . . . . . . . . . . . . . . . . . . . . . $360-500

Figure, 12⅛" l., Meiji period, figure of a tiger in stalking position, apparently roaring, signed Seiya in rectangular reserve . . . . . . . . . . . . . . . . . . . . . . . . . . . . . . . . . . . . . . . . . $133-265

Figure, 12½" l., striding figure of an elephant, trunk upraised and naturalistically cast, cast mark Seiya chu . . . . . . . . . . . . . . $500-630

Figure, 13½" l., third quarter, 19th century, seated figure of bear on his haunches with head turned to one side, fine detail, signed . . . . . . . . . . . . . . . . . . . . . . . . . . . . . . . . . . . . . $900-1,200

Figure, 14½" h., Meiji period, kneeling figure of archer, right leg stretched and balancing on left knee, holding a bow and outstretched arrow, a sword on his waist, and wearing a kimono over his armor . . . . . . . . . . . . . . . . . . . . . . . . . . . . . . $850-1,115

*Figure, 17½" h., early 19th century, seated Kannon, her soft robes loosely falling to the floor, her hand on right knee, her elaborately coiffed hair covered with a cowl, dark reddish brown patina painted on the bronze. (Illus.) . . . . . . . . . . . . . . . . . . . . . . . . $1,300

*Figure, 23" h., late 19th/early 20th century, standing figure of elderly woman holding a grain sifter in her outstretched hands, stooping forward, her hair in a tight bun. (Illus.) . . . . . . . . . . . . . . . . . . $2,600

*Figure, 24" l., late 19th century, standing figure of a buffalo pawing the ground, his head lowered and looking to the left with naturalistically incised detailing on hide. Dark matte patina, signed Ganko. (Illus.) . . . . . . . . . . . . . . . . . . . . . . . . . . . . $2,000

Figure, 43⅜" h., 19th century, standing figure of Kannon, gilt and polychrome, on a single lotus base, dressed in graceful Bodhisattva robes, hands in varada and vitarka mudra, holding lotus . . . . . . . . . . . . . . . . . . . . . . . . . . . . . . . . . . $2,200-3,800

Figures, pair, 10" l., late 19th century, standing figures of rhinoceros, in combat stance with heads lowered; well cast details of skin, signed . . . . . . . . . . . . . . . . . . . . . . . . . . . . $600-1,130

Figures, pair, 12½" h. and 13½" h., late 19th century, pair of geese, one with its head held in haughty pose, each with naturalistically cast plumage; cast mark . . . . . . . . . . . . . . . . . . . . $700-800

*Figures, pair, 48¾" h., late 19th century, standing figures of Samurai looking to the right and left, one holding a trident, the other a pike, and each wearing complete suit of armor. Finely cast details simulating lacquer, the metal exhibiting various gilt and sepia colorations on highlights, detachable rockwork bases and swords. (Illus.) . . . . . . . . . . . . . . . . . . . . . . . . $42,000

Hibachi, 11⅝" x 9⅜" x 8¼", 19th century, four relief panels of landscapes with Chinese sages, two looped handles of maple branches on the shoulder; pierced domed cover similarly decorated . . . . . . . . . . . . . . . . . . . . . . . . . . . . . . . . . . . $400-500

Incense burner, 11¼" h., 19th century, rounded square shape with Chinese immortals and warriors design, stylized dragons applied at each corner, and recumbent kirin on the pierced domed cover . . . . . . . . . . . . . . . . . . . . . . . . . . . . . $800-1,065

Incense burner, 22" h., late 19th century, dragon in swirling clouds inlaid with silver; animal-mask and upright handles on shoulders in contrasting tones of silver, gilt, and bronze; shi-shi knop on domed cover, on pierced tripod stand . . . . . . . . . . . . . . $3,000-3,500

Jar, 16" dia., 19th century, scaly dragon pursuing flaming pearl cast in relief on globular form body . . . . . . . . . . . . . . . . . . . . $250-380

Koro, 15" h., late 19th century, figures of cloud-borne gods cast on faceted ovoid body, dragon handles, tiger finial on cover, on bird-shaped legs above canted square base . . . . . . . . . . . $200-265

*Japanese bronze figure, 7 1/5" h.*

*Japanese bronze figure, 17½" h.*

*Japanese bronze figure, 23 1/10" h.*

*Japanese bronze pair of figures, 48¾" h.*

*Japanese bronze pair of vases, 19½" h.*

Lamps, pair, 13" h., 19th century, relief birds in flight on slender ovoid body, gilded mounts; wired for electricity . . . . . . . . . . . . . . . . . . . . . . . $300-433

Stand, umbrella, 23¾" h., low-relief lilies tinged with gilt on archaistic ground, cylindrical body with central knop . . . . . . . . . . . . . . . . . . . . . . . $265-530

Stirrups, pair, 10" l., early 19th century, inlaid with silver dragonflies and celestial hare, inscription on shaft, red lacquer interior . . . . . . . . . . . . . . . . . . . . . . . . . . . . . . . . . . . . . . . . . . . . . . . . . $1,000-1,300

Stirrups, pair, 11" l., 19th century, inlaid silver fleurette-diaper design; inscription and buckle on the pierced shaft, interior with suishu lacquer . . . . . . . . . . . . . . . . . . . . . . . . . . . . . . . $600-865

Urn, 29½" h., third quarter, 19th century, shishi among clouds on the shouldered ovoid body, tripod shishi on rockwork base legs, archaic style border around neck and shoulders, lion handles; cloud designs on pierced cover surmounted by a shishi and rockwork base . . . . . . . . . . . . . . . . . . . . . . $2,000-2,300

Vase, 9⅛" h., 19th century, tall slender flaring neck applied with a locust, squat globular shape, signed Shuko kansei . . . . . . . . . . . . . . . . $125-200

Vase, 9½" h., 19th century, tall, slender, flaring neck with applied grasshopper, squat globular shape, signed Shuko kansei . . . . . . . . . . . . . . . . . . . . . . . . . . . . . . . . . . . . . . . . . . . . . . . . . . $125-200

Vase, 9⅝" h., c. 1900, morning glories and fence in relief copper, silver, and bronze on brown ishime ground, ovoid shape . . . . . . . . . . . . . . . . . . . . . . . . . . . . . . . . . . . . . . . . . . . . . . . . . . . $665-750

Vase, 11¼" h., late 19th century, long flaring neck with cast design of two frogs, one climbing the shoulder and the other surfacing from a pond; tapered, oviform body, drilled base . . . . . . . . . . . . . . . . $105-158

Vase, 13½" h., 19th century, goose among chrysanthemums, bamboo, and grasses; bronze hirazogan and takazogan, on slender oviform body, signed Tatsuoki . . . . . . . . . . . . . . . . . . . . . . . . . . $465-600

Vase, 18¾" h., 19th century, high and low relief design of carp and iris on the bulbous shape, originally finished in orchid tone patina. Artist's seal, silver cartouche on base . . . . . . . . . . . . . . . . . $2,000-2,400

Vase, 23¾" h., panels of Samurai on an ovoid body, stem with rings and bird and foliate motifs raised on three feet above circular base, detachable bird handles, shallow flared dish with butterfly and orchids cast design; copper and silver inlay details . . . . . . . . . . . . . . . . . . . . . . . . . . . . . . . . . . . . . . . . . . . . $600-865

*Japanese bronze figure, 24" l.*

*Japanese bronze figural group, 21 5/6" h.*

*Japanese bronze vase, 24½" h.*

\*Vase, 24½" h., second half 19th century, high relief design of scholar utensils, tea ceremony ware, archaistic bell and baluster vase, all applied in colored metals on slender tapering baluster shaped body. Signed on the base. (Illus.) .................. $1,600-2,000

Vases, pair, 5½" h., Meiji period, silver and gold design of hens, chicks, and cockerel on the slender upright body; silver foot and rim, signed ........................................ $800-1,000

Vases, pair, 7" h., late 19th century, two panels of peony sprays with bird in flight above on baluster body, applied dragon handles, high spreading foot ........................................ $200-400

\*Vases, pair, 19½" h., late 19th century, design of armored Samurai, a lady on a terrace, a swordsman in fighting posture before a waterfall, a dragon and demon in combat in panels; birds in flight cast in low relief on the detachable flat tops; scrolling floral pierced handles; on five-legged domed bases depicting stylized foliage. Some gilding on details. Signed Kaga ju Murasawa Kuninori. (Illus.) .................................. $4,200

Vessel, 7¼" h., late 19th century, tripod, with design of Kannon astride a dragon in gold and silver takazogan and takanikubori; lotus finial on cover, signed at back of cover .................. $3,800-4,800

## Bronze
*(Javanese)*

Figure, 2½" h., 8th/10th century, seated Bodhisattva in dhyanasana with hands in abhaya and vitarka mudras, elaborate diadem, yellow patina, wood base .............................. $800-1,100

Figure, 3⅝" h., 8th/10th century, seated Avalokitesvara Padmapani in lalitasana on lotus throne, dressed in elaborate jewelry and high chignon, his right hand in varada mudra, wood base .................................................... $1,000-1,500

Figure, 4¼" h., 8th/10th century, seated figure of Kubera in dhyanasana, his hands in vitarka mudra, wearing elaborate diadem and Bodhisattva jewelry, the figure on a double lotus throne, wood base .................................................... $1,000-1,500

## Bronze
*(Korean)*

Bowl, 5⅞" dia., Silla Dynasty, footed, steep sided bowl with mild flare near rim; some azurite encrustations on the bright malachite patina ..................................................... $300-530

Figural group, Silla Dynasty, standing figure of a Bodhisattva wearing flowing robe on a pierced stand which extends before him, a snake at his feet .............................................. $400-650

Figure, 4⅝" h., Silla Dynasty, c. 8th century, standing figure of Avalokitesvara on a double lotus ivory base, right hand up and left hand lowered ................................................. $425-650

Mirror, 4" dia., Koryo Dynasty, four striding lions and foliage about a central boss, bordered by ropework and ribbed rim, some silver ......................................................... $700-1,200

Mirror, Koryo Dynasty, four phoenixes and foliage molded into sunken well, with raised flat lip decorated with foliate sprays, wood box ....................................................... $1,100-1,500

Vase, 11⅜" h., c. 12th century, plain, tear-shaped vase with flared mouth and raised on a thin ring foot .............................. $875-1,300

Vase, 12" h., Silla Dynasty, pear-shaped body with trumpet neck decorated with raised flange, cylindrical foot cast with horizontal bands, some malachite encrustation ............................ $500-765

Vase, 12⅛" h., Koryo Dynasty, tear form with flaring mouth and high ring foot .................................................... $1,000-1,800

# Bronze
## (Nepalese)

*Nepalese bronze Uma-Mahesvara group, 6¼" h.*

*Nepalese bronze figure, 16½" h.*

*Figural group, 6¼" h., 15th/16th century. Uma-Mahesvara group; seated on the back of recumbent Nandi, one of the god's arms raised in abhaya mudra, the other around the waist of his consort, his remaining two hands holding a string of beads and trisula, all on an openwork lotus base. (Illus.) ..................................................... $1,650

Figural group, 14½" h., Bhairava manifestation of Shiva depicted sitting on a dwarf, on a lotus base ..................... $133-266

Figure, 3¼" h., 13th/14th century, seated gilt figure of Vasudara, seated in lalitasana, dressed in Bodhisattva jewelry and garments, holding various attributes, traces of gilding on the softly worn figure ........................................ $1,300-1,700

Figure, 4⅞" h., 15th century, standing gilt figure of Garuda, hands in anjali mudra, folded wings, wearing snake ornaments, sash, and dhoti, with high headdress surmounted by three-leaf crown .............................. $1,400-1,800

Figure, 6¼" h., seated figure of Suryea, left hand in vitarka and right hand in varada, on double lotus base, faint traces of blue pigment ...................................................... $150-250

Figure, 6½" h., seated gilt figure of Brahma with three heads and eight arms, seated on a double lotus throne ................. $150-155

Figure, 7¾" h., standing figure of Maitreya, left hand in vitarka, right hand in varada, with stylized stupa in crown, atop double lotus base on four-footed platform ................... $40-65

Figure, 8" h., seated gilt figure of Manjusri holding a sword in one of his four arms, on a double lotus throne, with open flame mandorla; traces of red, orange, white, and blue pigment .............................................................. $300-500

Figure, 8¼" h., standing gilt figure of Padmapani, left arm in vitarka with single lotus bloom entwined, right hand in varada, on circular double lotus base; some red, white, and blue pigment traces ..................................................... $130-260

Figure, 9" h., early 19th century, seated figure of Suryea, hands in vitarka and abhaya mudra, on elaborate tiered lotus throne backed by pierced mandorla with an animal mask and birds, traces of gilt and blue pigment .......................... $265-400

Figure, 10½" h., standing gilt figure of Tara wearing high jeweled diadem and pendant earrings, red and blue pigment on her face, on a single lotus base ............................. $500-625

Figure, 12¼" h., 19th century, seated figure of Padmapani, leaning back on left arm on a double lotus throne, right hand on his knee, brightly polished metal ............................ $200-330

Figure, 13" h., seated figure of Padmapani, hands in vitarka and abhaya mudra, wearing jeweled diadem and high flame usnisa, upon a double lotus base, dark patina ...................... $200-265

Figure, 16½" h., standing gilt figure of Lokesvara, hands in vitarka and varada mudra, his right arm entwined with lotus blossom, wearing a long ungilded dhoti and high crown with small seated Buddha upon it, on circular double base. Traces of black, blue, red, and white pigment. (Illus.) ................. $800-1,050

Figure, 17" h., late 16th/early 17th century, seated gilt figure of Dhyanibuddha Amitayus wearing elaborate Bodhisattva garments, jewelry set with turquoise, and elaborate five-leaf diadem, seated dhyanasana on double-lotus throne engraved with flowers and foliage ....................................... $12,500-14,000

Figure, 17½" h., standing figure of Suryea, hands in vitarka and abhaya mudra, each arm entwined with lotus blossom, on circular double lotus base ...................................... $93-120

Figure, 17¾" h., standing figure of Padmapani, left hand in vitarka mudra, right hand by his side, wearing jeweled diadem in his elaborate high hair, on double lotus base, hollow cast .............................................................. $93-133

Figure, 21½" h., standing figure of Tara, left hand in vitarka mudra, right hand in dancing posture over the head, wearing pierced, jeweled diadem and sheer lower garment, legs in crossed position, on lotus base . . . . . . . . . . . . . . . . . . . . . . . . . . . . . . . . . . . . . . . $266-400

Figure, 31½" h., modern, seated gilt figure of Shakti, hands in vitarka and varada mudra, with lotus blossom entwined about each arm, wearing high jeweled diadem, seated on double lotus base, blue, red, and white pigments. (Illus.) . . . . . . . . . . . . . . . . . . . $3,500-5,000

*Nepalese bronze figure, 31½" h.*

*\*Sino-Tibetan bronze figural group, 6¾" h.*

\*Figural group, 6¾" h., early 19th century, dressed in armor, seated on recumbent roaring lion crouched on a single lotus base cast with a mound of pearls, holding small mongoose in his left hand, his right hand raised in vyakhyana mudra, with green, red, and black polychroming remaining over the heavy gilding. (Illus.) . . . . . . . . . . . . . . . . . . . . . . . . . . . . . . . . . . . . . . . . . . . . $1,650

Figural group, 15" h., Shiva embracing Shakti, each wearing elaborate openwork diadems, seated on lotus base in yab-yum; part of one leg missing . . . . . . . . . . . . . . . . . . . . . . . . . . . . . . . . . . . . . $130-265

Figure, 4 1/16" h., 17th/18th century, seated figure of Buddha in dhyanasana, hands in bhumisparsa and dhyana mudra, wearing simple robe and tightly curled hair, on double lotus throne . . . . . . . . . . . . . . . . . . . . . . . . . . . . . . . . . . . . . . . . . . . . . . . . . . . . . $200-350

Figure, 4½" h., seated gilt figure of Sarasvati, her hands in vitarka and varada mudra, a lotus blossom beneath her right foot and two branches of lotus on either side, seated on lotus base . . . . . . . . . . . . . . . . . . . . . . . . . . . . . . . . . . . . . . . . . . . . . . . . . . . . . . . . . $265-330

\*Figure, 5½" h., 18th century, of Birvapa-Virupa Lama, seated on ovoid lotus base leaning back on his right arm, his left arm raised in vitarka mudra, strings of turquoise-encrusted necklaces falling over his belly tied with a yogapatta, the hair painted blue, moustache and inlaid eyes detailed in black, a Tibetan inscription on the reverse designating his name. (Illus.) . . . . . . . . . . . . . . . . . . . . . . . . . . . . . . . . . . . . . . . . . . . . . . . . . . . . . $5,500

Figure, 6⁷⁄₁₆" h., standing, of the eight-armed Aryavalokitesvara, the eleven heads in a tiered pyramid, standing on a single lotus padmasama . . . . . . . . . . . . . . . . . . . . . . . . . . . . $600-800

# Bronze
## (Sino-Tibetan)

*\*Sino-Tibetan bronze figure, 5½" h.*

*Sino-Tibetan bronze figure, 9¾" h.*

Figure, 6⅞" h., 17th/18th century, of Sitabrahma, his right hand in vitarka mudra, holding a kapala in his left, seated on his white horse which is stepping across human figures ........................ $900-1,100

Figure, 8⅛" h., second half 18th century, seated gilt figure of Dhyanibuddha Amitayus, wearing Bodhisattva garments and jewelry, backed by separate double nimbus, seated dhyanasana on elaborate architectural base ................................... $475-740

Figure, 8½" h., seated gilt figure of a Shivite, its hands in vitarka mudra, the detachable figure seated sideways atop a coiled dragon above a bed of flames and a rat; inlaid with red glass and turquoise, mounted on a single lotus base, red and white pigment ...................................................... $400-665

*Figure, 9¾" h., late 18th century, gilt figure of Mahakala trampling a horse and demon on rounded rectangular double lotus base, dressed in heavy Y-pattern incised armor, wearing long skull garland and five-skill tiara backed by flaming red hair; some white, black and blue polychroming remaining. (Illus.) ................................................ $1,870

Figure, 10¼" h., 17th century, seated gilt figure of Avalokitesvara Padmapani, wearing Bodhisattva jewelry, garments and five-leaf diadem; his hands in varada and vitarka mudra, holding stem of a padma; seated dhyanasan on a double-lotus base, wood base ...................... $1,400-2,100

Figure 10¾" h., gilt figure of Buddha, ornate robe inlaid with beads seated on a double lotus base placed on a high throne decorated with a frieze of elephants and a vase, red, white, and blue pigment .............................................. $400-530

Figure, 11½" h., 16th/17th century, seated figure of Dhyanibuddha Amitavus, hands in dhyana mudra, waring Bodhisattva jewelry and garment in dhyanasana on double lotus throne .............................................. $500-830

Figures, pair, late 19th century, gilt figures of Buddha, hands raised in vitarka and varada mudra, seated on double lotus bases. Each cast from same mold ............................ $200-265

Pipe case, 15½" l., incised scale pattern on the fluted sides, gilded, two loops on the case and fitted cover, worn gilding .................... $100-200

## Bronze
### (Sokuthai)

Figure, 3 1/3" h., 13th century, head with finely cast details, tightly knotted hair; bright green malachite inclusions, traces of gilding, wood stand ......................... $450-650

Figure, 7½" h., 15th/16th century, Buddha's hand, its fingers raised in abhaya mudra; finely cast with extensive traces of gilt ...................................................... $650-850

Figure, 10¼" h., 15th century, Buddha's head, tightly curled hair on the finely cast but degraded head ...................... $500-830

Figure, 10⅜" h., standing figure of Buddha depicted walking, the left hand in vitarka mudra, right hand lowered, pendant ears, introspective face, tightly curled hair, and flame usnisa, on wood base ...................................... $350-400

Figure, 10⅞" h., probably 17th century, seated figure of Sakyamuni, his hands in his lap, hair tightly curled, seated on triangular double lotus throne ...................... $1,000-2,500

Figure, 12¾" h., 13th century, head of Buddha with tightly curled hair, usnisa, and inlaid eyes, wood stand .................. $1,800-2,500

Figure, 31³⁄₁₆" h., head of Buddha with closed eyes, a mound usnisa formed by the hair curled in tight knots, and a meditative expression on face, dark patina, fixed wood stand ................ $2,300-3,400

Figure, 4⅞" h., 16th/17th century, head of Buddha, a formal diadem above the serene face, wood base .................................... $200-350

Figure, 5½" h., 15th/16th century, head of Buddha with pendant ears, tightly curled hair about the elongated face, stone base ................................................... $350-480

Figure, 6" h., 10th/12th century, seated figure of Buddha, Khmer-style, hands in dhyana mudra, wearing elaborate Bodhisattva jewelry; seated dhyanasana on oval support, wood base ...................................................... $700-1,000

Figure, 6" h., 17th century, Ayudha period, head of Buddha with high scrolling eyebrows, ear pendant and meditative expression, wearing an elaborate flanged and squared band on forehead ...................................................... $650-850

Figure, 9" h., late 19th century, gilt seated figure of Buddha, elongated ears, high flame usnisa, introspective face; draped in ornate garment; seated dhyanasana on triangular double lotus base ..................................................... $450-650

Figure, 10½" h., 16th/17th century, gilt seated figure of Buddha, hands in dhyana mudra, wearing towering diadem and elaborate jewelry, seated dhyanasana on cushion base ..................... $300-565

Figure, 13" h., dancer balancing on right leg, wearing spiked hat and pointed shoes, the right hand raised, touching hat and the left hand on hip, wood base ..................................... $150-200

Figure, 13" h., 14th/15th century, Buddha with hands in dhyana and bhumisparsa mudra, seated on plinth pierced with eight rounded quatrefoils, dressed in well defined sheer and simple sanghata, the face framed by pendant crescent ears and the tightly curled hair ending in a mound and high flame usnisa, all under a deep moss green jadelike patina with faint traces of gilt remaining. (Illus.) ............................ $10,000-15,000

Figure, 16" h., including base, seated figure of Buddha, his hands in dhyana and bhumisparsa mudra, tight curls formed into an usnisa, pendant ears, serene face, seated dhyanasana on rounded base, wood base .............................................. $150-415

Figure, 21" h., 18th/19th century, gilt standing figure of Buddha, his hands in abhaya mudra, dressed in elaborate diadem and robe, on a tiered base ...................................... $450-780

Figure, 38" h., early 19th century, gilt standing figure of Buddha, his left hand in abhaya mudra and right hand by his side, wearing elaborately brocaded robes and diadem with a towering finial, wood base .................................... $1,500-2,000

Figure, 69" h., 20th century, seated figure of Buddha, his hands in dhyana and bhumisparsa mudra, pendant ears, tightly curled hair, and downcast eyes; seated in dhyanasana on raised lotus plinth decorated with rows of overlapping lotus petals, wearing simple robes, his hair rising to a tall usnisa, with elaborate mandorla behind him; the base decorated with kneeling figures and mythical beasts ....................... $4,000-4,700

Figures, pair, 9¾" h., seated figures of Buddha, Ayudha style, in dhyana and bhumisparsa, meditative faces framed by pendant ears and flame usnisa, on lotus base supported by four legs ................................................... $80-105

Figures, pair, 33" h., 19th century, seated figures of lions inlaid with glass in stylized design, mouths open .......................... $500-1,030

Figures, pair, 33⁵⁄₁₆" h., seated figures of foo dogs, colored glass and quartz inlays on body, flamelike protuberances on head, open mouth revealing fangs, on haunches .......................... $600-1,130

Figures, pair, 36¼" h. x 23⅜" d., 18th/19th century, gilt praying figures, kneeling, hands raised in prayer; serene faces with tight curls, wearing simple robes, on partially lacquered rectangular bases, each cast with an inscription, worn surfaces ................................................... $6,000-8,500

# Bronze
*(Thai)*

*Thai bronze Buddha, 13" h.*

# Bronze
## (Tibetan)

*Tibetan bronze figural group, 8" h.*

*Tibetan bronze figure, 9¾" h.*

*Tibetan bronze set of three figures, 4" h.*

Bell, 7" h., 18th/19th century, of simple design, the bell (ghanta) has a multiple stringing set, and a handle of lotus design with a vajra rising from it . . . . . . . . . . . . . . . . . . . . . . . . . . . . . . . . . . $400-600

Figural group, 6½" h., gilt yab-yum group, with the six-armed Shakti wearing a skull tiara and holding various attributes on an oval lotus base and Vishnu as a boar, embracing Shakti . . . . . . . . . . . . . . . . . . . . . . . . . . . . . . . . . . . . . . . . . $105-160

*Figural group, 8" h., 19th century, gilt bronze Siddha group, the Siddha seated in lalitasana on mythical animal pelt draped over back of prostrate demon, flanked by female devotees with hands in abhaya and kartarimukha mudras and holding skullcup, on lotus base, with heavy parcel gilding, red, blue, black, and white polychroming and turquoise inlaid jewelry. (Illus.) . . . . . . . . . . . . . . . . . . . . . . . . . . $3,520

Figure, 3³⁄₁₆" h., gilt seated figure of a Bodhisattva, with eight hands, two of which hold vajra and ghanta, and four heads, seated dhyanasana on a double lotus throne. . . . . . . . . . . . . . . . . . . $525-800

Figure, 6⅛" h., 18th/19th century, gilt seated figure of Usnisavijaya, hands in varada and vitarka mudra, one holding a small Adibuddha shrine, seated dhyanasana on a double lotus throne . . . . . . . . . . . . . . . . . . . . . . . . . . . . . . . . . . . . $600-975

Figure, 6⅜" h., 18th century, gilt seated figure of Dhyanibuddha Amitayus, with hands in dhyana mudra holding kalasa, wearing Bodhisattva jewelry and garments and a five-leaf diadem on his high chignon, seated dhyanasana on double lotus throne . . . . . . . . . . . . . . . . . . . . . . . . $425-550

Figure, 7" h., 18th/19th century, standing gilt figure of Kalacakra with six arms, a ferocious face with flaming hair and a diadem of skulls, wearing an elephant skin on his shoulders; standing on Ganesha, on a single lotus throne . . . . . . . . . . . . . . $1,500-1,900

Figure, 7¼" h., 18th century, seated gilt figure of Buddha with pendant ears, tightly knotted hair culminating in an usnisa, a flower held in his right hand, and his chest draped with scarves, on a waisted lotus plinth . . . . . . . . . . . . . . . . . . . . . . . $900-1,200

Figure, 7¾" h., seated figure of a Bodhisattva holding a rat with his left hand and a flame mount in his right, in lalitasana on a lotus base, with Ch'ien lung mark incised, and of the period. Oxidized copper patches on the well-patinated metal, part of diadem missing . . . . . . . . . . . . . . . . . . . . . . . . . . . . . . . $450-750

Figure, 9½" h., seated gilt figure of Mahakala wearing garland of severed heads and scarf, holding a chopper and a skull cup in his hands, seated upon the bodies of two humans on double lotus throne, traces of red paint . . . . . . . . . . . . . . $200-330

*Figure, 9¾" h., 18th century, gilt figure of Yamantaka trampling a row of geese and buffalo set onto a separately cast double lotus base formed with five prostrate demons, holding chopper, skullcup, skull, and shield in his four principal hands and assorted weapons in his remaining thirty, wearing a long garland strung with human heads and tied with snake, inlaid with turquoise with some red and blue polychroming remaining. (Illus.) . . . . . . . . . . . . . . . . . . . . . $6,600

Figure, 10½" h., standing figure of female deity, her hands in vitarka and varada mudra, lotus stem and blossom entwined about her arm, large flower petals decorating her ears and her five-flower crown above her high headdress, standing on a double lotus throne, traces of polychrome on the head . . . . . . . . . . $150-280

Figure, 10¾" h., 16th/17th century, western Tibet, seated figure of Dhyanibuddha Aksobhya with hands in bhumisparsa and dhyana mudra, wearing a towering chignon and diadem and elaborate Bodhisattva jewelry, seated dhyanasana on double lotus throne . . . . . . . . . . . . . . . . . . . $2,400-4,000

Figure, 20¾" h., late 18th century, gilt figure of Mahamayavi-Jayavahini, with three primary heads, trampling rows of beasts with her legs, her hands raised in katakamukha mudra, the right holding a chakra, the high beehive headdress formed from skulls and cast with a line of ten faces, copper repoussé series of hands on her shoulders, inlaid with turquoise, with extensive red and blue polychroming. (Illus.) . . . . . . . . . . . . . . . . . . . . . . . . . . . . . . . . . $7,000-9,000

*Figures, set of three, 4" h., 18th century, gilt figures of Kubera, seated on rectangular pillows in lalitasana and holding a gada, parasu, and pasa, respectively, in their right hands, each with a mongoose to the left, a long necklace resting on their bellies, gilding on the faces rubbed away to reveal black lacquer undercoat and hair with some blue pigment; the reverses of each with an inscription. (Illus.) . . . . . . . . . . . . . . . . . . . . . . . $3,300

Stupa, 5⅞" h., 15th/17th century, stepped and tiered in the usual form, monster and foliate arches above four of the five Tathagatas, set on rectangular base . . . . . . . . . . . . . . . . . . . . . . . . . . . . . . . . $900-1,700

Vajra, 5⅝" l., 18th/19th century, a single bolt form, used as ritual object . . . . . . . . . . . . . . . . . . . . . . . . . . . . . . . . . . . . . . . . . . . . . . . . . $150-250

*Tibetan bronze figure, 20¾" h.*

Café au lait (tzu chin) is a coffee brown glaze which originated in the K'ang Hsi reign. The color appears in a range of browns from a pale golden shade to a deep coffee tone. This lustrous brown glaze may be crackled. It is sometimes found applied over engraved decoration. It may also appear on objects decorated with reserve panels, a style of decoration most frequently associated with "powder blue."

# Café au Lait
*(Chinese)*

Bowl, 4" h., 18th century, with steep sides and a lipless rim, the exterior glazed with a lustrous coffee brown color, the interior glazed white . . . . . . . . . . . . . . . . . . . . . . . . . . . . . . . . . . . . . . . . $500-700

Bowl, 6" h., Kuang Hsu mark and period, with a pale brown glaze . . . . . . . . . . . . . . . . . . . . . . . . . . . . . . . . . . . . . . . . . . . . . . . . . . . . . . . $500-600

Bowl, 7" dia., Ch'ien Lung seal and period, covered inside and out with a lustrous brown glaze; the rim and base glazed in white . . . . . . . . . . . . . . . . . . . . . . . . . . . . . . . . . . . . . . . . . . . . . . . . . $1,500-2,000

Censer, 6" h., Ch'ien Lung period (unmarked), set on three short legs with a flared rim and loop handles, covered with a rich lustrous brown glaze . . . . . . . . . . . . . . . . . . . . . . . . . . . . . . . . . $550-650

Dish, 6" dia., K'ang Hsi period, with three reserves of flowers in famille verte palette set on a ground of rich, lustrous brown . . . . . . . . . . . . . . . . . . . . . . . . . . . . . . . . . . . . . . . . . . . . . . $400-500

Dish, 8" dia., Ch'ien Lung underglaze blue seal mark and period, a barbed rim, decorated all over with a brilliant lustrous coffee brown glaze, the base glazed in white . . . . . . . . . . . . . . . . . . . $2,400-2,800

Stem cup, 6½" h., 18th century, exterior covered in a brilliant coffee brown glaze; the interior in white . . . . . . . . . . . . . . . . . . . . . . . . . . $1,000-1,200

Vase (miniature), 2½" h., 18th century, double gourd shape, covered with an iridescent brown glaze . . . . . . . . . . . . . . . . . . . . . . . . . . . $200-300

Vase, 10" h., 18th century, pear shaped, with a deep, rich brown glaze, the bulbous bottom with three reserves of famille rose florals . . . . . . . . . . . . . . . . . . . . . . . . . . . . . . . . . . . . . . . . . . $900-1,200

Vase, 11" h., Ch'ien Lung period, mei ping form, covered with a rich, coffee colored glaze, the lip and interior glazed white . . . . . . . . . . . . . . . . . . . . . . . . . . . . . . . . . . . . . . . . . . . . . . . . . . . $1,200-1,600

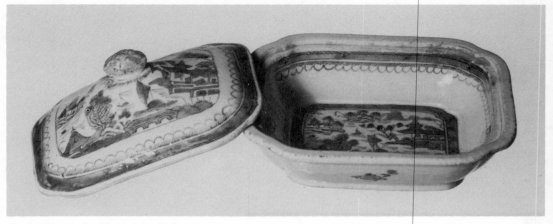

*Canton blue and white tureen, 8" l.*

# Canton (Blue and White)
## (Chinese)

*Canton blue-and-white covered jar, common ware, 19th century*

Canton blue and white wares usually have a border band containing diagonal lines followed by a scalloped motif to finish the band. The central motif is usually a form of the willow pattern (also called "Island" or "Island and Bridge"). This design contains trees, houses, mountains, boats, and bridges. Within the willow pattern used on Canton blue and white, one usually finds figures seen through an open window of a teahouse. Most of the Canton ware found today may be attributed to 19th century production, which is of lesser quality than the blue and white wares of earlier periods.

(See: Nanking Blue and White)

| | |
|---|---:|
| Bowl, 8" dia., late 19th century | $100-125 |
| Bowl, 12" dia., c. 1800 | $350-400 |
| Bowl, 14½" oval, mid-19th century | $300-350 |
| Creamer, 6" h., late 19th century | $100-150 |
| Cup and saucer, mid-19th century | $30-40 |
| Cups and saucers (set of twelve), late 19th century | $400-500 |
| Dish, 6" l. (leaf shape), c. 1840 | $70-90 |
| Dish, 10" sq. (deep veg. dish) | $130-150 |
| Dish, 12" oval (deep veg. dish) | $150-175 |
| Dish, 14½" l. (oval) divided into eight lobed sections, early 19th century | $200-250 |
| Ginger jar, 6" h., late 19th century | $40-50 |
| Ginger jar, 8" h., late 19th century | $75-100 |
| Jar (with cover), 6" h., 19th century, common ware, with a freely drawn scene of a house and landscape, similarly decorated on lid. (Illus.) | $100-150 |
| Pitcher, 7" h., early 19th century | $175-200 |
| Plate, 6" dia., late 19th century | $40-50 |
| Plate, 10" dia., late 19th century | $40-50 |
| Platter, 10" dia., mid-19th century | $80-100 |
| Platter, 14" dia., c. 1800 | $400-450 |
| Platter, 16" dia., c. 1870 | $400-500 |
| Platter, 17" dia., with fitted strainer, mid-19th century | $300-350 |
| Teapot, 6" h., mid-19th century | $75-100 |
| Teapot, sugar, creamer, mid-19th century | $200-225 |
| Tureen, 6" l., boar's head knop on lid, fine deep blue color | $275-350 |

Tureen, 8″ l., late 19th century. (Illus.) . . . . . . . . . . . . . . . . . . . . . . . . . . . . . . . . . . . . . . $200-225

Tureen, 9″ oval, with acorn knop, late 19th century . . . . . . . . . . . . . . . . . . . . . . . . . . $150-175

Tureen, 12″ l., (rectangular) x 8″ h., acorn knop on lid, early
19th century . . . . . . . . . . . . . . . . . . . . . . . . . . . . . . . . . . . . . . . . . . . . . . . . . . . . . . . . . . . . . $275-350

Celadon glazes were first introduced during the Chin Dynasty (265-420 A.D.). The celadon green glaze was an attempt to imitate the color of jade, which is very precious to the Chinese. During the Sung period these wares became one of the most important exports to the Near East, Persia, and Egypt. The fabled origins of the French word "celadon" are many: Celadon was the name of a French character in a play who wore green; he was a shepherd who donned green ribbons; he was a nobleman who wore pale green clothes; he was a collector of green glazed porcelain. (If he were all of these or none, "a rose by any other name would smell as sweet," and so celadon it is, irrespective of all the suggested fanciful origins.) The color is achieved by adding a small amount of iron oxide to the felspathic glaze. The depth of color depends on the amount of iron present in the glaze, the iron content of the body, and the type of fuel used. Northern Chinese celadons were fired with a coal fuel and are darker than the southern celadons, which were fired with wood. (See: Korean Ceramics; Lung-Ch'uan; Seiji; Thai Ceramics; Yuan; Yüeh)

*Chinese celadon lotus bowl. 6¼″ dia., Sung Dynasty*

*Chinese celadon lotus bowl with flared rim, Sung Dynasty*

Bowl, 6″ dia., Ming Dynasty, six-character mark of Wan Li, lipped rim, undecorated, with a thick, pale, bluish green glaze . . . . . . . . . . . . . . . . . . . . . . . . . . . . . . . . . . . . . . . . . . . . . . . . . . . . . . . . . $1,000-1,200

Bowl, 6″ dia., Ming Dynasty, Chekiang celadon, undecorated, with a blue glaze . . . . . . . . . . . . . . . . . . . . . . . . . . . . . . . . . . . . . . $400-600

*Bowl, 6¼″ dia., Sung Dynasty, Lung Hsuan celadon lotus bowl, Southern Sung, fine glaze, rim chip. (Illus.) . . . . . . . . . . . . . . . . . . . . . . . . . . . . $1,650

Bowl, 6¼″ dia., Sung Dynasty, with lotus leaf design on exterior, matte glaze. (Illus.) . . . . . . . . . . . . . . . . . . . . . . . . . . . . . . . . . . . . . . . . $500-700

Bowl, 6½″ dia., Sung Dynasty, shallow form, with carved decoration of overlapping petals on the exterior, glazed in a pale olive green . . . . . . . . . . . . . . . . . . . . . . . . . . . . . . . . . . . . . . . . . . . . . . . . . . $800-1,200

Bowl, 7″ dia., 18th century, rounded sides that turn in at the rim, with white slip decoration around the body depicting a bird on a berry branch, a prunus spray, and a butterfly . . . . . . . . . . . . . . . . . . . . . . $600-800

Bowl, 10″ dia., Yuan Dynasty, Lung-ch'üan celadon with molded decoration of scrolls . . . . . . . . . . . . . . . . . . . . . . . . . . . . . . . . . . . . . . . . $900-1,100

Bowl, 14″ dia., early Ming, c. 1400, with incised key pattern, calligraphy and peony scrolls. (Illus.) . . . . . . . . . . . . . . . . . . . . . . . . . . $2,500-3,500

*Chinese celadon bowl, 14″ dia., incised decoration, early Ming Dynasty*

Brush pot, 6″ h. x 7″ dia., K'ang Hsi period (unmarked), exterior with carved decoration of foliage under a grayish green glaze; interior and base glazed white . . . . . . . . . . . . . . . . . . . . . . . . . . $1,300-1,600

Brush washer, 4¾″ h., Yuan Dynasty, Lung-ch'üan celadon, with a fluted interior, ribbed exterior, and recessed base with unglazed ring . . . . . . . . . . . . . . . . . . . . . . . . . . . . . . . . . . . . . . . . . . . . . . . . . . $800-1,000

Bulb bowl, 10″ h., Ming Dynasty, Lung-Ch'üan celadon thickly potted and raised on three mask and paw tabs, the "eight trigrams" carved on the exterior, glazed in pale gray green . . . . . . . . . . . . . . . . . . . . . . . . . . . . . . . . . . . . . . . . . . . . . . . . . . . . . . . . . . . . . $600-900

Censer, 6½″ h., 18th century, molded with dragons between incised petal borders; key fret border at the top, interior glazed white . . . . . . . . . . . . . . . . . . . . . . . . . . . . . . . . . . . . . . . . . . . . . . . . . . . $600-800

*Chinese celadon dish, 16" dia., with overall crackle, Ming Dynasty*

*Chinese celadon vase, 22" h., yen yen shape, 19th century*

Dish, 4½" dia., Sung Dynasty, molded with bands of petals; the unglazed base ring burnt red in firing . . . . . . . . . . . . . . . . . . . . . . . . . . . . . . . . . . . . . . $350-450

Dish, 5" dia., early Ming Dynasty, Lung-ch'üan celadon, undecorated, molded with a lipped rim and rounded sides . . . . . . . . . . . . . . . . . . $400-600

Dish, 5" dia., Sung Dynasty, Lung-ch'üan celadon, molded in the center with two fish, the exterior with carved petals in a band, glazed pale green . . . . . . . . . . . . . . . . . . . . . . . . . . . . . . . . . . . . . . . . . . . . . . . . . $400-500

Dish, 6" dia., Sung Dynasty, Lung-ch'üan celadon, with an everted rim and upturned edge, molded with two fish and incised foliage scrolls on the interior, covered with a crackled glaze . . . . . . . . . . . . . . . . . . . . . . . . . . . . . . . . . . . . . . . . . . . . . . . . . . . . . . . . . . . . . $600-800

Dish, 8" dia., Sung Dynasty, Lung-ch'üan celadon; interior molded with two fish, the underside with incised leafy scrolls . . . . . . . . . . . . . . . . . $600-800

Dish, 8¾" dia., Yuan Dynasty, single fish design, blue green crackle glaze. (See Color Section) . . . . . . . . . . . . . . . . . . . . . . . . . . . . . . . . . . $600-800

Dish, 8¾" dia., Yuan Dynasty, twin fish design, olive brown glaze. (See Color Section) . . . . . . . . . . . . . . . . . . . . . . . . . . . . . . . . . . . . . . . . $600-800

Dish, 9" dia., Sung Dynasty, Lung ch'üan celadon, with slightly curved sides and a flanged rim; the interior molded with two fish, the exterior with molded petals and incised outlines, covered with a grayish green glaze . . . . . . . . . . . . . . . . . . . . . . $900-1,200

Dish, 10" dia., Ming Dynasty, molded with a center floral and honeycomb design, covered with a green, translucent glaze . . . . . . . . . . . . . . . . . . . . . . . . . . . . . . . . . . . . . . . . . . . . . . . . . . . . . . . . . . $600-700

Dish, 10½" dia., Ch'ien Lung seal mark and period, fluted rim, molded with a geometric design and lotus fleurette border, covered with a pale, grayish green glaze . . . . . . . . . . . . . . . . . . . . . $500-700

Dish, 11" dia., early Ming Dynasty, Lung-ch'üan celadon with an incised center of trellis pattern, radiating ribs extending to a barbed rim, yellow green glaze . . . . . . . . . . . . . . . . . . $700-1,000

Dish, 11" dia., Ming Dynasty, Lung-ch'üan celadon, of square shape, undecorated, covered with a heavy, transparent olive green glaze . . . . . . . . . . . . . . . . . . . . . . . . . . . . . . . . . . $1,000-1,200

*Dish, 11¾" dia., Ming Dynasty, 15th century, molded with a central trellis pattern, with a floral incised border, covered in a pale olive glaze . . . . . . . . . . . . . . . . . . . . . . . . . . . . . . . . . . . . . . . . . . . . . $800-1,000

Dish, 12" dia., Ming Dynasty, Lung-ch'üan celadon with a barbed rim, molded with a central lotus spray surrounded by scrolls . . . . . . . . . . . . . . . . . . . . . . . . . . . . . . . . . . . . . . . . . . . . . . . . . . . . . . . . . $600-800

Dish, 13" dia., Ming Dynasty, Chekiang celadon, molded with a large flower in the center, with foliate clusters on border, covered with a deep green glaze; foot rim burnt orange in the firing . . . . . . . . . . . . . . . . . . . . . . . . . . . . . . . . . . . . . . . . . . . $1,200-1,500

Dish, 13" dia., Ming Dynasty, Chekiang celadon molded with a floral pattern surrounded by incised lotus scroll, covered in an olive green glaze . . . . . . . . . . . . . . . . . . . . . . . . . . . . . . . . . . . . . . . . . . . . $600-900

Dish, 13" dia., Yuan Dynasty, Lung-ch'üan celadon, molded wave and dragon motif interior; underside with band of lotus petals, covered with a pale green glaze . . . . . . . . . . . . . . . . . . . . . . . . $900-1,200

Dish, 14" dia., Ming Dynasty, Lung-ch'üan celadon, with a light floral impression in the center, covered in a heavy olive green glaze . . . . . . . . . . . . . . . . . . . . . . . . . . . . . . . . . . . . . . . . . . . . . . . . . $900-1,200

Dish, 16" dia., with crackle overall and faintly incised leaf patterns under glaze, burnt orange firing rim on base. (Illus.) . . . . . . . . . . $1,400-1,600

Dish, 20" dia., Ming Dynasty, with large dragon in relief chasing the flaming pearl, ribbing on the cavetto, heavily potted with burnt orange rim on the unglazed portion of the foot rim. (See Color Section) . . . . . . . . . . . . . . . . . . . . . . . . . . . . . . . . . . . $4,000-5,000

Figure, official, 12" h., Ming Dynasty, Lung-ch'üan celadon, shown seated on throne, covered in a thick olive green glaze . . . . . . . . . . . . . . $1,200-1,400

*Incense burner (censer), 10" h., Ming Dynasty, globular body
on three short legs, incised with three lotus sprays extending
down to the legs, with two rope handles, covered in a pale
green glaze . . . . . . . . . . . . . . . . . . . . . . . . . . . . . . . . . . . . . . . . . . . . . . . . . . $2,000

*Jar, 9" h., Sung Dynasty, Lung-ch'üan celadon with applied
dragons chasing the flaming pearl set around the narrow
neck, covered in a thick, pale green glaze . . . . . . . . . . . . . . . . . . . . . . . . . . . . $1,900

Stem cup, miniature, 3½" h. x 3" w., early Ming Dynasty,
Lung-ch'üan celadon, with carved lotus petals on the
exterior, covered with a yellow green glaze . . . . . . . . . . . . . . . . . . . . . . . . . . . . $650-850

Stem cup, 4½" h., Ming Dynasty, Lung-ch'üan celadon
molded with two relief bands above the stem, covered with a
sea green glaze . . . . . . . . . . . . . . . . . . . . . . . . . . . . . . . . . . . . . . . . . . . . . . . . . . $900-1,200

Vase, 5" h., Ch'ien Lung seal mark and period, of ovoid
shape, molded with a coiled rope design, covered with a pale
and even green glaze . . . . . . . . . . . . . . . . . . . . . . . . . . . . . . . . . . . . . . . . . . . . . $1,200-1,600

Vase, 7" h., 18th century, mei ping shape, undecorated,
covered with a pale green glaze with a brown stained crackle;
brown wash on the foot rim . . . . . . . . . . . . . . . . . . . . . . . . . . . . . . . . . . . . . . . $800-1,000

Vase, 7½" h., Ming Dynasty, Chekiang celadon, of thick
walled, ovoid shape with concave neck and foot, incised with
a trellis pattern under a crackled sea green glaze, the glaze
somewhat degraded . . . . . . . . . . . . . . . . . . . . . . . . . . . . . . . . . . . . . . . . . . . . . $200-300

Vase, 8" h., K'ang Hsi period (unmarked), pear-shaped with
a molded allover dragon and floral design covered with a
translucent, pale green glaze . . . . . . . . . . . . . . . . . . . . . . . . . . . . . . . . . . . . . . $600-800

Vase, 8½" h., Ming Dynasty, baluster form, incised in a
trellis pattern under a pale green glaze . . . . . . . . . . . . . . . . . . . . . . . . . . . . . $1,000-1,500

Vase, 10" h., Ming Dynasty, Chekiang celadon, incised with
ribbing and peony blossoms . . . . . . . . . . . . . . . . . . . . . . . . . . . . . . . . . . . . . . . $800-1,000

Vase, 10½" h., Yüan Dynasty, yen yen shape, with a flaring
neck, undecorated, with a crackled, pale green glaze, the foot
unglazed . . . . . . . . . . . . . . . . . . . . . . . . . . . . . . . . . . . . . . . . . . . . . . . . . . . . . . . . $1,200-1,400

Vase, 12½" h., Ming Dynasty, rounded sides and flared rim,
freely incised with floral sprays beneath an olive green glaze . . . . . . . . . . . . . . . $1,100-1,200

Vase, 14" h., 19th century, bottle form, the body molded in
low relief with dragons above lappets . . . . . . . . . . . . . . . . . . . . . . . . . . . . . . . $500-700

Vase, 14¾" h., Ming Dynasty, the front and back have shield
reserves containing floral designs, the foot rim is burnt
orange in the firing. (See Color Section) . . . . . . . . . . . . . . . . . . . . . . . . . . . . . $3,000-3,500

Vase, 16" h., K'ang Hsi period (commemorative Cheng Hua
mark in underglaze blue), with bulbous body, tall cylindrical
neck, decorated with incised dragons in pursuit of flaming
pearl among clouds, covered in a pale gray green glaze . . . . . . . . . . . . . . . . . . $800-1,000

Vase, 20" h., 18th century, lobed shape with eight ribs
extending to the base, interior and base glazed white . . . . . . . . . . . . . . . . . . . $800-1,000

Vase, 21" h., Ming Dynasty, Chekiang celadon, yen yen
shape with incised trellis pattern, covered with a translucent,
crackled green glaze . . . . . . . . . . . . . . . . . . . . . . . . . . . . . . . . . . . . . . . . . . . . . . $1,600-1,800

Vase, 22" h., 19th century, yen yen form. (Illus.) . . . . . . . . . . . . . . . . . . . . . . . $2,000-2,500

The art of Champlevé postdated cloisonné in both China and Japan. It is
comprised of a metal body (usually bronze or brass) which is stamped,
etched, or graved to form depressions into which enamel is placed; then
the item is then fired. Cruder in appearance than cloisonné, it is thought
by many to antedate that craft, but this is not so. It is commonly found in

## Champlevé
### (Chinese)

large pieces such as umbrella stands, lamps, bowls, etc., in the form of a band or two of enameled design with much bare metal exposed. Occasionally, items with complex designs are found, or those made of more precious metals (although this is rare, as there is much wasted metal).

Incenser, 8½" h., 19th century, tripod form on cylindrical feet with deeply rounded body, upright handles, and domed cover. Design of lotus blossoms and scrolls on a turquoise blue ground; cover pierced with cash motifs and topped by bud finial. . . . . . . . . . . . . . . . . . . . . . . . . . . . . . . . . . . . . . . . . . . . . . . . $225-400

Urn, 10¾" h., 19th century, globular form set on four bird supports; domed cover, spout in form of bird head; U-shaped swivel handle. Foliate and lappet bands on the body; narrow enameled band on cover which has a seated monkey atop it . . . . . . . . . . . . . . . . . . . . . . . . . . . . . . . . . . . . . . . . . . . . $500-600

Vase, 5⅜" h., Ch'ien Lung, gilt bronze vase with design of flowering prunus branch in shaded pink and yellow with red and green centers, black branch with mottled white bark; black enameled 14-character inscription . . . . . . . . . . . . . . . . . . . . . . . . $1,250-1,700

## Champlevé
### (Japanese)

Figure, 8¼" w., 9⅝" h., 18th century, chariot in shape of phoenix, cast bronze base; blue green and deep russet enameling of the wheels and body; stylized head feathers . . . . . . . . . . . . . . . $925-1,100

Urn, 7" h., handled, iris and mons design on bronze ground, marked Japan . . . . . . . . . . . . . . . . . . . . . . . . . . . . . . . . . . . . . . . . . . . . . . $90-125

Vase, 14" high, dragon handles, phoenix design on bronze . . . . . . . . . . . . . . . . . . . $195-250

## Ch'êng-hua
### (Chinese)

Ch'êng-hua was a Ming Dynasty emperor who ruled during the years 1465-1487. This period is celebrated for the innovation of the beautiful tou-ts'ai enamels, particularly the so decorated "chicken cups" of the period. Of the scarce and rare items of this period that can be found today, the underglaze blue and white wares are the most likely to be encountered. Copies of the wares of this period were made during succeeding reigns, often using the Ch'eng-hua reign mark.

(See: Ming Dynasty)

## Chia Ching
### (Chinese — Ming Dynasty)

The Chia Ching reign (1522-1566) is celebrated for the special quality of its cobalt blue, which is dark and brilliant, tending to violet or purple. An innovation of this reign was the introduction of wu-ts'ai (five-color) enameled ware. A novelty of the time was the application of gold leaf tracery designs on green or red backgrounds, subsequently named "Kinrande" by the Japanese. Porcelains so decorated may also appear with cutout and incised decoration. Blue and white wares predominate in the porcelain production of this reign.

(See: Ming Dynasty)

## Ch'ien Lung
### (Chinese)

The Ch'ien Lung reign (1736-1795) was a productive time for innovative and novel techniques in porcelain design as well as being famous for its "remakes" of old styles, particularly: Imperial style celadons, "Ting" white porcelain, Lung-Ch'üan celadons, Ching Pai, Chün, Ming style blue and white wares, and wu-ts'ai. There was an assortment of monochromes. Flambé was a specialty of this period, as were tea dust, iron rust, robin's egg, and gilded and enameled porcelain made to resemble old bronze forms. Rose pink enamels were used as monochromes, background colors, or painted on as decoration. Included in this production is the rose enameled export patterns decorated in Canton. Lacework, rice pattern, and openwork carving were also specialties of this period. Lac Burgauté was also produced. Although the technical excellence in decoration and fineness of modeling were at their peak during this reign, the production of novelties and the demands of the export trade resulted in a reduction of quality toward the end of the period. The close of the Ch'ien Lung period, therefore, is regarded by connoisseurs as the beginning of the decline of porcelain art in China.

(See: Topic headings mentioned in the above for Ch'ien Lung examples; also Peach Bloom)

*Ch'ien Lung shallow bowl, 7¾" dia., tou-ts'ai decoration*

Bowl, 7¾" dia., mark and period, the shallow bowl decorated with emblems surrounding a central stylized pomegranate design, the exterior with stylized floral motif, all executed in tou-ts'ai technique. (Illus. here and in Color Section) .................................................. $1,400-1,800

Bowl, 13½" dia., unmarked, exterior decorated with a blue glaze with four gilt sprays of peony blossoms outlined in iron red on white reserves, rim decorated on both sides with gilt floral and geometric borders ........................................... $1,800-2,200

Bowl, 16" l. x 8¼" h., on well carved, wooden lotus leaf stand, unmarked, decoration in famille verte colors, interior decorated with figures in boats on a river landscape with a wide border of reserves of river scenes and birds separated by diaper and floral designs, exterior with four reserves, women on a floating pavilion; a kylin; a foo dog; men playing checkers ....................................................... $3,800-4,200

Dish, 6" dia., seal mark in underglaze blue, tou-ts'ai enamel decoration, center decorated with dragon chasing flaming pearl, outer rim decorated with five cloud forms and a dragon with filled in colors of red, green, lavender, and yellow, underside of dish with waves and cloud motifs .................... $2,000-2,500

Dish, 7⅛" dia., seal mark in underglaze blue, decorated with two dragons and flaming pearls in green enamel on a bright yellow background ...................................................... $2,500-3,000

Dish, 10" dia., mark and period, the center with a leaping dragon chasing a flaming pearl amidst clouds and flames, enclosed by two dragons and pearls around the border, the pattern repeated underside above lappet border, all picked out in lemon yellow enameled on a washed blue ground, six-character mark in underglaze blue. (Illus.) ............................ $2,500-3,000

Dish, 15" dia., unmarked and unglazed base, blue and white decoration of floral scroll and a ju-i border ............................... $1,000-1,200

Figure, 10" h., rooster, unmarked, depicted resting with legs on either side of a brown glazed rockwork base, rooster glazed white with a red comb, yellow legs, and underglaze blue eyes ....................................................... $800-1,000

Figure, 14" h. x 12" l., foo dog, including wood stand, (unmarked), heavy solid porcellaneous figure of a female with cub on her back, decorated with a blue mane and tail on an incised coffee glazed body, white teeth and ruff on neck ....................................................... $2,500-3,000

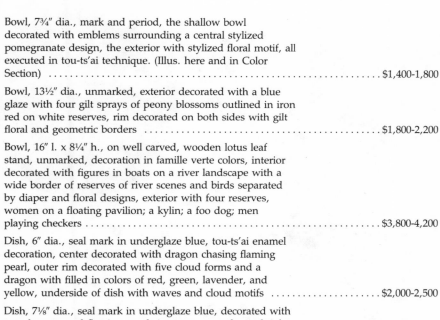

*Ch'ien Lung seal mark in underglaze blue*

*Ch'ien Lung dish, 10" dia., blue and yellow dragon motif*

Figure, 15½" h., Liu Hai standing on a toad, unmarked, decorated in polychrome and gilt with famille rose pink enamel under the toad's neck, the figure holding a water dropper pointing towards the toad's open mouth, a gold coin in the other hand . . . . . . . . . . . . . . . . . . . . . . . . . . . . . . . . . . . . . . . $1,900-2,200

Incense burner, 24" h., unmarked, modeled as a pagoda; base separates from building, glazed in green, cream, brown, and blue. (See Color Section) . . . . . . . . . . . . . . . . . . . . . . . . . . . . . . . $1,500-1,700

Jar, 14¾" h., unmarked, globular body, painted on the exterior with elaborate lotus heads and foliage below a small band of ju-i heads at the shoulder . . . . . . . . . . . . . . . . . . . . . . . . . . . . . $4,500-5,500

Pot stand, 6" h., unmarked, square-waisted shape with flat, pierced top, decorated with wu-ts'ai enamels, design of alternating panels of phoenixes and dragons among cloud scrolls . . . . . . . . . . . . . . . . . . . . . . . . . . . . . . . . . . . . . . . . . . . . . . . . . . $1,400-1,800

Saucer dish, 3½" dia., seal mark in underglaze blue, glazed a bright lemon yellow on the surface, underside glazed white . . . . . . . . . . . . $5,500-6,500

*Ch'ien Lung seal mark in underglaze blue*

*Ch'ien Lung vase, celadon, 5" h.*

*Ch'ien Lung vase, 9¼" h., iron red glaze*

Vase, 4½" h., unmarked, 18th century Ch'ien Lung, double-gourd form with vertical ribbing, covered with a thick creamy white glaze ending above foot rim . . . . . . . . . . . . . . . . . . . . . . . . . . . . . . . $200-300

Vase, 5" h., mark and period, celadon glaze, of squat form, incised underglaze with a motif of leaves above a key fret band, the body with ribbed design, with applied handles at shoulders. (Illus.) . . . . . . . . . . . . . . . . . . . . . . . . . . . . . . . . . . . . . . . . . . . . . $800-1,000

Vase, 6" h., unmarked, pear-shaped form covered with a deep purple glaze . . . . . . . . . . . . . . . . . . . . . . . . . . . . . . . . . . . . . . . . . . . . $600-700

Vase, 6" h., unmarked, 18th century Ch'ien Lung, bottle-shaped, covered with a turquoise glaze over biscuit . . . . . . . . . . . . . . . . . . $300-400

Vase, 6" h., unmarked, 18th century Ch'ien Lung, mei ping form covered with an unusual turquoise shade of robin's egg blue, lightly crackled, base and interior glazed white . . . . . . . . . . . . . . . . . . $700-900

Vase, 9¼" h., mark and period, iron red decoration with applied dragon wrapped around tall neck. (Illus. here and in Color Section) . . . . . . . . . . . . . . . . . . . . . . . . . . . . . . . . . . . . . . . . . . . . $900-1,200

Vase, 11" h., unmarked paint bottle with raised decoration of dragons and scrolling hibiscus in underglaze of copper red

and blue and set in relief against a thick brown ground, with
bands of squares and ju-i lappets at the top and bottom . . . . . . . . . . . . . . . . . . . . $800-1,000

Vase, 12½" h., unmarked, pear shaped, crackled greenish
gray glaze, the slightly flaring neck with a single raised rib
and applied with two openwork, stylized, elephant head
handles . . . . . . . . . . . . . . . . . . . . . . . . . . . . . . . . . . . . . . . . . . . . . . . . . . . . . . . . . . . $1,000-1,200

Vase, 14" h., unmarked, 18th century Ch'ien Lung, squat,
round body with a flaring mouth over a single-ring-decorated
long neck, covered with a glassy blue glaze which stops short
of the unglazed foot, with a rim chip . . . . . . . . . . . . . . . . . . . . . . . . . . . . . . . . $600-800

Vase, 16" h., unmarked, yen yen form, with a celadon
ground and white slip decoration in a design of branches and
peony and prunus blossoms . . . . . . . . . . . . . . . . . . . . . . . . . . . . . . . . . . . . . . . $1,200-1,600

Vase, 18" h., mei ping-shaped, covered with an overall glaze
of yellow . . . . . . . . . . . . . . . . . . . . . . . . . . . . . . . . . . . . . . . . . . . . . . . . . . . . . . . . . . $1,500-1,800

Vase, 19" h., seal mark in underglaze blue, blue and white
decoration, baluster form with scroll handles set at the neck,
decoration around the center of large flowers and ling chih
fungus, with a band of petal lappets at the shoulder and a
ju-i band at the base . . . . . . . . . . . . . . . . . . . . . . . . . . . . . . . . . . . . . . . . . . . . . . . $5,000-6,000

Vase, 24" h., unmarked, baluster form with two gilt, stylized
dragon handles mounted on neck, covered with a bright
green enamel with a continuous design of dragons in rose,
yellow, green, purple, and blue chasing flaming pearls
among pink, white, and blue cloud scrolls, decorative border
at lip and base, interior covered with a green tinted white
glaze, enameled with pink roses, damage to one handle . . . . . . . . . . . . . . . . . . . $3,000-3,500

## Ch'ien Yao
### (Chinese)

Ch'ien yao (named "Temmoku ware" by the Japanese) was first produced in China during the Sung Dynasty. Temmoku is named after t'ien-mu-shan, a Japanese name for a sacred Buddhist mountain. Ch'ien yao wares were used in the tea ceremonies of Japan and are held in high esteem by today's collectors. They have a lustrous, brown black glaze which may have tints of purple or blue. Within the glaze appear mottled streaks of blue, green, or brown which disappear into the black, giving the appearance known as "hare's fur." There are other rarer specimens which are speckled all over with silver and have the appearance of "oil spots."

*Ch'ien yao bowl, 4¼" dia., Sung Dynasty

Bowl, 4" dia., Sung Dynasty, glazed in black streaked with
brown, shading to a light olive tone on the rim, the
underside left unglazed . . . . . . . . . . . . . . . . . . . . . . . . . . . . . . . . . . . . . . . . . . . . $500-700

Bowl, 4" dia., Sung Dynasty, flared sides covered with a
brown to black glaze, the glaze falling short of the unglazed
reddish ware foot . . . . . . . . . . . . . . . . . . . . . . . . . . . . . . . . . . . . . . . . . . . . . . . . $900-1,000

*Bowl, 4¼" dia., interior with three dark "paper cutout," oval
quatrefoil panels on a white and mottled brown ground; the
exterior with a darker glaze; restored . . . . . . . . . . . . . . . . . . . . . . . . . . . . . . . $1,400

Bowl, 4¼" dia., Sung Dynasty, conical form with a
brown-to-black mottled glaze ending short of the buff ware
unglazed base; some kiln grit on the foot . . . . . . . . . . . . . . . . . . . . . . . . . . . $350-450

Bowl, 4¾" dia., Sung Dynasty, covered with a dark brown
glaze with iridescent "oil spots" . . . . . . . . . . . . . . . . . . . . . . . . . . . . . . . . . . . $1,000-1,200

Bowl, 5" dia., 19th century, copy of Sung bowl with a leaf
impression inside and a dark black glaze ending above an
unglazed foot rim . . . . . . . . . . . . . . . . . . . . . . . . . . . . . . . . . . . . . . . . . . . . . . . . $400-450

Bowl, 5" dia., Sung Dynasty, deeply potted form, the glaze a
dark brown to black at the center and rim with red brown
"hare's fur" and green streaks . . . . . . . . . . . . . . . . . . . . . . . . . . . . . . . . . . . . . $1,100-1,300

Bowl, 5" dia., Sung Dynasty, flared sides covered with a red brown glaze with blue black streaks of "hare's fur" ........................ $1,500-2,000

## Chinese Carpets and Rugs

The craft of making carpets and rugs was introduced to China via Persia (Iran) and India. In China, carpets and rugs have been used as floor coverings, pillar coverings, and on the K'ang (a platform upon which one slept). Carpets and rugs were also used as wall coverings or hangings, not only for their beauty, but to keep warmth within the home. Until the mid-19th century, subtle colors (sometimes only two hues) were used. Blue was predominant and was used for patterns set against ecru and brown grounds. Yellow was the imperial color and was used for carpets and rugs made for the imperial court. After the mid-19th century, color ranges changed, with brighter and more varied hues being introduced to conform with the tastes of Western markets. The two main knots used in Chinese carpets and rugs are the Sehna and Ghiordes. The Sehna is usually found at the ends of rows. Chinese rugs and carpets have a deep pile which can be either embossed or incised. (Embossing: knotting the carpet or rug on two levels with one set of knots being shorter. Incising: cutting the pile to accentuate the pattern.) Note: carpets are generally over ten feet — rugs are generally under ten feet.

Carpet, 11' x 10', light yellow field with sun medallion and dragons within a vine border ........................................... $4,500-6,000

Carpet, 11'2" x 7'9", tan field with flowering urns, butterflies, and scattered birds within a blue outer border containing foliage .......................................................... $295-340

Carpet, 11'3" x 7'2", blue field with blue and beige medallions filled with Shou symbols, within a deep blue border containing vines and butterflies .......................................... $800-1,400

Carpet, 11'5" x 9'8", deep green field with blossoming tree having red, blue, orange, and lavender flowers ......................... $1,400-1,900

Carpet, 12'4" x 9'7", gold field containing "hundred antiques" within an ivory border containing floral sprigs within an outer border of blue ................................................ $5,000-$7,000

Carpet, 14' x 9', maroon field with motif of peony blossoms and birds perched on branches, within a deep yellow border containing floral sprigs ............................................... $400-650

Carpet, 14'2" x 12', blue field within a blue outer border containing gold leaves ............................................. $2,300-3,000

Carpet 19'6" x 12'9", cream field filled with "hundred antiques" motif, floral ivory border within an outer border of deep blue ..................................................... $12,000-15,000

Carpet (Peking), 12' x 9', blue field with a central pagoda within a medallion, surrounded by flowering spandrels within a gold outer border ....................................... $1,500-2,200

Carpet (Peking), 15' x 11', blue field with symbolic motifs, within a pale orange border containing birds and scrolls, within an outer border of butterflies on a brown ground ................ $2,750-3,300

Carpet (Peking), 15'7" x 12'8", deep blue field with a central vase filled with flowers, scattered flowers throughout, within a beige border filled with flowers and scrolling vines, within a deep blue outer border ......................................... $2,500-3,850

Carpet (round), 12' dia., T pattern, peony medallions, blue border ...................................................... $7,000-9,000

Carpet (round), 18' dia., beige field with central motif of blue Shou symbols .............................................. $3,000-4,000

Mat, 2' x 3', deep red field having a green border containing
birds perched on tree branches . . . . . . . . . . . . . . . . . . . . . . . . . . . . . . . . . . . . . . . . . . . . . . . . . . . . . . . . $200-265

Mat, 2'9" x 2', deep green field with overall floral motifs . . . . . . . . . . . . . . . . . . . . . . . . . . . $65-85

Mat, 3'7" x 3', ivory field with motif of flower vases . . . . . . . . . . . . . . . . . . . . . . . . . . . . $120-140

Mat, 4'2" x 2'1", red field containing butterflies, within a deep
blue border containing flowers . . . . . . . . . . . . . . . . . . . . . . . . . . . . . . . . . . . . . . . . . . . . . . . . . . . $225-300

Mat, 4'7" x 2'11", red field with blossoming trees and
butterflies within a burgundy border . . . . . . . . . . . . . . . . . . . . . . . . . . . . . . . . . . . . . . . . . . $150-185

Mat, 4'9" x 3", deep blue field with multicolored florals . . . . . . . . . . . . . . . . . . . . . . . $200-300

Mat (oval), 4' x 2'5", deep blue field with urn filled with
flowers within a deep brown border . . . . . . . . . . . . . . . . . . . . . . . . . . . . . . . . . . . . . . . . . . $120-150

Mat (oval), 5' x 2'3", scalloped border, beige field with
multicolored floral motifs . . . . . . . . . . . . . . . . . . . . . . . . . . . . . . . . . . . . . . . . . . . . . . . . . . . . . . . $300-425

Mat (round), 2', scattered floral motifs on a blue ground . . . . . . . . . . . . . . . . . . . . . . $30-45

Rug, 3' x 3', yellow with five dragons and waves . . . . . . . . . . . . . . . . . . . . . . . . . . $2,000-2,750

Rug (Peking), 5' x 3', blue field with flowering vases within a
green outer border . . . . . . . . . . . . . . . . . . . . . . . . . . . . . . . . . . . . . . . . . . . . . . . . . . . . . . . . . . . . . . $500-800

Rug (silk), 8' x 4', five swirling dragons in shades of blue,
gold, and ivory with ivory cloud bands within a blue and
white wave border . . . . . . . . . . . . . . . . . . . . . . . . . . . . . . . . . . . . . . . . . . . . . . . . . . . . . . . . $6,000-10,000

# Chinese Export
## (Chinese)

Prior to the 16th century the Chinese exported their ceramic wares to India, Persia, and Egypt. The first European trade was established with the Portuguese who founded Macao in the 16th century. In 1602 the Dutch East India Company captured the Portuguese vessels and took over the sea routes, sailing to Asia and other European ports. By the end of the 17th century whole cargoes of blue and white wares were carried to Europe. Soon thereafter customers of other newly formed East India companies gave orders along with patterns and designs to be filled in China. During the 18th century vast amounts of porcelain characterized by European shapes were exported to the West. Tureens, vegetable dishes, sauceboats, creamers, were popular orders as well as figural pieces depicting people, animals, and birds. Such wares continued to flow from China into the late 19th century, fashioned in style, shape, and color to suit Western tastes.

(See: Armorial; Canton; Fitzhugh; Kraak; Nanking; Rose Canton; Rose Mandarin; Rose Medallion)

*Chinese export vases, mounted as lamps, late 18th century*

Bowl, armorial, 12" dia., 18th century, interior with an
English crest; exterior with two English crests on either side
separated by two floral sprays . . . . . . . . . . . . . . . . . . . . . . . . . . . . . . . . . . . . . . . . . . . . . $1,000-1,200

Charger, 18" dia., 18th century, painted in famille rose
enamels, decorated with a central floral medallion and five
floral sprays, with a gold and iron red spearhead border . . . . . . . . . . . . . . . . . . $1,200-1,500

Cream pitcher, 6" h., early 19th century, iron red decoration,
helmet-shaped . . . . . . . . . . . . . . . . . . . . . . . . . . . . . . . . . . . . . . . . . . . . . . . . . . . . . . . . . . . . . . . . . . $300-400

Cup and saucer, Fitzhugh pattern, late 19th century, green . . . . . . . . . . . . . . . . . . . . $100-125

Dish, 11" dia., 18th century, blue and white decoration with a
central village and river scene, the cavetto with a trellis
pattern separating four floral reserves, and four other floral
groups spaced around the border, the underside in white
glaze. (Illus.) . . . . . . . . . . . . . . . . . . . . . . . . . . . . . . . . . . . . . . . . . . . . . . . . . . . . . . . . . . . . . . . . . . . $400-600

Dish, 15" dia., 18th century, octagonal shape, the center with
flowers, surrounded by a floral border; in colors of pink,
blue, green, and gold . . . . . . . . . . . . . . . . . . . . . . . . . . . . . . . . . . . . . . . . . . . . . . . . . . . . . . . $1,200-1,300

*Chinese export dish, 11" dia., blue and white, 18th century*

Dishes (pair), 8½" dia., 18th century, with strawberry motif and reticulated border trimmed with gilt .......................... $300-400

Figure, Kuan Yin, 22" h., 19th century, molded on a rockwork base, decorated in bright enamels ........................ $600-700

Figures, cockerels (pair), 19th century, rockwork bases in colors of pink, blue, green, yellow, and ruby red ................ $880-1,000

Figures, dogs, 9" h., early 19th century, covered with a turquoise glaze, on aubergine rockwork ....................... $300-400

*Garniture set, 18th century, covered baluster vase and two similar, pear-shaped vases, with mandarin medallions and leafy scrolls in relief, decorated in pink, iron red, green, turquoise, and gilt enamels ................................... $1,800

Grotto figure, 12" h., 18th century, modeled as a Buddhist sage in a mountain enclosure below pines and pierced rockwork, with beaker vases, jardinieres, and archaic vessels ... $600-800

Mug, 5" h., late 18th century, cylindrical shape with underglaze blue borders of flowers and leaves, famille rose enamels of flowers and butterflies ........................ $400-450

Mug, 5" h., 18th century, cylindrical shape, decorated in famille rose colors with women and children in a garden, gilt rim border ............................................. $450-550

Mug, 5" h., late 18th century, barrel-shaped, decorated in famille rose colors with floral sprays and a pink scale band at the foot .............................................. $400-500

Pitcher, 12" h., decorated in famille rose enamels with a scene of ladies playing musical instruments surrounded by men and children ...................................... $400-600

Planters (pair), 6" h., late 18th century, the square bodies decorated with two Europeans wearing robes and flat hats while standing on a terrace, blue and white decoration ...... $500-700

Plate, Fitzhugh pattern, 9" dia., 18th century, orange American eagle in center with red, white, and blue shield ... $1,000-1,200

Plate (warming dish), Fitzhugh pattern, 12" dia., 18th century, orange, with hollow base and two tabs at either side for hot water, the center with initials in a center monogram .... $1,100-1,200

Plates (set of 8), armorial, 9" dia., with a Scotch crest in the center in iron red, green, grisaille, brown, and gilt, with a gilt scroll border ........................................ $800-1,200

Platter, Fitzhugh pattern, 12" oval, early 19th century, green ... $1,100-1,200

Platter, armorial, 15" l., rectangular, 18th century, with single central crest "en grisaille" and gilt, with a border of gilt and iron red ........................................... $500-700

Sugar bowl and cover, 8" h., 18th century, the body decorated with two double-looped handles and two sepia wreath reserves containing urns beneath willow trees ...... $400-500

Teapot, 5" h., mid-18th century, decorated with insects and flowers "en grisaille" and gilt .......................... $150-200

Teapot, 11" h., 18th century, decorated with a scene of ladies and gentlemen in a court setting in iron red, blue, orange, green, and gilt ........................................ $450-600

Tureen, 14" l., late 19th century, figural, in the form of a pig, painted in orange with gilt highlights, with two central panels in famille verte colors .......................... $600-800

Vase, 6" h., 19th century, lotus bottle form, double gourd shape, relief molded and enameled in famille rose ......... $300-400

Vase, 10" h., 18th century, double bottle form, blue and white decoration of flowers, the two spiraling bottles with outcurving necks to serve as oil and vinegar containers ... $300-400

*Vases (pair), 42" h., late 18th century, tall, flattened, pear-shaped bodies, each vividly enameled with colors and

molded in relief with two panels of figures on each side, the
sides with smaller panels, all in dense black, iron red and gilt
pattern ground, mounted as lamps. (Illus.) .................................... $4,000

Wall pockets (pair), 11" h., 19th century, decorated with
bands of floral and ju-i heads at top and bottom, all in blue
and white glaze ....................................................... $400-500

# Chinese Paintings

The 7th and 8th centuries brought the emergence of great Chinese
painters such as Yen Li-pen, Wu Toa-Tzu, Wang Wei, et al. During this
early time, artists preferred to paint on rolls. Paintings were basically
landscapes, although some artists preferred animals. The art of figure
painting reached an elegant state during the T'ang Dynasty. Court life,
historical subjects, animals, as well as human figures were depicted. It
was during the Sung Dynasty that portrait paintings emerged and the
technique of monochrome ink paintings was developed. During the
Yuan Dynasty painting was a most important art form and was regarded
as one of the superior forms of expression. During the Ming Dynasty,
there was encouragement of the arts. Schools of painting arose, including
Wu and Che. Among the superb painters of this period were Tung Ch'i-
Ch'ang, Shen Chow, and Tai Chin. The Ch'ing Dynasty brought a high
level of technical competence. There were great imitations of Yuan
masters produced, and paintings were executed in both dry and wet
brush techniques. Elegant calligraphic interpretations of poems often
accentuated picture formats and paintings were produced on cloth, silk,
and paper.

*Album of Sung and Yuan Dynasties paintings. (Illus.) ......................... $330,000

Ancestral portrait, 27" x 24⅛", ink and colors on paper, late
19th century. Court lady seated on chair, her attire showing a
mandarin square signifying sixth rank. (See Mandarin
Squares) ....................................................... $800-1,200

Ancestral portrait, 35" x 20", 19th century, ink and colors on
silk, Mandarin gentleman seated on chair .................................... $600-800

*From album of Sung and Yuan dynasty paintings: "Worshipping the stars in the palace of the Han Dynasty." Round fan, ink and colors on silk, late 12th century. Sold at Christie's, New York, for $330,000.*

Ancestral portrait, 42″ x 19″, framed size, colors on paper. Court lady seated . . . . . . . . . . . . . . . . . . . . . . . . . . . . . . . . . . . . . . . . . . . . . . . . . . . . . . . . . . . . . . . . . . . . . . . . $500-700

Hanging scroll, 79″ x 39″, ink and colors on silk, eighteen figures in pavilions . . . . . . . . . . . . . . . . . . . . . . . . . . . . . . . . . . . . . . . . . . . . . . . . . . . . . . . . $1,800-2,500

Hanging scroll, 13″ x 13″, late 19th century, ink and primary colors on silk, scholar seated by a river bank . . . . . . . . . . . . . . . . . . . . . . . . . . . . . . . . . . . $275-375

Hanging scroll, 16″ x 10″, 19th century, ink and colors on paper, two women on a balcony engaged in conversation . . . . . . . . . . . . . . . . . . . . . . $400-550

Hanging scroll, 26½″ x 12″, 19th century, ink on paper, ladies and rabbits in a garden . . . . . . . . . . . . . . . . . . . . . . . . . . . . . . . . . . . . . . . . . . . . . . . . . $500-700

Hanging scroll, 36⅜″ x 13½″, ink and colors on silk, landscape with pavilions and courtesans . . . . . . . . . . . . . . . . . . . . . . . . . . . . . . . . . . . . . . . . $170-185

Hanging scroll, 39″ x 20½″, ink and colors on silk, landscape featuring three brown horses and two white horses . . . . . . . . . . . . . . . . . . . . . . $250-350

Hanging scroll, 50″ x 28″, 20th century, mounted on board, seated Buddha . . . . . . . . . . . . . . . . . . . . . . . . . . . . . . . . . . . . . . . . . . . . . . . . . . . . . . . . . . . . $400-600

Hanging scroll, 54″ x 28½″, ink and colors on paper, celestial deities . . . . . . . . . . . . . . . . . . . . . . . . . . . . . . . . . . . . . . . . . . . . . . . . . . . . . . . . . . . . . . . . . . $300-475

Hanging scroll, 57″ x 28″, 19th century, ink and colors on silk, Lohan in poses . . . . . . . . . . . . . . . . . . . . . . . . . . . . . . . . . . . . . . . . . . . . . . . . . . . . . . . . $350-450

Painting, erotic, framed size 18″ x 24″, early 20th century, ink and colors on paper . . . . . . . . . . . . . . . . . . . . . . . . . . . . . . . . . . . . . . . . . . . . . . . . . . $250-325

Painting, fan, approximately 10½″ x 10″, 18th century, ink and colors on silk, songbird and Lichees . . . . . . . . . . . . . . . . . . . . . . . . . . . . . . . . . . $400-600

Painting on silk, approximately 50″ x 21″, ink and colors, late Ch'ing Dynasty, women and children on terraces . . . . . . . . . . . . . . . . . . . . . . $165-190

# Chinese Robes and Other Apparel

From the Ming Dynasty onward, Chinese embroidered garments have been admired as works of art. There are two basic robes; those worn in the winter and those worn in the summer. Imperial robes were produced in the imperial silk factories and robes for other officials were produced in private establishments. The ceremonial imperial dress (robe) had a five-clawed dragon and the flaming pearl as its central motif. The summer garments were made of lightweight silk, linen, or gauze. Such a garment was gathered around the waist with a silk girdle and was usually fastened in front with a jade or agate clasp. The winter garments were loose fitting and worn over a long dress made of either crepe or silk. Over these garments was worn a long sleeved coat which was usually elaborately embroidered with silk needlework.

Apron, late 19th century, gold couching and multicolored
embroidery with floral motifs . . . . . . . . . . . . . . . . . . . . . . . . . . . . . . . . . . . . . . . . . . . . $250-300

Apron, pink satin panels with gold couched phoenix, wave
border with silver couching . . . . . . . . . . . . . . . . . . . . . . . . . . . . . . . . . . . . . . . . . . . . . . $400-500

Coat, late 19th century, lotus and butterflies in satin stitch,
sleeve bands with blue and green embroidered flowers . . . . . . . . . . . . . . . . . . . . . . . $700-900

Coat, c. 1900, silk with gold couching stitch and satin stitch,
butterflies and birds . . . . . . . . . . . . . . . . . . . . . . . . . . . . . . . . . . . . . . . . . . . . . . . . . . . . $600-800

Coat, late 19th century, blue silk, embroidered butterflies and
flowers, satin and Peking stitches . . . . . . . . . . . . . . . . . . . . . . . . . . . . . . . . . . . . . . $875-1,000

Jacket, 20th century, white satin, rose flowers, couching in
blue . . . . . . . . . . . . . . . . . . . . . . . . . . . . . . . . . . . . . . . . . . . . . . . . . . . . . . . . . . . . . . . . . . $225-350

Jacket, late 19th century, black silk, wave border, gold and
white couching surrounded by multicolored embroidery in
floral motifs . . . . . . . . . . . . . . . . . . . . . . . . . . . . . . . . . . . . . . . . . . . . . . . . . . . . . . . . . . $450-500

Jacket, early 20th century, red satin, embroidered motifs of
flowers and butterflies . . . . . . . . . . . . . . . . . . . . . . . . . . . . . . . . . . . . . . . . . . . . . . . . . $250-320

Robe (child's), blue silk, eight dragons and clouds, bats with
border of waves and carp, gold couching . . . . . . . . . . . . . . . . . . . . . . . . . . . . . . . . $300-375

Robe (child's), c. 1900, yellow satin and gold couching,
dragons and peonies in blue, red, yellow, and green . . . . . . . . . . . . . . . . . . . . . . . $290-325

Robe (child's), early 19th century, blue silk, fish and wave
border with stitching in shades of red, blue, and green . . . . . . . . . . . . . . . . . . . . . $250-325

Dragon robe, late 19th century, black silk, gold couching, five
dragons on collar, dragon reserves on cuffs . . . . . . . . . . . . . . . . . . . . . . . . . . . . . . $400-500

Dragon robe, black satin, eight medallions of peonies, border
in gold couching . . . . . . . . . . . . . . . . . . . . . . . . . . . . . . . . . . . . . . . . . . . . . . . . . . . . . . . $800-950

Dragon robe, early 19th century, blue silk, four-clawed
dragon, cranes, and clouds in white, blue, and red satin
stitch, border on sleeves with gold dragons . . . . . . . . . . . . . . . . . . . . . . . . . . . . . . $300-400

Dragon robe, mid-19th century, black silk, dragons, bats, and
clouds. (Illus.) . . . . . . . . . . . . . . . . . . . . . . . . . . . . . . . . . . . . . . . . . . . . . . . . . . . . . . . $900-1,200

Dragon robe, c. 1910, red silk, gold couched dragons, blue
satin bands on sleeves with small dragon motifs . . . . . . . . . . . . . . . . . . . . . . . . . . $400-500

Dragon robe, early 20th century, light purple gauze,
five-clawed dragon in gold and longevity (Shou) symbols
throughout with border of black gauze . . . . . . . . . . . . . . . . . . . . . . . . . . . . . . . . . . $350-450

Dragon robe, red silk, Shou symbols, cranes, clouds, in
yellow and green with blue and purple satin stitches, gold
neck and border with black silk sleeves . . . . . . . . . . . . . . . . . . . . . . . . . . . . . . . . . $450-550

Dragon robe, red silk, multicolored flowers, dragon, Shou
symbols, and Buddhist symbols with gold couching, blue
satin neck and cuffs . . . . . . . . . . . . . . . . . . . . . . . . . . . . . . . . . . . . . . . . . . . . . . . . . . . $600-800

Dragon robe, late 18th century, yellow silk, nine dragons,
gold couching, bats, clouds, wave border . . . . . . . . . . . . . . . . . . . . . . . . . . . . . . $4,000-5,000

Dragon robe, yellow satin, brocaded dragons and Shou
symbols in gold, turquoise waves . . . . . . . . . . . . . . . . . . . . . . . . . . . . . . . . . . . . . . . $400-575

Shawl, black silk, dragon and flaming pearl in pink with
heavily knotted fringe . . . . . . . . . . . . . . . . . . . . . . . . . . . . . . . . . . . . . . . . . . . . . . . . . . $400-500

*Dragon robe, mid-19th century, black silk, blue and yellow clouds, bats and waves in colors*

**Ch'ing Dynasty**
*(Chinese)*

The Ch'ing Dynasty spanned the years 1644-1912, ending when the Republic of China was formed. There were eleven emperors who reigned during this period.

| | |
|---|---|
| Shun Chih | 1644-1661 |
| K'ang Hsi | 1662-1722 |
| Yung Chêng | 1723-1735 |
| Ch'ien Lung | 1736-1795 |
| Chia Ch'ing | 1796-1820 |
| Tao Kuang | 1821-1850 |
| Hsien Fêng | 1851-1861 |
| T'ung Chih | 1862-1874 |
| Kuang Hsü | 1875-1908 |
| Hsüan T'ung | 1909-1912 |

(See: Ch'ien Lung; K'ang Hsi; Nineteenth Century; Yung Chêng)

**Ching Pai**
*(Chinese)*

"Ching pai" is the term for a particular glaze which appeared at the close of the Sung Dynasty. The glaze is a thin, pale blue applied on a white body. Such wares were probably produced in the area of Ching-tê-chên.

Similar to Ting ware and northern celadons in decoration, the Ching pai porcelains have beautifully carved designs under the glaze.

(See: Ying-Ch'ing)

Chün yao is a ware first produced in the Honan province during the Sung Dynasty. The typical glaze is a sky blue with furnace transmutation flambé which varies from green to purple to copper red. The highest quality wares had a white body. Gray, red, or yellow bodies were used in common ware. The transformation to splashes of flambé within the glaze was accomplished during the firing by adding a copper compound to the glaze.

## Chün Yao
### (Chinese)

Bowl, 4¼" dia., Sung Dynasty, deep rounded sides, with allover glaze of pale, greenish blue, the unglazed foot rim burnt red in the firing ................................................. $800-1,000

Bowl, 6¼" dia., Yüan Dynasty, blue glaze with a large purple splash on interior and exterior along with many iron spots, the unglazed foot revealing the buff brown clay body. (Illus.) ............... $1,000-1,200

Bowl, 6½" dia., Yüan Dynasty, shallow form with rounded sides, with an opaque, gray-blue, thick glaze, the foot unglazed ........................................................ $450-600

Bowl, 8" dia., Sung Dynasty, rounded sides, lavender blue color with a splash of purple on one side of the bowl's interior ......................................................... $800-1,000

Bowl, 8" dia., Yüan Dynasty, interior and exterior with a streaked, turquoise blue glaze turning to aubergine at the rim ............... $2,500-3,000

Bowl, 10" dia., Yung Chêng period, incised, four-character seal mark, quatrafoil shape, with a streaked flambé glaze on the exterior and a bright milky blue Chun glaze on the interior, the blue changing to greenish brown at the ribs, the base with a yellow brown wash ......................................... $1,200-1,500

Censer, 4½" h., Yüan Dynasty, globular body on three short legs, a short neck, and slab handles at the sides of the rim; the body with a molded fleurette pattern, glaze a milky blue with a purple splash ................................................ $800-1,000

Dish, 4½" dia., Sung Dynasty, with slightly turned down rim, glazed in a pale lavender blue, with repair to the foot rim ...................................................... $800-1,000

Dish, 6½" dia., Sung Dynasty, with rounded sides, the glaze a blue-gray and falling short of the base ................................... $600-800

Dish, 7" dia., Sung Dynasty, with pale blue glaze shading to greenish buff towards the rim .......................................... $1,300-1,500

Dish, 7" dia., Yüan Dynasty, with flat, narrow rim, covered with a milky, blue-gray glaze shading to a light olive brown at the rim .................................................... $1,300-1,500

Jar, 5" h., Sung Dynasty, heavily potted with two small loop handles at the sides of the short neck, with a milky blue glaze overfired to a red brown, with a rim repair .......................... $900-1,100

Jar, 5" h., Yüan Dynasty, globular form with a short lipped rim; two flared handles and molded rings on the shoulders, covered with a pale blue glaze with brown crackle, with a purple splash on one side, buff pottery foot left unglazed .................. $3,000-3,500

Jar, 5" h., Yüan Dynasty, globular shape with a short neck and wide mouth, with two lug handles at each side, covered with a heavy grayish blue glaze, the foot burnt brown in the firing .................................................... $1,000-1,200

Jar, 6½" h., Sung Dynasty, globular shape with four looped handles, covered with a thick, grayish blue glaze ......................... $1,400-1,600

*Chün yao bowl, 6¼" dia., blue ground with purple splashes, Yuan Dynasty*

*\*Chün yao saucer dish, 4¼" dia., Southern Sung*

*Saucer dish, 4¼" dia., Southern Sung, with flared sides.
(Illus.) ........................................................................... $1,870

Vase, 6" h., Yüan/Ming Dynasty, pear shaped, glazed in a
pale blue with one purple splash on the body ...................... $1,200-1,400

## Cinnabar
*(Chinese)*

Chinese carved lacquer is found in many colors; however, the term Cinnabar refers to the red-vermillion hue which is most popular among collectors. By building up layer upon layer (sometimes as many as two hundred layers) over a metal or wood base, the lacquer becomes thick enough to carve. Early pieces tend to be more of a reddish brown color, whereas later pieces are a bright red.

Box, 5½" h., 19th century, of rounded form with lid showing
an official, with a trellis patterned background .................... $300-350

Box, 10" sq., marked "China," decorated with figures in a
garden setting .......................................................... $80-100

Box, 12" dia., 19th century, shaped like a leaf, the cover
showing a scene of a pavilion with small cartouches of
flowers ................................................................. $500-600

Box, 15" dia., Ch'ien Lung period, of compressed circular
form, with eight floral medallions on lobed body, the cover
having an intricately carved village scene ...................... $3,800-4,200

Box, 16" dia., 19th century, circular form, carved with a
basketweave design, the inside covered with black lacquer ...... $350-450

Brush pot, 7" h., 19th century, deeply carved showing a
mounted warrior on one side and women preparing tea on
the reverse ............................................................. $550-700

Dish, 8" dia., early 18th century, carved with a scene of
maidens in a mountain landscape; the underside decorated in
a diaper pattern (Illus.) .............................................. $300-400

Ju-i sceptre, 16" l., 19th century, with a low relief carving of a
sage and attendants at the terminal, the shaft carved with
Chinese emblems ...................................................... $700-900

Plate, 9" dia., Ch'ien Lung seal mark on inlaid brass plaque
set in back, carved with two dragons in pursuit of the
flaming pearl on a brass foundation, the reverse with diaper
patterns ................................................................ $600-800

Tray, 12" oval, late 19th century, carved with dragons in
clouds .................................................................. $250-300

Vase, 10" h., marked "China," carved with figures in a
landscape .............................................................. $60-80

Vase, 15", early 20th century, decorated with prunus
blossoms and figures in a garden ................................. $100-150

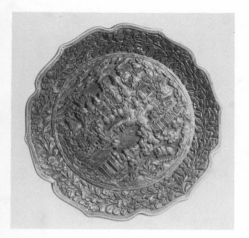

*Cinnabar dish, 8" dia., on brass*

## Clair de Lune
*(Chinese)*

The clair de lune (pale blue) glaze was developed in the early 18th century at the imperial kilns of Ching-tê Chên. The color was obtained by using a very small quantity of cobalt blue in the glaze. It is called "yüeh-pai" (moon white) by the Chinese.

Dish, 8" dia., 18th century, with the glaze thinning to a pale
blue white at the rim ................................................. $300-400

Dish, 9" dia., Yung Chêng period, six-character mark in
underglaze blue; glaze of pale blue green with an incised key
fret border; damaged ................................................. $600-700

Vase, 6¼" h., 18th century, baluster form, with two molded rings around the body and mask ring handles at the shoulders . . . . . . . . . . . . . . . . . . . . . . . . . . . . . . . . . . . . . . . . . . . . $300-500

Vase, 8½" h., 18th century, mei ping form, with the glaze thinning to white at the neck . . . . . . . . . . . . . . . . . . . . . . . . . . . . . . . . . . . . . . . . $600-800

Vase, 10" h., late 19th/early 20th century (commemorative Yung Chêng mark in underglaze blue), ovoid form body with incised, stylized phoenix . . . . . . . . . . . . . . . . . . . . . . . . . . . . . . . . . . . . . . $100-150

Vase, 10" h., 19th century (Kuang Hsü six-character mark in underglaze blue), mei ping form . . . . . . . . . . . . . . . . . . . . . . . . . . . . . . $600-700

Vase, 10¾" h., late 19th century (commemorative Ch'ien Lung seal mark in underglaze blue), incised handles and central medallions on the flattened, molded body . . . . . . . . . . . . . . . . . . . . . . . . $250-350

Vase, 12" h., 19th century (Kuang Hsü six-character mark in underglaze blue), archaic bronze form with two lug handles on the neck, with a shallow, relief-molded design of flowers on either side, covered with a crackled glaze . . . . . . . . . . . . . . . . . . . . . . . . . . . $600-800

Vase, 15" h., 18th century, baluster shape with pale violet blue glaze . . . . . . . . . . . . . . . . . . . . . . . . . . . . . . . . . . . . . . . . . . . . $1,000-1,500

Vase, 18½" h., late 18th, early 19th century, the unusual form having a pale blue glaze, with a lighter blue under the base. (Illus.) . . . . . . . . . . . . . . . . . . . . . . . . . . . . . . . . . . . . . . . . . . . . . $500-600

*Clair de lune vase, 18½" h., late 18th/early 19th century*

# Cloisonné

A painstaking combination of vitreous enamel and metal wires on a body material usually of metal composition, cloisonné is an artcraft which requires great technical knowledge as well as the ability to produce an aesthetically pleasing item. The wires are arranged in designs upon the metal body, into the compartments of which the enamels are packed (high temperature enamels first); the item is fired repeatedly to bring the enamels above the level of the wires, and the article is then buffed and polished many times. Many variations exist such as cloisonné on ceramics, "wireless" cloisonné in which the wires are removed prior to firing, baseless (pliqué à jour) cloisonné, etc. The process is known to have existed in Mycenaean Greece in 1300 B.C., and has been practiced throughout the world with notable success in Byzantium, France, Russia, China, and Japan. Cloisonné is currently produced in the People's Republic of China, Nationalist China, and Japan. Most items on the market today are of Chinese, Japanese, or Russian origin.

# Cloisonné
## (Chinese)

Known in China as Ch'ing tai-lan, the earliest verified examples date back to the 14th century. Chinese cloisonné is generally recognizable by its use of primary colors, thick gilded bronze, brass, or copper wires, and the presence of pitting in the enamels. Pitting is profuse in older pieces; today's examples are practically pit-free except for those made in imitation of the older wares. Enamels are generally opaque with a soft gloss finish. Designs incorporate stylized florals, dragons, geometrics, etc. Variations such as Openwork, silver wires, and translucent enamels exist.

Animal, 5" h. (without stand), 7" l., 20th century, camel with lift-off hump; blue, yellow, red design on turquoise ground; one of a pair. (Illus.) . . . . . . . . . . . . . . . . . . . . . . . . . . . . . . . . . . . . . . . . $700-800

*Chinese cloisonné animal, 5" h., from a private collection*

*Chinese cloisonné bowl, 9¼" dia.*

*Chinese cloisonné vessel, 6½" dia.*

*Chinese cloisonné box, 2½" dia. x 1½" h., from a private collection*

*Chinese cloisonné animal, 14" h. x 12" l. Courtesy of Sign of the Crane*

Animal, 7″ l. x 4″ h. x 3½″ w., mythological bearded dragon, covered, scroll design in multicolors on green ground, bronze antlers. ............................................................. $650-750

Animal, 11¾″ h., late 18th/early 19th century, goose, standing, beak open, head turned to one side, white plumage; yellow, blue, and green wing and tail feathers; gilded beak, webbed feet, and crest. Some pitting ......................... $1,300-1,500

Animal, 14″ h., 12″ l., late 19th century, dragon with ball of wisdom in shades of blue enamel, heavy gilding. (Illus.) ..................... $900-1,500

Animals, pair, 6¾″ l. x 4″ h., including base, 19th century, elephants, arabesque design in multicolors on turquoise ground. ............................................................ $1,700-2,100

Animals, pair, 9¼″ x 7″, phoenixes, urns on backs, multicolor pastels on light blue ground .......................... $1,700-2,100

Bowl, 7⅝″ dia., 19th century, shallow rounded sides, everted scalloped rim. Lotus scroll band on sides, a central shou medallion surrounded by floral scrolls, all on turquoise ground. Two character mark Ta Ming ........................ $500-650

Bowl, 9¼″ dia., 4½″ h., probably K'ang Hsi period, wan bowl. Eight galloping, flaming horses in dark red, yellow, cobalt blue, and light green among cloud diapers above waves around exterior; five rabbits (two yellow, one white, one dark red, and one pinkish) on ground with plants, moon overhead in inside center; sides of interior has "Three Friends" (pine, bamboo, and plum) in dark green and brown, yellowish brown, pale and dark green, and dark red, pink, white, and dark brown respectively. Also on interior sides, yellowish deer with white spots; red-crested crane (white with red legs, beak, crest, and eye, and black tail); dark green century plant with dark red and pink flowers, pale green leaves. Copper wires. Ch'ing tai reign mark enameled on bottom. (Illus.) .............................. $1,200-1,700

Bowls, pair, 5⅔″ w., late 18th century, four chased panels of characters on bat-scroll grounds; domed covers with wide-shaped flat rims decorated with formal lotus sprays, interlocking bats and four ruyi heads around a knop finial, on turquoise ground. Enamels slightly damaged .......................... $800-1,200

Box, 2½″ dia., 1½″ h., Ch'ien Lung, covered, round; red and blue lotus flowers on turquoise ground, gilded wires. Impressed mark on bottom reads "Ch'ien lung ko." (Illus.) ................... $800-1,000

Box, 3¾″ dia., 2¼″ h., Ch'ien Lung, round shape with cobalt blue and rust-red dragon with flaming pearl on cover, cloud cloisons on ground, with wave border; blue enameled interior and bottom ........................................ $175-250

Box, 6″ h. x 2⅞″ x 4″, late 18th century, rectangular, flower design on sky blue ground, with poem in black enamel, "Spring is coming and the buds are opening to the warmth." (See Color Section) ....................................... $800-950

Box, opium, 10½″ x 7¾″ x 2″ h., c. 1850; 1,000 flower design in shades of blue, gold, yellow, on black background, gilded finials. (Illus.) ............................................. $1,200-1,600

Box, 12⅜″, late 19th century, circular, cushion shape, with broad band of lotus scroll design on bottom and base in red, blue, yellow, green, and white on turquoise ground; a circular reserve of dragon chasing flaming pearl, clouds, on white ground surrounded by broad band of lotus scroll .................... $1,000-1,100

Box, 15¼″ dia., 20th century, covered, round; confronting dragon and phoenix design on cover; overall design in shades of blue and lavender with touches of yellow and red on blue ground, gilded handles. (Illus.) ............................. $4,000-4,500

Brush holder, 2¾″ dia. 5″ h., 19th century, five-clawed dragon and flaming pearl design on cloud-diapered black ground; ju-i border at top; blue and green wave design at bottom ........................................................ $300-500

*Chinese cloisonné box, 15¼″ dia., from a private collection*

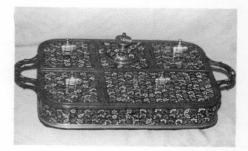

*Chinese cloisonné opium box, 10½″ x 7¾″ x 2″ h. Courtesy of Recollection Gallery, Brighton, Mich.*

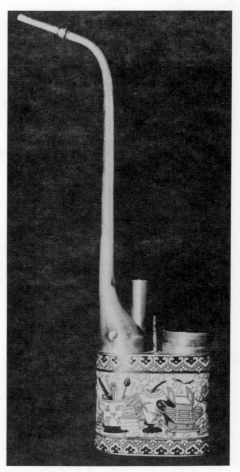

*Chinese cloisonné water pipe, 10¾″ h.*

*Chinese cloisonné figure, 12" h. Courtesy Ron Roberts, Tulsa, Okla.*

*Chinese cloisonné ginger jar, 6½" h., from a private collection*

*Chinese cloisonné figure of oxcart, 20½" l. x 11¾" h. Courtesy Zora's Antiques*

Candlesticks, pair, 8¼" h., Ch'ien Lung, pricket type, scrolling lotus, interlocking cloud collar and ju-i lappets in dark and light blue, red, green, yellow, and white on turquoise ground. Circular domed base, a double baluster stem, umbrella-form drip pan, and surmounted by small sconce with central pricket. Gilt-bronze rims . . . . . . . . . . . . . . . . . . . . . . . . . . . $1,200-1,400

Candlesticks, pair, 9¼" h., prunus florals on rust ground, marked "China," small nick . . . . . . . . . . . . . . . . . . . . . . . . . . . . . . . . . $230-300

Censer, 10" h., rectangular with t'ao t'ieh mask designs, flanges, and upright handles at rim, pierced cover in design of scrolling lotus, large knop finial, pink, yellow, white, blue, red, green, and black on turquoise ground . . . . . . . . . . . . . . . . . . . . . . $650-900

Figure, 12" h., 20th century, seated human figure, aqua blue background, gilded face, yellow on shoulders and head. (Illus.) . . . . . . . . . . . . . . . . . . . . . . . . . . . . . . . . . . . . . . . . . . . . . . . . . . . . $450-600

Figure, 20½" l. x 11¾" h., 19th century, oxcart; top opens to form receptacle; multicolors on turquoise background. (Illus.) . . . . . . . . . $1,200-1,600

Incense burner, 4½" l., Ch'ien Lung period. Ting shape, globular, compressed body with tripod feet; design of lotus scrolls between blue petal borders on turquoise ground. Everted rim gilded and set with two upright handles. Four-character Ch'ien Lung mark . . . . . . . . . . . . . . . . . . . . . . . . . . . . $1,200-1,850

Incense burner, 4¾" h., Ch'ien Lung period, U-shaped deep body, gilded tripod elephant feet; cover gilded and pierced with scrolls, Buddhist emblems and Buddhist lion knop . . . . . . . . . $850-1,400

Jar, ginger, 6½" h., 20th century; white lotus blossoms on blue background; marked "China." (Illus.) . . . . . . . . . . . . . . . . . . . . . $150-200

Jar, ginger, 8" h., plum blossoms on beige ground, from People's Republic of China . . . . . . . . . . . . . . . . . . . . . . . . . . . . . . . $160-250

Napkin ring, red, pink, and yellow florals on green, red ground, marked "China" . . . . . . . . . . . . . . . . . . . . . . . . . . . . . . . . . . $25-40

Plate, 8" dia., 20th century; 1,000 flower design in vivid multicolors on dark green background, petaled shape. (Illus.) . . . . . . . . . $150-200

Plate, 10" dia., 20th century; design of children playing on rocking horse with buildings in distance; greens, blues, flesh tones. (Illus.) . . . . . . . . . . . . . . . . . . . . . . . . . . . . . . . . . . . . . . $150-200

Screen, table, 24½" h. x 14" overall (cloisonné 11½" x 8"); design of vase of flowers, planter, scroll, compote, etc., in multicolors on black ground. (Illus.) . . . . . . . . . . . . . . . . . . . . . . $900-1,200

Snuff bottle, 2½" h., overall blue, green, black, and red floral design; matching stopper . . . . . . . . . . . . . . . . . . . . . . . . . . . . . $185-250

Vase, 8¼" h., Ch'ien Lung period, Ku form, decorated with t'ao t'ieh masks between pendant and rising stiff leaves, on turquoise ground, gilded borders, base, and interior . . . . . . . . . . . . . $2,500-3,500

Vase, 9½" h., allover floral design in green, yellow, and pink on rust-red ground, marked "China" . . . . . . . . . . . . . . . . . . . . . $200-275

Vase, 9½" h., slender neck, bulbous base, multicolored flowers on blue and green ground, marked "China" . . . . . . . . . . . . . $200-250

Vase, 13¼" h., multicolored lotus flowers, double-T fretwork on green ground . . . . . . . . . . . . . . . . . . . . . . . . . . . . . . . . . . . . $200-300

Vase, 14" h., 20th century; white chrysanthemums and medium blue leaves on lighter blue ground. (Illus.) . . . . . . . . . . . . . . $250-350

Vase, 21⅝" h., 19th century, hexagonal, with tall flaring neck, design of prunus, chrysanthemums, and peonies alternating with panels of bats on scrolling floral ground in turquoise, lapis blue, reddish brown, yellow and white; double panels of lotus around shoulder and base; t'ao t'ieh mask band above foot, gilt fretwork around rim and base . . . . . . . . . . $800-1,200

Vase, 23" h., ovoid, long neck, design of Mandarin ducks in pond with flowering lotus and fronds up to the neck, dragonflies above the rim; double gilt line border . . . . . . . . . . . . $1,900-2,000

Vases, pair, 12" h., inverted bell-shaped body, long neck with garlic-form mouth, design of dragons above waves between formal borders on white ground; flower scrolls on the neck, wood stands .......................................................... $375-500

Vessel, 3¼" h., Ch'ien Lung period, Ting shape, gilt dragon-head supports; t'ao t'ieh masks in blue, red, white, and black on turquoise ground on the sides; gilt-bronze foo lion finial on the cover, two legs repaired ................................. $300-500

Vessel, 6½" dia. at opening, 7¾" h., Ting shape, three-legged, design of dark red, yellow, and green lotus flowers, with scroll and leaf intertwining, on turquoise ground, t'ao t'ieh masks on cobalt blue ground on round knob cloisonné handles, probably K'ang Hsi. (Illus.) ...................... $1,050-1,600

Water pipe, 10¾" h. to top of stem, multicolored scholar's symbols, cobalt blue bands at top and bottom with stylized design in black, white, and yellow, on turquoise ground, implements missing. (See Color Section) ..................................... $125-200

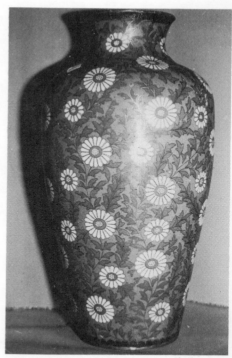

*Chinese cloisonné vase, 14" h. Courtesy Kathleen E. Norton, Norton's Objets d' Art*

*Chinese cloisonné plate, 10" dia., from a private collection*

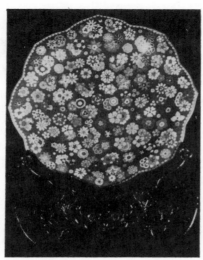

*Chinese cloisonné plate, 8" dia., from a private collection*

*Chinese cloisonné table screen, 24½" h. x 14", from a private collection*

# Chinese Openwork Cloisonné

*Chinese openwork cloisonné vase, 5⅝" h.*

The main difference between ordinary Ch'ing tai-lan and Openwork is the background. In Openwork the background is devoid of enamel. Oftimes, the bare metal is finely textured to give a granulated effect. Openwork is usually done in a lotus/arabesque design, and the overall effect is rather three-dimensional.

Box, 1⅜" h., 2¾" dia., 18th century, round, footed, 1,000 flower design of blue and carnelian flowers on top and base; design of blue and green beads on foot; turquoise counterenamel. Covered . . . . . . . . . . . . . . . . . . . . . . . . . . . . . . . . . . . . . . . . . . . $275-325

Bucket, 6¼" h., 18th century, high stationary handle, red, white, royal blue, and aqua florals on scroll-covered ground, several stylized butterflies, twisted rope wires used throughout. (Illus.) . . . . . . . . . . . . . . . . . . . . . . . . . . . . . . . . . . . . . . . . . . . . . . . $300-450

Jar, temple, 11" h., 18th century, chrysanthemums, leaves, scrolls, etc.; gold colored finial on top . . . . . . . . . . . . . . . . . . . . . . . . . . . . . . . . . . . . $600-800

Jewelry, charm bracelet, three large openwork charms, six semiprecious stone charms . . . . . . . . . . . . . . . . . . . . . . . . . . . . . . . . . . . . . . . . . . . $150-200

Snuff bottle, 2½" h., overall floral design in black, red, green, and blue, seal signed on base . . . . . . . . . . . . . . . . . . . . . . . . . . . . . . . . . . . . . . . . $180-250

Vase, 5⅝" h., double scrolls in red, green, light blue, dark blue, and white; lotuses in blue/dark blue and white/pink/red, with green leaves. (Illus. here and Color Section.) . . . . . . . . . . . . . . . . . . . . . . . . $400-650

Vases, pair, 9¼" h., pastel hues of blue, pinks, greens, yellow, and white in lotus scroll design . . . . . . . . . . . . . . . . . . . . . . . . . . . . . . . . . $800-1,200

# Cloisonné
## *(Japanese)*

*Japanese cloisonné clock. Courtesy Renee's Antique Shoppe, Winthrop, Mass.*

Known in Japan as Yusen-shippo (wired enamel), Shippo-yaki (enameled artcraft), or Shippo (enamel); the more precise term is Yusen-shippo.

A few verified examples of Yusen-shippo date back to the 15th century; these were mainly small crosses and items for the church. However, production of cloisonné began in earnest during the 16th century when the Hirata family began turning out small examples to be set into sword furnishings, for use as handles for paper sliding doors, or as nailhead covers. It was not until the 1830s when Kaji Tsunekichi became interested in the art that items such as vases, boxes, bowls, plates, etc., began to be made on a very small scale. As Tsunekichi taught others, and as the craft spread, others became masters of the art also.

At first producing an extension of Chinese shapes, designs, and methods, by the end of the 19th century the Japanese were creating Yusen-shippo that was distinctly different. Very fine (usually silver) wires were used; Japanese motifs were adopted; and the greatly refined enamel exhibited a glassiness, almost devoid of "pinholes," that had never before been attained. Additionally, new types were produced such as Shōtai-shippo (pliqué à jour), Totai-shippo (ceramic-bodied), Moriage (a relief effect), Musen-shippo (wireless), Yu-musen shippo (combination of wired and wireless), etc.

With the exception of the World War II period, Yusen-shippo has been produced steadily since the late 16th century and is being produced today at two locations in Japan.

Box, 1⅜" h., 2⅝" w. x 3⅜" l., rectangular, with rounded corners; pink mums and green foliage surrounded by blue flowers, cream scrolls, green leaves on the goldstone ground top; white flowers with blue foliage and red scrolls on sides .................... $125-200

Box, 4" x 5" w., 2½" h., semioval shape, hinged, and footed, colorful design of birds, flowers, and a duck in water on turquoise ground cover; intricate floral designs on sides in multicolors, giving a terrazo effect on the white and gray ground .................... $200-250

Charger, 12" dia., design of crabs eating rice fan, with vase of grapes, leaves, etc. Ornate 1" band around edge .................... $350-550

Charger, 18" dia., c. late 19th century, intricate designs in deep and light turquoise, pink, white, gray, and dark red on a green goldstone ground .................... $600-800

Clock, 4⅞" h., 19th/early 20th century, design of multicolored butterflies on black ground; brass wires, dull finish. (Illus.) .................... $500-600

Dish, 7½" dia., Meiji period, alternate barbed and lobed outline with design of fantailed fish below pendant wisteria .................... $700-900

Handle, walking stick or umbrella, 12" l., 19th century, pastel floral design on turquoise blue ground, butterfly at end of knob .................... $70-90

Jar, 3 11/16" h., late 19th century, flattened, oviform shape decorated with two reserves of a dragon and phoenix on pale salmon and khaki aventurine grounds alternating with two reserves of karashishi on mustard and black grounds; flowerheads and roundels on swirl aubergine ground on cover with gilt, chrysanthemum-head finial .................... $1,500-2,600

Jar, 5" h., covered, three metal feet, 20th century, black with dragon design in grays, lavender, etc. (Illus.) .................... $400-600

Jar, 9⅛" h., late 19th century, hexagonal bulbous shape with constricted foot and neck, decorated with reserves of peonies, cockerel, dragon, chidori, landscape, and falcon, all on brocade ground, chip on edge of one panel .................... $850-900

Jar, 35" h., late 19th century, slender, with design of birds, cherry blossoms, kiku, and other flowers on blue ground, some restoration. Wood stand .................... $850-1,015

Jar, tobacco, 5¼" h., c. 1900, cylindrical body with design of flying birds, flowering plum trees, bamboo, and chrysanthemum; formal foliate border and spherical knop with paulownia sprays and leafy scrolls on cover; all against midnight blue ground. Slight warping along the rim .................... $500-650

Koro, 2½" h., late 19th century, depressed globular body with design of large plum blossoms on coral red ground; three stubby feet with formal foliate scrolls; chrysanthemum bud finial on the domed cover .................... $175-300

Koro, 4⅞" h., late 19th century, globular silver body with paulownia and encircling dragon designs in applied cloisonné; ho-o cloisonné enamel bird on cover .................... $2,300-2,600

Napkin ring, ho-o bird with colorful florals and geometric designs .................... $75-85

Netsuke, 1⁷⁄₁₆" dia., Kagamibuta type, red/black, red/blue/black/yellow geometric diaper designs, and yellow/blue flowers with red/black/white arabesque design. Probably early 19th century; some pitting, black wood outer portion. (Illus.) .................... $400-600

Plaque, 13⅝" l., rectangular, with design of large circles with various emblems and archaic script, in red, pink, blue, yellow, white, green, aubergine, and black on turquoise ground, some chipping, mounted in wood frame and backed with wood .................... $150-300

Plaque, 14¼" dia., late 19th century, circular, with design of duck in pale blue water, foliage and dark aubergine sky;

*Japanese cloisonné netsuke, 1 7/16" dia.*

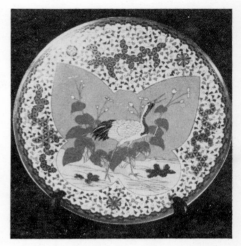

*Japanese cloisonné plate, 12" dia., from a private collection*

*Japanese cloisonné table screen, from a private collection*

*Japanese cloisonné jar, 5" h., from a private collection*

*Japanese cloisonné vase, 9" h., from a private collection*

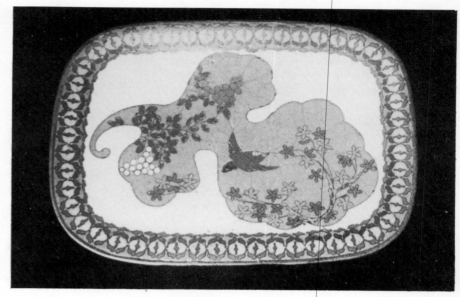

*Japanese cloisonné tray. Courtesy Jade Butterfly, Chicago, Ill.*

border of brown palmettes . . . . . . . . . . . . . . . . . . . . . . . . . . . . . . . . . . . . . . . $650-900

Plate, 11¾" dia., late 19th century, design of colorful ho-o bird within a border of panels of florets, stylized ho-o bird, mons, and dragons, in pastel beige, brown, blue and gray, on black ground, some goldstone, foliated rim . . . . . . . . . . . . . . . . . . . . . $550-750

Plate, 12" dia., early 20th century, black and white, red-crested crane design on blue, butterfly-shaped reserve, white background with brocade design; gilded wires. (Illus.) . . . . . . . . . . . . . . . . . . $450-500

Plate, 12" dia., late 19th century, circular, scalloped rim, and a central design of plum and peony blossoms on gold-speckled brown ground; fleurettes and abstract ornaments borders . . . . . . . . . . . . . . . . . . . . . . . . . . . . . . . . . . . . . . . . $350-550

Plate, wall, 17¾" dia., late 19th century, design of ho-o bird in center in blue, surrounded by diaper band border; a wide border of diaper design and circular panel chains of foliate motifs in gray, white, and brown, on black ground; some goldstone . . . . . . . . . . . . . . . . . . . . . . . . . . . . . . . . . . . . . . . . . . . $750-1,000

Potpourri, miniature, three-footed, covered, design of butterflies, variegated leaves, mons, flowers, and goldstone, unmarked . . . . . . . . . . . . . . . . . . . . . . . . . . . . . . . . . . . . . . . . . . . . . . . . . $100-175

Screen, table, 18" x 30" (cloisonné 12" dia.), design in black, greens, yellow, rust, on blue gray background. (Illus.) . . . . . . . . . . . . . . . $1,200-1,500

Teapot, 3" h., butterflies design on cobalt and maroon ground; floral design on cover; some goldstone . . . . . . . . . . . . . . . . . . . . . . . . $200-300

Teapot, 3½" h., finely detailed flowers and butterflies on midnight blue reserves and goldstone, bronze flower finial . . . . . . . . . . . . . . . . . . . $250-325

Teapot, 7" h., to top of handle, three ball feet. Design of rocks, waves, and florals in muted colors on salmon ground. Movable handle decorated with tiny florals, matching finial on lid. (See Color Section.) . . . . . . . . . . . . . . . . . . . . . . . . . . . . . . . . . . $550-800

Tea set, five pieces: teapot, two demitasse cups and saucers, creamer, and sugar. All five are covered with gilt wire in scroll pattern (type known as "Kyoto Jippo"), with many colorful mons, flowers, and other symbols. Signed by Takahara Komojiro of Kyoto . . . . . . . . . . . . . . . . . . . . . . . . . . . . . $1,500-2,000

Tray, 7⁵⁄₁₆" x 5⁵⁄₁₆", 19th century, floral and bird design in rusts, greens, with a turquoise, leaf-shaped reserve on white ground; scroll diaper on reverse; matte finish. (Illus.) . . . . . . . . . . . . . . . . $450-550

Tray, 11½" sq., design of cockerel, hen, and chick on pale blue ground; pink and gray band of foliage border. Signed

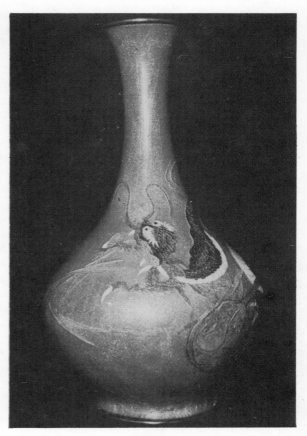

*Japanese cloisonné vase, 9½" h. Courtesy Interiors Unlimited, Goodlettsville, Tenn.*

*Japanese cloisonné vase, 9¾" h., from a private collection*

*Japanese cloisonné vase, 7" h., from a private collection*

*Japanese cloisonné vase, 12" h., from a private collection*

Shotei (for the painting); reverse inscribed Deakin Bros. & Co., Yokohama . . . . . . . . . . . . . . . . . . . . . . . . . . . . . . . . . . . . . . . . . . . . . . . . $1,000-1,400

Urns, pair, 3½" h., c. 1880, florals and butterfly on rust and blue ground; goldstone; flower finial on cover . . . . . . . . . . . . . . . . . . . . . . . . . . . $300-325

Vase, 3½" h., c. 1900, ovoid, with a brass ring foot and slightly rolled brass lip; white chrysanthemums and forest green leaves on navy blue ground; deep green counterenamel . . . . . . . . . . . . . . . . . . . . . . . . . . . . . . . . . . . . . . . . . . . . . . $90-150

Vase, 4¾" h., 19th century, four goldfish and marine plants on green and coral ground . . . . . . . . . . . . . . . . . . . . . . . . . . . . . . . . . . . . . . . . . $200-400

Vase, 4¾" h., two cranes on midnight blue ground, Kyoto school . . . . . . . . . . . . . . . . . . . . . . . . . . . . . . . . . . . . . . . . . . . . . . . . . . . . . . . . . $200-350

*Japanese akasuke cloisonné, 6 1/16" h.*

Vase, 6" h., 3" dia., flowers and leaves in brown, aqua, green, and blue swirl panels; some goldstone . . . . . . . . . . . . . . . . . . . . . . . . $200-400

Vase, 6" h., 19th century, pale, bluish gray dragon with white and red accents on black ground, signed . . . . . . . . . . . . . . . . . . . . . $300-500

Vase, 7" h., late 19th/early 20th century; turquoise vase with flowers and bird design in white, pink, yellow, green, and brown; spray of flowers on reverse. (Illus.) . . . . . . . . . . . . . . . . . . . . . . $500-650

Vase, 9" h., dragon on black reserve panel on black ground; arabesques in pink, chartreuse, blue, and green; reverse shows iris and water design on red reserve panel. (Illus.) . . . . . . . . . . . . . . . . $800-900

Vase, 9½" h., reserve design of birds and maple leaves against sky blue; other reserves: leaves and tendrils on gray ground, fan-shaped scenic reserve in pale yellow, blue, gray, leafy branch on tan, bare wisteria branches on pink, against pale gray ground. (Illus.) . . . . . . . . . . . . . . . . . . . . . . . . . . . . . . . . . . . . $1,000-1,200

Vase, 9¾" h., marked "Ito," green dragon design on translucent red ground, damaged by cracks. (Illus.) . . . . . . . . . . . . . . $200-250

Vase, wall, 10½" h., butterflies and flowers with much goldstone, on black ground . . . . . . . . . . . . . . . . . . . . . . . . . . . . . . . . . . . . $175-290

Vase, 12" h., late 19th/early 20th century, design of three Lohans in soft multicolors on black ground. (Illus.) . . . . . . . . . . . . . . . $850-1,000

Vase, 12¼" h., three shield-shaped panels with designs of phoenix, dragon, and bird with colorful mums, with florals, scrolls, etc., between the panels; butterflies on shoulder, much goldstone . . . . . . . . . . . . . . . . . . . . . . . . . . . . . . . . . . . . . . . . . . . . . . $400-600

Vases, pair, 4¾" h., allover design of flying birds in browns and pale grays. Geometric designs on top and bottom in bluish gray, brown, and beige, all on dark red ground. Some silver wires highlighted with gilding. (See Color Section.) . . . . . . . . . . $500-800

Vases, pair, 6⅜" h., c. 1900, slender ovoid shape with design of two delicate strands of chrysanthemums interspersed with tall grasses in rust, lavender, and mint green, above which flies yellow butterfly, on midnight blue ground . . . . . . . . . . . . . . . . . . . . . . . $800-1,100

## Akasuke — Pigeon Blood

Akasuke is a type of Yusen-shippo whereby a copper body is punched, often into an overall stippled design. Usually simple designs such as bamboo, birds, etc., are impressed by means of repoussé. The copper must be meticulously clean and brilliantly polished, whereupon transparent red enamel (hence the term Pigeon Blood) is applied over the entire object. The combination of the red transparent enamel and the bright copper results in a deep reflective look which Westerners have found quite pleasing. Opaque cloisonné designs (usually fairly simple flowers, on one side of the object only) are often, but not always, added. The finished object is generally bound with silver or a silver-type metal.

Curiously enought, purple, green, and yellow transparent enamels are incorporated in an identical process, but somehow Pigeon Blood does not accurately reflect these colors. Ōta Kan-noe is credited with the invention of Akasuke in 1880-81.

Bowl, 5" dia., cloisonné roses on pigeon blood ground . . . . . . . . . . . . . . . . . . . . . . . . $125-175

Jars, pair, 6" h., bamboo, butterfly, and dragonfly design on pigeon blood ground, silver rims and base . . . . . . . . . . . . . . . . . . . . . . . . . . . . . . . $200-350

Lamp, 13" h., 26" overall, including two-socket brass fixture. Profusion of flowers, leaves, and vines with stipple on pigeon blood ground. Not converted vase, but made as a lamp . . . . . . . . . . . . . . . . . . . . . . . . . . . . . . . . . . . . . . . . . . . . . . . . . . . . . . . . . . $300-450

Vase, 5" h., 3" w., shaded pink, white, and red flowers, shaded leaves and stems cover front, basse-taille bird and palm, silver rims . . . . . . . . . . . . . . . . . . . . . . . . . . . . . . . . . . . . . . . . . . . . . . . . . . $110-200

Vase, 6¹⁄₁₆" h., pink and white roses on pigeon blood ground with basse taille birds and bamboo. (Illus. here and Color Section) . . . . . . . . . . . . . . . . . . . . . . . . . . . . . . . . . . . . . . . . . . . . . . . . . . . . . . $150-275

Vase, 11" h., c. 19th century, four birds in gray, brown, and white enamels near a tree . . . . . . . . . . . . . . . . . . . . . . . . . . . . . . . . . . . . . . . . . . . $200-350

Vases, pair, 10" h., large pink and white roses with green fiiage, basse-taille palm trees, silver rims . . . . . . . . . . . . . . . . . . . . . . . . . . . . . $450-600

## Ginbari — Foil Cloisonné

Ginbari began in an effort to conserve silver and to avoid the cracking that can occur when silver is fired. A sheet of silver foil is wrapped around a brass or copper body and is usually stippled into a repetitive design. Transparent and/or translucent enamels are used over the foil with great effect. For purposes of consolidation, pieces are also listed below which have only small foil areas.

Bowl, 9½" dia., scalloped, red roses on interior and exterior on blue foil ground, silver and copper wires . . . . . . . . . . . . . . . . . . . . . . . . . . . . . $300-400

Box, 2⁷⁄₈" h., 5" dia., pink and blue flowers, green leaves against bright blue foil in center of cover; sides covered with small flowers in pink, blue, yellow, and red on green ground . . . . . . . . . . . . . . . . . . . $125-200

Jar, 16½" h., late 19th century, ovoid shape supported on tripod feet with iris and lilies rising beside fronds design reserved on a pale blue ground which diffuses to red; butterflies design and button knop (with some damage) on the domed cover . . . . . . . . . . . . . . . . . . . . . . . . . . . . . . . . . . . . . . . . . . . . $800-900

Jewelry (belt buckle), 3" x 2", shape of butterfly with colorful flowers and flying butterflies; fish-scale foil . . . . . . . . . . . . . . . . . . . . . . . . . . . . . . . $75-125

Platter, 12½" l., c. 1900, oval shape with design of orange and purple foil carps swimming among green and turquoise water reeds on royal blue ground, signed . . . . . . . . . . . . . . . . . . . . . . . . . . . . . $600-800

Teapot, 3" h., butterflies and flowers on blue ground . . . . . . . . . . . . . . . . . . . . $200-275

Teapot, 6" h., design of peonies and blossoms in blues, pinks, yellow, greens, and white on fish-scale teal blue ground with four brass ball feet . . . . . . . . . . . . . . . . . . . . . . . . . . . . . . . . . . . . $750-850

Vase, 5¾" h., lilies and buds with leaves design in red/white, purple/white, green and turquoise foil on opaque, gray green ground. (See Color Section) . . . . . . . . . . . . . . . . . . . . . . . . . . . . $150-250

Vase, 6" h., classical shape, fish-scale, blue, purple, orange blooming orchids, green fernery, with mountain scene in distance . . . . . . . . . . . . . . . . . . . . . . . . . . . . . . . . . . . . . . . . . . . . . . . . . . . . . $200-250

*Japanese ginbari cloisonné vase, 24" h. Courtesy Chase Gilmore Art Galleries*

*Japanese ginbari cloisonné vases, 7½" h., from the collection of TK Oriental Antiques of Williamsburg*

Vase, 6" h., egret design on pale green suffusing to pale aqua fish-scale ground. (See Color Section) ...................................... $125-250

Vase, 6" h., 19th century, white bird on brown tree branch, green leaves, red, orange, and yellow flowers on pale blue and white foil ground, signed ........................................... $200-300

Vase, 7¼" h., three foil fish swimming on green foil ground .................. $300-500

Vase, 24" h., two swimming carp, one red, one black, with overhanging branch of hydrangea in white, pink, lavender, green, on pale blue fish scale ground shading to deeper tone at neck. Some age and firing cracks. (Illus.) ................................. $600-800

Vases, pair, 4¾" h., yellow, white, and pink foil flowers on black ground ............................................................. $300-475

Vases, pair, 7½" h., pink flowers with green leaves on pale blue foil ground; stamped "C.P.O." on rim, marked in foil on base "Shibataro." (Illus.) ....................................... $1,000-1,200

Vases, pair, 11⅝" h., 19th century, baluster shape, matched pair, design of iris in vivid purple, blue, and pink on a shaded white-to-blue foil ground; cracks on one vase ......................... $400-600

*Close-up of Japanese moriage cloisonné vase, 9½" h.*

## Moriage — "Cameo" Cloisonné

Moriage is a type of Yusen-shippo whereby — either by piling on additional enamel or by repoussé — certain areas of a piece are worked in relief. The relief areas are usually worked in opaque enamel. Moriage is credited to Ando Jubei and Kawada Shibatarō, who invented it in 1903-1910.

Bowl, 3" h., 3" dia., covered, floral design ..................................... $300-450

Vase, 9½" h., pink and white flowers with blue centers (two of the flowers are moriage), on pale silver green grading to deeper green fish-scale ground. (Illus.) ......................... $350-475

Vases, pair, 9¼" h., c. 1900, pale violet and yellow flowers, various shades of green leaves and branches, on dark gray ground, signed Ando of Nagoya ...................................... $1,000-1,800

## Shōtai — Pliqué à Jour Cloisonné

More commonly known by the name given it by French art historians in the 18th century, Shōtai is a type of Yusen-shippo in which transparent/translucent enamels are used exclusively, and the entire method of production is the same until after firing. After the piece has been fired, the metal body is removed by means of a resist or by acid-etching. (Acid-etching seems to be a popular means, as a frosted effect is usually noticeable.) After removal of the metal body, the resulting object is transparent (often compared to stained glass by writers) and very fragile. Bound in silver or silver-type metal, it is extremely subject to cracks and/or breakage. For this reason, most of the Shōtai on today's market is of recent origin. Ando Jubei is credited with the invention of Shōtai in 1897.

*Japanese Shōtai cloisonné bowl, 5" dia., from a private collection*

Bowl, 2" h. x 3⅝" dia., shallow bowl with design of creamy yellow prunus blossoms on pale green ground, wood stand . . . . . . . . . . . . . . . . . . $300-400

Bowl, 5" dia., 2¾" h., pink and white blossoms, dark green leaves on pale green ground. (Illus.) . . . . . . . . . . . . . . . . . . . . . . . . . . . . . . . . . $900-1,000

Jar, 3½" h., light, medium, and dark green overall floral design on pale green ground. Silver rim and base. Fitted wood box. (See Color Section) . . . . . . . . . . . . . . . . . . . . . . . . . . . . . . . . . . . . . . $550-650

Napkin ring, floral design . . . . . . . . . . . . . . . . . . . . . . . . . . . . . . . . . . . . . . $125-175

Vase, 3" h., ovoid, with multicolor floral design on pale green ground . . . . . . . . . . . . . . . . . . . . . . . . . . . . . . . . . . . . . . . . . . . . . . . . . . . . . $450-500

Vase, 5" h., blooming pastel florals on pale green ground . . . . . . . . . . . . . . . . . . . $500-600

Vase, 5" h., two angelfish facing each other; goldfish and marine plants on pale green ground . . . . . . . . . . . . . . . . . . . . . . . . . . . . . . . . . . $500-600

## Totai — Ceramic-bodied Cloisonné

Totai is distinguishable from ordinary Yusen-shippo in that it is not fired upon a metal body; rather, a pottery or porcelain body is used, over which "soft" cloisonné enamels and wires are placed. The colors are usually subdued and have a matte finish rather than the glossy one associated with Yusen-shippo, and the enamels exhibit depressions not found in the ordinary wares. After having gained great popularity in the late 19th century, Totai gradually lost its appeal because of subsequent crazing of the enamels.

One of the most prolific producers of pottery Totai was Kinkozan, who is also known for Satsuma wares. A great many of Kinkozan's wares exhibit great similarities: a dull, grayish-blue ground, bean-shaped diapers, and scattered flowers and butterflies in subdued pastels.

*Japanese Totai cloisonné bowl, 3½" h., from the collection of Bob Law*

An interesting type of Totai, dubbed "tree bark" by Westerners, is usually found on porcelain and is notable for its brown "bark" texture and matte inlays of Totai; the enamels used are non-vitreous, very thin, and quite liable to breakage. In keeping with the brown bark ground, the enamel colors are usually autumnal. Totai was first created in the 1860s by Tsukamoto Kaisuke.

Bowl, 3½" h., 5" w., two-handled, 19th century porcelain, dull greens, rose, bluebird and leaf, flower design on dark brown ground; flying bird, flower and leaves on reverse; brass wires, some flaking, marked. (Illus.) . . . . . . . . . . . . . . . . . . . . . . . . . . . . $350-450

Bowl, 4" h., 6" dia., covered, scattered flowers and bean-shaped cloisons on light blue ground, signed Kinkozan . . . . . . . . . . . . . . . . . . $200-300

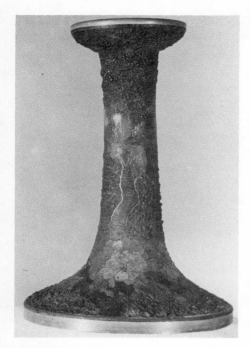

*Japanese Totai cloisonné "treebark" candlestick, from the collection of Bob Law*

*Japanese Totai cloisonné vases, 6⅛" h., from a private collection*

*Japanese Totai cloisonné cup. Courtesy E & E Collectables & Antiques*

Box, 5½" dia., 3¼" h., covered, footed, rust flowers and green leaves on black and gold ground (cover); sides of red and black; on porcelain ............................................... $200-300

Candlestick, 6⅜" h., 4¼" dia. base, treebark, early 20th century; marked "Hand painted Nippon" with green wreath; floral design in red, orange, green, and brown on brown ground, brass wires. (Illus.) ............................................... $350-500

Cup, 4" h., porcelain, grape and leaf design in plum, white, pink, greens, blue, and gold on turquoise; blue and white foot with design of different insects, damaged. (Illus.) ......... $150-200

Cup and saucer, colorful fleurettes on blue pottery ground, handleless cup ............................................... $200-300

Jar, ginger, 5½" h., brick red and other colors of large snowflakes on dark brown "tree bark" ground ................... $250-350

Jar, ginger, 5¾" h., design of robin searching for worm; florals, on "tree bark" ground, lidded ........................ $325-450

Jar, ginger, 5¾" h., 5¼" w., bulbous, with colorful flowers all outlined in white in irregular medallions of ultramarine on the charcoal ground; tightly knit, heart-shaped cloisons; butterflies design on inner cover. Signed on base; pottery ........ $375-500

Jar, 6" x 6", delicate butterflies, leaves, and fretwork on "tree bark" ground (pottery) ........................................ $300-375

Plate, 6⅜" dia., ceramic, late 19th/early 20th century, painted design in center of flowers, butterflies on cream; blue rim with bean-shaped cloisons, scattered single flowers; signed Kinkozan. (Illus.) ............................................... $450-550

Pot, brush, floral and butterfly design on cloisonné scene on top; blue design on white footed base (bottom) ................. $300-400

Tea caddy, 4" h., covered, with inner liner, bean-shaped diaper design, scattered flowers in whites, blues, dark reds, and yellow on powder blue ground; two lavender panels outlined in black, with floral design. Signed. (See Color Section) ............................................... $350-450

*Japanese Totai cloisonné plate, 6⅜" dia., from a private collection*

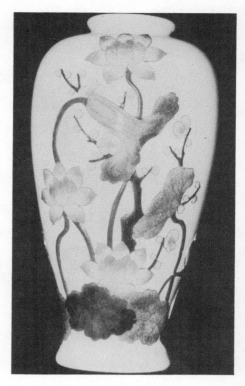

*Japanese Totai cloisonné vase, 6" h. Courtesy I Ching Antique Gallery*

Tea container, 7½" h., 19th century, on porcelain, covered, red maple leaves and waves in three shaped, textured panels, giving the leaves a relief effect. The wave and floral medallions on deep olive ground. Top has wave form border, foot and cover have geometric borders, cover restored . . . . . . . . . . . . . . . . . . . . . . . . . $250-375

Vase, 6" h. on Satsuma, slightly raised cloisonné on glazed Satsuma; pink, white, and pale green flowers, green leaves on cream ground. (Illus.) . . . . . . . . . . . . . . . . . . . . . . . . . . . . . . . . . . . . . . . . . . $1,200-1,500

Vase, 8½" h., c. 1900, ovoid body with design of bird, cherry branch, garden flowers in shaded orange, green, burnt sienna, silver, and gold on brown "tree bark" ground; porcelain . . . . . . . . . . . . . . . . . . . . . . . . . . . . . . . . . . . . . . . . . . . . . . . . . . $450-600

Vase, 10½" h., c. 1900, ovoid body with butterflies, anemones, and chrysanthemums in red, brown, and green enamels on brown "tree bark" ground; porcelain . . . . . . . . . . . . . . . . . . . . . . . . . . . $450-625

Vases, pair, 6⅛" h., stemmed, porcelain; aqua reserves with duck swimming, another of pair of birds flying above waves, against medium blue ground with spiral cloison diaper interspersed with geometric designs in rose, rust, brown, yellow; florals painted on inside and base in blue, green, red, and blue and green respectively. Blue and white base. (Illus.) . . . . . . . . . . . . . . . . . . $300-400

Vases, pair, 18¼" h., late 19th century. Pear-shaped bodies with various flowering plants between intricate borders, in blue, white, and gilding; diaper design, double kiku handles; on porcelain . . . . . . . . . . . . . . . . . . . . . . . . . . . . . . . . . . . . . . . . . . . . . . . . . . . . $1,000-1,400

Box, 6½" sq., with rounded corners, "tree bark" finish (pebble surface on black ground), tan peony, dark red buds, bright red larger bud, dark and medium green leaves, and yellow and orange butterfly. Black lacquer interior . . . . . . . . . . . . . . . . . . . . . . . . . . . $175-300

*Japanese cloisonné on lacquer tray, 13" x 18". Courtesy Kelly's Worldwide Antiques, Alexandria, Va.*

## Cloisonné on Lacquer

Tray, 13" x 18", fan designs in blues, greens, golds, rusts on black ground; border of gold lacquered butterflies. (Illus.) ...................... $500-650

## Copper
*(Chinese)*

Kettle, sake, 7¾" h., Ch'ien Lung, design of vegetal forms in gold and other metals on alternating fluted panels of melon-shaped pot, lid, and base of warming stand. Hinged support arms which fold inward, reticulated spherical finial ..................... $550-650

Tea set, four pieces, brass trim, marked "China." ............................ $65-80

Toothpick, 3" x 2¼" x 2¼" h., fluted shape, blue enameled interior, marked "China." ................................................. $20-25

Urns, pair, 11" h., 20th century, solid copper, lidded, marked "China." .................................................................. $40-50

## Copper
*(Japanese)*

Box, 7¼" x 3¾", relief design of dragon encircling Buddhistic arch handle on hinged cover; continuous band of iris design on sides; wooden insets on the interior, silvered ..................... $65-105

Figure, 9½" l., Meiji period, model of an articulated lobster, sectioned claws and feelers, two-character signature ...................... $550-650

Figures, pair, 5 1/10" l., late 19th century, crayfish, finely modeled and articulated, signed Hiromi ...................... $265-400

Humidor, 7" h., late 19th century, cylindrical body, hand-hammered, with silver overlay suggestive of natural crevices along the rim; ivory finial (added later) depicting three monkeys mocking a hanging scroll showing a moon rising over trees. One monkey has fine cracks ...................... $350-600

Incense burner, 5" h., 18th century, barrel shape with etched details of thatched ties and reeds, rope fittings about the barrel; pierced cover. Carved, footed wooden stand ...................... $275-325

Incense burner, 8" l., rectangular with incised design of lakeside huts and fish swimming among deep sea plants; pierced cover with prunus roundel and movable handle ...................... $80-130

Ladles, marriage (pair), 17th/18th century, standard form. One with long-handled double spout, and one with small wing-handle single spout; each with design of black pine, cranes, minogame and bamboo lacquered design ...................... $375-500

Ojime, ovoid with silver-toned design of crab amidst applied sea grasses, unsigned ...................... $125-150

Tsuba, 3⅛" dia., 19th century, oval, with butterflies design applied in silver, gold, shibuichi, shakudo, mother-of-pearl, kozukahitsu ...................... $750-1,000

Tsuba, 3¼" dia., 1863, rounded square shape, irregular lip, carved design of clouds and pierced full moon design; applied design of a dancing tanuki in brass. Signed Higashiyama, sealed Motonobu on a gold censer, and dated 1863 ...................... $700-1,400

Tsuba, 3⅝" dia., Meiji period, rounded square shape with lipped edge. Design of a demon clutching a tama and a tanuki emerging from a cloud overhead molded in high relief with gold highlights; reverse done in similar way depicting a tempest blowing past a pine. Signed Nara Schicho Sairyuken Toshiyoshi ...................... $1,000-1,650

Vases, pair, 4⅝" h., late 19th century, flattened oval flask form on spreading rectangular bases. Design of cockerels beneath cherry trees and butterflies in peonies, surrounded by key fret design in iro-e hirazogan; clematis design on the sides. Marked "No" (Hattori Shoten) ...................... $750-1,100

Vases, pair, 7½" h., 19th century, tapering baluster shape, each with design of a cockerel and hen in silver and gilt relief, badly dented ...................... $160-240

*Nepalese copper figural group, 6½" h.*

*Nepalese copper figural group, 6" h.*

## Copper
### (Nepalese)

*Figural group, 6" h., 16th/17th century, gilt Uma-Mahesvara group, the god seated in lalitasana with his consort perched on left knee and holding attributes of Shiva with his eighteen flailing arms, some traces of gilt, a crescent in the high coiled hair. (Illus.) ..................................................................$1,870

*Figural group, 6½" h., 12th/13th century, Uma-Mahesvara group, the god and consort seated in lalitasana on lotus mound atop tiered base, two of his arms around Uma, the other two raised in vitarka mudra and holding prayer beads, with extensive gilding, some red pigment remaining on well-worn patina. (Illus.) ......................................................$7,150

Figural group, 7¼" h., a man and woman seated in yab yum, on lotus base; traces of gilding and red pigment remain ...................$65-100

Figure, standing, of Padmapani, on a circular double lotus base, his hands in varada and vitarka mudra, his left arm entwined by a lotus and wearing a high jeweled diadem ......................$265-400

## Copper
### (Sino-Tibetan)

Figure, 4½" h., gilt thunderbolt held in place by Garuda heads, mounted loosely on a circular double lotus base ........................$105-160

Figure, 7¼" h., seated gilt figure of Shiva with multiple arms, two of them raised to form trisula, incised shou medallions on the knees, seated on a double lotus base ..................................$90-130

Figure, 7½" h., 19th century, gilt seated figure of a Lokesvara, hands in dhyanasana, holding a flame jar, shou medallions incised on the robe, seated on triangular lotus base; traces of faint red and blue pigments visible ............................$130-260

67

Figure, 7⅝" h., 18th/19th century, seated gilt figure of Dhyanibuddha Amitayus, in dhyanasana, hands in dhyana mudra, wearing flowing Bodhisattva robes, a five-leaf diadem above the introspective face, seated on a double lotus throne . . . . . . . . . . . . . . . . . . . $400-600

Figure, 7⅞" h., 18th/19th century, gilt seated figure of Dhyanibuddha Amitayus, hands in dhyana mudra, holding kalasa, a double chignon atop his head, on double lotus throne . . . . . . . . . . . . . . . . . . . . . . . . . . . . . . . . . . . . . . . . . . . . . $375-700

Plaques, votive (pair), 4¾" h., c. 1770, each plaque portraying a seated Dhyanibuddha Amitayus, in dhyanasana, hands in dhyana mudra holding cintamani, a shaped prabha behind, on double lotus throne . . . . . . . . . . . . . . . . . . . . . . . . . . . . . . . . . . $500-700

## Copper
### (Tibetan)

Figure, 8¾" h., seated figure of Suryea, gilt, hands raised in vitarka mudra, wearing cowl hat and seated on high semicircular base . . . . . . . . . . . . . . . . . . . . . . . . . . . . . . . . . . . . . . . . $150-200

Figure, 9⅞" h., 18th century, seated figure of Sakyamuni, gilt, in dhyanasana, wearing monastic robe, his hands in bhumisparsa and dhyana mudra, seated on double lotus throne; base engraved with visvavajra . . . . . . . . . . . . . . . . . . . . . . . $1,000-1,665

Gahu, 5¼" h., 19th century, standard form ritual object which contains painted figure of Hevajra . . . . . . . . . . . . . . . . . . . . $400-525

Gahu, 7⅛" h., gilt roundels and two celestial dragons on interior frame; silver cover with repoussé massed foliage, pierced . . . . . . . . . . . . . . . . . . . . . . . . . . . . . . . . . . . . . . . . . . . . . . . $400-650

Mandala, 12" x 10¾", 19th century, Wheel of Life, Eight Trigrams, and astrological diagram repoussé in center of cosmic frog's belly, with three deities and other mandalas surrounding . . . . . . . . . . . . . . . . . . . . . . . . . . . . . . . . . . . . . . . . . . . $600-932

Mandala, 13⅛" x 11⅛", seated gilt figure of Buddha within architectural frame; the frame with carved coral, turquoise, mother-of-pearl, pearls, and colored glass . . . . . . . . . . . . . . . . . . . $450-715

Teapot, 10¾" h., 19th century, dragon spout and handle; domed cover and shoulders with lotoid and foliate overlay design . . . . . . . . . . . . . . . . . . . . . . . . . . . . . . . . . . . . . . . . . . . . . . . . . $250-400

## Copper Red
### (Chinese)

The copper red colors are achieved through the use of copper oxide, which, when fired in a *reducing* atmosphere, produces various hues of red. Copper oxide fired in an *oxidizing* atmosphere produces various shades of green. Variations in kiln atmosphere, whether accidental or a matter of deliberate experimentation, have produced a number of magnificent color developments in the history of Chinese porcelain decoration.

(See: Underglaze Red)

## Copper Red
### (Chinese — Monochromes)

Bowl, 10" dia., Ch'ien Lung seal mark in underglaze blue, the bowl interior glazed white . . . . . . . . . . . . . . . . . . . . . . . . . . . . . . $600-700

Saucer dish, 6" dia., Yung Chêng six-character mark in underglaze blue, covered with pale enamel . . . . . . . . . . . . . . . . . . . $600-800

Stem bowl, 5" h. x 7" dia., Yung Chêng six-character mark and period. Bowl with rounded sides and lipless rim, with a hollow stem, the interior and base glazed with a grayish white tint . . . . . . . . . . . . . . . . . . . . . . . . . . . . . . . . . . . . . . . . . . $1,600-2,000

Stem cup, 4½" h., Yung Chêng six-character mark and

period. Glazed in a deep red which thins to white at the rim, the interior and foot glazed white . . . . . . . . . . . . . . . . . . . . . . . . . . . . . . . . . . . . . . . . . . . . $2,900-3,200

Vase, 6¼" h., K'ang Hsi period (unmarked). Bronze form with four mask-and-ring handles at the shoulders; body in red glaze with patches of gray; the handles and rim in a white glaze. Rare . . . . . . . . . . . . . . . . . . . . . . . . . . . . . . . . . . . . . . . . . . . . . $900-1,300

Vase, 6½" h., Ch'ien Lung underglaze blue seal mark and period. Pear-shaped, with red shading lighter towards the rim; interior and base in a white glaze . . . . . . . . . . . . . . . . . . . . . . . . . . $1,800-2,200

Vase, 8½" h., Yung Chêng six-character underglaze blue mark and period. Mei ping shape covered with a beautiful, deep crimson glaze, the lip and base in a grayish blue-white tint . . . . . . . . . . . . . . . . . . . . . . . . . . . . . . . . . . . . . . . . . . . . . . . . . . $5,500-6,500

Vase, 10½" h., 18th century, pear shaped, with finely mottled cherry red glaze, the lip and interior glazed white . . . . . . . . . . . . . . . . . . $1,000-1,200

Vase, 12¼" h., pear shaped, Ch'ien Lung mark and period, covered with an even, finely pitted dark cherry glaze. (Illus.) . . . . . . . . . . . . . . . $1,200-1,500

Vase, 12¾" dia., fading rim, 18th century, pear-shaped, the cherry red color fading to pink at the foot, with a white glazed interior and rim, with base unglazed . . . . . . . . . . . . . . . . . . . . . . . . . . . . . $1,000-1,200

*Chinese copper red vase, 12¼" h., Ch'ien Lung*

# Coralene
## *(Japanese)*

Japanese coralene is a term used to describe porcelain objects which have motifs executed in glass beads. The glass beads were applied to the porcelain with a fixative. The beads are colorless and reflect the hue of the coloring agent which was added to the fixative. These wares were produced during the Nippon era, Made in Japan era, and post WW II. There are several markings associated with these wares (see Marks Section). Another form of coralene used on pottery is just beginning to gain recognition. When used on pottery objects, the glass beading forms outlining and border ornamentations. The beading used on pottery wares is opaque white, and such was inserted into the soft clay so that the beads are only half to three quarters visible. This type of glass beading was usually painted turquoise, gold, pink, blue, or green. Pottery wares having this form of coralene usually have moriage motifs and such were made during the Nippon and Made in Japan eras.

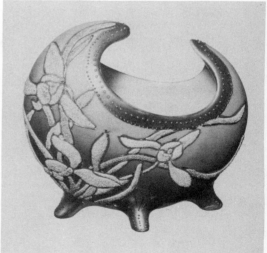

*Crescent shaped vase marked "Patent Applied for No. 38257"*

Basket, 5" x 3½", three legs, cobalt and gold trim, loop handle, blue, rust, pink with white daisies and green leaves on a white ground, marked "Pat. Pend. Feb. 9, 1909" . . . . . . . . . . . . . . . . . . . . . . . . . . . . $80-110

Bowl, 1½" x 8", plums, leaves in greens, white, pinks, yellows, blue matte ground, marked "Pat. Pend. Feb. 9, 1909" . . . . . . . . . . . . . . . . . . . . . . . . . . . . . . . . . . . . . . . . . . . . . . . . . $165-190

Box, 1½" x 2" x 3", pink, lavender, and green thistles on copper toned matte ground, marked "Kinran Pat. 16132 Japan" . . . . . . . . . . . . . . . . . . . . . . . . . . . . . . . . . . . . . . . . . . . . . . . $95-115

Crescent vase, 4½" h., four legs, shaded gold matte ground, irises in pinks and yellow with green leaves, marked "Patent Applied for No. 38257" (Illus.) . . . . . . . . . . . . . . . . . . . . . . $150-175

Plate, 8½" dia., white lilies, green leaves on finished porcelain ground, unmarked . . . . . . . . . . . . . . . . . . . . . . . . . . . . . $85-110

Vase, 4" h., butterflies in orange, tan, yellow, and rust with pink/blue/lavender shaded matte ground, marked "Pat. Applied for No. 38257" . . . . . . . . . . . . . . . . . . . . . . . . . . . . . . . $250-275

Vase, 4" h., jonquils and leaves in shades of green, yellow, tan, and pink, copper toned matte ground, marked "Feb. 9,

1909''  . . . . . . . . . . . . . . . . . . . . . . . . . . . . . . . . . . . . . . . . . . . . . . . . . . . . . . . . . . . . . . . . . . . . $135-150

Vase, 4¾'' h., cobalt trim, morning glories, apricot to tan
matte ground, unmarked  . . . . . . . . . . . . . . . . . . . . . . . . . . . . . . . . . . . . . . . . . . . . . . . $110-125

Vase, 8'' h., scalloped and fluted rim, bulbous body, cream,
pink, green, and yellow snapdragons, lavender to light blue
matte ground, marked ''Feb. 9, 1909''  . . . . . . . . . . . . . . . . . . . . . . . . . . . . . . . . . $200-235

Vase, 10'' h., pink matte ground, green and brown geometric
motifs on shoulders which trail downward to form panels,
marked ''Feb. 9, 1909''  . . . . . . . . . . . . . . . . . . . . . . . . . . . . . . . . . . . . . . . . . . . . . . $175-200

Vase, 12'' h., handled, scalloped rim and base, trees and
grass in shades of copper with copper matte ground, marked
''Feb. 9, 1909''  . . . . . . . . . . . . . . . . . . . . . . . . . . . . . . . . . . . . . . . . . . . . . . . . . . . . . $250-325

# Dolls
## Hakata

Elderly man, 8'' h., seated with legs crossed and playing a
samisen  . . . . . . . . . . . . . . . . . . . . . . . . . . . . . . . . . . . . . . . . . . . . . . . . . . . . . . . . . . . $90-110

Elderly man, 10'' h., seated on tatami mat and holding rice in
his hand  . . . . . . . . . . . . . . . . . . . . . . . . . . . . . . . . . . . . . . . . . . . . . . . . . . . . . . . . . . $100-145

Two men seated with legs crossed, beside them a basket of
persimmons  . . . . . . . . . . . . . . . . . . . . . . . . . . . . . . . . . . . . . . . . . . . . . . . . . . . . . . . $200-250

Young woman, 9'' h., seated on a mat  . . . . . . . . . . . . . . . . . . . . . . . . . . . . . . . . $100-120

## Made for Export

Doll, 3½'' h., dressed in cloth kimono with jointed arms and
legs and painted shoes and socks  . . . . . . . . . . . . . . . . . . . . . . . . . . . . . . . . . . . . $60-80

Doll, 4½'' h., dressed in Western garb, jointed arms and legs  . . . . . . . . . . . . . . $50-60

Doll, 9'' h., blue sleep eyes, dimples, jointed body marked
''Japan''  . . . . . . . . . . . . . . . . . . . . . . . . . . . . . . . . . . . . . . . . . . . . . . . . . . . . . . . . . . . $90-100

Doll, 10½'', brown sleep eyes, jointed baby body, marked
''Made in Japan''  . . . . . . . . . . . . . . . . . . . . . . . . . . . . . . . . . . . . . . . . . . . . . . . . . . $110-125

Doll (celluloid), boy doll 4½'' h., blowing a trumpet and
dressed in sailor suit with red hat, paper label marked
Nippon  . . . . . . . . . . . . . . . . . . . . . . . . . . . . . . . . . . . . . . . . . . . . . . . . . . . . . . . . . . . . $45-50

Doll (bisque), bride doll 4½'' h., crepe paper gown and satin
hat trimmed with flowers, impressed NIPPON on back  . . . . . . . . . . . . . . . . $125-145

Doll, stoneware (bisque finish), white head, no hair, marked
''Made in Japan''  . . . . . . . . . . . . . . . . . . . . . . . . . . . . . . . . . . . . . . . . . . . . . . . . . . . $30-35

## Traditional

Doll, 3½'' h., early 20th century, Japanese bandleader,
eggshell lacquer face, glass eyes, paper body. (Illus.)  . . . . . . . . . . . . . . . . . . $200-250

Doll, 4'' h., archer, eggshell lacquer face, glass eyes, red gold
brocade garb, paper body. (Illus.)  . . . . . . . . . . . . . . . . . . . . . . . . . . . . . . . . . . $200-250

Doll, 7'' h., Chinese, grandmother, silk garb, composition
face, cloth body  . . . . . . . . . . . . . . . . . . . . . . . . . . . . . . . . . . . . . . . . . . . . . . . . . . . $190-225

Doll, Bijin (all silk), wearing blue kimono and gold obi  . . . . . . . . . . . . . . . . . $160-195

Doll, Bijin, 21'' h., wearing a kimono with motif of boats . . . . . . . . . . . . . . . . $140-180

Doll, Geisha, 20'' h., wearing kimono with silver brocade obi
and holding a closed fan  . . . . . . . . . . . . . . . . . . . . . . . . . . . . . . . . . . . . . . . . . . . $150-200

Doll, Geisha, 23'' h., wearing red silk kimono and holding a
lantern  . . . . . . . . . . . . . . . . . . . . . . . . . . . . . . . . . . . . . . . . . . . . . . . . . . . . . . . . . . . $200-220

Doll, Japanese Boy Festival, paper and cloth body, lacquer
face  . . . . . . . . . . . . . . . . . . . . . . . . . . . . . . . . . . . . . . . . . . . . . . . . . . . . . . . . . . . . . . $190-225

Doll, Samurai 8'' h., c. 1900, standing, wearing full suit of
armor  . . . . . . . . . . . . . . . . . . . . . . . . . . . . . . . . . . . . . . . . . . . . . . . . . . . . . . . . . . . . $120-170

Doll, Samurai 11'' h., seated and wearing complete suit of
armor  . . . . . . . . . . . . . . . . . . . . . . . . . . . . . . . . . . . . . . . . . . . . . . . . . . . . . . . . . . . . $150-210

Doll, Samurai 12" h., late 19th century, in full suit of armor . . . . . . . . . . . . . . . . . . . . . $175-225

Dolls, 4" h., early 20th century, Chinese babies, movable
eyes, paper squeakers on stomach. (Illus.) . . . . . . . . . . . . . . . . . . . . . . . . . . . . . each $125-150

*Japanese archer doll (left); Japanese bandleader doll (right). Courtesy collection of Jean Keats*

*Chinese grandmother (left); Japanese Boy Festival doll (right). Courtesy collection of Jean Keats*

*Chinese babies, chop on neck, 4" h. Courtesy collection of Jean Keats*

Eggshell porcelain is so light and thin that it reminds one of the fragile shell of an egg. When held to the light it is so translucent that it appears to be made of glaze alone. Its production goes back to the 18th century. Most pieces being sold in today's market are representative of the late 19th/early 20th century.

(See: Made in China; Nineteenth Century)

## Eggshell Porcelain
### *(Chinese)*

# 18th Century Porcelains
## (Chinese)

The 18th century production of Chinese porcelain covers the reigns of late K'ang Hai, Yung Chêng, Ch'ien Lung and early Chia-Ch'ing. But the porcelains listed in this category cannot be directly attributed to any of these reigns.

(See: Ch'ien Lung, Copper Red, Flambé, Imari (Chinese), K'ang Hsi, Peking Glass, Powder Blue, Sang de Boeuf.)

Bowl, 10⅜" dia., the interior and exterior both covered with petal-shaped streaks of reddish purple and milky lavender . . . . . . . . . . . . . . . . . . . . $200-300

Bowl, 15½" dia., early to mid-18th century, with large reserves of mythological animals separated by two ju-i bordered floral and scroll reserves, all on an iron red mosaic background, with an inside border of repeated floral patterns and a central design of flowers and leaves, decorated in overglaze enamels of iron red, yellow, green, and turquoise. (Illus.) . . . . . . . . . . . . . . . . . . . . . . . . . . . . . . . . . . . . . . . . . $2,000-2,500

Chop block, 4" h. x 6" l., commemorative Wan Li mark, wu t'sai decoration, modeled as an iron red painted, double-headed foo lion atop a block with a dragon and flaming pearl motif. (Illus.) . . . . . . . . . . . . . . . . . . . . . . . . . $1,200-1,500

Stem cup, 3½" h., incised rose pink enamel ground with a design of phoenix in flight among clouds below a band of key pattern . . . . . . . . . . . . . . . . . . . . . . . . . . . . . . . . . . . . . . . . . . . . $200-250

Teapot, 13½" h., rectangular form, decorated with scrolling branches and bands of lappets, with bats among clouds, all in a blue and white glaze . . . . . . . . . . . . . . . . . . . . . . . . . . . . . . $1,000-1,200

Vase, 5½" h., mei ping shaped, etched and reserved with flowering branches of brown, aubergine, yellow, and white on a speckled leaf green ground . . . . . . . . . . . . . . . . . . . . . . . . $700-900

Vase, 6¾" h., blue and white, baluster form, with a short trumpet neck, painted with a riverside village scene . . . . . . . . . . . . . . . . . . . . . . $500-600

Vase, 7½" h., bottle form, covered with a pitted white glaze . . . . . . . . . . . . . . . . $175-225

Vase, 9½" h., commemorative mark of Wan Li on outside rim, beaker form, transitional style of a court scene above a center band of table settings, the lower half with flowers. (Illus.) . . . . . . . . . . . . . . . . . . . . . . . . . . . . . . . . . . . . . . . . . . . . . . . $800-1,000

*Eighteenth century vase, 9½" h., beaker form, transitional style*

*Eighteenth century vase, 17" h., transitional style*

*Eighteenth century Chinese bowl, 15½" dia.*

*Eighteenth century chop block, 6" l., wu ts'ai decoration*

## Eiraku
### (Japanese)

Collectors appear interested in Eiraku porcelains produced from the twelfth generation (1824) on. (The Zengoro line of potters.)

**Forms:**

1. Red ground with gold designs.
2. Red ground with gold/silver designs.
3. Red ground with gold/silver designs in combination with under the glaze blue and white motifs (often an underglaze blue-and-white medallion).

Incense burner, 5" h., 19th century, cylindrical form, motif of grasses in medallions of underglaze blue on a red and gilt/silver ground . . . . . . . . . . . . . . . . . . . . . . . . . . . . . . . . . . . . . . . . . . . . . . . . . . . . . . . . . $500-700

Sake cup, red, gilt, and silver ground with medallion of landscape motif in underglaze blue in center of cup and matching underplate . . . . . . . . . . . . . . . . . . . . . . . . . . . . . . . . . . . . . . . . . . . . . . . . . . . . . $250-325

## Enameled Brass
*(Chinese)*

Box, 3" x 4", heavily enameled design of birds, trees, and insects, marked "China." . . . . . . . . . . . . . . . . . . . . . . . . . . . . . . . . . . . . . . . . . . . . . . . . $40-60

Box, 3½" l., hinged, colorfully enameled flowers on blue ground on three of the sides and top lid . . . . . . . . . . . . . . . . . . . . . . . . . . . . . . . . . . $20-30

Chatelaines, pair, 1¼" dia. of plaques, early 19th century. Each circular plaque painted with European subjects — a man and woman courting; a man holding a cask while a woman blows on a horn, a building in the background, etc. A monster mask holding the loop of the metal mount in its mouth. Some restorations . . . . . . . . . . . . . . . . . . . . . . . . . . . . . . . . . . . . . . . . . . . . . . $900-1,290

Silent butler, 6½" x 5", top and handle enameled with butterflies and flowers, carnelian bead . . . . . . . . . . . . . . . . . . . . . . . . . . . . . . . . . . . . $40-65

## Enameled Copper
*(Chinese)*

Enameled copper, called yang-tz'u ("foreign porcelain") by the Chinese, was introduced to China in the late 17th century. The method of production is to coat the copper surface with an opaque enamel and then to paint the treated surface with enamel colors. Although many traditional motifs were incorporated, the object of production was to export the wares; therefore, a surprising number of European subjects are to be found. "Canton Enamel" and "Peking Enamel" are two names attributed to these wares, reflecting their cities of origin.

Basin, 17¾" dia., late 18th/early 19th century, Canton. Design of carp and grapevines on sides; interior depicts pair of Mandarin ducks in pond with lotus, blue rocks, and overhanging tree peonies; all painted in famille rose palette. Stylized dragons and dragon medallions on everted foliate rim, on yellow ground. Chips, cracks . . . . . . . . . . . . . . . . . . . . . . . . . . . . . . . . . . . $650-915

Bowl, 7¼" dia., late 18th/early 19th century, Canton. Stylized lotus blossoms on foliate scroll in famille rose colors on exterior, dragon in center flanked by two other four-clawed dragons on interior; on lemon-yellow ground with cloud scroll designs. Dragon medallion in blue on the base. Cracked, rubbed, some restoration . . . . . . . . . . . . . . . . . . . . . . . . . . . . . . . . . . . $2,100-3,400

Bowl, 7 2/5" w., late 18th century, Canton. Oblong, octagonal body. Birds and peony with rockwork on yellow ground with lotus scroll and bat design; key pattern on neck; kuei dragon handles at sides; monster mask feet; and foliate panels, plantain leaf designs on cover, with kuei dragon finial. Wood stand . . . . . . . . . . . . . . . . . . . . . . . . . . . . . . . . . . . . . . . . . . . . . . . . . . . . . . . . . . . $2,300-3,500

Box, 7" dia., 19th century, Canton. Butterflies and plants

between petal borders on apricot ground; similar design on cover which is topped with flower-painted button knop. Body of compressed globular shape. Green interior .......................... $125-260

Cup, wine, 3" dia., Canton. Three reserves painted with European subjects in famille rose palette, on scrolling foliage ground; single flower on interior and base on white ground. Restored ........................................................ $130-266

Cup and saucer, early 19th century, Canton. Shape of a peach, the stems comprising the handle; design of fruiting and flowering sprigs .................................................. $275-305

Dish, 8½" dia., 18th century, Canton. Central design of entwined flowers with flying bat and butterfly encircled by border of lotus, on lavender diaper ground; formal lotus scroll design on yellow ground on sides; emblems and peonies between foliate scroll borders on exterior; phoenix medallion on base. All in famille rose palette. Chips ......... $1,600-2,200

Dish, 14" dia., 19th century, Peking. Circular, the exterior painted in apple green; an ornate phoenix and dragon chasing flaming pearl, yellow and blue clouds, and four reserves with dragons, phoenix, and Ch'i-lin, on blue ground on interior ....................................................... $400-530

Ewer, 10½" h., 19th century, Canton. Pear-shaped body painted in brown, pink, and blue on greenish-yellow ground with panel on archaic vases against foliate ground, border of blue and white scrolls at base and yellow and green scrolls just above foot; band of plantain leaves at neck, and the cover with a petal design. Slender spout and loop handle, both with crazed design. Some wear ........................... $150-300

Ewers, wine (pair), 13½" h., 19th century, Canton. Persian-influenced shape, enameled in famille rose palette with two raised leaf-shaped panels of Shoulao attending a dignitary and others beneath pine, on the pink and yellow peony ground, formal scrolling tendrils, with bands of plantain leaves on neck; carved wood domed covers pierced with foliage. Both restored. (Illus.) ............................... $500-700

Snuff bottle, Canton, continuous design of garden flowers in famille rose enamels on green ground, formal borders on neck. Restoration and chipping on neck ......................... $50-75

Snuff bottle, Canton, multicolored design of a figure in a landscape on one side; a woman at a table near a window through which can be seen another man and woman apparently talking on the reverse ............................. $80-105

Snuff bottle, Canton, two reserves depicting people in landscape settings on speckled yellow ground. Red, four-character Ch'ien Lung mark. Some chipping ................ $50-80

*One of a pair of Japanese enameled silver vases, 7 3/5" h.*

*Pair of Canton enameled copper wine ewers, 13½" h.*

Snuff bottle, Peking, Ch'ien Lung mark and period. Design of two black-and-white magpies on branches of plum blossoms, butterfly, peony trees, rockwork, within stylized ch'ih dragon borders; two small landscapes in black and white on the sides; formalized bandings on the neck and foot, all in famille rose palette. Four-character Ch'ien Lung mark in blue on base .................................................. $4,750-5,500

Snuff bottle, Peking, Ch'ien Lung period. Two portraits of European women in landscapes surrounded by foliated gilt copper borders of kylin, peaches, and pomegranates; floral and petal lappet bandings on the waisted neck; all in famille rose palette on pale green, black-speckled ground ......................... $8,000-9,000

Snuff bottle, Peking, reserves showing two young ladies in pavilion setting, an attendant waiting on the Immortal Lan Ts'ai-ho, and a mother and child in a garden, on yellow floral ground ...................................................... $100-135

Tray, 8⅕″ w., late 18th century, Canton. Oblong, hexagonal shape with daisy, peony, and orchid blooms, rockwork and bird in flight on turquoise ground. Slightly crackled enamels ................. $800-1,000

## Enameled Silver
*(Chinese)*

Bank, shape of a seated Oriental man ....................................... $90-150

Snuff bottle, flattened spade shape, with flowering plants and butterflies enameled in turquoise, pink, and blue on the front and back ...................................................... $150-215

Snuff bottle, hinged, enameled floral design with Oriental characters on back, engraved sides .............................................. $85-110

Snuff bottle, oviform with design of numerous ladies and children on pavilion terrace molded and decorated in turquoise, aubergine, and blue enamels, matching stopper ..................... $150-200

Vase, 8″ h., c. 1900, baluster body with mask and ring handles, with chased and applied design of a bough of peaches and a gingko branch enameled in bright yellow, pink, and lime green, impressed marks ...................................... $50-180

Vases, pair, 7¼″ h., design of Shou characters, flowering plants, and cash ...................................................... $200-250

## Enameled Silver
*(Japanese)*

Incense burner, 6″ h., 19th century, four corner feet; flowers and butterflies design pierced in vessel, some picked out in colored enamels; a flower knop on the domed cover. Liner ................. $2,000-2,200

Koro, 8″ h., late 19th century, hexagonal, with six panels of flower baskets and birds/flowers in Shibayama style; six elephant head loose-ring handles applied to the shoulders; cloisonné flower garlands on the domed cover, surmounted by a finial of two silver mandarin ducks. Finial damaged, with some inlay missing. Signed Chuichi ............................... $1,650-2,050

Vase, 8″ h., 19th century, slender ovoid shape, waisted neck, with relief design of iris decorated with colored enamels. Signed ...................................................... $1,200-1,450

Vases, pair, 7 3/5″ h., late 19th century, pear-shaped, with slender flaring neck; colorfully enameled clumps of iris on the bodies and lappets of stylized flowers incised on the neck. Body signed Yoshiaki horu, impressed mark Mitsuyuki. Dents. (Illus.) ...................................................... $850-1,100

## Fa Hua
*(Chinese)*

Fa hua wares were an innovation of the Ming Dynasty. Polychrome enamel colors were applied between threads of clay or slip, which served as partitions, much like the style of cloisonné. The background colors are a deep cobalt blue or a brilliant turquoise. The enamels are mainly green, aubergine, and yellow ("san-t'sai" three-color ware).

(See: Ming)

*Fa hua jar with lid, 17" h., Ming Dynasty*

Figure, 6½" h., Kuan Yin, Ming Dynasty, seated on a wave-splashed rockwork base, her robe glazed in turquoise, with an ocher glaze overall ................................................................. $300-400

Fish bowl, 27" dia., 18th century, with floral and lotus scroll main design under a ju-i border, the overall glaze of turquoise, filled in with yellow and aubergine to complete the floral decor ................................................................. $2,600-3,200

Jar, 12" h., Ming Dynasty, baluster form with a straight short neck with lipped rim, the motif of musicians (the faces unglazed and left in the biscuit) playing various musical instruments, with formal borders at shoulder and base, the background color a purple blue, the design filled in with blue, yellow, aubergine, and white ................................................................. $3,500-4,500

Jar and cover, 15½" h., Ming Dynasty, the ovoid body pierced with designs of birds and peonies glazed in cream, aubergine, turquoise, and yellow, the cover with a conical knop and incised with flower sprigs and flower heads, leaves and branches left in the biscuit ................................................................. $5,000-6,000

Jar and cover, 17" h., Ming Dynasty, with a motif of fish and ducks in lotus ponds, decorated in aubergine, yellow, turquoise, and white on a blue ground; some areas left in biscuit; the lid in lotus form. (Illus.) ................................................................. $10,000-12,000

Jardiniere, 10" h., Ming Dynasty, rounded form, with design of "sages" and cloud forms, a floral band encircling the rim, covered in tones of brown, cream, green, purple, and turquoise glazes ................................................................. $2,000-3,000

Jardiniere, 12" h., Ming Dynasty, rectangular form, decorated with scroll design, colors of purple and turquoise on blue ground ................................................................. $2,000-2,400

Vase, 10½" h., 19th century, quadrangular beaker form, with a bulbous center and raised unglazed foot, decorated with blue and green glazes within raised slip borders on a deep purple glazed ground ................................................................. $275-325

Vase, 13" h., 18th century, mei ping form with a lipped rim, with a lily pad and floral motif separated from the neck and base by wide borders; glazed in blue, white, yellow, turquoise, and green ................................................................. $600-800

Vase, 13½" h., 16th century, double gourd shape, with pierced design of sages in a garden on each bulbous portion, decorated in aubergine, yellow, turquoise, and white on a blue ground; some of the areas left in the biscuit ................................................................. $4,000-5,000

Wine jar, 13" h., Ming Dynasty, decorated with a continuous pattern of riders on horseback among clouds, with a top border of large flower designs, with arches as a border design near the base, the dominant, overall color turquoise, the filled in areas dark violet, yellow, aubergine, and white ................................................................. $6,000-7,000

## Famille Jaune
*(Chinese)*

Famille jaune (yellow family) decoration first became popular during the reign of K'ang Hsi (1662-1722). Basically, these porcelains use the same techniques as famille noire and famille verte, but the background color is yellow. In order of rarity, the yellow is first, followed by black and lastly, green.

(See: Famille Noire; Famille Rose; Famille Verte)

*Famille jaune wine pot, 8¾" h., K'ang Hsi*

Dish, 9½" dia., Kuang Hsü mark and period, depicting dragons in pursuit of flaming pearls in enamels of green, red, aubergine, and black outline, all on a lemon yellow ground .................... $250-350

Jardiniere, 14" dia., late 19th century, with incurved sides decorated with flowers in black on a yellow background ....................... $400-500

Jardiniere, 14" dia., 19th century, painted with eight officials in the famille verte palette on a yellow ground, the borders with iron red floral design ...................................................... $500-700

Planters (pair), 6" h. x 10" l., c. 1900, enameled with birds and wisteria on a yellow ground .......................................... $800-1,000

Vase, 18" h., 19th century, wide shouldered baluster form painted with enamel design of a kylin, all on a yellow ground ................................................................... $600-700

Vase, 24" h., 19th century, square shape with a flared neck, with design of peony and prunus branches with birds, all in colors of turquoise, green, black, and aubergine on a yellow ground ................................................................... $800-1,000

Wine pot, 8¾" h., K'ang Hsi period (unmarked). Modeled in graceful, open design and decorated in famille jaune; the motif of floral patterns painted in aubergine, white, and green are bordered by black lines, the center with a scene of a sage being offered gifts by a boy; the reverse with a wise man leaning on his staff along with a crane; two smaller panels with flower-filled vases beneath each main panel, with repairs and restorations (Illus.) ......................................... $4,000-5,000

## Famille Noire
*(Chinese)*

Famille noire (black family) decoration became popular during the reign of K'ang Hsi (1662-1722). The color was obtained by decorating the porcelain with a black pigment, which was then covered by a transparent green glaze. This resulted in an iridescent sheen known as "oil slick," which throws off a violet purplish hue. A typical decoration of famille noire includes rocks and tree branches laden with prunus blossoms and birds enameled in green, yellow, and aubergine. Production of vases, bowls, and plates in the black, yellow, and green families continued to be popular in the 18th and 19th centuries. The late examples do not command the prices of the original wares.

(See: Famille Jaune; Famille Rose; Famille Verte)

Brush pot, 8" dia., K'ang Hsi period, with continuous design of dragons chasing flaming pearls among cloud scrolls, all above swirling waves. (Illus.) .......................................... $1,400-1,600

Jardiniere, 14" dia., 19th century, decorated with two maidens in a garden setting ............................................ $400-500

Vase, 9" h., 19th century, baluster form with a turned out neck decorated with birds and flowering branches in famille verte colors ....................................................... $400-500

Vase, 15" h., late 19th century, bottle form, decorated in famille verte enamels with a scene of flowering prunus, with birds perched on the branches ......................................... $1,200-1,400

Vase, 17" h., 19th century, with scene of warriors astride horses. (Illus.) ................................................. $1,000-1,200

Vase, 18" h., K'ang Hsi period, six-character mark in underglaze blue. Quadrangular form with a flaring neck,

*Famille noire brush pot, 6½" h., K'ang Hsi*

*Famille noire vase, 17" h., 19th century*

*Famille rose bowl, 14¾" dia., rare, late Ch'ien Lung*

decorated with vividly enameled peony blossoms and foliage in yellow, green, aubergine, and iron red, heightened with gilding on a thick black ground, the shoulders with peonies on a black stippled green ground .................................... $15,000-20,000

Vase, 20¼″ h., 19th century, quadrangular form decorated with the four seasons on separate panels in colors of green, yellow, and aubergine ................................................ $900-1,200

Vase, 36″ h., 19th century, yen yen shape decorated with the "hundred birds" pattern, with two large phoenixes standing on the rocks with cranes in the trees overhead; the reverse of vase with magpies and other birds perched in trees, enameled in colors of aubergine, yellow, green, and white .................. $2,800-3,400

Vases (pair), 15¾″ h., 18th century, Chia-Ch'ing period. Bottle form with bulbous mouths, decorated with foo dogs trailing ribbons among cloud scrolls in colors of aubergine, yellow,and green .................................................. $3,000-3,500

Famille rose (pink family) decoration refers to a group of enamel colors in which the pink color predominates. Although the color pink was discovered in Europe in the mid-1600s, it was not adopted by the Chinese until the Ch'ing Dynasty. This "foreign" color first gained recognition in the Yung Chêng period, but became most firmly established in the reign of Ch'ien Lung. The famille rose palette consists of a rose pink accompanied by yellow, green, blue, aubergine, and black. The items listed under this heading are 18th century examples. (Note: The later export wares which were given the pattern names of Rose Mandarin, Rose Canton, and Rose Medallion are listed under individual topic headings.)

(See: Famille Jaune; Famille Noire; Famille Verte)

# Famille Rose
## (Chinese)

*Famille rose vase, 16″ h., 18th century*

Barber's bowl, 10½″ dia., enameled with a central vase of flowers, the rim having three camellia sprays ............................. $800-1,000

Bowl, 10½″ dia., Ch'ien Lung period (unmarked), decorated with tree peonies and magnolia emerging from rocks and with a bird perched on a branch, the interior with a red and pink peony ....................................................... $1,800-2,200

Bowl (lotus), 10½″ dia., enameled in gilt and iron red with a large central peony branch below alternating feather scrolls and bellflower at the rim; the exterior has a similar pattern ................... $800-1,000

Bowl, 14″ dia., Ch'ien Lung period (unmarked), decorated with butterflies, chrysanthemums, bats, and birds on a blue ground .......................................................... $1,200-1,400

*Bowl, 14¾″ dia., late Ch'ien Lung, scene of foreign concessions at Canton, cracked and riveted, rare. (Illus.) ...................... $22,000

Compotes (lotus, pair), 7″ dia., the lotus petal molded bowls with turquoise interiors, standing on tall stems with flower scrolls above breaking green waves ...................................... $1,500-1,800

Dish, 4½″ dia., Yung Chêng period, six-character mark in underglaze blue, delicately painted with a peony and three different floral sprays in colors of pink, yellow, turquoise, and green on a white ground .............................................. $800-1,200

Dish, 8½″ dia., Yung Chêng mark and period, shallow dish with peach branches bearing fuit and flowers, enameled in pink, yellow/green, and white, with small cracks ........................ $3,500-4,500

Flower holder, 8″ h., wall pocket, molded as a tall pink lotus pod above a green stalk and decorated with a gilt bow ........................ $400-500

Pitcher, 14″ h., pear shaped, painted with a large panel of birds in flight and perched on brown rockwork beside peonies and chrysanthemums, all within a gilt scroll border below a band of spearheads .......................................... $1,200-1,400

*Punch bowl, 15" dia., Ch'ien Lung period, enameled in colors and gilt with four alternate panels of court figures and laborers on pavilion terraces, with a pair of cockerels and a pair of sparrows on a millefleur ground ............................ $2,200

Saucer dish, 8" dia., the center enameled with a long flowering plum blossom branch beside peonies, all below radiating lotus petals divided by small gilt flower sprays at the rim; back enameled with lotus petals ...................... $1,000-1,200

Vase, 10" h., Ch'ien Lung period (unmarked), bottle form, with a long neck, enameled with flower blossoms on one side and butterflies and birds on the reverse .................... $800-1,000

Vase, 12" h., 18th century, melon-shaped form with a bulbous body, the ribs extending from the body up the short, slightly flared neck, decorated with a tree branch and flowers in green, pink, brown, and white enamel with gilt highlights ............... $1,800-2,200

Vase, 16" h., 18th century, Ch'ien Lung seal mark in underglaze blue, nine peach decoration with flowering branches ............................................................. $2,500-3,000

Vase, 19" h., Ch'ien Lung period, seal mark in underglaze blue, decorated with two panels of oval form reserved on a marbled, bluish green ground, one panel containing a mountain landscape, the other with a blooming tree and floral sprigs ............................................................ $2,500-3,000

Vase, 26" h., bulbous body with elongated neck, mark and period of Ch'ien Lung, decorated with a pair of phoenixes with bright pink, green, yellow, and blue plumage, surmounted by a large blossoming tree peony and flowering peach trees ........................................................ $15,000-18,000

## Famille Verte
### (Chinese)

Famille verte (green family) decoration became popular during the reign of K'ang Hsi (1662-1722). Although predominantly green, famille verte decoration also uses underglaze blue, with transparent, on-glaze enamels which can include shades of yellow, aubergine, green, and coral red. Famille verte (famille jaune as well) may also exhibit a luster or "oil slick" similar to the famille noire. The designs were done in landscapes, florals, garden settings, and whimsical figures of animals (foo dogs, kylins, etc.).

(See: Famille Jaune; Famille Noire; Famille Rose)

Bowl, 7" h., K'ang Hsi mark and period, decorated with Buddhist emblems, symbols, teapots, and instruments on a white ground ......................................................... $1,500-2,000

Bowl, 8" dia., 18th century, interior decorated with a floral spray medallion, the exterior with chrysanthemums, peonies, rockwork, and butterflies .......................................... $500-700

Bowl, 16" l. x 8¼" w., oval shape, on carved wood lotus leaf stand, Ch'ien Lung period (unmarked), with interior decorated with figures in boats on a river landscape with a wide border of reserves of river scenes and birds separated by diaper and floral design; exterior with four reserves of women on a floating pavilion, a kylin, a foo dog, men playing checkers ....................................................... $3,800-4,200

Brush pot, 5½" h., K'ang Hsi period, unusual relief design of mountain and river landscape within a reserve, the bottom signed with three green enameled artemis leaves. (Illus.) ................... $1,200-1,400

Brush pot, 6" h., 19th century, decorated with a river landscape, figures in boats, pavilions, and pine trees ......................... $300-400

*Famille verte brush pot, 5½″ h., K'ang Hsi*

*Famille verte dish, 8½″ dia., K'ang Hsi*

Dish, 8½″ dia., K'ang Hsi period, decorated in san t'sai palette with both sides showing frolicking horses among swirling waves, with five good luck symbols in the center, rim restoration, signed with a commemorative Chia-ching mark. (Illus.) .............................................. $3,000-4,000

Dish, 8¾″ dia., K'ang Hsi period (unmarked), with center design of chickens in a garden, with rim reserves of fish and "antiques" on a black-stippled green ground .............................. $600-800

Dish, 9″ dia., K'ang Hsi period (unmarked), octagonal shape, the center decorated with an exotic bird on a flowering camellia branch, the border with medallions of insects reserved on a black-speckled green ground, the underside decorated with flower sprays .............................................. $700-900

Dish, 14″ dia., K'ang Hsi period, decorated in the center with two phoenix birds in a garden setting, with floral sprays on the border, on a white ground ........................................ $1,000-1,200

*Garniture set (three pieces), 12″ h., K'ang Hsi period, consisting of two trumpet-necked vases and a covered center vase, the bodies of each pear shaped and of oval quatrefoil lobed section; variously enameled with birds and butterflies among prunus and peonies between bands of floral panels, the rims restored, the cover not a match. (Illus.) ............................... $1,900

Ginger jar, 8½″ h., early 19th century, ovoid shape with reserves of figures in indoor and outdoor settings on a background of symbols and emblems, with a domed lid ....................... $175-250

Jar, 9″ h., K'ang Hsi period (unmarked), ovoid shape with a floral design emerging from rockwork with numerous birds and butterflies .................................................... $600-800

Plates, 23″ dia. and 11¾″ dia., K'ang Hsi period (unmarked), both mounted and set in an 18th century English Chippendale table 29½″ h. The large plate is set as the table top with the smaller one set below at the juncture of the legs (photograph presents aerial view of large plate). Both plates decorated with insects and flowering branches with a border of flowers set among diaper patterns; these patterns interrupted by partitions of floral sprays set on a black-stippled green ground ........................................... $12,000-15,000

*Famille verte dish with commemorative Chia Ching mark within double concentric circles in underglaze blue*

81

Syrup pot, 12" h., K'ang Hsi period (unmarked), cylindrical form with a tiara top, painted on the biscuit in famille verte colors, decorated with Buddhist symbols, waves, and phoenix birds, with the original dragon head spout and three foo dog head mask handles at the back. (See Color Section) ............... $2,500-3,000

Vase, 7" h., 19th century, double gourd shape decorated with a floral and mountain landscape ......................................... $300-400

Vase, 12½" h., 19th century, baluster form decorated with a male and female peacock among flowering branches and rockwork, the neck with rocks and flowers along with scrolling fleurettes on a black-stippled ground ..................... $400-600

Vase, 18" h., 18th century, Chia-Ch'ing period (commemorative mark of K'ang Hsi in underglaze blue). Quadrangular form decorated with birds, prunus blossoms, and rockwork in famille verte enamels ..................... $2,000-2,500

Vase, 20" h., 18th century, yen yen form, with flared rim, four reserves of birds on branches and four smaller similar reserves on the neck ............................................ $1,500-1,800

Vase, 20" h., 19th century, yen yen with two reserves of birds, and rockwork set on an iron red diaper ground ........................ $500-600

Wine pot, 8¾" h., K'ang Hsi period (unmarked), in the form of a foo dog with one foot on a ball standing in an upright posture and leaning against a vase form pot with a long curved spout, with a foo dog finial on the pot cover, all set on square base, decorated with two reserves of table settings which are surrounded by a floral motif, with a chip on the spout ..................................................... $4,000-5,000

*Famille verte garniture set, 12" h., K'ang Hsi*

**Fans**    The three most common forms of Chinese fans are:
1. Brise (folding fan).
2. Screen fan (stationary fan).
3. Short stick fan.

Common forms of Japanese fans are:

1. Hi-ogi (the slatted fan/folding fan).
2. Sensu (made of silk or paper, with wood, ivory or bamboo ribs).
3. Tessen (a folding fan with metal ribs used by the samurai and occasionally ornamented with the moon on one side and the sun on the other).
4. A Kome ogi (used by women and having approximately 39 ribs, usually decorated with floral motifs).

During the last half of the 19th century, fans from Asia were in vogue in the West. Generally large, most fans had motifs of flowers, dragonflies, lace, silk, and feathers, used singularly or in combination. During the last quarter of the 19th century, the wooden block print fans were popular in America. This style of fan was made by gluing two perfumed sheets together. Such fans generally had wooden ribs. Many of the fans exported from China, from the 18th century on, had motifs and designs based on European styles and motifs. For the most part, Chinese fans were produced in Canton. The principal places of manufacture for the Japanese fans were Nagoya, Kyoto, and Tokyo.

## Chinese

Fan, 7½", c. 1880, gauze leaf embroidered with dragons, ivory sticks, fitted lacquer box . . . . . . . . . . . . . . . . . . . . . . . . . . . . . . . $175-225

Fan, 10", brise with appliqued silk . . . . . . . . . . . . . . . . . . . . . . . . . . . . . . . . . $75-100

Fan, 10", 19th century, lacquered sticks, paper painted with landscape . . . . . . . . . . . . . . . . . . . . . . . . . . . . . . . . . . . . . . . . . . . . . . . . . . . . $225-300

Fan, 11", c. 1880, leaf painted with figures, ivory faces, silk clothes, lacquer sticks, in fitted lacquer box . . . . . . . . . . . . . . . . . . . . . $200-300

Fan, 11", mid-19th century, leaf painted with figures with ivory faces and silk clothes, on a terrace, lacquer sticks . . . . . . . . . . . . . . . $310-365

Fan, 11½", mid-19th century, ivory brise carved with dragons, bats, and landscapes, red guard sticks . . . . . . . . . . . . . . . . . . . . . . . $200-275

Fan, c. 1800, leaf painted with a man and boy fishing, pierced ivory sticks . . . . . . . . . . . . . . . . . . . . . . . . . . . . . . . . . . . . . . . . . . . . $400-500

Fan, woven ivory with applied stained ivory birds, flowers, and foliage, handle set with hardstones . . . . . . . . . . . . . . . . . . . . . . $2,800-3,500

*Japanese fan, late 19th century, 9¼" w.*

## Japanese

*Fan (Hi-ogi), 9¼", late 19th century, gilt lacquer motif of peacocks, tail of peacocks, and guard sticks in Shibayama style, tasseled cord and ojime (Illus.) . . . . . . . . . . . . . . . . . . . . . . . . . . . . . . . $580

Fan (Hi-ogi), late 19th century, lacquered ivory sticks, motif of flowers and berries in tones of brown, and gold, guard sticks with motif of birds and bamboo, overall Shibayama style decoration . . . . . . . . . . . . . . . . . . . . . . . . . . . . . . . . . . . . . . . . . . . $900-1,200

Handscreen, painted feathers . . . . . . . . . . . . . . . . . . . . . . . . . . . . . . . . . . . . . $75-125

## Southeast Asia

A pair of fans (as above) with silk tassels . . . . . . . . . . . . . . . . . . . . . . . . . . . $100-125

A pair of feather handscreens, ivory handles with silk and mother-of-pearl rosettes . . . . . . . . . . . . . . . . . . . . . . . . . . . . . . . . . . . . . . . . $125-175

Fitzhugh is one of the three major export patterns imported when America and China began direct trade (just after the American Revolution). The Fitzhugh pattern has intricate trellis work in the border band,

## Fitzhugh Pattern
(Chinese)

with four split pomegranates and spread-winged butterflies. The center reserve contains four groups of flowers (and emblems) surrounding either an oval monogram or a medallion. The central motif can also be found with a post and spear ornamentation and posts and spears can also be found in the border. Blue, green, and orange are the most common colors. The name Fitzhugh is derived from the family for which the first dinner service was made.

(See: Chinese Export)

### Flambé
### (Chinese)

Flambé is a furnace transmutation glaze which changes deep red (sang de boeuf) into a tangle of streaks and shadings which can be green, brown, gray, blue, or crimson. The catalyst for this change is copper oxide reacting to a rapid change of atmosphere in the kiln caused by the introduction of wood smoke during the firing. This technique was perfected in the 18th century. (Although flambé is evident in the K'ang Hsi period, we must suppose it was a matter of kiln "accident" at that time.) As in sang de boeuf, the late 17th century flambé had controlled glazes that did not run over the foot. The 18th century examples will probably show evidence of grinding at the foot rim, since the art of controlling the glaze was lost. The 19th century examples often have a very rough footing with glaze running over the foot rim. They show evidence of having to be chipped away from the kiln floor. These late pieces may have the base and foot rim glazed with a burnt orange/brown wash which was applied in imitation of iron oxide in order to suggest that they were earlier period wares.

*Flambé bowl, 8½" dia., 18th century*

Bowl, 8½" dia., 18th century, with a streaked purple, blue and white glaze, unglazed foot rim, with coffee glaze under foot. (Illus.) ............................................................ $600-700

Conch shell, 5½" dia., 18th century, realistically modeled with blue and purple flambé glaze thinning to tan at the high spots ............................................................ $400-600

Jar, 12" h., 19th century, ovoid form, glazed in a deep streaky purple shading to a lighter color at the ringed neck .......................... $250-300

Moon flask, 10" h., Yung Chêng incised, four-character seal mark, flattened sides with peach-shaped panels and short cylindrical neck with looped handles, covered with a bright crimson/blue streaked glaze, damaged .................................... $600-800

Stand, 15¼" h., Ming Dynasty, with blue transmutation glaze over an open, hollow, vase form stand ..................................... $275-350

Stem cup, 7½" h., 18th century, decorated with a mottled violet/red glaze, the lip glazed in white .............................. $1,400-1,600

Vase, 8" h., 18th century, mei ping body, covered with a streaked red glaze which thins to white at the top and terminates in a thick roll above the base ............................ $500-600

Vase, 8" h., Ch'ien Lung seal mark and period, ovoid shape with a small, lipped rim, set with double loop handles with scroll terminals, glazed in deep purple with two streaks of blue, ground at the foot ...................................... $800-1,000

Vase, 12" h., 19th century, bottle form with glaze and streaked in tones of lavender and milky blue, the base with a café au lait wash .............................. $500-600

Vase, 12" h., Ch'ien Lung period, baluster form, with a blue glaze streaked with white ............................ $800-1,000

Vase, 12" h., late 18th century, with molded and applied stylized elephant head and ring handles, impressed factory mark on the lip rim, glaze ground down at the foot rim, underfoot glazed brown. (Illus.) .......................... $500-600

Vase, 15" h., Ch'ien Lung period, seal mark in blue, with melon-ribbed bulbous bottom, elephant head mask and ring handles at the neck, and an incurving flared rim, with seven raised studs above the shoulders, glazed in a blue to purple glaze, the interior glazed in a lustrous brown color ...................... $1,400-1,800

Vase, 15" h., early 18th century, baluster form set on an unglazed foot rim, covered with a purple and blue streaky glaze, the interior with a white crackled glaze ........................... $850-1,000

Vase, 15" h., 19th century, baluster form covered with a deep crimson glaze with lavender blue streaks, the interior with a white glaze, chipped on the foot rim ..................................... $400-600

Vase, 18" h., Ch'ien Lung period, yen yen shape, with a dark, purplish red flambé glaze, the base with brown glaze ................. $1,600-1,800

Vase, 21" h., late 19th century, yen yen shape, with a streaky purplish glaze thinning to pale celadon at the rim, with thick glaze chipped off around the foot rim ..................................... $400-500

Vase, 24" h., late 19th century, squared with a red streaked and mottled glaze thinning to white at the rim and forming in puddles at the foot .................................................. $350-500

*Flambé vase, 12" h., late 18th century*

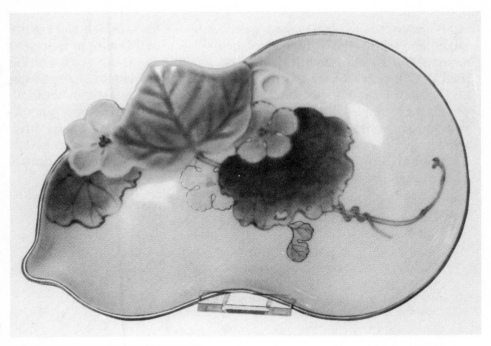

*Fukagawa dish molded in relief, signed*

The Fukagawa family began working in Hizen province about 1650. After 1868, porcelain wares were specifically made for Western export. Wares most available today date from the late 19th century. The porcelain is generally of fine quality, and occasionally motifs were molded in relief. Overall colors are of the Imari palette. The Mt. Fuji mark is associated with Fukagawa and these wares are still being produced.

## Fukagawa
*(Japanese)*

Bowl, 9" dia., polychrome and gilt flowers, signed Fukagawa sei .................................................................. $300-400

85

Dish, 19th century, motif in blue, yellow, and gilt. (Illus.) ...... $200-250

Plate, hexagonal, underglaze blue with iron red and gold,
two carp leaping through waves, signed Fukagawa sei ...... $600-700

Plate, 6" dia., motif of samurai in shades of orange, blue, red,
and gold, signed ...... $125-150

Vase, 18" h., flowers in colors, signed (cracked) ...... $200-300

Vase, 19½" h., beaker form with hexagonal contour,
riverscapes and women in gardens, neck and base containing
a border of scrolls and medallions of phoenix birds ...... $800-1,100

Vase, 61" h., shouldered ovoid body in polychrome,
medallions containing children at play with alternating panels
of irises on a ground of wave motifs, a waisted neck with
mon of cranes on a diapered ground (slight damages) ...... $2,500-3,750

Vases (pair), 13½" h., ovoid bodies, flared necks, florals,
courtiers and butterflies in hues of red and orange, signed ...... $500-700

Vases (pair), 38" h., baluster form, baskets of flowers,
phoenix, and flowering branches on a geometric diapered
ground, polychrome and gilt, signed ...... $9,000-15,000

Vases (pair), 48½" h., ovoid with painting in polychrome
enamels and gilding, flared ruffled rim, panels of birds and
foliage alternating with panels of samurai, overall motifs of
brocade diapers and mons with dragons on the panel
borders, signed Fukagawa sei (one neck repaired) ...... $5,000-7,000

## Funerary Objects
### (Chinese — Tomb Articles)

Funerary applies to objects made specifically for tomb burial. During the Shang and Chou dynasties such objects were usually made to represent animals and were placed in the tombs as offerings to the gods. During the Han Dynasty, funerary articles of pottery were made, usually taking on forms of farm animals, dancers, etc. Perhaps the most famous tomb objects were made during the T'ang Dynasty. Taking on forms such as women, warriors, camels, horses, birds, etc., and ranging in size from mere inches to several feet in height, they are the apex of the glazed pottery funerary wares. Aside from pottery, funerary wares were made of such materials as wood, bronze, jade, silver, etc.

(See: Han Dynasty; T'ang Dynasty; Sung Dynasty)

## Furniture
### (Chinese)

*Altar table, 42" h., c. 1900, inlaid mother-of-pearl. (Illus.) ...... $3,520

Cabinet (black lacquer), 39" h., late 19th century, D-shaped
front, doors inlaid with ivory and painted in gilt with motif
of children at play ...... $1,000-1,500

Cabinet, 2'6" x 1'11", early 20th century, red lacquer, doors
painted with landscapes ...... $500-650

Cabinet, 2'6" x 2', early 20th century, black lacquer, two
cupboard doors with hardstone inlay in motif of landscapes ...... $450-625

Cabinet, 2'9" x 2'6", (hardwood), early 20th century, two
cupboard doors above a single drawer, overall carving of
adults and children, square legs ...... $400-600

Cabinet (side), 4' x 2'8", early 20th century, two cupboard
doors with overall motif of women, birds, and flowering
trees set with hardstones on a black lacquer ground
highlighted with gilt ...... $800-1,200

Chair (armchair), hardwood, 40" h., back carved with
dragons, half dragon arms, animal mask legs ...... $600-800

Chair (side), 38½" h., back carved with sage and attendants,

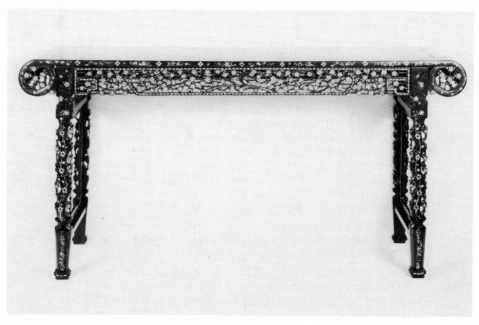

*Altar table inlaid with mother-of-pearl

shaped seat with scroll band, cabriole legs .................................. $400-600

*Chairs (armchairs/pair), 38" h., hardwood, splat carved with
vases, the arms on openwork panels (Illus.) .................................... $990

Chairs (armchairs/pair), 17th century, horseshoe backs,
curved toprail, cane seats .............................................. $8,000-12,000

Chairs (armchairs/pair), Huang Hua-li, yoke back, concave
splats, curving armrests ................................................. $5,000-7,000

Chest (camphor wood), 39" w., rectangular with overall
carving of birds, bamboo, and foliage ...................................... $500-750

Chest, 2' x 2', black lacquer, one drawer above two cupboard
doors, gilt and polychrome motifs of flowers and foliage ...................... $375-450

Etegere (rosewood), 4'8" x 2'11", set with asymetrical
shelving, border of gilt and black lacquer ................................... $800-1,200

Etegere (rosewood), 5' x 3', scroll and pierced crest rail above
shelving (asymetrical) with two cupboards at the base, ball
and claw feet ......................................................... $1,500-1,700

Firescreen, 3' h., 19th century, rectangular embroidered form
with motif of court figures and flying cranes within a
rosewood frame inlaid with mother-of-pearl in a floral motif ................... $500-700

Mirror, 35" h., black lacquer with polychrome landscapes ...................... $110-130

Mirror, 39" w., frame inlaid with shell forming peony scrolls ................... $300-395

Mirror (mahogany), 51" x 63", rectangular frame, carved and
pierced with two dragons and flower heads .............................. $900-1,350

Screen, hardwood, early 20th century, four panel, panel size
4' x 1'6", carved and pierced with dragons in reserves
surrounded by flower and Shou symbols ..................................... $300-400

Screen, 19th century, six panel, panel size 6'2" x 8'7",
continuous motif of landscape with adults and children on
pavilion terraces, black lacquer ground with hardstone
decoration ......................................................... $2,600-3,500

Screen, two panel, panel size 72" x 31", inlaid with ivory and
continuing motifs of birds and flowering branches with
carved and pierced border on a black lacquer ground ...................... $1,200-1,600

Screen, coromandel, six panel, panel size 6'1" x 17", carved and gilt with scenes of pavilions, bridges, willow trees and landscapes, lower panel sections having vases filled with flowers . . . . . . . . . . . . . . . . . . . . . . . . . . . . . . . . . . . . . . . . . . . . . . . . . $2,500-3,500

Screen, coromandel, two leaf, leaf size 6'3" x 2'10", carved polychrome motif of temples, trees, and priests, bordered with cinnabar carved with motifs of peony blossoms and branches . . . . . . . . . . . . . . . . . . . . . . . . . . . . . . . . . . . . . . . . . . . . . . . . . . . . $1,200-1,800

Screen, coromandel, eight panel, panel size 8' x 1'11", brown lacquer ground with continuing motif of Tsai Wen-shi's return home, panels bordered with polychrome seasonal flowers . . . . . . . . . . . . . . . . . . . . . . . . . . . . . . . . . . . . . . . . . . . . . . . . . . $2,900-4,100

Screen, six panel, panel size 7' x 1'11", carved red lacquer with overall motif of mythological animals within an ebonized frame . . . . . . . . . . . . . . . . . . . . . . . . . . . . . . . . . . . . . . . . . . $2,600-3,400

Screen, four panel, panel size 5'8" x 1'6", black lacquer inlaid with hardstones forming flowering trees within a frame painted with polychrome birds . . . . . . . . . . . . . . . . . . . . . . . . . . . . $1,200-1,500

Sewing table, 19th century, black lacquer with gilt landscapes, lyre trestle legs . . . . . . . . . . . . . . . . . . . . . . . . . . . . . . . $1,200-1,500

Stand, 19" h., inlaid marble top, frieze pierced with pomegranate sprays . . . . . . . . . . . . . . . . . . . . . . . . . . . . . . . . . . . . . . . . $300-400

Stand, 29" h., frieze with carp dragons . . . . . . . . . . . . . . . . . . . . . $300-400

Stand, 33" h., inlaid marble top, frieze carved with ju-i lappets below flower scrolls . . . . . . . . . . . . . . . . . . . . . . . . . . . . . . . . . $400-500

Stand, 35" h., inlaid marble top, octagonal on a frieze carved with vines . . . . . . . . . . . . . . . . . . . . . . . . . . . . . . . . . . . . . . . . . . . . . . $350-450

Stand, 35" h., marble inlaid top, frieze pierced and carved with gourds, cabriole legs . . . . . . . . . . . . . . . . . . . . . . . . . . . . . . . . . . $350-470

Stand, 35½" h., inlaid marble top, three tiers, frieze carved and pierced with peonies . . . . . . . . . . . . . . . . . . . . . . . . . . . . . . . . . $350-450

Stand, 108" h., hardwood, with inlaid shell, carved and inlaid with figures and flower heads, center insert having embroidered panel . . . . . . . . . . . . . . . . . . . . . . . . . . . . . . . . . . . . . $2,700-3,600

Table, 30" h., hardwood, quatrefoil top with relief carvings of prunus blossoms . . . . . . . . . . . . . . . . . . . . . . . . . . . . . . . . . . . . . . . . . $400-425

Table, 30" h., hardwood, rectangular, concave sides carved with phoenix, knees having lion masks, ball and claw feet . . . . . . . . . $1,200-1,600

Table, 32" h., hardwood, pedestal, inlaid marble top, pedestal reticulated with vines and foliage and ending in three legs . . . . . . . . . . . $500-600

Table, 32" h., top carved with flower scrolls . . . . . . . . . . . . . . . . . . $300-400

Table, 36" l., oval, top carved with warriors on horseback and pavilions, glass cover, one drawer . . . . . . . . . . . . . . . . . . . . . . . . . $1,200-1,500

Table, 44" l. (lacquer), low, black, motifs of landscapes, ladies, hardstones and enamel, glass top . . . . . . . . . . . . . . . . . . . . $800-1,200

Table, 54", dia., hardwood, inlaid marble top, curving frieze carved with foliage, four masked legs with ball and claw feet . . . . . . . . . . . . . . . $1,700-2,300

Trunk, 1'8" x 2'5", leather, brass mounts, polychrome motifs of women and pavilions . . . . . . . . . . . . . . . . . . . . . . . . . . . . . . . . . . . . $275-350

*One of a pair of armchairs, 38" h.*

# Furniture
## (Indian)

Armchair (rollback), back carved with scrolls, dragon head handrest, legs mounted with dogs, overall pierced and carved motifs of vines . . . . . . . . . . . . . . . . . . . . . . . . . . . . . . . . . . . . . . . . $900-1,200

Desk, six drawers above a slant front, raised on two pedestals, each having three drawers, overall carving of birds and vines . . . . . . . . . . . . . . . . . . . . . . . . . . . . . . . . . . . . . . . . . . . . . . . $800-1,000

Screen, four-fold, fold size 1'8", sandalwood with pierced and carved motifs of flowers and foliage . . . . . . . . . . . . . . . . . . . . . . . . . $135-195

Table, 2'6" x 2', octagonal top, overall carving of foliage and scrolls in concentric panels on a pierced and carved eight panel base (sandalwood) .................................................. $100-125

Table (as above), with overall inlay of ivory ................................. $500-625

Writing table, 4'2", pierced and carved scrolling vines, flowers and birds above five drawers, slant top, pierced and carved apron, raised on standard having lion head feet ...................... $800-1,000

## Furniture
### (Japanese)

Armchair, early 20th century, (hardwood), flanged crest rail above panel having carved dragon, dragon armrests, tambour seat, claw and ball feet .................................................. $1,500-2,000

Armchair, early 20th century, (hardwood), scrolled crest rail with carved vines, tambour back and seat with dragon medallion, winged griffin supports, dragon armrests ....................... $1,200-1,600

Armchair, late 19th century (hardwood), pierced and carved motif of prunus, dragon armrests, serpentine seat, cabriole legs ............................................................. $500-700

Cabinet, 3' x 2' (black lacquer), center door surrounded by panels, raised on bracket feet (Shibayama style), slight chipping, some inlay missing ................................................. $500-700

Cabinet, early 20th century, moon back, circular, carved red foliage and dragons, rectangular plinth ................................... $800-1,200

Chest, 2' x 2', lift top, brass mon and hinges ............................... $300-375

Chest, 2' x 2" x 2'6", lift top, iron hinges, shaped legs, shallow drawer ....................................................... $400-600

Chest (Tansu), 2' x 4" x 4', domed top, iron mounts, lock and bail handles, painted with black mons ................................... $1,900-2,400

*Desk, rolltop, 86" h., c. 1900, overall relief carving of foliage. (Illus.) ............................................................. $1,980

Screen, 19th century, four fold, fold size, 65" x 25", painted with depiction of children playing blindman's bluff on a gilt ground ........................................................... $1,200-1,900

*Settee, c. 1900, 57" l.

*Rolltop desk, c. 1900

Screen, 19th century, four fold, fold size, 65" x 25", motif of falcon in polychrome on a gilt ground .......................... $1,400-1,800

Screen, 19th century, six fold, fold size, 5'9" x 2'3", painted polychrome motifs of gardens and courtesans ......................... $1,600-2,100

*Settee, 57" l., c. 1900, serpentine back, dragon arm rests, seat with dragons and clouds, skirt carved with scrolls. (Illus.) ...................... $1,320

Stand, 2'8" h., c. 1900, hexagonal top, skirt carved with prunus blossoms, cabriole legs ......................... $300-400

Table, 1'5" x 2', 20th century, serpentine top with painted motif of dragons, skirt carved and pierced with foliage, cabriole legs ......................... $150-200

Table (nest of four), black lacquer, size of largest table, 2'2" x 1'1", motifs of pine, plum, and bamboo in gilt ......................... $500-700

*Tansu (chest), overall h. 64", overall w., 40", carved red cinnabar lacquer, inlaid in shibayama ......................... $3,000-4,000

*Writing table, 54" h., late 19th century, upper part surmounted by carving of Mt. Fuji, which is encircled by two dragons, top enclosing two cabinets and an open letter rack, glass top writing surface, mythical animal knees, cabriole legs, scroll feet (Illus.) ......................... $800-1,200

*Writing table (Japanese), late 19th century, 54" h.

# Furniture
## (Korean)

Chest, 49" h., lacquer inlaid with tortoiseshell to form continuous motif of swirling dragons and clouds ......................... $1,800-2,400

Chest (elmwood), 4'8" x 3', upper section having four small drawers and lower section having two cupboard doors, butterfly hinges, and bracket feet ......................... $600-800

Chest on chest, 3'5" x 2'5", each chest with two doors
and brass mounts .................................................. $200-320

Chest on chest, 4'3" x 2'8", wrought iron bale handles and
four doors ......................................................... $300-400

Screen, four fold, fold size, 5' x 1'9", leather with polychrome
landscapes and figures on a brown ground ...................... $3,000-5,000

Screen, six fold, fold size, 2'1", embossed paper with
continuous motif of gardens, silk border, black lacquer frame,
brass mounts ...................................................... $600-800

## Furniture
*(Thai)*

Table (hardwood), 1'4" x 5'6", oblong top carved with
elephants, shaped skirt, cabriole legs ........................... $400-600

## Furniture
*(Vietnamese)*

Armchairs (pair), pierced cresting above inlaid splat flanked
with brackets and scrolled arms, drop-in seat, scrolled legs,
overall inlay of mother-of-pearl ............................... $2,500-3,500

Cabinet (black lacquer), 5'5" x 2'8", mirrored back, beveled
sides, inlaid mother-of-pearl forming motifs of gardens and
flowers .......................................................... $1,100-1,600

Table, 1'8" x 2'10", carved and inlaid with mother-of-pearl
forming motifs of warriors ........................................ $500-700

## Geisha Girl Chinawares

Among the newly recognized collectibles are chinawares which feature standing and/or seated figures of Bijin (Japanese beauties). These wares are commonly referred to as "Geisha Girl Chinawares." Basically tablewares; occasional and ornamental objects were also produced. And . . . among these special pieces are chocolate sets, vases, coffee services (both standard, doll, child's sizes and miniatures). There are many border colors, including blue, brown, yellow, green, orange, orange/red, etc. Some of these border colors are used in combination with gold. This is one of the types of wares where markings are the least consideration. When matching pieces, the only criteria are color, pattern, and comparable porcelain. The motifs used on Geisha Girl Chinawares were hand painted, and hand painted in combination with the use of stencils and occasionally decals. This is the first time these wares have been listed as a specific category in any price guide, therefore the descriptions are augmented with basic descriptions of the patterns.

### Basket Pattern

The underlying design is orange with four Bijin who are found in various poses (depending upon design). Within the motif are baskets, Mt. Fuji, and dwellings.

Gravy boat, apple green trim with gold lacing in trim and
motif. Bijin picking flowers ....................................... $45-50

Plate, 8½" dia., green trim, women appear to be washing
clothes .............................................................. $20-30

## Butterfly Pattern

The underlying design is orange. The motif consists of Bijin and children catching butterflies. Within the pattern are pink cherry blossoms and often Mt. Fuji is seen in the distant background. On occasion this pattern will contain a more scenic motif, including the use of houses and pavilions. Border trims of apple green or blue with gold highlights appear to be the most expensive.

Berry set, one large bowl, six smaller ones, all with three
turned-out legs, red/orange trim .......................................... $40-50

Bowl, 7¾" dia., four curled legs, fluted/scalloped rim,
red/orange trim .......................................................... $35-40

Bowl, 8¼" dia., scalloped rim, blue/gold trim ........................... $55-65

Cake plate, 6" dia., fluted melon swirl and scalloped rim,
blue/gold border ........................................................ $24-31.50

Cake plate, 6" dia., fluted melon swirl and scalloped rim,
green border ............................................................ $22-34

Cake plate, 6¼" dia., red/orange border ................................ $12-15

Chocolate pot, 8" h., button finial, curved handle, green trim ......... $85-110

Chocolate pot, 8" h., spire knob finial, red/orange trim ............... $55-70

Chocolate pot, 9¼" h., looped finial, curved handle, swirled
contour, blue/gold trim ................................................. $90-115

Chocolate pot, 9½" h., open bowl finial, blue trim .................... $70-85

Chocolate set, pot 8" h., four cups and saucers, red/orange
trim, .................................................................... $45-60

Chocolate set, pot 9¼", six cups/saucers, blue/gold trim, open
finial ................................................................... $145-150

Coffee set, pot, covered sugar, open creamer, six cups and
saucers, blue/gold trim, on interior of cups a painted flower ......... $110-125

Coffee set, pot, open creamer, covered sugar, six cups and
saucers, six cake plates, button finial on pot and sugar bowl,
red/orange trim ......................................................... $70-80

Teapot, 6½" h., green/gold trim ........................................ $65-75

Urn, 7¾" h., domed lid with spire finial, two inverted U
handles, scalloped base ................................................. $150-165

Vase, 8" h., orange trim on rim and base .............................. $85-95

*Courtesan Processional Pattern cake plate, 6" dia.*

## Courtesan Processional Pattern

Perhaps one of the most interesting of the patterns, in that pieces with this pattern can be traced to the late 19th century. It can be found with backstamps indicating pre-Nippon era, Nippon era, and Made in Japan. The underlying design can be orange or red/orange. The motif consists of varying numbers of Bijin, and other courtesans, bridge(s), dwellings, Mt. Fuji (on occasion), a lake or river (on occasion), and trees (often cherry trees). Markings are not the criterion for matching pieces; however, the first piece listed bears a Green M in Wreath Nippon backstamp.

Bowl, 6½" dia., square with indented corners, orange trim,
touches of gold throughout .............................................. $50-75

Bowl (circular), 8" dia., fluted rim, blue/gold trim, gold
throughout .............................................................. $70-90

Bowl (circular), 9¾" dia., fluted rim, four legs, blue/gold
border .................................................................. $95-112

Bowl, 11" dia., red/orange trim with gold highlights .................. $140-165

Box, 3" x 2" x 3¼", blue trim ......................................... $95-100

Cake plate, 6" dia., apple green trim . . . . . . . . . . . . . . . . . . . . . . . . . . . . . . . . . . . . . . $20-26.50

Cake plate, 6" dia., deep blue trim. (Illus.) . . . . . . . . . . . . . . . . . . . . . . . . . . . . . . . . $15-17.50

Cake plate, 6" dia., orange trim, gold highlights . . . . . . . . . . . . . . . . . . . . . . . . . $35.50-47.50

Creamer, 3" h., open, deep green trim . . . . . . . . . . . . . . . . . . . . . . . . . . . . . . . . . . . $15-17.50

Cup and saucer, cup 1⅞" h., saucer 5½" dia., deep green
trim . . . . . . . . . . . . . . . . . . . . . . . . . . . . . . . . . . . . . . . . . . . . . . . . . . . . . . . . . . . . . $18.50-25.50

Dinner plate, 9½" dia., blue/gold trim . . . . . . . . . . . . . . . . . . . . . . . . . . . . . . . . . . $23.50-34.50

Hatpin holder, blue trim . . . . . . . . . . . . . . . . . . . . . . . . . . . . . . . . . . . . . . . . . . . . . . . . $40-55

Pitcher, 5" h., orange trim highlighted with gold throughout . . . . . . . . . . . . . . . . . . $45-67.50

Teapot, 4½" h., deep green trim, button finial, bulbous
contour . . . . . . . . . . . . . . . . . . . . . . . . . . . . . . . . . . . . . . . . . . . . . . . . . . . . . . . . . . . . . $60-75

Teapot, 5" h., blue/gold trim open finial, squat contour . . . . . . . . . . . . . . . . . . . . . . . $65-80

Teapot, four cups and saucers, red/orange trim with gold
highlights . . . . . . . . . . . . . . . . . . . . . . . . . . . . . . . . . . . . . . . . . . . . . . . . . . . . . . . . . . . $95-110

Teapot, six cups and saucers, open creamer and covered
sugar, blue/gold trim . . . . . . . . . . . . . . . . . . . . . . . . . . . . . . . . . . . . . . . . . . . . . . . . $125-165

## Flower Arranger Pattern

Underlying design is orange. Bijin in a garden. Occasionally one will find
a man in this pattern.

Egg cup, 2½" h., green trim . . . . . . . . . . . . . . . . . . . . . . . . . . . . . . . . . . . . . . . . . . $15-17.50

Egg cup, 2½" h., orange trim . . . . . . . . . . . . . . . . . . . . . . . . . . . . . . . . . . . . . . . . . . $6-7.50

## Kago and Flowers Pattern

Kago is a sedan chair, and an adaptation of this form is used in this
pattern. The underlying design is orange. The flower arrangements in
the kago are usually offered by a courtesan on the left to a Bijin on the
right. The Bijin generally wears an ornate kimono.

Bowl, 8" dia., three stub feet, yellow trim . . . . . . . . . . . . . . . . . . . . . . . . . . . . . . . . . $40-45

Hatpin holder, swirled contour, green/gold trim . . . . . . . . . . . . . . . . . . . . . . . . . . . . . $65-80

Salt and pepper shakers, green top and neck with gold
lacing. Salt with scalloped base, pepper with straight base . . . . . . . . . . . . . . . . . . $20-27.50

## Lantern Pattern

Underlying design is orange. Bijin in a garden with hanging lanterns
overhead. Within the design are cherry blossoms and occasionally one
finds Mt. Fuji in the distant background, as well as a lake with two boats.

Chocolate pot, 8½" h., blue/gold trim, open finial,
swirled/fluted . . . . . . . . . . . . . . . . . . . . . . . . . . . . . . . . . . . . . . . . . . . . . . . . . . . . . . . $75-90

Chocolate set, pot 8½" h., three cups and saucers, blue/gold
trim, straight form . . . . . . . . . . . . . . . . . . . . . . . . . . . . . . . . . . . . . . . . . . . . . . . . . . $110-110

Chocolate set, pot 9" h., six cups and saucers, all
fluted/scalloped rims and swirled contours, blue/gold trim . . . . . . . . . . . . . . . . . . $135-145

Coffeepot, 7⅝" h., green trim, open finial . . . . . . . . . . . . . . . . . . . . . . . . . . . . . . . . . $85-95

Hatpin holder, red/orange trim . . . . . . . . . . . . . . . . . . . . . . . . . . . . . . . . . . . . . . . . $20-22.50

Plate (cake), 6" dia., blue/gold trim . . . . . . . . . . . . . . . . . . . . . . . . . . . . . . . . . . . . $30-37.50

Plate, 8½" dia., orange trim, gold lacing throughout. (Illus.) . . . . . . . . . . . . . . . . . . $34.50-45

Plate (set of six set into rattan holders), blue/gold trim . . . . . . . . . . . . . . . . . . . . . . . $60-70

Vase, 10" h., four legs, blue trim . . . . . . . . . . . . . . . . . . . . . . . . . . . . . . . . . . . . . . . $130-145

*Lantern Pattern plate, 8½" dia.*

### Meadow Pattern

Generally four Bijin and a child in a meadow, with Mt. Fuji, dwellings, and trees.

Bowl, 6″ dia., turquoise trim with handle at the side looping over the rim . . . . . . . . . . . . . . . . . . . . . . . . . . . . . . . . . . . . . . . . . . . . . . . $50-65

### Umbrella Pattern

Within the motif are reserves generally outlined in the same hue as the border trim. There can be up to four reserves, though most common are two or three. The reserves may take on several different contours within the pattern or they may have the same contour. Within the reserves are two Bijin with an umbrella and a Bijin and child in a dwelling. This pattern is similar to another which has reserves featuring Bijin and children in various poses but without umbrellas. Prices for each pattern are comparable, with apple green and the blue/gold border trim appearing to be the most expensive.

Bowl, 7¾″ dia., red/orange trim . . . . . . . . . . . . . . . . . . . . . . . . . . . . . . . . . $22.50-27

Bowl, 8″ dia., blue/gold trim . . . . . . . . . . . . . . . . . . . . . . . . . . . . . . . . . . . $40-47.50

Cake plate, 6″ dia., blue/gold trim . . . . . . . . . . . . . . . . . . . . . . . . . . . . . $22.50-27.50

Cake plate, 6¼″ dia., red/orange trim with gold highlights throughout . . . . . . . . . . . . . . . . . . . . . . . . . . . . . . . . . . . . . . . . . . . . . . . . $32-42.50

Chocolate pot, 10″ h., spire finial, red/orange trim, straight form . . . . . . . . . . . . . . . . . . . . . . . . . . . . . . . . . . . . . . . . . . . . . . . . . . . . $50-65

Chocolate set, pot 9″ h., fluted bases on pot and cups, blue/gold trim with small flower on interior of cups . . . . . . . . . . . . . . . . . $145-165

Chocolate set, pot 10½″ h., six cups and saucers, orange trim with gold highlights throughout . . . . . . . . . . . . . . . . . . . . . . . . . . . . . . $95-115

Coffeepot, 8¾″ h., blue/gold trim, button finial . . . . . . . . . . . . . . . . . . . $70-100

Cracker jar, 8½″ dia., blue trim, four small legs, turned out position trimmed in blue . . . . . . . . . . . . . . . . . . . . . . . . . . . . . . . . . . . . $120-130

Hair receiver, 4½″ dia., red/orange trim with gold highlights . . . . . . . . . . . . . . . . . . . . $60-70

Hair receiver, 5″ dia., blue trim . . . . . . . . . . . . . . . . . . . . . . . . . . . . . . . . . $60-65

Nut set, main bowl, 7″ dia., 6 small bowls, 3″ dia., blue/gold trim . . . . . . . . . . . . . . . . . . . . . . . . . . . . . . . . . . . . . . . . . . . . . . . . . . . . . $70-75

Teapot, 7″ h., red/orange trim with gold highlights throughout . . . . . . . . . . . . . . . . . . . . . . . . . . . . . . . . . . . . . . . . . . . . . . . . . $85-100

Tea strainer, 6″ l., blue trim with gold throughout . . . . . . . . . . . . . . . . . $30-35

## Han Dynasty
*(Chinese)*

The Han Dynasty (206 B.C. - 220 A.D.) potters used a low-fired lead glaze of translucent greenish yellow. When this was applied to the reddish or slaty gray porcelaineous stoneware it produced color variations of green, brown, and yellow. Han decoration is stamped, incised, molded, and may have applied ornamentation (strips of clay). Funerary and figural pottery items were produced to meet the need for tomb furnishings. During this period a black unglazed pottery was made in Szechuan. Other major kiln sites were found in Fukien and Hopei provinces. When examined today, Han products often have a flaky iridescence which is the result of many years of burial.

Dish, 7″ dia., with a silvery, iridescent green glaze . . . . . . . . . . . . . . . . $600-800

Dish, 8″ dia., with a heavy iridescent green glaze, three spur marks on the unglazed base . . . . . . . . . . . . . . . . . . . . . . . . . . . . . . . . . $2,500-3,000

Figure, 5" h., boar, posed in a reclining position, unglazed, buff-colored pottery with earth encrustations .............................. $1,000-1,200

Figure, 8" h., attendant, depicted in a standing posture, unglazed buff pottery ..................................................... $900-1,200

Figure, 8½" l., ox, with traces of white slip and earth encrustations .......................................................... $3,000-4,000

Figure, 10" l., dog, shown with mouth open, tail curled, with collar and harness, with some traces of pigment and iridescent glaze ....................................................... $4,000-5,000

Figure, 10¼" l., dog, cylindrical body on tall legs, the mouth open and wearing a harness, green glazed with degradation and chips, on a wood stand .......................................... $2,800-3,000

Granary jar, 11" h., of cylindrical form, with sloping roof and set on tripod feet, with a degraded glaze of pale green with silvery iridescence ...................................................... $1,200-1,500

*Incense burner, 8½" h., with relief decoration of hunters and dogs on modeled mountain peaks, with an iridescent green glaze ................................................................... $2,500

Jar, 5⅝" h., with cover, of gray pottery painted with red pigment, traces of earth encrustation ..................................... $1,100-1,600

Jar, 6" h., standing on three molded bear feet applied to the base, decorated around the center in molded relief with tigers, deer, and running human figures among hills; covered with a deep green glaze and silvery iridescence overall ..................... $4,000-5,000

*Jar, 7" h., molded with vertical bands of herringbone pattern, with shallow, knife-cut ribs .................................................. $1,200

Strainer, 6½" dia., the top in the form of a circular bowl with five large holes in it, set on a hollow foot with an arched, shaped opening on one side, with a streaked and mottled green glaze over red pottery, fired upside-down, showing three spur marks on the bowl rim ....................................... $2,400-3,000

Vase, 8" h., shaped with a waisted neck and foot, rare gray pottery with slip decoration of dragon scrolls and triangular lappets with traces of white and red pigment ............................ $3,000-5,000

Vase, 20" h., with globular body and tall neck with a flared, everted rim, the neck with four ribs, the body with two rib bands, set on a splayed foot, of red unglazed pottery ...................... $1,500-2,000

*Vessel, 13" l., rare, molded as a ram in recumbent position, with openwork curled horns. (Illus.) ......................................... $11,000

Wine jar, 14½" h., with monster mask handles, the green glaze showing silvery iridescence ......................................... $1,800-2,200

*Han Dynasty vessel, rare

Haniwa, 7½" h., Tumulus period

Pottery head, 7" h., Jomon period, terra cotta, stylized eyes, applied earrings .............................................................. $800-1,100

Pottery head, 7½" h., Tumulus period, terra cotta. (Illus.) ................... $1,500-2,000

Water carrier, Jomon period, terra cotta (partial torso) ...................... $2,500-3,500

# Haniwa
*(Japanese)*

# Hardstones

**Agate.** Carved agate can be found in a variety of hues and forms. Red agate has been used extensively for the carving of figures and ornamental objects.

**Amber.** Amber, although not a hardstone, is closely associated with hardstones. Amber has been transformed into jewelry, snuff bottles, and ornamental objets d'art. It has been extensively used by the Chinese, although supplies have come from areas such as Burma. It is difficult for the layman to detect true amber from amberine and other compositional substances (plastics). True amber will feel warm to the touch and is a conductor of electricity to a small degree. After rubbing true amber with a woolen cloth, it should give off a bit of electric static. Plastic compositions which resemble amber may be penetrated with the point of a hot needle or pin.

**Aventurine.** Aventurine is a form of quartz, which has mineral silicates. These tiny specks sparkle and such is often referred to as "natural goldstone."

**Bowenite.** Bowenite is often mistaken for jade. Bowenite is frequently referred to as Soo Chow Jade. Commonest among the hues for bowenite are pale yellowy green and white. Bowenite has been used in the same manner as jade and soapstone.

**Carnelian.** Carnelian is a hard, tough stone, reddish in color and used most often in the creation of jewelry.

**Coral.** Coral has been used extensively for jewelry, the carving of ornamental objects, and for the embellishment and ornamentation of various art forms, including metalwares. Coral is a hard substance formed from the skeletons of anthozoan polyps (marine animals). It is recognized by its rich, red color; however, coral can be found in other hues, including pink, white, and black.

**Lapis lazuli.** The color of lapis lazuli is opaque blue. It has been extensively used for items of personal adornment, carvings, and for the ornamentation of other art forms, including metalwares. Lapis should not be confused with sodalite, which is more of a purple hue. (It should be noted that objects of sodalite are being exported by the Chinese, at present.)

**Malachite.** Malachite is a green-veined stone which can be either opaque or translucent. It has been used for embellishments of objects in many art forms. Its most common usage has been in the creation of jewelry and ornamental objects.

**Quartz.** The quartz family consists of many varieties, including clear quartz (rock crystal), amethyst (shades of purple/violet), rose quartz (pink), smoky quartz, blue quartz, and green quartz. Quartz has been used for the carving of ornamental and occasional objects such as figures, animals, snuff bottles, vases, etc. Quartz has also been used as ornamentation on various art forms.

**Serpentine.** Serpentine is often mistaken for jade. It is occasionally referred to as Soo Chow Jade, as are bowenite and soapstone. Commonest among the hues for serpentine are white, light green, and brown. Serpentine can be found in dark green and it can also have a mottled appearance. Serpentine has been used in much the same manner as jade, especially during the first quarter of the 20th century.

**Soapstone.** Soapstone (also called Soo Chow Jade) is a soft stone, having a soapy feel. Its composition is basically talc, chlorite, and, on occasion, magnetite. Soapstone has been used for ornamental carving, figures, seals, occasional objects, etc. It has been used as a less expensive embellishment than jade.

### Agate

*Agate figure of Kuan Yin, 11" h.

Bowl (smoky), 6" l., curled leaf form entwined with vines and fruit . . . . . . . . . . . . . . . . . . . . . . . . . . . . . . . . . . . . . . . . . . . . . . . . . . . . . . . . . . . $525-700

Box and cover, 4" l., oblong with birds, bats, prunus, and
peaches (slight chipping) . . . . . . . . . . . . . . . . . . . . . . . . . . . . . . . . . . . . . . . . . . . . . . $200-300

Brush washer (gray), 4½" h., carved as a tree trunk with
perched birds . . . . . . . . . . . . . . . . . . . . . . . . . . . . . . . . . . . . . . . . . . . . . . . . . . . . . . . . . $300-400

Figure, bird (pink), 4" h., erect pose . . . . . . . . . . . . . . . . . . . . . . . . . . . . . . . . . . . . . $200-300

Figure, 4¼" h., Pu tai, holding staff and fan . . . . . . . . . . . . . . . . . . . . . . . . . . . . . . . $150-200

*Figure, 11" h., Kuan Yin, holding a vase and wearing rosary
beads (russet/gray). (Illus.) . . . . . . . . . . . . . . . . . . . . . . . . . . . . . . . . . . . . . . . . . . . . . . . $520

Vase (brown/purple), 6" h., covered, tapering form carved
with t'ao t'ieh masks, foliage, and two dragons, loose ring
handles and domed cover with foo lion finial . . . . . . . . . . . . . . . . . . . . . . . . . . . . . $125-175

Vase (smoky), 7" h., covered ovoid form entwined with vines
and flowers . . . . . . . . . . . . . . . . . . . . . . . . . . . . . . . . . . . . . . . . . . . . . . . . . . . . . . . . . . . . $450-575

Wine pot (blue/gray), 5⅛" h., curved spout, loop handle and
domed cover . . . . . . . . . . . . . . . . . . . . . . . . . . . . . . . . . . . . . . . . . . . . . . . . . . . . . . . . . . . $125-175

# Amber

Figure, Li Tai-po, 1½" l., holding cup and wine pot, in
reclining position . . . . . . . . . . . . . . . . . . . . . . . . . . . . . . . . . . . . . . . . . . . . . . . . . . . . . . $90-110

Figure, Shou Lao, 3" h., carrying peach branch . . . . . . . . . . . . . . . . . . . . . . . . . . . . $200-300

Figures, foo dogs (pair), 6" h., male with ball and female with
cub . . . . . . . . . . . . . . . . . . . . . . . . . . . . . . . . . . . . . . . . . . . . . . . . . . . . . . . . . . . . . . . . . . . $225-325

Group, 3" h., Buddha and two immortals on rockwork base . . . . . . . . . . . . . . . . . . $300-400

Mountain landscape, 3' h., with pavilions and figures,
reverse with pine trees and figures in woodland scene . . . . . . . . . . . . . . . . . . . . . . $325-500

# Aventurine

Figure (green), 7½" h., Kuan Yin, flowing robes, hairdo with
tiara and holding a peony blossom . . . . . . . . . . . . . . . . . . . . . . . . . . . . . . . . . . . . . . . $165-185

Figure, rhinoceros (goldstone), 3" h., standing upright and in
a stride . . . . . . . . . . . . . . . . . . . . . . . . . . . . . . . . . . . . . . . . . . . . . . . . . . . . . . . . . . . . . . . $175-300

# Bowenite

Table screen, 12" h., inlaid with lapis lazuli, carnelian, coral,
and rock crystal with large peony branch and crane upon
rockwork . . . . . . . . . . . . . . . . . . . . . . . . . . . . . . . . . . . . . . . . . . . . . . . . . . . . . . . . . . . . . . $350-450

# Carnelian

Figure, elephant, 4" h., with raised trunk standing in upright
position . . . . . . . . . . . . . . . . . . . . . . . . . . . . . . . . . . . . . . . . . . . . . . . . . . . . . . . . . . . . . . . . $220-300

Figure, Kuan Yin, 4" h., holding ling chih spray with long
flowing robes and hair in topknot . . . . . . . . . . . . . . . . . . . . . . . . . . . . . . . . . . . . . . . . $265-320

Figure, parrot, 3" h. . . . . . . . . . . . . . . . . . . . . . . . . . . . . . . . . . . . . . . . . . . . . . . . . . . . . . $100-200

# Coral

Figure, child, 1½" h., astride a carp . . . . . . . . . . . . . . . . . . . . . . . . . . . . . . . . . . . . . . . $125-140

Figure, child, 2" h., riding an elephant . . . . . . . . . . . . . . . . . . . . . . . . . . . . . . . . . . . . $125-150

Figure, Kuan Yin, 2" h., holding a vase . . . . . . . . . . . . . . . . . . . . . . . . . . . . . . . . . . . . $120-150

Figure, Kuan Yin, 8¾" h., holding small bird, wearing
flowing robes with flowers in her hair . . . . . . . . . . . . . . . . . . . . . . . . . . . . . . . . . . . $2,000-2,800

Figure, Mei jen (young woman), 9" h., holding peony branch . . . . . . . . . . . . . . . . $600-800

Group, 8" h., young woman holding peony flower with two boys kneeling beside her ............................................. $1,300-1,650

Group, 12" h., woman and child (deep pink), child holding a peach and woman holding a lotus blossom, mounted as lamp ............................................................. $1,750-2,000

## Lapis Lazuli

Figure, foo dog, 4" l., recumbent, holding a ribbon-tied ball ...................... $275-375

*Group, lions, 8" l., one lion at play with two cubs, incised and detailed (Illus.) ......................................................... $700

Mountain, 7¾" l., low relief, one side with four boys and pine trees and bridge, reverse with deer and pine trees ............... $1,600-2,300

Vase, 5" h., cylindrical carved with bands of dragons, elephant head handles, carved foliage on neck (slight chipping at base) ........................................................ $100-125

Vase, 8" h., covered, baluster form, elephant head handles with loose rings, carved circular medallion on each side with dragon and pearl ..................................................... $500-800

Vase, 8" h., covered, relief carving of t'ao t'ieh masks, bands of lotus blossoms and two lion mask handles, domed cover with foo dog finial ...................................................... $900-1,300

*Lapis lazuli group, Buddhist lions, 8" l.*

## Malachite

Figure, 2" h., parrot, rockwork base ....................................... $150-175

Figure, 3¼" h., dragon of the North and flaming pearl ...................... $120-145

Figure, 4⅝" h., Mei jen holding a basket and peony branch ................... $120-220

Vase, 3½" h., brush holder form, relief foliage ............................. $300-400

## Quartz

### Amethyst Quartz
Vase, 7" h., covered, baluster body with relief work of peach trees and birds, with domed cover ................................... $250-275

### Green Quartz
Figure, 10¼" h., Kuan Yin holding peony branch ........................... $75-120

Group, 4⅜" h., two young men holding string of carp ...................... $125-170

Group, 11" h., Kuan Yin and attendants mounted as a lamp ................. $220-250

Vase, 12" h., tapering form, carving of birds on rockwork (chipped) ................................................................ $300-500

### Rock Crystal
Ball upon stand, 7" h., carved with three recumbent foo dogs ................ $900-1,700

Figure, 5" l., water buffalo reclining with boy on his back ................... $175-265

Figure, 6" h., Kuan Yin wearing flowing robes and cowl .................... $400-600

Figure, 6" h., ram recumbent, head upright .............................. $100-1,200

Figure, 7" l., horse, recumbent with foreleg raised to chin, bushy tail and mane .................................................... $1,800-2,800

Figure, 7" h., Kuan Yin holding lotus blossom and wearing flowing robes with hair in topknot ...................................... $115-140

Figure, 10⅝" h., Lu Tung-pin wearing hat, sword on his back, and holding fly whisk .............................................. $850-1,200

Figures, ducks, 4½" h. ................................................. $400-600

Vase, 8" h., domed cover with phoenix finial, relief carving of dragons of the North and flaming pearls with loose ring handles ............................................................... $900-1,100

**Rose Quartz**

Brush pot, 4" dia., flanked by four male figures ............................... $100-125

Figure, crane, 5" h., with incised plumage and head turned
back, holding lotus branch in its beak ....................................... $300-425

Figure, elephant, 23" h., trunk raised, mahoot, mounted as
lamp ..................................................................... $150-200

Figure, Kuan Yin, 12" h., holding a vase and beside her,
perched upon a peony branch, is a phoenix holding a peony
in its beak ............................................................... $110-1,500

Figure, parrot, 14" h., perched upon a rock ............................... $285-320

Figure, woman, 9" h., with flowing robes and hairdo in
topknot, holding flowering branch .......................................... $300-400

Vase, covered, 8" h., oviform, high relief carving of woman
upon pierced rockwork base, with boy finial ................................ $225-275

Vase, covered, 8" h., with phoenix finial, body carved with
peonies and buds .......................................................... $475-575

**Smoke Crystal**

Figure, Pu tai holding sack and carrying fly whisk in seated
position .................................................................. $120-140

Group, 5¼" h., water buffalo recumbent with two small
boys, finely detailed ...................................................... $11-1,400

## Serpentine

Beaker, 6⅜" h., archaistic styling with flanges (mottled
brown) ................................................................... $225-375

Bowl (deep green), 6" dia., lotus form with trailing vines all
around ................................................................... $175-225

Bowls (pair), 6" dia., green/brown, plain with flaring sides ................ $100-125

Figure, 3" h., bearded official (brown) .................................... $100-125

Figure, 5⅜" h., Mei jen wearing flowing robes ............................. $75-95

Group (mottled brown), 2¼" h., boy with food and cub ..................... $400-700

Incense burner (pale green), 7¼" h., three mask feet, dragon
head and loose ring handles, domed cover with dragon finial ............... $800-1,350

Libation cup (pale yellow), 8¼" l., tapering body, dragon fret
handle, curved spout with loose ring and domed cover ...................... $300-350

Mountain (green/white), 10¾" h., one side with two
Immortals and landscape; the reverse with figures, pavilions,
pine trees ................................................................ $650-900

Vase, covered (yellowy green), 6½" h., panels of t'ao t'ieh
masks, lappets, two dragon head handles, domed cover ...................... $200-300

Vase (yellowy green), 10" h., cover with foo dog finial,
dragon mask handles, and loose rings, carved key fret,
leaves, and t'ao t'ieh masks .............................................. $200-320

## Soapstone

Brush washer, 5" l., pale yellow, leaf form with peony
blossoms .................................................................. $300-400

Figure, 5¼" h., Pu tai in reclining position holding a sack
and fly whisk ............................................................. $250-400

Figure, 8" h., Kuan Yin, flowing robes (chipped) .......................... $125-175

Figure, 15½" h., Shou Lao standing on pierced rockwork
base ..................................................................... $350-425

Group, 8" h., Pu tai with three children (russet) ......................... $120-180

Mountain, 5' h., boulder form carved on both sides with
Lohans and dragon (gray/white/brown) ...................................... $200-325

Seal, 3" h., carved with phoenix and clouds ............................... $60-90

Seal, 4¼" h., carved with dragons and clouds ................................... $70-95

Table screen, 15½" x 11½", riverscape with fishermen in high
relief (light green/red mottlings) ........................................... $175-250

**Turquoise**

Figure, 2½" h., dancer holding a fan and flower (slightly
damaged) ................................................................. $250-350

Group, 3¼" h., mother and child upon rockwork (slight
restoration) .............................................................. $350-400

Group, 4" h., Immortal beside a Buddhistic lion ......................... $350-425

Group, 4" h., Kuan Yin and young boy, carved in openwork;
Kuan Yin holding a peony branch ....................................... $300-375

# Hirado (Mikawachi)
*(Japanese)*

*Hirado plate, late 19th century*

The productions of Hirado (Mikawachi), from 1750 A.D. on, rank among
the best of Japanese porcelains. Before 1868, the productions were
intended for the sole use and discretion of Matsura Shizunobo (Daimyo
of Hirado). It was not until the Meiji restoration (1868) that Hirado wares
were made for domestic sale and Western export. Among the Hirado
wares available on today's market are small ornamental objects with
pierced openwork as well as motifs which are molded in relief. One
particular pattern associated with these wares consists of Chinese
children at play. Many past published authors attested that the greater
the number of children, the better the quality of the piece.

Bulb bowl, 13" dia., late 19th century, three stub feet, white
Shishi and peony blossoms molded in relief against a blue
ground .................................................................. $485-515

Figure, 5" h., Shishi, white (chipped) ................................... $200-300

Incense burner, 5" h., late 19th century, square form,
supported by four boys with boy finial, underglaze blue and
white .................................................................... $295-340

Incense burner, 5½" h., late 19th century, in form of a Shishi
and pierced tama, underglaze blue on white ground .................... $325-450

Incense burner, 12" h., 19th century, Bijin leaning against a
lantern, pierced openwork, underglaze blue and white ................. $600-750

Jar, covered, 5" h., c. 1900, landscape motif, Shishi finial ............. $400-600

Plate, 8" dia., late 19th century. (Illus.) ............................... $200-300

Wine pot, 4¾" h., 19th century, in form of Fukurokuju and a
sack ..................................................................... $400-460

# Honan
*(Chinese)*

Honan wares are believed to have been produced in and around the
capital of Honan in the latter part of the Sung Dynasty. These wares have
a dark brown to black glossy glaze.

(See: Sung Dynasty)

# Hsüan Tê
*(Chinese)*

Hsüan Tê was a Ming Dynasty emperor who reigned during the years
1426-1435. The Chinese regard these years as the peak of their porcelain
perfection. This short reign was a time of relative peace and prosperity.

The production of porcelain was encouraged by the emperor. Blue and white porcelain was made, and the imperial wares employing the vivid Mohammedan blue pigment were produced. Popular floral motifs included peonies, lotus blossoms, and chrysanthemums. Another popular design was dragons chasing flaming pearls. Underglaze copper red decoration appeared on the famous stem cups and bowls of the period. The favored designs of these items were fish, pomegranates, and dragons in a white field that had the appearance of "congealed fat." (These items were extensively reproduced during the reign of Ch'ien Lung.) The copper red monochromes that have reported origins in this period were copied in the reign of K'ang Hsi and often bear Hsüan Tê reign marks, the originals having been lost to us through the centuries. Polychrome decoration was also popular in the period featuring san-ts'ai colors. The practice of using reign marks was first established during this period. These reign marks were often copied, sometimes on wares unrelated to the production of the time. These later items are often found in today's auction market.

(See: Ming Dynasty)

I-Hsing wares were and are being made at potteries in Yi-Hsing Hsien in the Kiangsu province of China. They are famous primarily for their unglazed stoneware teapots found in a variety of red, brown, and buff shades of clay. The early 16th and 17th century decorations may be etched, in relief, stamped, or pierced. Later wares may be partially or fully enameled. There are about fifty factories involved with ceramic production today. Some items may be found to bear Han inscriptions copied from roof tiles of the period.

(See: Made in China)

# I-Hsing
*(Chinese)*

*I-Hsing teapot, 4½" h., enameled, 20th century*

Figure, Kuan Yin, 9¾" h., 18th century, posed resting on rockwork with a crackled, light yellow glaze falling short of the base . . . . . . . . . . . . . . . . . . . . . . . . . . . . . . . . . . . . . . . . . . . . . . . . . . . . . . . . . . . . . . $600-800

Gourd, 3½" l., modeled in double gourd form in yellow clay, with stem of dark brown clay, impressed potter's mark . . . . . . . . . . . . . . . . . . . . . . . . $400-500

Tea bowls (pair), 4" h., 19th century, with covers and stands, of beige clay, etched with calligraphy of famous poems, the interior with a gray-white crackled glaze . . . . . . . . . . . . . . . . . . . . . . . . . . . . . . . . . . . $100-150

Teapot, 4¼" h., 19th century, of tree trunk form with branch handle, spout, and open knop on lid, with applied flower sprigs, red clay, impressed potter's mark . . . . . . . . . . . . . . . . . . . . . . . . . . . . . . $175-225

Teapot, 4½" h., marked "China," decorated in colored enamels with a foo dog knop on lid. (Illus.) . . . . . . . . . . . . . . . . . . . . . . . . . . . . . . . . $60-75

Teapot, 4½" h., 19th century, double teapot in the form of two drums tied together with a ribbon, lid with lizard form knop, impressed potter's mark . . . . . . . . . . . . . . . . . . . . . . . . . . . . . . . . . . . . . . . . . $175-225

Teapot, 5½" h., 19th century, cylindrical shape with a long handle, straight spout, and domed cover, inscribed with the date "ping shên" (1836) . . . . . . . . . . . . . . . . . . . . . . . . . . . . . . . . . . . . . . . . . . . $600-800

Teapot, 6" h., dark brown pottery molded in relief with a dragon chasing a flaming pearl on one side and a sea monster on the reverse, with scaled loop handle and a short spout, the cover with a dragon . . . . . . . . . . . . . . . . . . . . . . . . . . . . . . . . . . . . . . . $350-450

Teapot, 6" h., late 18th century, covered with a robin's egg blue glaze, the interior and base in a dark brown biscuit, impressed potter's mark . . . . . . . . . . . . . . . . . . . . . . . . . . . . . . . . . . . . . . . $1,500-1,700

Teapot, 6" h., 19th century, decorated with a carved spray of chrysanthemums, the reverse side inscribed with a poem, with impressed potter's mark ............................................ $200-300

Teapot, 6" h., 19th century, molded in form of a lotus pod with stalk handle, lid in form of a lily pad ........................................ $175-225

Teapot, 6½" h., red-brown pottery with tan flecks, short straight spout, and ear-shaped loop handles, signed Shih Ta-pin ...................................................... $1,200-1,400

Teapot, 8" h., 19th century, red-brown pottery with dark brown specks, straight handle, curved spout, with a domed lid .............................................................. $150-200

*Teapot, gnarled pine bark form, marked with Kung Ch'un seal. (Illus.) ...................................................... $1,210

*Teapot, lozenge shaped with dome cover, signed Shih Ta-pin. (Illus.) ...................................................... $990

*Teapot, petal form with shallow flower cover, signed Shih Ta-pin. (Illus.) ...................................................... $1,430

(L. to R.) *I-Hsing teapot, lozenge shape, signed. *I-Hsing teapot, knarled pine bark form, signed. *I-Hsing teapot, petal form, signed

## Imari
### (Chinese)

Although production of Chinese Imari began at the end of the 18th century it did not gain momentum until the mid-19th century in an effort to capture part of the popular Western export market of Japan. Although the Chinese patterns are the same as the Japanese, there are differences in appearance: The Chinese Imari porcelain is crisp and has a greenish tint glaze; the biscuit may have a slightly brown foot rim; there is no evidence of spur marks; the underglaze blue is lighter and does not run; the red tone used is a coral red.

Chinese Imari dish, 8½" dia., 18th century

Dish, 8½" dia., early 18th century, underglaze blue-red and gilt decoration of two women under a parasol with reserves of birds and figures in border. (Illus.) .................................... $800-1,000

Dish, 9" dia., 18th century, with central motif of flowers in a vase and large radiating panels of flowers, and an iron red painted diaper border .................................................. $700-800

Dish, 14" l., 18th century, floral motif in the center with radiating panels of flowers along with trellis patterns and floral borders, painted in blue, red, yellow, and gilt highlights .............................................................. $600-800

Tankard, 6¼″ h., 18th century, with iron red diaper border at the rim and two flower-filled vases on either side, in colors of iron red, underglaze blue, and gilt . . . . . . . . . . . . . . . . . . . . . . . . . . . . . . . . . . . . . . . . . . . $550-650

Tankard, 6½″ h., 18th century, decorated with two swimming carp in river under prunus branches, executed in underglaze blue and gilt, with an iron red trellis diaper border at rim . . . . . . . . . . . . . . . . . . . . . . . . . . . . . . . . . . . . . . . . . . . . . . . . . $550-650

# Imari
## (Japanese)

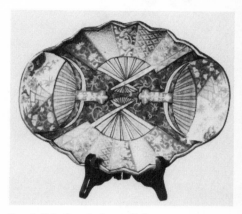

*Imari dish, fans in low relief*

The port of Imari is synonymous with certain classes of Japanese porcelains which are also termed Imari. Imari porcelain wares were produced in northwest Kyushu, Hizen province (modern prefecture, Saga). Early Imari productions were influenced by styles associated with Korean blue-white (Yi Dynasty) and wares of the Ming Dynasty. Imari can be classified by several groupings.

1. Kakiemon (see Kakiemon)

2. Sometsuke, underglaze blue and white (see Japanese blue and white)

3. Arita (see Arita)

4. Sansai (three-color ware): Three color ware can be either underglaze blue with overglaze red on a white ground, or overglaze green and red on a white ground. Both aforementioned varieties can have gilt embellishments.

5. Gosai, five-color ware

6. Nishikide (brocade-patterned wares), similar to Gosai but the motifs are more intricate.

Japanese Imari is grayer and heavier than its Chinese counterpart. The glaze is thicker and sometimes contains minute pinholes. On the earlier Imari wares, there is sometimes evidence of spur marks (caused by the supports used in the kilns). The blue on Japanese Imari tends to be runny and is darker than that used on Chinese Imari. Japanese Imari has a thick, Indian red opaque enamel as compared to a thinner coral red hue used on Chinese Imari. It is not unusual to find Japanese Imari (certain varieties) which have ornamentations executed in lacquer and/or enamel.

*Imari covered bowl, late Edo period*

*Imari figure posed for blindman's bluff*

Bottle, 10¼" h., late 17th century, baluster form with flat shoulder and cylindrical neck, Kutani style ........................... $12,000-15,000

Bottles (pair), 11" h., 19th century, sake squared with sloping shoulder and narrow mouth, fan form roundels, birds and grapes, stylized leaves on neck with red foliate ground ..................... $1,200-1,600

Bowl, 7" dia., c. 1900, Sansai, border panels of birds and flowers, center reserve of riverscape ................................. $100-175

Bowl, 8" dia., c. 1900, fluted, Gosai, panels of floral scrolls and lotus medallion in center ..................................... $150-165

Bowl, 8¼" dia., fluted rim with panels of flowers ..................... $75-100

Bowl, 8½" dia., late 19th century, Sansai, radiating panels of diapers, florals, and trellis motifs .............................. $300-350

Bowl, 8¾" dia., late 19th century, Gosai, fluted rim, floral medallion and panels of gardens ................................. $175-220

Bowl, 9⅜" dia., 19th century, Kinrade (red predominating), Dutch scenes with medallion of ship surrounded by other ships, diapered ground ....................................... $2,300-2,750

Bowl, 9¾" dia., late 19th century, flared rim, Sansai, scroll panels of florals and birds with alternating panels of dragons and clouds ..................................................... $175-250

Bowl, 11" dia., late 19th century, Gosai, diapered ground with foliate scrolls ................................................ $700-800

Bowl, 11¼" dia., interior with panels of cranes and riverscape, key fret border; exterior with diapered panels of stylized butterflies ................................................ $500-575

Bowl, 11½" dia., late 19th century, fluted rim, Sansai, center medallion of dragon with radiating panels of diaper, floral, and bird motifs .................................................. $350-475

Bowl, 12⅜" dia., late 19th century, fluted rim, Gosai, medallion of peony and plum blossom in a vase, radiating panels containing Shishi, scrolls, and diapers with overlapping mons .................................................. $225-400

Charger, 24½" dia., late 19th century, Sansai with central roundel of flowers, fluted rim with panels of birds and flowers, chips on rim .............................................. $450-625

Dish, 7½" dia., c. 1900, Gosai, floral, and birds in narrow panels, scalloped rim ............................................ $100-120

Dish, 8" dia., peach form, Gosai, landscape, gilt embellishments ................................................... $350-500

Dish, 9½" dia., Gosai landscape panels and scalloped rim ........... $110-125

Dish, 12" dia, c. 1900, leaf-shaped, Sansai with gold carp on ground of flowers ................................................ $400-500

Dish, 12" dia., fish form, Sansai .................................. $180-225

Dish, 13" dia., early 18th century, Sansai, chrysanthemum scroll and band of birds and foliage ............................. $800-1,000

Dish, 14" dia., Sansai, panels of butterflies and flowers ............. $75-110

Dish, late 19th century, fans in low relief. (See Back Cover and Color Section) ............................................... $500-650

Figure, 8" h., Edo period. (Illus.) ............................... $900-1,200

Fish bowl, 19½" dia., 19th century, depressed ovoid form, Gosai and gilt, octagonal panels of lotus, dragons, wave and diaper motifs, with butterflies on the interior, minor restoration ...................................................... $350-575

Jars (pair), 16⅞" h., baluster form with domed covers and pear finial, Sansai with scattered foliage (one having some restoration) .................................................... $3,500-4,200

Jars (pair), 40¼" h., early 19th century, double gourd, red and polychrome enamels, panels of courtesans within a black border, six panels of landscapes .......................................... $3,000-4,000

Rice bowl, covered, Edo period. (Illus.) .................................... $250-350

Teapot, late 19th century. (See Color Section) .............................. $225-285

Vase, 14″ h., ovoid, Sansai, panels of stylized bats, floral
ground .................................................................... $300-380

Vase, 15½″ h., late 19th century, ovoid, Sansai, hexagonal
panels of flowers, dragons, and courtesans, mounted as a
lamp ..................................................................... $300-450

Vase, 16″ h., 18th century, double gourd, Sansai, leaf and fan
shaped floral reserves, chip on foot rim ................................... $800-1,000

Vase, 26¼″ h., late 19th century, ovoid form with flaring
neck, red and gold, warrior on a key fret ground, signed
Hichozan Shin-po ......................................................... $1,500-2,100

Vases (pair), 15½″ h., bulbous with floral panels, Gosai ................... $1,600-2,000

Vases (pair), 22″ h., late 19th century, oviform with trumpet
neck and dragons molded in relief, fan-shaped panels of
flowers on a red ground with gilding ...................................... $1,500-2,450

*Inro, ivory, Buddha motif (left); lacquer inro with dragon and cloud motif (right). Courtesy the Rosett Collection*

## Inro
### (Japanese)

The inro is a personal accessory in the form of a tiered box. It was used as a container for such items as medicine, herbs, pills, etc. The inro has separate compartments which fit one into another. These compartments were fastened together with a cord (the cord running through tubes on either side of the inro). The ojime (string fastener) allowed for adjustment of the cord. This was followed by the netsuke, which secured the cord and its attachments and kept them from slipping through the obsi (sash). (See: Netsuke, Ojime. For terminology for lacquered inro see Lacquer, Japanese and Shibayama.)

Single case, late 19th century (lacquer), oval form, hiramakie,
takamakie, with tiger on rockwork, reverse having a dragon
and clouds, lacquer netsuke of Daruma attached (slightly
damaged) ................................................................. $350-480

*Inro, lacquer motif of tree and mountain (left); inro, lacquer motif of landscape (right). Courtesy the Rosett Collection*

Single case (lacquer), 19th century, motif of Emma-o with reverse motif of Oni, gold, red, and silver ............................ $1,800-2,000

Single case (lacquer), 19th century, hiramakie, takamakie, motif of Daruma with eyes inlaid with glass, ivory ojime and wood netsuke (three masks) attached ........................ $325-400

Single case (mini-2"), undecorated white metal, ivory bead ojime and ivory netsuke, kakyuku ............................... $200-225

Two-case (copper), pitchfork motif, manju netsuke, woven metal ............................................................. $750-900

Two-case (long), late 19th century (lacquer), gold hiramakie on red ground with motif of boy riding an ox ..................... $220-275

Two-case, 19th century (metal), inlaid with coral, motifs of peony blossoms and bats with gold inlay, coral bead ojime and cloisonne disk netsuke attached .............................. $600-900

Two-case, 19th century, ivory (artist's inro), two wells for color, two wells for water, bone ojime, bamboo brush and holder ......................................................... $800-900

Three-case (ivory), ojime, Buddha and landscape. (Illus.) ........ $2,700-3,000

Three-case, late 19th century (lacquer), gold hiramakie trees and mountain, wood ojime. (Illus.) ........................... $700-800

Three-case, 19th century (lacquer), gold hiramakie, motif of hat and plow with ivory bead ojime attached ................... $120-150

Four-case (lacquer), gold, landscape, signed Kajikawa. (Illus.) ....... $900-1,000

Four-case, late 19th century (ivory), Shibayama style, motif of Sambaso dancer ............................................... $1,600-2,100

Four-case (large size, 16"), ivory carved and pierced with quails, ivory bead ojime, ivory netsuke study of quails attached ........................................................ $800-12,000

Four-case, 19th century (lacquer), dragon and clouds, signed. (Illus.) ........................................................ $800-900

Four-case, late 19th century, ebony, relief carvings of Chinese sages ........................................................... $400-500

Four-case, late 19th century (lacquer), red and gold hiramakie, motif of dragons and waves, amber bead ojime and ivory netsuke in form of a drum attached ...................... $600-800

Four-case, early 19th century, motif of sage seated beside a tree on a wood with tortoiseshell inlay ....................... $500-600

Four-case, late 19th century (lacquer), continuous carved brocade patterns with lacquer netsuke (manju) carved with vines attached ................................................. $400-600

Four-case, 19th century (lacquer), takamakie, landscape in low relief, on reverse prunus blossoms ..................... $300-400

Four-case (lacquer), oval form, Shibayama style, landscape motifs with reverse having two Shishi ....................... $3,000-4,000

Four-case, late 19th century (pottery-Kutani grayware), diamond-shaped reserves containing thirty-six poets ........... $900-1,200

Four-case, late 19th century (ivory), Shibayama style, both sides having four mons containing floral sprigs ............... $1,200-1,800

Four-case, late 19th century (lacquer), black ground with gold falcon, glass bead ojime, stained ivory netsuke in the form of two birds perched on branch ................................ $200-300

Four-case, 19th century (ivory), Shibayama style, contour of a star, applied horn, red lacquer, mother-of-pearl, with motif of peacock and kiku, inlaid plaque signed Shibayama ......... $6,000-8,000

Four-case, late 19th century, wood with inlaid motifs of toys, Shibayama style ............................................... $800-1,000

Five-case, early 19th century (lacquer), gold and silver hiramakie, takamakie, riverscape motif ....................... $2,000-3,000

Censer, 5½" h., late Ming Dynasty, squared fang ting shape, covered, and inlaid with silver, t'ao t'ieh masks on leiwen ground on either side and on the short legs; upright loop handles from the rim. Four pairs of confronting birds separated by short flanges radiating from rectangle upon which a pierced oval knop with silver wire inlaid details is placed ........................................................ $900-1,200

Figure, 5⅝" h., Ming, 16th/17th century, head of Buddha with long, slender ears, round cheeks, and wearing a diadem; extensive traces of lacquer and colored pigments on surface, some old damages. Wood stand ..................................... $450-800

Figure, 7½" h., Ming Dynasty, head of Bodhisattva, hollow cast, with delicate features and precise curls, high chignon which was pierced for placement of diadem; blue, black, and green traces of pigment over gesso on the rust-brown surface ................ $1,300-1,965

Figure, 9⅞" l., Ming Dynasty, standing figure of horse, hollow cast, with short legs, bridle, saddle blanket, and trappings; center seam ..................................... $400-530

Figure, 30" h., Ming, dated 1483, kneeling Taoist immortal, cast in nine sections, with small beard, moustache, heavy eyebrows, his left hand resting on knees and right hand holding small dragon, wearing tight, simple robes; long inscription on back; rusted surface and repaired neck ....................... $2,500-4,000

Gong, temple, 4'3½" h., 33½" wide ........................................ $625-900

# Iron
## (Chinese)

Dish, 3⅜" dia., late 19th century, footed, lobed, shallow dish with shrine complex design in mass gold zogan within a central roundel upon grape leaf ground, surrounded by a key fret border which has additional roundels in which famous Kansai area sights are depicted, Komai style ............................. $700-1,000

Figures, pair, 9½" l., horses, their heads raised and adorned with saddles and trappings decorated with flower medallions .................... $65-105

Jar, water, 8⅛" h., 19th century, cast design of turtles and temple complex on the bulbous form ...................................... $140-200

Jar, water, 8⅜" h., 19th century, cast design of butterflies on a finely ribbed cylindrical form ............................................ $140-200

Koro, 4⅓" h., 19th century, four Tokugawamon on flowering foliage in hirazogan on the irregularly shaped body; pierced silver cover with two Tokugawamon, scrolling foliage, traces of rust .............................................................. $550-815

Kozuka, design of millet heads and bird rattle in shakudo and gold, signed Issai Tomei with kakihan ............................... $3,250-3,900

Netsuke, 18th/19th century, a smoker's accessory in the form of an ovoid iron flint lighter, with design of silver and copper flower heads, a metal ring for attachment, and hinged case which opens to reveal the lighter .......................................... $325-460

Ojime, tiny Noh mask applied on the iron front; reverse silvered and applied with a seal ............................................... $65-70

Tsuba, 2¼" x 2½", 19th century, repoussé leaf design with incised vine motif, copper and brass detail ................................ $200-300

Tsuba, 2½" dia., 17th century, pierced circular guard with design of thick stalk of bamboo, leaves, ryu-hitsu, unmarked .................... $390-550

Tsuba, 2⅔" dia., 19th century, Choshu type; oval with molded and carved flowers on mokume ground, ryu-hitsu, unmarked, cloth pouch .................................................. $225-355

Tsuba, 3" dia., early 19th century, oval, gilded edge with hannya mask eboshi and staff in shakudo, gold, and copper, signed .................................................................. $375-640

Tsuba, 3" dia., 18th/19th century, Choshu type, circular with

# Iron
## (Japanese)

a water dragon and waves design finely and deeply carved, ryu-hitsu, signed Chohan Shunyoken tsukuru . . . . . . . . . . . . . . . . . . . . . . . . . . . . . . $500-765

Tsuba, 3⅛" dia., 19th century, design of eight sages, pines, and bamboo molded and carved, with applied silver, shakudo and gold; gold-rimmed ryu-hitsu, signed Gashu Hikone (no) ju Soheishi Nyudo Soten sei . . . . . . . . . . . . . . . . . . . . . . . . . . . . $1,100-1,300

Tsuba, 3⅕" dia., 19th century, circular with carved cockerel design highlighted with copper wattle and comb and gold beak; reverse depicts a butterfly in shakudo, sealed in gold hon-zogan . . . . . . . . . . . . . . . . . . . . . . . . . . . . . . . . . . . . . . . . . . . . . . . . . . . . $1,100-1,400

Vases, pair, 12½" h., late 19th century, baluster shape with monkeys catching octopus on the beach design in iro-e takazogan, circular stylized birds and flaming jewels design in gold nunome zogan on the base and neck, some rust . . . . . . . . . . . . . . . . . $2,600-3,000

## Iron Rust
### (Chinese)

The iron rust color was invented during the Ch'ien Lung reign. It has metallic specks on a deep red brown glaze.

Censer, 8" h., 18th century, round body, glazed in deep red-brown with iridescent flecks . . . . . . . . . . . . . . . . . . . . . . . . . . . . . . . . . . . $800-1,000

Stem cup, 5½" h., late 18th century, deep red-brown glaze with iridescent black flecks; rim edged in white . . . . . . . . . . . . . . . . . . . . . . . $600-800

Vase, 5" h., 18th century, bulbous form with flared lip, interior and lip glazed white . . . . . . . . . . . . . . . . . . . . . . . . . . . . . . . . . . . $600-800

Vase, 5½" h., 18th century, red-brown glaze and iridescent brown and black flecks . . . . . . . . . . . . . . . . . . . . . . . . . . . . . . . . . . . . . . . . $220-300

Vase, 7½" h., Ch'ien Lung period, bottle form on splayed foot with long tapered neck, with black and silvery specks on a good deep red-brown glaze . . . . . . . . . . . . . . . . . . . . . . . . . . . . . . . . . $800-1,000

Vase, 8" dia., 18th century, pear shaped, medium brown glaze with dark flecks, the underfoot having a café au lait glaze, with a white glazed lip and interior . . . . . . . . . . . . . . . . . . . . . . . . . $750-900

Vase, 9" h., 12" dia. at shoulder, Ch'ien Lung period (unmarked), well potted, wide-shouldered baluster body with a short lipped rim, finely glazed in a deep violet brown and covered with a minutely speckled metallic glaze (Illus.) . . . . . . . . . . . . . . . . . $2,800-3,200

Vase, 11" h., 20th century (character mark and period of Hsüan T'ung), rounded, squat body with cylindrical neck, reddish brown glaze . . . . . . . . . . . . . . . . . . . . . . . . . . . . . . . . . . . . . . . . . $400-500

Vase, 18" h., Ch'ien Lung period, mei ping type, with overall dark reddish brown glaze and mottled, iridescent black overglaze . . . . . . . . . . . . . . . . . . . . . . . . . . . . . . . . . . . . . . . . . . . . . . $3,000-3,500

Vase, 23" h., 18th century, globular body with wide sloping shoulders and cylindrical neck flaring slightly towards the rim, covered with a reddish brown glaze having iridescent, silvery black mottling, the base unglazed . . . . . . . . . . . . . . . . . . . . . . . $12,000-15,000

*Iron rust vase, with fine glaze, 9" h.*

## Ivory
### (Chinese and Japanese)

Perhaps the most superior carved ivories come from China and Japan. Chinese ivories date as early as the Shang Dynasty. However, most of the pieces available on today's market date from the Ch'ing Dynasty. It was during the reign of K'ang Hsi that ivory workshops were established in Canton. It is likely that it was in these workshops that the well known puzzle ball was first produced and created. The puzzle ball having anywhere from three to thirty-two revolving spheres within one hollow outer sphere is one of the most popular forms of Chinese carved ivory, followed by human and animal figures, and carvings of palaces and pagodas, etc. Chinese ivory can be lacquered, decorated in polychrome enamels, stained, etched, or left in its natural hue. Japanese ivory carvings tend to be more naturalistic, as seen in the form of the netsuke. As one collector so aptly put it, "Carved Japanese ivory figures speak to you because they are so realistic." Japanese ivory carvers used lathes which were simple and rough, and they had great skill with the fiddle bow drill. The end result of their expertise is unsurpassed.

**Identification** (looking at a cross section):

**Elephant tusk.** Upon examination one will find a series of zigzag lines (patterns). Elephant ivory has a mellow color and darkens slightly with age. It can split as it ages, and such splits will be found to form parallel lines.

**Walrus tusk.** Walrus tusk will have a dark granular core.

**Narwhale.** When checking a cross section of Narwhale one will find a pattern of concentric circles.

**Bone.** Since bone is hollow and filled with marrow, one will find a pattern of minute holes which sometimes look like dark dots.

**Antler.** Antler resembles bone, but it has a series of irregular holes.

**Celluloid.** A man-made material used as a facsimile of ivory and often termed "ivorene." One should find mold marks on ivorene and there will be no grain as found in the above forms of ivory. Ivorene will have a pattern consisting of a series of straight lines. Ivorene is flammable, so the point of a hot needle or pin should melt away a small indentation.

## Ivory (Burmese)

Burmese carved ivory usually consists of the whole tusk, which may be ornamented with motifs of carved animals, flora, and fauna.

Chess set, 18th century, kings seated on chairs, queens
kneeling on chairs, kings 3¾" h., pawns 1⅛" h. .......................... $9,000-12,000

## Ivory (Chinese)

Brush pots, 8¼" h., curving oval section carved and pierced
with dragons and scrolls ................................................. $350-425

Buddhist shrine, 17" h., low relief carving with dragon and
floral panels, interior with seated Buddha ................................ $800-1,200

Buddhistic lions, 5" h., on double lotus base ............................ $475-675

Buddhistic lions, 14" h., male with reticulated ball, female
with a cub, rectangular, elaborately carved bases ....................... $1,500-2,000

Candleholders, 5½" h., formed like Kylins .............................. $300-500

Ewer (wine pot), 15" h., oval hexagonal, curving spout,
dragon and cloud scroll panels ......................................... $650-800

Horses, 5" l., saddles ornamented with coral and turquoise
cabochons ............................................................. $225-450

Kylins (pair), 3¼" l., turquoise inlaid eyes ........................... $175-350

Puzzle ball, 5" dia., eleven interior balls, various designs, link
chain ................................................................. $400-500

**Chess Sets:**
Macao, c. 1840, one side European royalty, kings 4¼" h.,
pawns 2⅛" h. ......................................................... $1,200-1,800

Natural and red-stained, circular bases, kings 4" h., pawns 2½" h. .................................................................. $550-750

Natural and red-stained, on puzzle ball bases, kings and queens as European and Chinese dignitaries, rooks as flag-bearing elephants, pawns as foot soldiers, kings 4" h., pawns 2¼" h. .............................................................. $450-650

Natural and red-stained, kings 5⅝" h., pawns 2⅝" h., circular puzzle ball mounts ..................................................... $450-550

**Female Figures:**

Doctor's model (so-called), 6½" l., head resting on one hand .................... $125-200

Immortal, 15" h., holding prunus spray and an elaborate pair of scissors ............................................................ $500-800

Kuan Yin, 10" h., 18th century, holding vase and rosary. (Illus.) ............................................................. $10,000-13,000

Musician, 15" h., holding a lute ........................................... $500-700

**Male Figures:**

Dignitary, 12" h., robes incised and stained with dragons and cloud scrolls ........................................................... $400-550

Dignitary, 25" h., holding a tablet of rank ................................. $1,000-1,550

Immortal, 14" h., bearded sage holding a basket of fish and book ............................................................. $650-825

Immortal, 21" h., bearded sage with dragon-headed staff beside a young acolyte holding a tea tray ............................. $1,000-1,400

Lohan, 6" h., flowing robes ............................................... $600-700

Shou Lao, 30" h., standing holding a peach branch and long staff with a deer at his feet (slight chipping) ...................... $1,050-1,625

Warrior, 9" h., standing with a sword and holding a spear .................... $500-600

**Figures — Pairs:**

Dignitary, 22" h., with sword hilt, consort with scepter (cracks) ............................................................. $2,000-2,800

Dignitary and consort, 13" h., robes incised and stained, with dragons and roundels above wave patterns ...................... $1,300-1,875

Dignitary and consort, 20" h., deep yellow hue ........................... $1,100-1,600

Dignitary and his lady, 41" h., he having a seal and sword, she holding a rolled scroll, washed in black (surface cracks) ................. $5,000-8,000

Emperor and empress, 7¾" h., dragon and phoenix thrones .................... $750-900

Emperor and empress, 9" h., seated on dragon and phoenix thrones ............................................................. $750-975

Emperor and empress, 24" h., on dragon and phoenix thrones, robes with phoenix (surface cracks) ........................... $5,500-7,000

**Immortals:**

Eight Immortals, 5" h., each holding his attribute, standing on floral plinth ........................................................ $2,000-2,500

Eight Immortals, 9" h., each holding his attribute ....................... $4,000-5,000

**Groups:**

Battle scene, 14" l., in pine grove, two warriors, three foot soldiers and pavilion .................................................. $1,500-1,875

Equestrian group, 8" h., military ....................................... $425-570

Fruit, 8" h., in gourd form ............................................. $400-500

Hanging vase, 22" h., oval with archaic masks ........................... $500-600

Incense burner, dragons in deep relief, upswept handles, loose rings, dragon finial ............................................. $375-420

Incense burner, 48" h., pagoda shape, three-tiered, pierced, and carved, having figures of dignitaries, double gourd finials, scroll handles, loose rings, and panels with eighteen lohans (minor cracks) ............................................. $1,500-2,500

**Tusks:**

Carved tusk, 20" h., with immortals, dancers, musicians on
three tiers . . . . . . . . . . . . . . . . . . . . . . . . . . . . . . . . . . . . . . . . . . . . . . . . . . . . . . . . . . . . $1,700-2,125

Carved tusk, 26" l., with figures and pavilion and wooded
mountains . . . . . . . . . . . . . . . . . . . . . . . . . . . . . . . . . . . . . . . . . . . . . . . . . . . . . . . . . . . . $1.600-1,975

Plain large tusk, 26" l. . . . . . . . . . . . . . . . . . . . . . . . . . . . . . . . . . . . . . . . . . . . . . . . . $600-800

*Chinese ivory Kuan Yin, 18th century.*
*Courtesy the Rosett Collection*

Box/cover, 2¾" h., late 19th century, gold hiramakie with
vine and birds . . . . . . . . . . . . . . . . . . . . . . . . . . . . . . . . . . . . . . . . . . . . . . . . . . . . . . . . . $350-570

Box/cover, 2¾" h., relief carving of birds, chrysanthemums,
and foliage with bee finial inlaid with horn . . . . . . . . . . . . . . . . . . . . . . . . . . . . . . $500-720

# Ivory
## *(Japanese)*

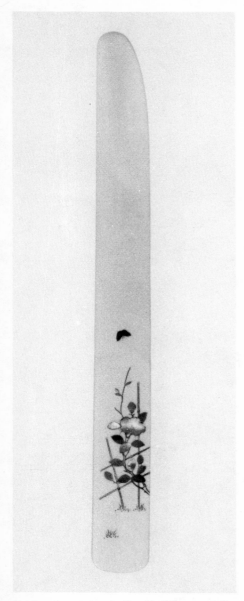

*Japanese ivory paper knife with shibayama inlay*

Box/cover, 3½" h., oval, motif of sparrows and chrysanthemums, Shibayama style . . . . . . . . . . . . . . . . . . . . . . . . . . . . . . . . . . . . . . . . $350-520

Box/cover, 3¾" h., pierced and carved with peonies and foliage . . . . . . . . . . . . . . . . . . . . . . . . . . . . . . . . . . . . . . . . . . . . . . . . . . . . . . . . . . . . . . . . . $250-400

Box/cover, 4" h., late 19th century, drum form, carved with the seven gods of good luck . . . . . . . . . . . . . . . . . . . . . . . . . . . . . . . . . . . . . . . . $700-900

Box/cover, 6" h., overall motif of masks (demons and deities) . . . . . . . . . . . . . . . . . $750-925

Box/cover, 6¼" h., cylindrical having panels carved in high relief, motif of Lohans, dragon finial, Shibayama style . . . . . . . . . . . . . . . . $700-950

Brush pot (tusk carving), 12" h., carved with continuous scene of boats, boatmen, trees, and foliage within a village . . . . . . . . . . . . . $1,800-2,400

Card case, 4¾" x 2½", motif of eagle and sparrows with pine, reverse motif of lilies and pheasant, Shibayama style . . . . . . . . . . . . . . . . . $750-1,175

Figure, basket seller, 8⅛" h., carrying baskets of various contours and sizes . . . . . . . . . . . . . . . . . . . . . . . . . . . . . . . . . . . . . . . . . . . . . . . . $1,200-1,800

Figure, Bishamon, 7" h., late 19th century, holding naginata and shrine . . . . . . . . . . . . . . . . . . . . . . . . . . . . . . . . . . . . . . . . . . . . . . . . . . . . . . . . . . . $300-500

Figure, boy, 3" l., in crawling position . . . . . . . . . . . . . . . . . . . . . . . . . . . . . . . . . . $350-450

Figure, Buddha, 2¾" h., seated upon lotus . . . . . . . . . . . . . . . . . . . . . . . . . . . . . . $150-200

Figure, Daruma, 5" h., wearing loose robes . . . . . . . . . . . . . . . . . . . . . . . . . . . . . $200-300

Figure, Jurojin, 5¼" h., late 19th century, holding a fan and scroll . . . . . . . . . . . . . . . . . . . . . . . . . . . . . . . . . . . . . . . . . . . . . . . . . . . . . . . . . . . . . . $300-430

Figure, Kannon, 7" h., holding a lotus blossom . . . . . . . . . . . . . . . . . . . . . . . . $800-1,100

Figure, man, 2¾" h., kneeling and holding a No mask, engraved and stained . . . . . . . . . . . . . . . . . . . . . . . . . . . . . . . . . . . . . . . . . . . . . . . . . . $450-700

Figure, umbrella seller, 2¾" h., seated beside folded umbrellas, holding one open umbrella . . . . . . . . . . . . . . . . . . . . . . . . . . . . . . . . . . . $450-635

Figure, woman, 4½" h., holding a samisen, engraving stained black . . . . . . . . . . . . . . . . . . . . . . . . . . . . . . . . . . . . . . . . . . . . . . . . . . . . . . . . . $500-700

Figure, woman, 12" h., late 19th century, holding a mirror . . . . . . . . . . . . . . . . . $1,200-1,800

Figure, woodcutter, 15" h., late 19th century, standing on a log which he is sawing with his right hand, holding a sake jar in his left hand . . . . . . . . . . . . . . . . . . . . . . . . . . . . . . . . . . . . . . . . . . . . . $2,500-3,750

Okimono, fisherman, 5½" h., holding a goy. (Illus.) . . . . . . . . . . . . . . . . . . . . . . . $500-600

Okimono, grasshopper on radish, 5" l. (Illus.) . . . . . . . . . . . . . . . . . . . . . . $1,500-1,700

Okimono, man, 6" l., with two Oni, cleaning abumi, which is carved in low relief with motifs of flowers and dragons. Oni holding brushes and buckets . . . . . . . . . . . . . . . . . . . . . . . . . . . . . . . . . . . . . . $1,250-1,700

Okimono, monkey, 2" l., with dog attempting to retrieve food from an elephant's trunk . . . . . . . . . . . . . . . . . . . . . . . . . . . . . . . . . . . . . . . . . $400-600

Okimono, Shoki and Oni, 4" l., signed Kokyudo. (Illus.) . . . . . . . . . . . . . . . . $8,000-10,000

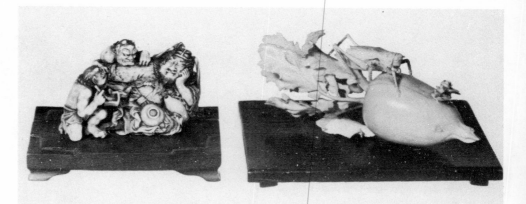

*Okimono of Shoki and Oni (left); okimono of grasshopper and radish (right). Courtesy the Rosett Collection*

Okimono, two coiled dragons in combat, signed Kiraku.
(Illus.) . . . . . . . . . . . . . . . . . . . . . . . . . . . . . . . . . . . . . . . . . . . . . . . . . . . . . . . . . $4,500-5,500

Paper knife, 19th century, Shibayama inlay. (Illus.) . . . . . . . . . . . . . . . . . . . . . $800-1,200

Takarabune (treasure ship), 16″ l., with various treasures . . . . . . . . . . . . . . . . . . $2,500-3,500

Tusk (carved), 14½″ l., seven gods of good luck
(Shichifukujin) in the form of a processional behind a cart
being drawn by an elephant . . . . . . . . . . . . . . . . . . . . . . . . . . . . . . . . . . . . . . . . $1,200-1,400

Vase (pair), 4″ h., cylindrical contour, relief carvings of
peony, chrysanthemum, and other flowers . . . . . . . . . . . . . . . . . . . . . . . . . . . . . . $350-550

Vase (tusk), 23¼″ h., 19th century, motif of pheasant and
cherry tree Shibayama style upon a carved wood stand . . . . . . . . . . . . . . . . . . . $1,500-2,250

*Japanese ivory of two coiled dragons (left); Japanese ivory of
fisherman and boy (right). Courtesy the Rosett Collection*

## Ivory
*(Indian)*

India is known for statues of religious figures, jewelry, and other adornments. In India, oftentimes an ivory tusk was split in half lengthwise, which is the explanation of why so many carvings have either a convex or concave contour. Indian ivory may be left in its natural state or it may be painted.

Box, 5½″ x 7½″ x 4½″, corners having cylindrical spires,
overall motif of concentric rings . . . . . . . . . . . . . . . . . . . . . . . . . . . . . . . . . . . . . . . $200-245

Chess set, natural and ebony stained, pierced openwork with
fluted baluster stems, kings 5″ h., pawns 2⅞″ h. . . . . . . . . . . . . . . . . . . . . . . . $900-1,100

Chess set (ivory and horn), natural and ebony stained, kings
4¼″ h., pawns 2¼″ h. . . . . . . . . . . . . . . . . . . . . . . . . . . . . . . . . . . . . . . . . . . . . . $425-570

Group, chariot and horse, 15″ l., with seated dignitary in the
chariot . . . . . . . . . . . . . . . . . . . . . . . . . . . . . . . . . . . . . . . . . . . . . . . . . . . . . . . . . . $275-400

Knife, 16″ l., with elephant on a vasiform base carved with
flowers, long flat blade with pierced motifs . . . . . . . . . . . . . . . . . . . . . . . . . . . . . $400-520

Musicians (pair), 7″ h., short tunics, pleated skirts (some
damage) . . . . . . . . . . . . . . . . . . . . . . . . . . . . . . . . . . . . . . . . . . . . . . . . . . . . . . . . . $200-300

## Bone

Chess set, early 20th century, kings 4" h., pawns 1⅝" h. . . . . . . . . . . . . . . . . . . . . . . . . . . . $150-200

Chess set (Chinese), king 4½" h., pawn 2½" h., Oriental and
European dignitaries . . . . . . . . . . . . . . . . . . . . . . . . . . . . . . . . . . . . . . . . . . . . . . . . . . . . $900-1,100

Kris, handle (Balinesian), 14" l., motif of stylized deities . . . . . . . . . . . . . . . . . . . . $75-100

Sword, Japanese, 15" l., early 20th century, hilt and sheath
carved with figures and pagodas . . . . . . . . . . . . . . . . . . . . . . . . . . . . . . . . . . . . . . . . . $275-320

## Rhinoceros Horn

Kuan Yin, 5" h., holding a scepter and prayer beads . . . . . . . . . . . . . . . . . . . . . . . . $400-600

Libation cup, 7" l., leaf form . . . . . . . . . . . . . . . . . . . . . . . . . . . . . . . . . . . . . . . . . . $3,500-4,500

Tusk, 3½" h., open lotus fond, leaves and buds . . . . . . . . . . . . . . . . . . . . . . . . . . $4,500-5,500

## Jade

Jade refers to nephrite and jadeite, and both are termed hardstones. The earliest jade carvings date from the Shang and Chou dynasties (1600-771 B.C.). During that time, animals were predominant forms. During the period of the Warring States, plaques with openwork designs were developed. Jade was used for sword furniture during the Han Dynasty. Jadeite or nephrite is so hard and tough that, when forcibly scratched with a stainless steel blade, one will find a black mark showing that the jade has scratched the stainless steel. Jadeite and nephrite require special cutting abrasives such as powdered garnets, rose quartz sand and carborundum. One can distinguish jadeite from nephrite with the aid of a jeweler's glass. Jadeite will have granular crystals and nephrite will show fibrous structures. Well known colors include spinach green, mutton fat (white), lavender, red, brown, pale blue, celadon, black, apple green, etc.

*Covered vase, mottled spinach green, 9" h.*

Beaker, 6" h., celadon, rockwork, waves, set with hardstone
plant . . . . . . . . . . . . . . . . . . . . . . . . . . . . . . . . . . . . . . . . . . . . . . . . . . . . . . . . . . . . . . $1,300-1,700

Belt hook, 4½" l., spinach green, carved dragon shaft with
dragon head terminal . . . . . . . . . . . . . . . . . . . . . . . . . . . . . . . . . . . . . . . . . . . . . . . . $200-300

Belt hook, 5" l., spatula form, dragon motif in low relief . . . . . . . . . . . . . . . . . . . $300-400

Bowl, 4½" dia., white dragons in low relief . . . . . . . . . . . . . . . . . . . . . . . . . . . . $1,000-1,300

Bowl, 5½" dia., spinach green, spread foot, black flecking . . . . . . . . . . . . . . . . $1,200-1,500

Box and cover, 3" l., mutton fat, oval, dragon entwining body
with dragon finial . . . . . . . . . . . . . . . . . . . . . . . . . . . . . . . . . . . . . . . . . . . . . . . . . . . . $250-300

Box and cover, 5" l., fei-ts'ui (bright green), notched corners,
with low relief carving of bird perched among flowering
branches . . . . . . . . . . . . . . . . . . . . . . . . . . . . . . . . . . . . . . . . . . . . . . . . . . . . . . . . . . . . $400-500

Box and cover, 5½" dia., spinach green, two dragon
medallions, mask and ring handles, dragon finial . . . . . . . . . . . . . . . . . . . . . . $2,000-3,100

Brush washer, 3" dia., spinach green, cylindrical body, relief
work featuring lotus blossoms . . . . . . . . . . . . . . . . . . . . . . . . . . . . . . . . . . . . . . . . $125-150

Brush washer, 5" dia., celadon, dragons in relief on shoulder . . . . . . . . . . . . . $1,500-1,800

Brush washer, 6" l., gray, leaf shape (Mogul), relief carving of
foliage . . . . . . . . . . . . . . . . . . . . . . . . . . . . . . . . . . . . . . . . . . . . . . . . . . . . . . . . . . . . . . $200-220

Candlesticks (pair), 15" h., spinach green, pricket, floral
motifs in relief with linked scrollwork on bases . . . . . . . . . . . . . . . . . . . . . . . $1,800-2,000

Cricket cage, 6" h., gray/white, pierced and carved with
dragons and plum blossoms . . . . . . . . . . . . . . . . . . . . . . . . . . . . . . . . . . . . . . . . . $700-925

Dish, 7" l., white, oval with butterfly handles and loose rings,
four cabriole legs, carved flower heads and ch'ih lung . . . . . . . . . . . . . . . . . . $3,700-4,200

Ewer, 6" h., celadon, bulbous with arched spout, dragon head handle and loose ring .................... $375-500

Figure (pair), birds, 7" h., on flowering branches ............................ $900-1,200

Figure (pair), birds, 9" h., russet, standing on rockwork (chipped) ................................... $1,250-1,300

Figure, boy, 4½" h., brown, holding a flower ................................ $700-900

Figure, Buddha, 7" h., celadon, Dhyanasana (meditation) .................... $2,500-3,000

Figure, dog, 2" l., green/gray/brown, incised hair, bushy tail .................... $400-520

Figure, dog, 3" l., gray/light brown, curly tail and mane, holding peony branch in its mouth .................... $400-500

Figure, dog, 3" l., moss green, recumbent .................... $300-475

Figure, dragon, 3" l., upon rockwork, white/pink .................... $675-800

Figures (pair), elephants, 4" h., spinach green, trunks curved downward between tusks .................... $600-800

Figure, female, 6" h., lavender, holding two fans .................... $2,000-4,500

Figure, horse, 2" l., white, standing erect, bushy tail and mane .................... $200-285

Figures, horses (pair), 6" l., spinach green, standing erect with curly tails .................... $400-575

Figure, Kuan Yin, 10" h., celadon, holding lotus blossom .................... $1,200-1,400

Figure, Kuan Yin, 12" h., fei-ts'ui, holding a peach branch and standing beside a phoenix .................... $5,500-7,000

Figure, Kuan Yin, 16" h., green/gray, holding basket of flowers with black and brown mottlings .................... $2,500-3,500

Figure, Kylin, 6¾" h., spinach green, turned horn and wings .................... $300-500

Figure, lady 6" h., holding a fan, blue/gray .................... $250-385

Figure, Lan Ts'aiho, 10" h., lavender .................... $4,500-6,000

Figure, Lohan, 5" l., brown/white, seated upon a leaf .................... $475-560

Figure, Mei Jin, 8" h., white, holding a staff and basket .................... $650-725

Figure, pig, 4" l., green/brown, archaic styling .................... $275-300

Figures, phoenix (pair), 12" h., fei ts'ui, standing upon rockwork bases with each holding a peony blossom in its beak .................... $5,500-7,000

Figure, Pu Tai, 9" h., apple green, holding rosary beads and ju-i scepter .................... $1,200-1,425

Figure, Pu Tai, 4¾" l., fei ts'ui holding a fly whisk and sack in a reclining position .................... $725-775

Figure, ram, 2" h., celadon .................... $150-170

Figure, Shou Lao, 5½" h., celadon, standing on rockwork base .................... $800-1,000

Figure, water buffalo, 9" l., celadon/brown, kneeling with motifs of archaic styled symbols .................... $1,500-2,000

Group, cornucopia with lilies, 4½" l., white .................... $275-300

Group, elephant and boys, 3" h., gray/white/brown, trunk turned downward with one boy on either side of the elephant's back, which supports a censer .................... $1,400-1,800

Group, female goat and her kid, 6½" h., on pierced rockwork, lavender .................... $3,000-3,750

Group, Lohan seated on foo dog, 7" h., Lohan with clasped hands, foo dog with turned horn, mutton fat .................... $700-850

Group, peaches, 5" l., white, in a cluster with leaves, branches, and flowers .................... $2,500-3,000

Group, phoenix, 9" h., apple green, two phoenixes on rockwork bases with tree peonies .................... $1,500-1,750

Group, monkey with two small monkeys, 2¾" h., in playful

*Covered vase, 18th century, pale celadon, 9½" h.*

*Covered vase, mottled green and brown, 6"*

115

pose, white/brown ........................................ $850-1,000

Group, sage holding a young boy, 2¾″ l., white ................... $200-285

Group, sparrows, 8″ l., green/white, perched on cucumbers
with grasshopper on one leaf ................................. $1,400-1,900

Incense burner, 5″ h., white/apple green/emerald green,
square form, key fret in relief with foo dog finial and four
masked feet ................................................ $750-900

Incense burner, 5″ h., celadon, contour like a petal with three
legs, tao t'ieh mask and C scrolls ........................... $2,800-3,325

Incense burner, 5″ h., quadrangular form, handles with loose
rings, cabriole legs, domed lid and foo dog finial, with motif
of dragon in low relief, fei-ts'ui ............................ $700-800

Incense burner, 12″ h., spinach green, elephant form with
pagoda cover with bells hanging from roof of pagoda,
carving in low relief ........................................ $1,700-2,100

Incense burner, 4″ h., celadon, carved tao t'ieh mask motif,
handles with loose rings, domed lid with two dragons and
three masked feet ........................................... $2,600-3,100

Libation cup, 4½″ l., boat shape, white, dragon looped
handles, curved spout, carving of vertical ridged flanges ..... $375-500

Mirror frame, 16¾″ x 13″, spinach green, boats and river
landscapes, mounted in metal ................................ $400-500

Mountain, 4″ l., fei-ts'ui, carved with deer, cranes, and
landscape ................................................... $900-1,200

Pi disc, 2¼″ dia., white, C scrolls and dots .................... $120-140

Pilgrim bottles (pair), 13″ h., spinach green, floral medallions
and ju-i scepter handles ..................................... $7,000-10,000

Plaque, 3″ dia., fei-ts'ui, dragon in relief with motifs of cloud
scrolls ...................................................... $600-670

Plaques (pair), 5″ h., fei-ts'ui, relief carving of kylin and
clouds encased in wood frames ............................... $1,400-1,500

Scroll weight, 6″ l., gray, oblong with motifs of flowers and
feathery leaves, toad at one end ............................. $1,200-1,500

Seal, 1½″ h., white, foo dog finial ............................ $90-110

Scepter, 14″ l., russet/celadon, carved and pierced with ling
chih branches ............................................... $900-1,200

*Vase, covered, 9½″ h., pale celadon, 18th century. (Illus.) ..... $2,800

*Vase, covered, 6″ h., Ch'ing Dynasty, mottled green and
brown. (Illus.) .............................................. $360

Table screens (pair), 5″ h., fei-ts'ui, relief carving of kylin and
clouds ...................................................... $1,400-1,500

Table screens, 12″ x 9″, green/white, carving of pavilions,
mountains, and figures ...................................... $3,000-4,000

Table screens (pair), moss green, landscape motif in low relief ... $5,000-6,000

Table screen, 12″ h., spinach green, low relief carving of
landscape with sage and pavilion ............................. $7,000-10,000

Vases (covered, pair), 6″ h., fei-ts'ui, tapered with panels of
peony blossoms, butterflies, and S scrolls .................... $600-800

Vases (double), 5″ h., spinach green, formed like hollow
bamboo stalk, carving includes rockwork, ling chih, and
butterflies .................................................. $200-225

Vases (hanging pair), 6″ h., spinach green, pear-shaped,
U-shaped handles, carving in low relief of lotus blossoms,
domed lid ................................................... $550-590

Vase, 6″ h., white, in form of a dragon/carp (upright position)
upon base of waves .......................................... $1,700-2,240

Vase, 6″ h., celadon, chain type with female figure in relief,
cover having stylized cloud formations ....................... $500-600

Vase, 9¼" h., celadon, beaker form with dragon handles and
loose rings, motifs include t'ao t'ieh masks ............................... $1,600-1,900

Vase, 6" h., lavender, baluster form, loose ring handles,
pierced fretwork, lions on shoulder, carved t'ao t'ieh masks ................. $2,200-3,750

Vases (covered, pair), 3" h., baluster form, lavender ........................... $600-650

Vase, 7¾" h., white, double gourd, relief work of vines,
tendrils, and gourds ...................................................... $1,800-2,700

Vase, white, ovoid form with relief work on band ........................... $600-700

Vase (covered), 14" h., spinach green, quadrangular form,
archaistic carving of birds, leaves, and peonies with domed
lid and dragon finial ...................................................... $600-725

Vase (covered), 5" h., celadon, loose ring handles, modeled
dragon and pearl entwining body with phoenix finial ..................... $1,600-2,200

Vases, deep green/brown, covered, flat tapering contour with
dragon/fret handles, motifs of birds and prunus tree, domed
lid with lotus finial ...................................................... $1,700-2,400

*Vase (covered), 9" h., mottled spinach green jade. (Illus.) ................ $1,000

Vases, 4¾" h., gray/white/brown, tree trunk form, hollow
carved and undercut with chih lung and two dragons ..................... $2,000-3,100

Vase, 7" h., gray/white, covered, high relief carving of lilies
and foliage, domed lid conforms to overall motif ......................... $1,500-1,900

Wine pot, 5" h., celadon, lotus form with leaf sprays and frog
finial ............................................................................. $400-65

## Japanese Clocks

The clock (as we know it) was introduced to Japan via European traders and missionaries sometime during the 16th century. It was during the Meiji period that the Western time standard was adopted, replacing the Japanese system. Before this period, time was measured either by the zodiac or by the rising and setting sun. Time spacing devised by the rising and setting sun were divided into six equal parts, which were equal to one another only at the equinoxes. Early clocks were similar to English lantern clocks. Spring-driven clocks were introduced in the early 1800s, as well as weight-driven pillar clocks. Many are familiar with the small spring-driven clocks which were placed in a case not unlike an inro and were then suspended on a cord with a netsuke. When trade was established with the West, Western clocks were imported, but before too long such was produced in Japan and also made specifically for Western export.

Pillar clock, 20" h., 18th century, glazed canopy revealing the
movement, with turned corner columns, pierced front plate,
and balance wheel with verge escapement, trunk with
adjustable chapters and additional scale ................................. $2,000-2,550

## Japanese Paintings

The introduction of Buddhism altered the course of Japanese art. It was during the Heian period that a secular art developed. The Yamato-e school specialized in scroll painting, which depicted landscapes and events taken from myth and legend. Kanga (pictures) in black, gray, and white were executed in varying enamels in Chinese style. During the Kakamura period, Sumi-e (Zen) and painted scrolls depicting battles and portraitures reached new heights. The Muromachi period painters were much influenced by the works of the Yuan and Ming dynasties. Motifs were pronounced, with a profusion of colors and gold. The Tosa school is

117

associated with the aforementioned style. The Kano school excelled in the technique of pen and ink. By the 15th century, Japanese art emerged from the influence of other Asian countries. The Momoyama period shows the Western influence in art for the first time, and the Edo period gave birth to Ukiyo-e (see Wood Block Prints). From the Meiji period on, Japanese paintings show both a traditional and Western influence. Many Japanese artists modeled their works upon European art and adopted the technique of oil painting. Among the later masters of Japanese art are Taikan (noted for screens and scrolls) and Kokei (known as a color stylist).

*Japanese hanging scroll, 17th century, of a standing beauty*

Hanging scroll, 42" x 22", ink and colors on silk, depiction of a school of carp with one leaping among waves ............................. $500-650

Hanging scroll, 40" x 20⅝", ink and colors on silk, depiction of a dying Buddha on a dais surrounded by Lohans and Bodhisattvas ...................................................... $1,800-2,450

Hanging scroll, framed size 42½" x 29", ink and colors on silk, a Lohan riding an elephant with a background of flowering trees and foliage ........................................ $750-900

Hanging scroll, 44½" x 16", 19th century, ink and colors on silk, depiction of monkeys at play on branches and vines ............. $500-800

Hanging scroll, 36" x 11½", colors on beige silk, depiction of irises and grasses ................................................ $155-190

Hanging scroll, 52" x 24½", 19th century, ink on paper, depiction of a forest and waterfall with many monkeys at play ............................................................... $600-800

Hanging scroll (Kano school), frame size 37" x 16", ink on paper, fisherman and his catch ...................................... $200-325

Hanging scroll, 36" x 14¼", colors on silk, depiction of a Lohan seated beside a tree .......................................... $125-200

*Hanging scroll, approximately 98" x 13", third quarter of the 17th century, sumi, gofun and colors on gilt paper with standing figure of a beauty (slightly retouched), fitted box. (Illus.) .................................................................. $1,100

Painting (Tosa style), 8½" x 6½", colors on gold ground, depiction of Samurai in battle ........................................ $325-500

Painting (Tosa style), 10" x 8¼", depiction of Kannon ............ $200-295

Painting (Edo period), frame size 60" x 36", ink on paper, depiction of a large leaping carp ............................... $1,000-1,200

Painting, 10¾" x 15¾", ink and colors on paper, depiction of a ferocious tiger .............................................. $900-1,000

Painting, 12" x 15", colors on paper, scenic with Dutch sailing ships ................................................................ $700-1,000

Watercolor, 13½" x 23¼", signed H. Yoshida, depiction of children at play within a street scene ........................ $1,700-2,000

Watercolor, 14½" x 10¼", signed Zenshin, depiction of leaping black and gold carp .................................... $1,100-1,500

Watercolor, 17¼" x 12", signed Hasui, depiction of thatched house on a river bank ......................................... $1,200-1,800

Watercolor, 18" x 13¾", signed Hasui, titled "Rain at Chihabara Canal" ............................................... $1,800-2,400

## Japanese Screens

Screens were used in Japanese homes as a protection from drafts and to secure privacy. They were also used as room dividers and served as movable walls. Folding screens were introduced to Japan via Korea and China sometime during the 7th century. The earliest screens had wooden frames covered with silk, paper, or woven fabric. Generally, cloth and paper screens were ornamented with calligraphy, pictures, and poetry. During the 14th century, hinges (introduced via Korea) were first used, thus allowing for a continuous surface. Perhaps the most beautiful and sought after screens date from the Edo and Meiji periods.

Two-leaf, leaf size 22½″ x 30½″, painted in sumi and colors on paper, motif of landscape and village ..................................... $150-225

Two-leaf, leaf size 46″ x 22½″, 19th century, painted in sumi and colors, motif of cranes, foliage, and flowers ............................... $450-650

Two-leaf (erotica), leaf size 56½″ x 31″, painted in sumi, gofun, and colors on paper, depiction of six Bijin bathing, one leaf shows a man and woman enjoying one another .................... $3,500-5,000

Four-leaf, leaf size 7′6″ x 5′, 18th century, painted in sumi, gofun, and colors on paper with depiction of Manchurian cranes, grasses, and reeds ...................................... $3,000-4,250

Four-leaf, leaf size 66″ x 64″ (Kano school), 19th century, painted in sumi, gofun, and colors on paper with gold leaf, depiction is of Narihira ................................................ $2,000-3,000

Six-leaf, leaf size 44½″ x 25½″ (Kano school), 19th century, painted in sumi, gofun and colors on paper, motif of riverscape ...................................................... $2,500-3,200

Six-leaf (Toasa school-Genji screen), early 19th century, painted in sumi, gofun, and colors on paper, six scenes from *The Tales of Genji* ............................................... $2,200-3,100

Six-leaf, leaf size 27½″ x 13½″, 19th century (pillow screen), painted in sumi, gofun, and colors on a gold ground, depiction of court figures and attendants ................................. $1,700-2,200

Six-leaf, leaf size 70″ x 24″, 19th century, painted in sumi, gofun, and colors on paper, cranes and pines ........................... $2,000-3,000

Six-leaf, leaf size 12′ x 6′, late 19th century, painted in sumi, gofun, and colors on gold paper, depiction of cranes flying and standing with riverscape ...................................... $6,000-7,000

Six-leaf, leaf size 12′ x 5′ (Kano school), 19th century, painted in sumi and colors on paper, depiction of landscape with houses, mountains, and river ...................................... $1,900-2,300

Six-leaf, leaf size 50″ x 22″, early 19th century, painted in sumi, gofun, and colors on paper, each leaf depicting karako at play ................................................................ $4,000-6,000

Six-leaf, leaf size 10′ x 4′10″, late 19th century, painted in sumi, gofun, and colors on paper, one side having scattered birds and flowers, the other having a landscape ......................... $1,500-1,700

Six-leaf, leaf size 12½′ x 4′10″, painted in sumi, gofun, and colors on paper, depiction of cranes, ducks, and other fowl in a riverscape ...................................................... $1,800-1,950

# Jewelry

Bracelet, 3¼″ dia., muttonfat, flowers in relief ............................... $400-500

Bracelets (pair), bangle, apple green jade with emerald patches .......................................................... $2,200-2,600

*Bracelets (pair), apple green and celadon jade (Illus.) ........................... $13,000

Brooch, yellow gold junk and boatman on an apple green jade sea .............................................................. $750-1,000

*Brooch, apple green jade, diamond terminals, platinum mount (Illus.) ........................................................ $3,800

Hairpins (set of seven), coral and gilt filigree with kingfisher feather ............................................................. $500-700

Necklace, 19″ l., coral beads, 14 kt gold clasp with oval bead .................... $150-200

*Bracelets, apple green and celadon jade*

Necklace, 24" l., twenty-seven graduated green jade beads with platinum clasp set with apple green jade cabochon flanked by small ruby cabochons . . . . . . . . . . . . . . . . . . . . . . . . . . . . . . . . . . . . . . . . . . . . . $110,000-125,000

Necklace, opal pendant, gold links, pendant in form of a snuff bottle . . . . . . . . . . . . . . . . . . . . . . . . . . . . . . . . . . . . . . . . . . . . . . . . . . . . . . . . . . . . . . . . . . . $350-575

Necklace, graduated coral beads and links with gold clasp . . . . . . . . . . . . . . . . . . . . . . . $250-400

Necklace, three rows of turquoise beads divided by gold links . . . . . . . . . . . . . . . . . $400-600

Necklace, heart-shaped lapis lazuli pendant and gold link chain . . . . . . . . . . . . . . . . . . . . . . . . . . . . . . . . . . . . . . . . . . . . . . . . . . . . . . . . . . . . . . . . . . . . . . . . $200-350

Pendant, carved amethyst quartz in the form of a peach . . . . . . . . . . . . . . . . . . . . . . . $175-200

Pin, 14 kt gold lady set with red coral . . . . . . . . . . . . . . . . . . . . . . . . . . . . . . . . . . . . . . . . . $30-50

Ring (man's), oval green jade cabochon in yellow gold mount, cabochon 10" x 7" . . . . . . . . . . . . . . . . . . . . . . . . . . . . . . . . . . . . . . . . . . . . . . $7,000-10,000

(See: Cloisonné)

*Brooch, apple green jade with diamond terminals*

## Kaga
### (Japanese)

Kaga wares are similar to Kutani, with both having been produced in Kaga province (modern prefecture, Ishikawa). Kaga wares are generally found with red designs on a white ground or red and gold designs on a white ground. Polychrome motifs are found on wares made from the late 19th century onward. Landscapes and multiplicity portraits are two of the most common motifs.

*Kaga plate, late 19th century*

Bottles, 6" h., late 19th century, pear-shaped, trumpet necks, overall motif of a multitude of figures . . . . . . . . . . . . . . . . . . . . . . . . . . . . . . . . . . . . . $250-325

Ewer, 12" h., late 19th century, pear-shaped, red and gold motif of figures on a terrace, loop handle, dragon finial . . . . . . . . . . . . . . . . . . . . . . . . $500-700

Ewer, 10½" h., late 19th century, red and gilt motif of riverscapes and figures, loop handle, dragon finial . . . . . . . . . . . . . . . . . . . . . . . . $400-600

Jar, covered, 12¼" h., late 19th century, red ground, two panels containing polychrome and gilt motif of karako, domed cover with Shishi finial . . . . . . . . . . . . . . . . . . . . . . . . . . . . . . . . . . . . . . . $700-900

Plate, 6" dia., late 19th century, red, gilt, black motif of Bijin in landscape reserves, key fret band on border. (Illus.) . . . . . . . . . . . . . . . . . . $250-300

Teapot, 9" across, late 19th century, phoenix handle and spout, paulownia blossom finial, panels having polychrome motif of landscapes . . . . . . . . . . . . . . . . . . . . . . . . . . . . . . . . . . . . . . . . . . . . . . . . . $125-175

Vases, 27" h., late 19th century, baluster form, polychrome motifs on red ground with gilt highlights; motif of standing and flying cranes among peony and lotus scrolls . . . . . . . . . . . . . . . . . . . . $600-900

Vases (pair), 4" h., late 19th century, baluster form, red ground with overall motif of figures in polychrome . . . . . . . . . . . . . . . . . . . . . . . . $300-350

Vases (pair), 12" h., red and gilt, birds, insects, foliage . . . . . . . . . . . . . . . . . . . . . . $400-500

## Kakiemon
### (Japanese)

Ranking among the finest of Japanese porcelains are those attributed to Kakiemon. Kizaemon Sakaida (known as Kakiemon) is credited with creating the first over-the-glaze colored enamels used in Japan on porcelain during the mid-1600s. There are three varieties of Kakiemon motifs.

1. Designs based on Ming and Ch'ing dynasties (Chinese).

2. Designs showing a European style (perhaps influenced by the Dutch).

3. Designs which are true Japanese (interpretations of nature). Kakiemon porcelain wares are of the most refined quality, and motifs are elegant although generally sparse.

Old Kakiemon is quite expensive. However, wares made in the style of Kakiemon, especially during the last quarter of the 19th century, are quite affordable.

(See: Imari, Japanese; Arita; Hirado; Sometsuke)

*Kakiemon plate, 7" dia., 18th century*

Bottle, 7" h., cranes in relief with blue clouds ............................. $1,500-2,000

Bowl, 6" dia., late 19th century, conical with fluted sides and petal lip, sprays of flowers and phoenix roundels on interior with a floral border, Kakiemon-style ...................................... $1,500-2,000

Bowl, 6" dia., 18th century, round contour with three floral sprays on exterior, chrysanthemum sprays on interior ...................... $4,500-5,500

Dishes (pair), 4" dia., floral reserves and diapers ........................... $900-1,100

Flask, 8" h., Kakiemon-style, 19th century, flattened form and rounded with small loop handles and a short mouth, decorated with pine, plum, and bamboo with a spray of peaches ...................................................................... $800-950

Plate, 7" dia., 18th century, with two figures crossing a bridge ............... $4,500-5,500

Vases (pair), 8" h., Kakiemon-style, double gourd with floral motif .................................................................................. $700-900

# K'ang Hsi
## *(Chinese)*

During the reign of K'ang Hsi (1662-1722) imperial patronage of the kiln at Ching-tê Chên encouraged the innovation of new decorative techniques. This period marks the beginning of an assembly line-type of decoration. Soft-paste porcelain (one that could be fired at a lower temperature) was discovered. Special translucent glazes were developed. Very fine cobalt techniques were employed on blue and white wares. Whitewares continued to be made, as were monochromes and crackle glazes. Great quantities of wares were produced: underglaze blues and copper reds, famille jaune (yellow family), famille noire (black family), and famille verte (green family). Also popular were the three-color enamels (green, yellow, and aubergine) with black outlines on biscuit. The paste of the period is gray-white in tone and marked by black spot imperfections. Iron oxide is in evidence on the unglazed base rims of porcelains.

(See: Blue and White Wares (Chinese); Famille Jaune; Famille Noire; Famille Verte; Mirror Black; Peach Bloom; Powder Blue; Sang de Boeuf)

*K'ang Hsi dish, 8½" dia., blue and white decoration*

Bowl, 5", six-character mark in underglaze blue, decorated in wu ts'ai enamels, the interior with a dragon in the center medallion, the exterior with two dragons among branches and a phoenix in flight .................................................. $1,400-1,800

Bowl, 7" dia., commemorative mark of Ch'êng Hua, blue and white decoration, decorated with a scene of six frolicking deer in a meadow landscape with pine trees and fungus ..................... $800-1,000

Condiment set, unmarked, consisting of eight pieces attractively arranged in a black lacquered wood box,

*K'ang Hsi figure, 17" h., seated official, Ming style*

*K'ang Hsi figure, 13" h., standing boy on carved wood stand*

including five 5⅛" hexagonal dishes and three 4⅝" pentagonal dishes, all decorated on the biscuit with a bird on a prunus branch in colors of green, yellow, and aubergine with black outlines ............................. $1,800-2,200

Dish, 6" dia., unmarked, decorated with an allover deep blue glaze ............................. $900-1,200

Dish, 8" dia., six-character mark in underglaze blue, decorated with wu ts'ai enamel colors, the design consisting of a large medallion of chrysanthemums, prunus, magnolias, peonies, and day lilies among scattered flowers enclosed by a double line border; rim with floral design as well ...................... $2,000-2,200

Dish, 8½" dia., commemorative Ming Ch'eng-Hua mark, blue and white, painted in a silvery blue with eight alternating panels of flowers and emblems around a central pattern, the exterior having eight panels of sketchy lines and circles. (Illus.) ............................. $500-600

Dish, 8⅝" dia., back marked with a commemorative Ch'eng-Hua mark, decorated in tou t'sai technique with a repeating pattern of flying bats on the back, the front showing a hare in the center along with deer and trees. (Illus. here and in Color Section) ............................. $800-1,000

Dish, 9" dia., unmarked, with a white ground, decorated with underglaze blue leaves and red and gilt chrysanthemums surrounded by a diaper border with four scrolling floral medallions painted in iron red and gilt ............................. $500-600

Dish, 14" dia., unmarked, decorated with wu ts'ai enamel colors; center of the dish decorated with chrysanthemums with an outer border band of ju-i lappets, everted rim decorated with peony blossoms amid floral scrollwork ............................. $1,200-1,400

Figure, 13" h., standing boy holding a vase with a child clinging to his side (a repair on the vase rim); glazed in white with iron red, green, and yellow decoration along with some outlining in black. (Illus. here and in Color Section) ............................. $2,200-2,500

Figure, 14" h., unmarked, decorated in famille verte colors depicting a woman wearing an apron and holding a flower, standing on a base decorated with flowers ............................. $2,200-2,500

Figure, 17" h., seated court official, with turquoise glaze applied to the biscuit with touches of brown and aubergine, unglazed biscuit face and hands; heavily potted in the Ming style, some hairline cracks. (Illus.) ............................. $2,000-2,200

Jar, 8¾" h., unmarked, of finely potted ovoid form with short neck and molded lip set on flat unglazed foot, glazed overall in a milky white glaze ............................. $1,000-1,400

*K'ang Hsi dish, 8⅝" dia., tou-ts'ai decoration*

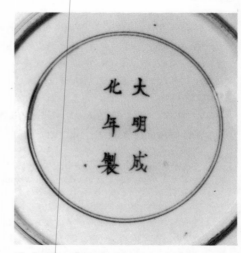

*Underside of K'ang Hsi tou-ts'ai plate, commemorative Ch'eng Hua reign mark*

Jar (covered), 18" h., unmarked (double circles in underglaze blue on the base), decorated in wu ts'ai enamels, the motif of two dragons (one in iron red) chasing a flaming pearl separated by two peony blossoms surrounded by stylized leafy scrolls; lid decorated with clouds and flaming pearls .................. $4,500-5,500

Saucer dish, 4½" dia., six-character mark in underglaze blue, with incised decoration of a phoenix and a dragon in a center medallion, the underside with two dragons in pursuit of flaming pearl, all under a canary yellow glaze; base of the dish glazed with a greenish tinted white glaze .......................... $5,000-6,000

Saucer dishes (pair), unmarked, glazed in a finely crackled allover turquoise color, base left unglazed, with a firing crack in one dish ...................................................... $700-1,000

Syrup pot, 12" h., unmarked, of cylindrical form with a tiara top, painted on the biscuit in famille verte colors, decorated with Buddhist symbols, waves, and phoenix birds, with the original dragon head spout and three foo dog head-mask handles at the back ............................................. $2,500-3,000

Vase, 16" h., unmarked, bottle form, decorated with three whimsical animals in copper red on a white glazed ground ................. $2,800-3,200

Vase, 18½" h., unmarked, blue and white decoration, yen yen shape, decorated with panels of the "hundred antiques," with a border of prunus blossoms ...................................... $1,800-2,200

Water dropper, 7" l., unmarked, in the shape of a frog crouching on his hind legs and holding a lotus leaf in his mouth, enameled in a bright turquoise on the biscuit ..................... $1,200-1,500

Wine pot, 7½" h., modeled in the form of a crayfish with three-color enamel on the biscuit. (Illus. here and in Color Section) ................................................................ $1,500-2,000

*K'ang Hsi wine pot, 7½" h., modeled as a crawfish*

## Karatsu
*(Japanese)*

Karatsu wares are prized by followers of Cha no yo (the tea ceremony). Early Karatsu wares have thick opaque glazes applied to a hard pottery. E-Karatsu wares had motifs painted in black or brown under the glaze. From the 17th century Karatsu wares were decorated in the Korean mishima technique. Designs were impressed into the biscuit and filled with slip. The motifs were repetitive and consisted of circles, half circles, conventional florals, and lines.

Bottle, 7½" h., 19th century, small mouth, concave band around middle, mottled black/brown glaze ................................... $125-165

Dish, 4" dia., plum blossoms and branches, iron oxide and blue ...................................................................... $200-250

Teapot (E-Karatsu), 9" h., round form, two loop handles, tapered spout, sunken lid, bands of foliage and flowers in brown ................................................................... $900-1,100

## Kenzan
*(Japanese)*

Ogata Kenzan (1662-1743) was a potter and poet. He was the brother of Ogata Korin (a famous painter and lacquer worker). Kenzan worked in Kyoto producing articles for Cha no yo. His designs were bold yet sketchy and quite unconventional for his day. He was a superb color stylist and used unusual combinations of color. He is one of the most famous of all Japanese potters and his works are found in major museums throughout the world.

Chawan (Kenzan style), calligraphy and flowers ............................. $400-500

Chawan (Kenzan style), Edo period, colors on hagi glaze.
(Illus.) ........................................................ $500-600

Dish, earthenware (purple/brown), early 18th century, white
slip with blue (Illus.) ........................................ $2,500-3,500

Jar, covered, 7″ h., Kenzan style. (Illus.) ........................ $250-350

Kenzan earthenware dish dating early 18th century

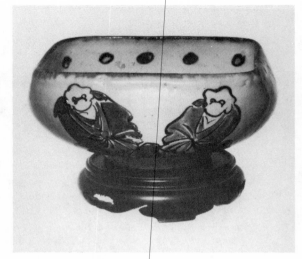

Kenzan-style chawan, Edo period

Kenzan-style jar

# Kiangnan Ting Wares
*(Chinese)*

124

These wares were produced in what was formerly called Kiangsu and Anhwei provinces, in an area north of Kuantung. This section is now called Kiangnan. Kiangnan wares are made of pottery with a thick, creamy, buff-colored glaze which is finely crackled and stained (in a darker hue). This often gives the surface an appearance somewhat like the surface of an ostrich egg. The pottery can appear unadorned or molded with relief ornamentation. Evidence points to the first appearance of these wares during the Ming Dynasty. They should not be confused with Ting Yao (a porcelain), or Ko Yao (crackleware), which has a different style of crackle and which were both in existence prior to the Ming Dynasty. Kiangnan wares appear with heavy coagulations in the glaze which are called "tear streaks."

Kiangnan Ting ware vase, 17½" h., 16th century

Vase, 13" h., 14/16th century, pear-shaped with a flared base, the center with molded decoration, with a copper sheathed lip, covered in a heavy creamy beige glaze with fine crackle, the glaze with heavy "tear streaks." . . . . . . . . . . . . . . . . . . . . . . . . . . . . . . . . . . . . $800-1,000

Vase, 16" h., 14/16th century, pear-shaped, undecorated, with a heavy "tear streaked" cream-colored glaze . . . . . . . . . . . . . . . . . . . . . . . . . . . $800-1,000

Vase, 17½", 16th century, pear shaped, with a finely crackled glaze over a heavy creamy glaze, and an unfired foot rim and base. (Illus.) . . . . . . . . . . . . . . . . . . . . . . . . . . . . . . . . . . . . . . . . . . . . . . . $600-800

## Kimono — Accessories
### (Japanese)

Literally, kimono means wear thing. This way of dressing dates back to the Tumulus period (200-552 A.D.). Early periods were influenced by both China and Korea. During the Nara period (552-794 A.D.) apparel was made of gauze or brocade (both silk) and such was worn with sashes. By the Hien period (794-1184 A.D.) clothing became more simple. The kimono with short and narrow sleeves was worn daily by the commoners. Court costumes consisted of layers of garments and long skirts. By 1333, clothing was simplified and the kosode and hakama were developed. Hakama are loose pants not unlike culottes and were worn with the kosode. Eventually the kosode was worn by women and the hakama was worn only by men. During the Momoyama and Edo periods, the kosode changed in being and became an elegant outer garment with elaborate motifs. This form of kosode is what is referred today as a kimono. Old kimonos are highly collectible, as are the obi (sashes worn with kimonos). Patterns can be hand-dyed, hand-embroidered, etc. Such apparel makes an elegant hostess robe or loungingattire.

Kimono, 61" l., blue ground, floral motif in silver and gold . . . . . . . . . . . . . . . . . . . . . $250-350

Kimono, 61" l., pale green, painted with large lilies and slightly embroidered with silver and gold threads . . . . . . . . . . . . . . . . . . . . . . . . . . $200-300

Kimono, 61" l., red, embroidered with fans and mums . . . . . . . . . . . . . . . . . . . . . . . $225-350

Kimono, 63" l., green ground, dragons in gold . . . . . . . . . . . . . . . . . . . . . . . . . . . . $280-350

Kimono, 63" l., shades of blue, clusters of flowers and lightly embroidered in gold and white silk threads . . . . . . . . . . . . . . . . . . . . . . . . . . . . . $350-400

Kimono, dyed silk, embroidered with cranes . . . . . . . . . . . . . . . . . . . . . . . . . . . . . . $150-175

Obi, silk brocade, gold and pale orange peonies on a green ground . . . . . . . . . . . . . . . . . . . . . . . . . . . . . . . . . . . . . . . . . . . . . . . . . . . . . . . . . . . $80-115

Obi, silk brocade, flowers, fans, and lattice designs in pale shades of blue . . . . . . . . . . . . . . . . . . . . . . . . . . . . . . . . . . . . . . . . . . . . . . . . . . . . . . . $75-120

Obi, silk brocade, fan-shaped panels of flowers with waves in shades of cream, lavender, and gold . . . . . . . . . . . . . . . . . . . . . . . . . . . . . . . . . . . . $175-220

Obi, silk brocade, panels of chrysanthemums and scenic motif in pale greens, cream, orange, and beige . . . . . . . . . . . . . . . . . . . . . . . . . . . . $175-250

Pouch, c. 1920, pigskin leather (lady's handbag), lined in
green suede, fitted with a mirror, bronze clasp . . . . . . . . . . . . . . . . . . . . . . . . . . . . . . $275-380

Priest's robe, blue silk, woven motif of huts (frayed) . . . . . . . . . . . . . . . . . . . . . . . . $200-300

## Kinrande
*(Chinese)*

Kinrande is the Japanese name for gold "brocade" decoration found on 16th century Ming porcelain decorated in red or green enamels and gilt tracery designs.

(See: Ming Dynasty)

## Kobe Toys

Kobe toy, 6½" l., twelve animations . . . . . . . . . . . . . . . . . . . . . . . . . . . . . . . . . . . . . . . $1,500-1,700

Kobe toy, double figures with four animations and wheel
movement . . . . . . . . . . . . . . . . . . . . . . . . . . . . . . . . . . . . . . . . . . . . . . . . . . . . . . . . . . . . . $400-500

Kobe toy, "watermelon eaters," clockwork wind with rotating
head (rare) . . . . . . . . . . . . . . . . . . . . . . . . . . . . . . . . . . . . . . . . . . . . . . . . . . . . . . . . . . . $3,000-4,000

## Korean Ceramics

During the period from 57 B.C. to 935 A.D. three small states were formed in the Korean peninsula, with the main state being Silla. The wares produced at Silla were made of an ash gray stoneware and were modeled in a style resembling Han bronze forms. They produced covered vases with cutout decoration at the foot and/or rims. The decoration was incised with circles, trefoils, chevrons, etc. Also made during this period were green glazed pottery tiles and greenish brown glazed stoneware.

The ceramics of the Koryo Dynasty (918-1392 A.D.) represent some of the finest wares produced in Korea. Although white and black ceramics were made, this period is most famous for its celadons, some of which are distinctively decorated with inlaid and reverse inlaid designs. Late in the dynasty, painted wares were produced which were influenced by the Chinese Tz'u-chou ware. The celadons dating from the mid-12th to the end of the 13th century are most highly regarded by today's collectors.

The Yi Dynasty extended many centuries from 1392 to 1910. A great variety of styles were produced early in the period, mostly in imitation of the earlier Koryo wares. A new product of the Yi Dynasty was Punchŏng ware. One style of decoration employed the use of white slip, which was either painted with iron brown or incised with sgraffito decoration. Another technique was to fill small, stamped impressions with white slip, which was then covered with a transparent celadon glaze. The blue and white ware of the period was produced at the Punwan potteries located southeast of Seoul. Although blue and white production began in the mid-15th century, some of the finest examples date from the early 1700s.

During the 500- odd years of the Yi Dynasty many other types of ceramics were produced, including black glazed wares, white glazed wares, porcelaineous pottery with bluish tint glazes, wares decorated with underglaze iron oxide or underglaze red, and pottery wares glazed in a variety of dull, pale tints of cream, blue, and green.

Bottle, 9¼" h., Yi Dynasty, blue and white decoration, bulbous form with a flared rolled lip, decoration consisting of a single, free brushstroke under a creamy, green-tinted glaze ................... $200-300

Bottle, 9½" h., Koryo Dynasty, 11th-12th century, mallet shaped, carved with three upright sprays of leafy foliage below a band of petals ................. $600-700

Bottle, 10" h., Yi Dynasty, 15th century, Punchŏng ware, tear form with two brown flower sprays painted on a white washed ground ................. $1,200-1,600

Bottle, 11" h., 13th century, Silla ware, ovoid shape with a flat, everted rim, covered with a gray ash glaze ................. $200-300

Bottle, 11" h., Koryo, 13th century, inlaid celadon, squat, bulbous body with long neck, flared mouth, with white inlay of lotus petals and chrysanthemums in a wide band, the leaves inlaid with black, covered with a crackled sea green glaze ................. $600-700

Bottle, 12" h., Yi Dynasty, 15th century, Punchŏng ware, tear form with a thick footing, carved with two large peonies on a hatched background, with stylized leaf bands around the neck ................. $3,000-5,000

Bottle, 12½" h., Koryo, 13th century, inlaid celadon, pear-shaped, inlaid in white with two floral sprigs and scroll band below a lappet collar ................. $500-600

Bowl, 5½" dia., Yi Dynasty, covered with a greenish blue, tinted white glaze, with kiln grit adhering to base and center of bowl ................. $175-225

Bowl, 6½" dia., Yi Dynasty, celadon, with molded floral decoration in the center, covered in a sea green glaze ................. $225-325

Bowl, 7" dia., Koryo Dynasty, 13th century, inlaid celadon, the interior with four white inlaid floral groupings and inlaid double rings in interior and on exterior. (Illus.) ................. $500-700

Bowl, 7½" dia., Koryo, 13th century, inlaid celadon, interior with white inlaid chrysanthemum petals and stylized leaf scroll, exterior with a double ring of black inlay above four chrysanthemums ................. $200-250

Bowl, 7¼" dia., Yi Dynasty, with a flared rim, set on a high unglazed foot, covered with a gray/buff crackled glaze containing small black specks, spur marks in the bowl center ................. $120-150

Bowl, 8" dia., Koryo, 12th century, delicately potted and molded on the interior with foliage, covered with a good green blue celadon glaze ................. $750-1,000

Bowl, 8" dia., Koryo, 13th century, thickly potted and molded on the interior with foliage, covered with a good green blue glaze ................. $350-500

Bowl, 8" dia., Koryo, 12th century, inlaid decoration, delicately potted, inlaid on the exterior with flowers, the interior decorated with pomegranate sprays and bands near the lip ................. $750-1,000

Bowl, 8" dia., Koryo, 12th century, incised with two parrots in flight, set on a ring foot, with three spur marks ................. $1,000-1,500

Bowl, 8" dia., Yi, 14th/15th century, Punchŏng ware, covered inside and out with massed punchwork covered with white slip ................. $350-550

Bowl, 8¼" dia., Yi Dynasty, celadon, molded, interior with a floral design and birds beneath a band of waving scroll; exterior of a peony within double circles, covered with a sea green glaze ................. $200-300

Cup, 4⅜" h., Sang'Gam, Koryo Dynasty, 13th century, decorated with chrysanthemums below a lightly incised border, with matching stand ................. $1,800-2,200

Cup stand and cup, 8" h., Koryo, 12th century, fluted stand

*Korean bowl, 7" dia., Koryo Dynasty*

*Korean jar, 3½" h., Koryo Dynasty*

with incised floral sprays; fluted cup incised around the lip .................... $1,000-1,500

Dish (ricecake dish), 3" h. x 5" dia., Yi Dynasty, set on a high splayed foot, covered with a brownish buff glaze ......................... $200-250

Ewer, 6½" h., Koryo Dynasty, 13th century, oviform body inlaid in each vertical lobe with a spray of three flower heads in black and white slip above a band of overlapping petals around the slightly recessed biscuit foot ......................... $1,200-1,500

Jar, 2" h., Yi Dynasty, baluster form, covered with a green spotted, deep brown glaze ......................... $100-150

Jar, 3½" h., Koryo Dynasty, 13th century, inlaid in black and white slip with alternate ju-i heads and floral sprigs, the shoulder having small daisy heads. (Illus.) ......................... $500-700

Jar, 3½" h., Koryo Dynasty, celadon, bulbous form on a riased ring foot, covered with a sea green celadon glaze ......................... $150-200

Jar, 4" h., Yi Dynasty, Punchŏng, baluster form with wide mouth, decorated on the shoulder with punchwork under white slip ......................... $1,500-2,000

Jar, 10" h., Yi Dynasty, blue and white decoration, decorated in underglaze blue with two large, freely drawn floral designs; glaze with a grayish tint ......................... $200-300

Jar, 9" h., Koryo, 13th century, inlaid decoration, baluster form, inlaid in black and white with flowers and bands at the rim and foot ......................... $750-1,000

Jar, 15" h., Silla, 8th/10th century, bronze form, the base with rectangular cutouts, the body incised with geometric designs, on a gray-black stoneware body ......................... $1,000-1,200

Oil bottle, 4" h., Koryo, 12th/13th century, inlaid decoration in black and white with a band of scrolling foliage around the shoulder ......................... $500-700

Stem cup, 3" h. x 4" dia., Yi, 15th century, Punchŏng, flaring cup set on a trumpet foot, exterior washed in a white slip, interior decorated with a cluster of flower heads within a band of circles centering on a hatched ground ......................... $1,000-1,200

Storage jar, 10" h., Yi Dynasty, blue and white decoration, bulbous form with a rolled lip, with underglaze blue floral and leaf clusters ......................... $150-200

Storage jar, 11" h., Yi Dynasty, with bulbous body and two lug handles, decorated in underglaze blue with large peonies with underglaze green leaves, on a white ground ......................... $225-300

Storage jar, 16" h., Yi, 18th century, baluster form with a wide short neck, covered with a pale bluish-white glaze ......................... $900-1,100

Vase, 15" h., 19th century, Koryo style, black and white inlaid medallions of flying cranes, with stiff leaf decoration at the base, and crackle overall. (Illus.) ......................... $400-500

Vase, 16" h., 20th century, celadon, mei ping shape, painted in black and white with "hundred cranes" in a center medallion, allover decoration of cloud scrolls, on a celadon ground of grayish green color ......................... $300-450

Wine pot (covered), 7" h., Koryo Dynasty, simple, lobed form with curved handle and spout, fitted with a domed, lobed cover, covered with a sea green celadon glaze ......................... $1,300-1,700

Wine vessel, 10" h., Koryo, 13th century, ovoid form with a short rolled neck, covered with green and brown mottled glaze ......................... $500-600

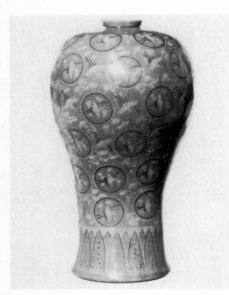

*Korean vase, 15" h., Koryo style, 19th century*

# Korean Paintings

Painting, approximately 36" x 54", late Yi Dynasty, ink and colors on paper, courtesans in gardens and pavilions ......................... $200-325

Painting, 46" x 76", late Yi Dynasty, colors on paper, figures in a garden setting ......................... $200-290

*Noritake Occupied Japan Wares*

*(L. to R.) Noritake cracker jar, 7½" h., Green M in Wreath mark, $175-$195. Noritake vase, 12" h., Green M in Wreath mark, $200-$220. Noritake humidor, elk motif, 6" h., Green M in Wreath mark, $195-$220. Occupied Japan couple, 12" h., SKG mark, $250-$275. Occupied Japan busts, Ardalt mark, 6½" h., $200-$235 pair. Occupied Japan water carrier, Ishihara China mark, 15" h., $500-$600 pair. Occupied Japan cherub with cart, Moriyama China mark, 8" l., $145-$165.*

*Kyoto Wares*

*(L. to R., front) Ko Kiyomizu sake bottle, 7" h., 18th century, $12,000-$15,000. Kyoto bowl 8" w., late 19th century, signed Shozan, $600-$800. Teapot, 3½" h., late 18th century (possibly Rokubei), $1,200-$1,500. Rear: Tea bowl (Chawan), 2½" h., early 19th century, $700-$900. Awata mizusashi (water jar), 6" h., c. 1830, signed Gasan Saku, $2,500-$3,500. Wine pot, 7" w., c. 1735-1750, $1,700-$2,200. Candlestick, 8¼" h., c. 1830, $900-$1,200. Awata mizusashi, early 19th century, 6" h., $2,250-$2,800.*

*Banko Wares, Sumida Gawa Wares*

*(L. to R., front) Banko kogo (box), c. 1840, $600-$800. Three Sumida Gawa figures, 3½" h., $350-$425, $500-$700, $350-$425. Banko bowl, impressed mark, late 19th century, $600-$850. Rear: Banko vase, 7¼" h., 19th century, $1,500-$1,900; Banko koro (incense burners), matched pair, 12" h., $2,800-$3,200. Ko Banko wine pot, late 18th century, $1,200-$1,500.*

*Early Chinese Pottery*
*(L. to R.) Figure, lady (rear), 8½" h., T'ang Dynasty, straw glaze, $1,200-$1,500. Figure, boar, 5½" l., T'ang Dynasty, $1,200-$1,500. Figure, court lady, 13½" h., T'ang Dynasty, $8,000-$10,000. Figure, court official, 12" h., Wei Dynasty, $1,500-$2,000.*

*Kutani and Imari*
(L. to R.) Kutani rose jar (front), late 19th century, $125-$150. Kutani plate with bird and floral motif, late 19th century, $125-$175. Kutani box in the form of Daikoku's bag, 19th century, $1,200-$1,500. Kutani vase with silver overlay, late 19th century, $220-$225. Imari cat incense burner (koro), (Arita), early 19th century, 10" w., $1,200-$1,500; Imari figure of man playing blindman's bluff (rear), mid-19th century, 9" h., $900-$1,200. Imari scalloped plate with fans in relief, late 19th century, $500-$650.

*Chinese Celadon*
(L. to R.) Vase, 14¾" h., Ming Dynasty, $3,000-$3,500. Charger 20" dia., dragon in relief, Ming Dynasty, $4,000-$5,000. Dish, 8¾" dia., Yuan Dynasty, twin fish design, $600-$800. Dish, 8¾" dia., Yuan Dynasty, single fish design, $600-$800.

*Miscellaneous Japanese Porcelains*
*(L. to R.) Vase, 8" h., late 19th century, signed Ryosai, $900-$1,200. Vase with motif of cranes, 9½" h., c. 1975-85, $600-$800. Vase with heron, signed Shofu, late 19th century, $450-$600. Vases (pair), motif of frogs in various poses, signed Hyochen-Tokyo, late 19th century, 8¼" h., $1,200-$1,400. Vases (pair), shark's skin glaze, early 20th century, 9½" h., $900-$1,200.*

*Chinese Monochromes*
*(L. to R.) Vase, iron red glaze, 9¼" h., Ch'ien Lung mark and period (see Ch'ien Lung), $900-$1,200. Vase, Powder Blue, 9" h., 18th century (see Powder Blue), $400-$600. Bowl, Peach Bloom, 5" h., 8" dia., Ch'ien Lung mark and period (see Peach Bloom), $1,000-$1,200. Stem cup, celadon 3¼" h., 5¼" dia., Yung Cheng mark and period (see Yung Cheng), $1,500-$2,000. Ginger jar, Mirror Black, 10½" h., K'ang Hsi period (see Mirror Black), $500-$700. Vase, white glaze (crackle), 6¾" h., 18th century (see Ko Yao), $400-$600.*

*Chinese Cloisonné*
*(L. to R.) Water pipe, 10¾" h., $125-$200. Openwork vase, 5⅝"., $400-650. Late 18th century box, 6" h., $800-$950.*

*Japanese Cloisonné*
*(Top, L. to R.) Shotai jar, 3½"h., $450-$500. Yusen teapot, 7" to top of handle, $550-$800. Totai tea caddy, 4"., $350-$450. (Bottom, L. to R.) Ginbari vase, 6" h., $125-$250. Yusen vase, one of a pair, 4¾" h., $600-$800 pr. Ginbari vase, 5¾" h., $150-$250. Akasuke vase, 6¹⁄₁₆" h., $150-$275.*

*Thai Ceramics*

*(L. to R.) Vase 15" h., Sawankhalok, $1,200-$1,400. Figure (rear), 9" h., Sawankhalok, $400-$600. Footed bowl, 10¾" dia., Sawankhalok, $600-$800. Bowl, 16" dia., Sawankhalok, $600-$800.*

*Early Ching Dynasty Porcelains*

*(L. to R.) Figure, boy, 13" h., K'ang Hsi period (see K'ang Hsi), $2,000-$2,500. Wine pot (rear, figural), crayfish, 7¾" h., K'ang Hsi period (see K'ang Hsi), $1,500-$2,000. Vase, 6¼" h., underglaze red, Ch'ien Lung mark and period (see Underglaze Red), $1,200-$1,500. Plate, 8⅝" dia., tou-ts'ai decoration (see K'ang Hsi), $800-$1,000. Bulb bowl, 3¼" h., 9" dia., tou-ts'ai decoration (see Yung Cheng), $3,000-$3,500. Bowl (shallow), 7¾" dia., tou-t'sai decoration, Ch'ien Lung mark and period (see Ch'ien Lung), $1,400-$1,800.*

*Satsuma*

(L. to R., front) Two figures, 3½" h., c. 1925, $160-$180 each. Seated figure with fan, 3½" h., signed Genzan, c. 1870, $1,500-$1,800. Teapot (Naeshirogawa), Edo period, $1,200-$1,500; Suiteki (water dropper), 2½" h., 18th century, $950-$1,250. Rear: Mizusashi (water jar), 6" h., late Edo period, $2,200-$2,800. Figure of a bijin, 5¼" h., $1,500-$1,800. Double gourd vase, signed Tanzan, early 20th century, $275-$325. Figure of Rakan, 5¼" h., c. 1860, $1,700-$2,100. Bottle/vase, shark's skin glaze, 18th century, $2,500-$3,200.

*Chinese Blue and White Wares*

(L. to R.): Vase, 12" h., K'ang Hsi mark and period, garlic top, $1,500-$1,700. Dish, 8¼" dia., K'ang Hsi period, $400-$500. Vase (with lid), 11¼" h., K'ang Hsi period, molded form, $900-$1,200. Vase, 10" h., Ch'ien Lung period, $1,000-$1,200.

Korean screens (Pyong P'ung) date as far back as the first century A.D., but it is screens dating from the Yi Dynasty that seem to be of interest to collectors. Before the 14th century, the folding screen was held together with cord, but from the 14th century on paper hinges were used. The Korean screen can have embroidered or painted panels with motifs. Motifs include landscapes, florals, animals, court scenes, etc.

(See: Furniture, Korean)

## Ko Yao
*(Chinese)*

Ko Yao, the famous Chinese crackleware, was a product of the Ko kilns run by two brothers during the Sung Dynasty. The crackling is caused by the glaze cooling and contracting at a different rate than the underlying body, thereby breaking into sections separated by fine surface lines or "cracks." Once discovered the technique was expanded and the potters could produce the crackle at will, to the point of regulating the size of the cracks. Pigment was then rubbed into the crevices to heighten the design. Many fine Ko pieces have a primary crackle outlined in black and a secondary, finer crackle outlined in brown. The glaze colors are typically gray to gray green. Ko Yao wares have continued in production since the Sung Dynasty.

*Ko Yao vase, 14½" h., 18th century*

Bowl, 10" dia., 18th century, covered with a grayish green glaze, the crackle stained with brown and black .............................. $500-600

Flask, 21" h., Yung Chêng period, six-character mark in underglaze blue, of quatrefoil shape with stylized scroll handles, covered with a fine gray glaze, the crackle stained in darker shades of gray and brown ..................................... $15,000-18,000

Vase, 6¾" h., 18th century, fish roe crackle on an opaque white glaze. (See Color Section) ............................................. $400-600

Vase, 8" h., Yung Chêng period, six-character mark in underglaze blue, of squat shape with a narrow neck and bulb-shaped mouth, molded with two animal mask and ring handles, covered with a thick, opaque, gray green glaze with a large crackle, with a brown wash on the foot .......................... $8,000-10,000

Vase, 14½" h., 18th century, crackle over opaque, grayish glaze, with dragon handles and copper rim. (Illus.) .......................... $800-1,000

## Kozuka
*(Japanese)*

The Kozuka is the small utility knife which was worn (carried) with the sword (wakizashi). They are highly decorated and may have applied silver, shakudo, relief carving, etc. Prices for Kozuka have escalated in the past few years.

**Terminology:**

**Shakudo** — copper with a small percentage of gold content.
**Nanako** — a ground punched with minute dots.
**Ishime** — a rough surface.
**Shibuichi** — a metal which has a large percentage of copper and a small percentage of silver.

Iron Kozuka, motif of gourds and vines of inlaid silver ........................ $200-220

Iron Kozuka, 19th century, inlaid copper fans ................................ $100-120

Iron Kozuka, 19th century, gold, bronze, and silver inlay of monkey and insects ................................................... $300-400

\*Iron and shibuichi, 19th century, gilt and silvered takazogan
with cat hiding among peonies watching a butterfly (Illus.) ........................$200

Shakudo Kozuka, 19th century, high relief motif of frog
(shibuichi) and lily pad (shakudo) ..........................................$400-650

Shakudo Kozuka, 19th century, gilt and silver inlay of dragon
and clouds and Mt. Fuji ................................................$2,000-2,250

Shakudo Nanako Kozuka, 19th century, motif of applied gold
and shakudo birds ......................................................$450-700

Shakudo Nanako Kozuka, halberd applied in gold, copper,
and shakudo ...........................................................$300-425

Shakudo Kozuka, relief motif of vegetables naturalistically
enameled ..............................................................$185-240

Shibuichi Kozuka, 19th century, gilt and silver geese in flight ..............$185-215

Shibuichi and iron Kozuka, 19th century, gilt and silvered
takazogan, motif of cat and peony .......................................$250-325

Shibuichi Kozuka, 19th century, gilt, motif of birds in flight .............$285-350

Shibuichi Kozuka, 19th century, gilt and shakudo motif of
flying cranes and waves .................................................$200-250

Shibuichi Kozuka, with sunken relief carving of a figure,
table, and book .........................................................$500-700

Shibuichi Kozuka, 19th century, motif of a figure and
waterfall applied in shakudo, gold, and copper, the backside
having a dragon .........................................................$380-470

Shibuichi Kozuka, 19th century, ishime ground with motif of
Mt. Fuji, quarter moon, and birds in flight, silver inlay ...............$600-800

*Kozuka, iron and shibuichi with a cat among peonies*

## Kraak Porcelain
### (Chinese)

*Kraak porcelain dish, 14½" dia., Wan Li period*

The name "Kraak" refers to a certain type of blue and white porcelain export ware of the 17th century. The Dutch traders gave it this name after their capture of the Portuguese ships (called Caraques) in 1602. Kraak ware consisted mostly of deep dishes or plates but also included water bottles, vases, bowls, and ewers. The porcelain is light and has a ringing tone when struck. There are small pittings in the glaze. Occasionally plates are marked on the back with an egret or a hare. A typical deep dish has a broad rim decorated with alternating broad and narrow panels which frame a central medallion that is decorated in designs including insects, animals, figures, or flower-filled vases. The rim panels are decorated with alternating birds, fruits, and emblems separated by narrow panels of ribbon or geometric designs. The distinctive decoration of Kraak wares sets it apart from other blue and white products of the period, particularly in regard to its dense and profuse overall designs.

(See: Blue and White; Chinese Export)

Bowl, 6" dia., a bird and insects encircled by a floral design,
with divisions of ju-i heads and emblems ...............................$500-600

Bowl, 7" dia., with deep sides, with birds and insects in the
center, surrounded by alternating panels of bamboo,
butterflies, and flowers, with fruit form and scroll panels on
the exterior ...........................................................$600-800

Bowl, 8" dia., the center decorated with emblems surrounded
by fruit and symbols, the exterior with a design of floral
panels .................................................................. $600-800

Bottle, 14" h., baluster form with panels of deer and
flowering branches below ju-i lappets, in gray blue glaze ..................... $1,000-1,200

Dish, 8" dia., center with a flower-filled vase, with alternating
panels of flowers and birds on rim ......................................... $400-600

Dish, 9½" dia., center decorated with two deer in a
landscape, border panels with alternating floral and fruit
design .................................................................. $800-1,000

Dish, 14½" dia., Wan Li period, water scene with ducks
surrounded by radiating panels enclosing fruits and
emblems. (Illus.) ....................................................... $800-1,000

Dish, 18" dia., with a barbed edge center medallion of a bird
near a pond, border with alternating panels of flowers and
emblems ................................................................ $800-1,000

Dish, 20" dia., with the center depicting a flower-filled vase
on a tripod, the borders with a floral design repeated
between lined panels; restoration on the rim ............................... $400-600

*Dish, 20" dia., densely patterned showing a bird in flight
near a large peony spray with two other birds standing on
rockwork below, with radiating border panels of scholars,
peach sprays, utensils, and Buddhist emblems, damaged ...................... $1,300

## Kuan
### (Chinese)

Kuan wares were first produced during the southern Sung Dynasty. The
name "Kuan" means official, royal, or imperial. This beautifully made
porcelain is set apart from other wares of the period by its brilliant,
gemlike luster. This thick shining glaze has colors varying from a bluish
to grayish green — from a greenish white to different shades of buff or
gray. With magnification countless minute bubbles can be seen in the
glaze. The large, prominent crackle that was used was of the "crab's
claw" variety. These wares may have spur marks similar to those found
on Japanese ceramics.

Bowl, 6" dia., Yung Chêng mark and period, covered with a
creamy glaze, with brown-black stained crackle ............................. $4,000-6,000

Dish, 8" dia., Yuan Dynasty, covered with a creamy crackle
glaze .................................................................. $1,200-1,400

Vase, 6¼" h., Sung Dynasty, of "hu" shape with tubular
handles, with underglaze slip scrollwork decoration at the
shoulders, covered with a blue green crackled glaze, a gold
lacquer repair at the lip ................................................. $1,000-1,200

Vase, 6½" h., Yung Chêng period, seal mark in underglaze
blue, with a bulbous body and a tall neck, covered with a
silvery gray glaze, with crackle in faint brown and black
stains .................................................................. $6,000-8,000

Vase, 7" h., Ch'ien Lung period, seal mark in underglaze
blue, pear-shaped with a bulbous mouth, the neck with two
rings in shallow relief, covered with a finely crackled
lavender blue glaze, the foot covered with a brown slip .................... $20,000-25,000

Vase, 8" h., Yung Chêng seal mark and period, ovoid form,
divided into six lobes, the short neck turned down and
fluted, set on a pedestal base, covered in a pale bluish-white
glaze, poorly crackled with brown stain ................................... $2,000-2,500

Vase, 13" h., 18th century, ovoid form, with a short neck and
thick molded lip, decorated in a grayish beige glaze with
brown and black crackle .................................................. $800-1,000

# Kuang-tung Stoneware
*(Chinese)*

*Figure, late 19th century, flambé glaze on brown stoneware, 11" h.*

Kuang-tung stoneware comes from the kilns located near Canton in Kuang-tung province. The body of the wares can be red, yellow, or buff. They are typically glazed in a thick, opaque, dark bluish glaze which is flecked and streaked with combinations of gray, purple, red, blue, or brown (similar to a flambé glaze). Information for dating its origins is scanty; some evidence indicates the Ming Dynasty; other evidence points to 18th century development.

Figure, 7" h., late 19th century, seated on rocks and holding a scroll, glazed in white and purple flambé on a brown stoneware body .................................................................. $150-200

Figure, 8" h., late 19th century, seated on rockwork with white and purple flambé glaze on a brown stoneware body ..................... $150-200

Figure, 11" h., late 19th century, wearing high hat, glazed in a white and purple flambé gla on a brown stoneware body (Illus.) ....................................................................... $150-200

Figure group, 14" h., 19th century, with a figure astride a foo dog, the hands left unglazed, revealing the dark brown clay, the rest with a heavy blue flambé glaze. (Illus.) ....................... $1,200-1,400

Jar, 8" h., 18th century, mei ping shaped, the reddish clay covered with a heavy purple-blue flambé glaze which ends in heavy puddles around the foot ............................................ $500-700

Jar, 9" h., 18th century, covered with a thick blue green streaked and mottled glaze fading to tan at the mouth, the glaze falling short of the foot, chips at the base ............................ $250-350

Vase, 14" h., 19th century, bottle form, covered with a mottled milky blue glaze ....................................................... $800-900

*Kuang-tung stoneware figure, 19th century*

# Kutani
*(Japanese)*

Kutani, in Kaga province (post Meiji prefecture, Ishikawa), is synonymous with beautiful and appealing porcelain wares. Kutani wares were first produced during the mid-1600s. Kutani may be divided into the following specific groups:

1. Ko Kutani (old Kutani or early Kutani) — the range of colors used on ko Kutani included bold and somewhat dark shades of red, green, purple, yellow, and brown.

2. Ao Kutani (green Kutani) — wares decorated with a green glaze and colors including green, yellow, and purple with black outlining.

3. Akaye Kutani — red designs on a white ground.

4. Akaji Kinja Kutani — a red ground with gold or silver designs.

5. Hachiroye Kutani — combining No. 3 (akaye) and No. 4 (akaji kinja) and/or a red ground with gold designs and motifs in under-the-glaze blue.

There are, of course, certain classes of Kutani wares made since 1875 for Western export which are enameled in every conceivable color and which have motifs styled for Western tastes.

*Kutani box, Daikoku's bag*

*Akaye Kutani tea caddy*

| | |
|---|---|
| Berry set, one large bowl, six small bowls, red and gilt border, courtesans in procession, Mt. Fuji in background, polychrome enamels | $165-210 |
| Berry set, one large bowl, four small bowls, each piece on four legs, deep red border, floral motif in polychrome enamels | $110-130 |
| Bowl, 5½″ dia., polychrome, red/gold border trim, governess and two children on picnic | $200-225 |
| Bowl, 7″ dia., akaye-1,000 faces | $75-90 |
| Bowl, 8″ dia., akaye, motif of mythological figures and ju-i lappets, exterior motif of flowers | $200-250 |
| Bowls (pair), 7″ dia., ao Kutani, central motif of carp, floral diapered border, exterior having stylized foliage | $600-800 |
| Box, 6″ dia., 19th century, Daikoku's bag. (Illus. here and on Front Cover) | $1,200-1,500 |
| Coffee pot, c. 1900, AO. (Illus.) | $800-1,200 |
| Coffee pot, late 19th century, red and gilt. (Illus.) | $600-800 |
| Dish, 7″ dia., ko Kutani, square form with motif of pine branch and perched bird | $1,100-2,000 |
| Dish, 7″ dia., red/gilt border, polychrome Kannon riding a dragon | $200-225 |
| Dish, 10″ dia., ao Kutani, band of birds and floral roundels | $250-300 |
| Dish, 10″ dia., polychrome and gilt figures against a riverscape, blue/gilt border | $120-150 |
| Figure, 12″ h., c. 1900, woman in flowered kimono holding an open fan, polychrome | $500-700 |
| Figure, 16″ h., woman holding a bird in her hand and wearing a kimono having geometric diapered pattern, polychrome and gilt | $800-1,100 |
| Incense burner, 7″ h., ao Kutani, square form with motif of phoenix and flowering trees, elephant head and loose ring handles | $600-800 |
| Plate, late 19th century. (See Color Section) | $125-175 |
| Tea caddy, akaye (Illus.) | $120-140 |
| Tea set, covered pot, sugar and creamer, six cups and saucers, orange trim, motif of various birds, double lotus finials | $150-175 |

Tea set, covered pot, sugar and creamer, six cups and saucers, six cake plates, orange/red trim, motif of woman and children in procession, double lotus finials . . . . . . . . . . . . . . . . . . . . . . . . . . . . . . . . . . . . . . . . . . . . . . . . . . . . . $150-200

Tea set, covered pot, sugar, open creamer, four cups and saucers, recessed lids, cobalt blue and gold with red roses . . . . . . . . . . . . . . . . . . . . . . $200-225

Tea set, akaye, covered pot, sugar, creamer, five cups and four saucers, one cake plate, motifs of birds and clouds . . . . . . . . . . . . . . . . . . . . . . $175-200

Tea set, teapot (right angle handle), five cups, gilt with motif of 36 poets . . . . . . . . . . . . . . . . . . . . . . . . . . . . . . . . . . . . . . . . . . . . . . . . . . . . . . $1,200-1,500

Tea set, covered pot, sugar, open creamer, 1,000 faces, polychrome with gilt trim . . . . . . . . . . . . . . . . . . . . . . . . . . . . . . . . . . . . . . . . . . . . $200-250

Vase, 12" h., AO, 19th century, Fuku mark. (Illus.) . . . . . . . . . . . . . . . . . . . . . . . . $300-400

Vase, 12" h., polychrome on a red ground. (Illus.) . . . . . . . . . . . . . . . . . . . . . . . . $150-200

Vase, 2½", polychrome and gilt, overall continuous motif of men on horseback . . . . . . . . . . . . . . . . . . . . . . . . . . . . . . . . . . . . . . . . . . . . . . . . . $300-400

Vases (pair), 18" h., octagonal, each panel containing medallions filled with beautiful women, akaye . . . . . . . . . . . . . . . . . . . . . . $1,200-1,500

Vase, 11" h., akaye, bulbous with elongated neck, elephant head and loose ring handles, continuous motif of scholars . . . . . . . . . . . . . . . $225-285

Vase, 10" h., polychrome and gilt, double gourd form, upper portions with chrysanthemoid mons, lower portion having lotus scrolls . . . . . . . . . . . . . . . . . . . . . . . . . . . . . . . . . . . . . . . . . . . . . . . . . . . . . . $225-300

Vase, 9" h., polychrome and gilt, floral motifs in fan-shaped reserves on a white ground . . . . . . . . . . . . . . . . . . . . . . . . . . . . . . . . . . . . . . . . . $100-150

Vase, 16" h., ovoid, polychrome (pastel hues) motif of a waterfall, mountains, and lake . . . . . . . . . . . . . . . . . . . . . . . . . . . . . . . . . . . . . . . $450-525

Vase, 25" h., akaye, reserve of Bijin and attendants, neck and base ornamented with cloud scrolls . . . . . . . . . . . . . . . . . . . . . . . . . . . . . $1,200-1,600

Vase, 7" h., silver overlay. (Illus. here and in Color Section) . . . . . . . . . . . . . . . . . . $200-225

*Kutani vase with silver overlay*

*Coffeepots, Ao (left), late 19th century (right). Courtesy Alan and Ina Sims*

*Kutani vase with red ground*　　　　*Kutani vase with scenic motif (Ao)*

This term refers to an extremely fine group of porcelains made by the imperial kilns during the 18th century. Literally translated the term means "ancient moon terrace," a description that does not seem to relate logically to the wares. These porcelains are rare. They bear red seal marks which precede and follow black enameled poems. There are one or two additional red seals on the sides. The detailing is extremely fine. The subject matter usually includes people, birds, or floral designs. These porcelains were diminutive in size, rarely exceeding 7″ in height. This style of decorating was copied in the 19th century on larger pieces of porcelain. The detail is painted in the same meticulous style as the originals. The style is also to be found on 20th century eggshell porcelain but the work is of inferior quality.

(See: Made in China)

# Ku Yüeh Hsuan
## (Chinese)

Box, 3½″ dia., 19th century, Ch'ien Lung, seal mark in overglaze blue, the cover with gnarled branches and prunus blossoms in black with black and red seals, the borders with overglaze, finely painted ju-i symbols . . . . . . . . . . . . . . . . . . . . . . . . . . . . . . . . . . . . . . . $400-500

Vase, 4″ h., Ch'ien Lung period, seal mark in overglaze blue enamel, pear-shaped body with bulbous "garlic" top; neck inscribed with a poem in black with three iron red seals; body decorated with two yellow flowers turned around two light brown enameled trees with pale sepia foliage and pink roses and birds, with single blue chrysanthemum having pale olive green leaves, delicately executed . . . . . . . . . . . . . . . . . . . . . . . . . . . . . . . . . . . . $35,000-40,000

Vase, 13¾″ h., 19th century (commemorative mark of Ch'ien Lung within a double square), of double gourd shape with intricate, black enameled borders at the neck, waist, and foot, with garden scenes in famille rose palette, with black enameled poems and red seals on the back, bearing the Castiglione signature . . . . . . . . . . . . . . . . . . . . . . . . . . . . . . . . . . . . . . . . . . . . . . . . . . . . . . . . $3,000-3,500

Vase, 16½" h., 19th century (commemorative Ch'ien Lung seal mark in overglaze blue within a double square), quadrangular shape with a circular base; neck and base with delicately enameled borders in blue, with four scenes of men in gardens with mythological beasts . . . . . . . . . . . . . . . . . . . . . . . . . . . . . . . . . . . . . . . . . . . $3,500-4,000

## Kyo Wares
### (Japanese)

Kyo wares (also called Kyoto wares) refers to the pottery and porcelain produced in the kilns in and around Kyoto, Japan.

(See: Eiraku; Kenzan; Ninsei; Satsuma)

*Kyoto mizusashi*

Bottle, 7" h. (Ko Kiyomizu), Edo period, blue, green, gilt. (See Front Cover and Color Section) . . . . . . . . . . . . . . . . . . . . . . . . . . . . . . . . $12,000-15,000

Bottle, 8" h. (Ko Kiyomizu), Edo period, pear shaped, blue, green and gilt flowers and hedges . . . . . . . . . . . . . . . . . . . . . . . . . . . . . . . . . . . $9,000-12,000

Bowl, 8" dia., late 19th century, signed Shozan. (See Color Section) . . . . . . . . . . . . . . . . . . . . . . . . . . . . . . . . . . . . . . . . . . . . . . . . . . . . . . . . . . . $600-800

Bowl, covered, Awata, Edo period, iron oxide and underglaze blue. (Illus.) . . . . . . . . . . . . . . . . . . . . . . . . . . . . . . . . . . . . . . . . . . . . . $600-800

Candlestick, 8¼" h., Awata, Edo period. (Illus. here and in Color Section) . . . . . . . . . . . . . . . . . . . . . . . . . . . . . . . . . . . . . . . . . . . . . . . . . . $900-1,200

Chaire, late Edo period, brown and blue motif of birds, ivory cover . . . . . . . . . . . . . . . . . . . . . . . . . . . . . . . . . . . . . . . . . . . . . . . . . . . . . . . $300-500

Chawan, 2½" h., early 19th century, blue, green, white and gilt with paulownia blossom on reverse. (Illus.) . . . . . . . . . . . . . . . . . . . . . . $700-900

Candlestick, 8¼" h., Awata, Edo period. (Illus. here and in Color Section) . . . . . . . . . . . . . . . . . . . . . . . . . . . . . . . . . . . . . . . . . . . . . . . . . . $900-1,200

Mizusashi, 6" h., late Edo period, signed Gosan saku. (Illus. here and in Color Section) . . . . . . . . . . . . . . . . . . . . . . . . . . . . . . . . . . . . . $2,250-2,800

Teapot, 3½" h., late 18th century. (Illus. here and in Color Section) . . . . . . . . . . . . . . . . . . . . . . . . . . . . . . . . . . . . . . . . . . . . . . . . . . . . . . $1,200-1,500

Wine pot, 7" dia., c. 1750. (Illus. here and in Color Section) . . . . . . . . . . . . . . . $1,700-2,200

*Kyoto (Ko Kyomidzu) bottle*

*Kyoto (Awata) candlestick*

*Kyoto chawan*

*Kyoto (Awata) bowl with cover*

*Kyoto wine (left) and teapot (right)*

## Lac Burgauté
### (Chinese)

The origin of Lac Burgauté probably dates back to the 18th century, although there are occasional references to its manufacture during the reign of K'ang Hsi. It is a biscuit porcelain which is covered with a black lacquer and inlaid with designs in mother-of-pearl.

(See: Lacquer)

> Bowl, 4¾" h., 18th century, with black lacquer sides in
> eight-petal lotus form, inlaid with iridescent mother-of-pearl
> in designs of flowers, Taoist emblems, and "hundred
> antiques"; interior and base lined with silver . . . . . . . . . . . . . . . . . . . . . . . . . . . . . . . . . . . $200-250

## Lacquer

Lacquer is derived from the sap of the lac tree, *Rhu vernicifera* (Urishi in Japanese). Lacquer may be applied to wood, metal, ceramics, papier-mache, or built up and carved.

**China:** The earliest Chinese lacquer wares date from the Han Dynasty (5 to 3 BC). It is the lacquered objects made since the start of the Ch'ing Dynasty that are most available on today's market. Chinese lacquer ware may be divided into three categories: 1. carved lacquer (including cinnabar — see Cinnabar); 2. furniture and screens; 3. ornamental objects. Furniture and screens (see: Furniture, Screens) can be found having inlaid or incised motifs. The Chinese have used mother-of-pearl, silver, gold, tortoiseshell, semiprecious stones (Lac Burgauté), etc., to form beautiful motifs on lacquered objects. Of special interest are coromandel screens. Coromandel screens derive their name from the Indian Coromandel coast, from where they were exported to Western markets. With the new relations established with the People's Republic of China, it is expected that new as well as collectible lacquer wares will soon become highly available in Western markets.

**Japan:** The technique for lacquer wares was obtained in Japan via China. During the Nara period, the lacquer art reached great heights. It was at that time the addition of coloring agents was developed as well as the technique for applying lacquer to various bases. Methods developed since that time have brought Japanese lacquer to a degree of excellence unsurpassed anywhere. The lacquer art form of Japan encompasses many varieties.

### Terminology:

**Maki-e** — application of gold and silver to a lacquered object.
**Hiramakie** — designs raised above the surface only to the height of the film of lacquer (a flat sprinkled picture).
**Takamakie** — relief lacquer decoration.
**Kinmakie** — lacquer with gold ornamentations.
**Ginmakie** — lacquer with silver ornamentations.
**Kirigane** — gold strips or squares applied to small areas.
**Negoro** — red lacquer over black.
**Shibayama** — named for its inventor, this style made use of ivory, tortoiseshell, coral, mother-of-pearl, etc., to build up the decoration.

**Korea:** Korean lacquer wares are believed to date as early as 440 A.D. In past years, very little Korean lacquer wares were exported to the West. It is however, lacquer wares of the late Koryo and Yi dynasties that appear to be of interest to dealers and collectors. The Korean artisans were skilled at inlay. Lacquered wares can have scrollwork of silver wires and/or inlay of mother-of-pearl, tortoiseshell, and/or Kwagak (painted ox horn). The ox horn was converted into sheets of various contours and sizes and then painted on the reverse, thus allowing the bright colors to last for centuries. Later pieces, dating from the Yi Dynasty, have intricate motifs and designs. Early pieces tend to have more simple motifs.

(See: Cinnabar; Furniture; Inro)

### Lacquer, Chinese

Brush holder, 4¾" h., early 19th century, cylindrical form, gilt on a brown ground, motif of wisteria scrolls . . . . . . . . . . . . . . . . . . . . . . . . . . . . . $160-220

Bowls (pair), 4½" dia., 18th century (Lac Burgauté), lotusform, black ground, floral motif of inlaid mother-of-pearl, silver lining (minor damages) . . . . . . . . . . . . . . . . . . . . . . $500-600

Bowls (pair), 6½" dia., (Lac Burgauté), early 18th century, mother-of-pearl inlay motifs forming pine and willow on a black ground, silver lining . . . . . . . . . . . . . . . . . . . . . . . . . . . . . . . . . . . . . . . . . . . . . $600-800

Box, 7" dia., 19th century, black with high relief carving of a dragon and the flaming pearl on black ground . . . . . . . . . . . . . . . . . . . . . . . . . . . $400-480

Boxes, covered (pair), 18" x 14", 19th century, gilt with
painted motifs of gardens and women strolling among
flowers and trees . . . . . . . . . . . . . . . . . . . . . . . . . . . . . . . . . . . . . . . . . . $1,000-1,200

Box, covered, 14" l., late 19th century, octagonal with
continuous motif of gardens within reserves having borders
filled with key fret in gold on a black ground (some chipping) . . . . . . . . . . . . . . . . . . $120-160

Cups (pair), 4" dia., 18th century, (Lac Burgauté),
blackground with S-shaped panels filled with flowers of
inlaid mother-of-pearl, silver lining (some inlay missing,
minor chipping) . . . . . . . . . . . . . . . . . . . . . . . . . . . . . . . . . . . . . . . . . . . . . $450-600

Figure, 13½" h., 19th century, Kuan ti executed in red and
gilt lacquer . . . . . . . . . . . . . . . . . . . . . . . . . . . . . . . . . . . . . . . . . . . . . . . . . . $220-250

Group, 16" l., early 19th century, boy upon a water buffalo,
buffalo being black with gilt highlights, boy executed in red
and black with gilt highlights . . . . . . . . . . . . . . . . . . . . . . . . . . . . . . . . . . $1,100-1,500

Panel, 24" x 10", late 19th century, gilt lacquer carved with
women waving at warriors on horseback (minor damage to
frame) . . . . . . . . . . . . . . . . . . . . . . . . . . . . . . . . . . . . . . . . . . . . . . . . . . . . . $100-135

Panel, 43" x 9", early 19th century, red and black with
painted figures and landscapes . . . . . . . . . . . . . . . . . . . . . . . . . . . . . . . . . . . . $100-125

Tea caddies (pair), 8" h., 19th century, black ground with gilt
motif of figures and flowers, pewter lining . . . . . . . . . . . . . . . . . . . . . . . . . . . . . $400-500

Tray, 14" dia., early 19th century, (Lac Burgauté), inlaid
mother-of-pearl floral motif of blossoming plum branches
with quarter moon above set on a brown ground, border
containing mother-of-pearl chrysanthemum scrolls (slight
chipping) . . . . . . . . . . . . . . . . . . . . . . . . . . . . . . . . . . . . . . . . . . . . . . . . . . . $900-1,000

## Lacquer, Japanese

Panels (two), 27" h., c. 1920, black lacquer, Shibayama style
motif of potted plants . . . . . . . . . . . . . . . . . . . . . . . . . . . . . . . . . . . . . . . . . . . $750-900

Shrine, 13" h., 19th century, black with gilt mounts, gilt
interior with Buddha seated on lotus base . . . . . . . . . . . . . . . . . . . . . . . . . . . . . $800-1,000

*Japanese Namban shrine, Momoyama period. Sold at Christie's, New York, for
$170,500

Suzuribako (box for ink stone, water dropper, and brushes), 8¼" x 6¾", 19th century, gold hiramakie, takamakie, kirigane, with landscape and waterfall . . . . . . . . . . . . . . . . . . . . . . . . . . . . . . . . . . . . . . . $1,200-1,500

Sword stand, 22½" h., 19th century, red lacquer with rectangular base, waved pole support carved with peacock and floral motif . . . . . . . . . . . . . . . . . . . . . . . . . . . . . . . . . . . . . . . . $300-350

Tray, 11" dia., late 19th century, R - bracket feet, gold and silver hiramakie with floral mons on a black ground . . . . . . . . . . . . . . . . . . . . . . . . . $250-300

Tray, 13" x 9", 19th century, plum and pine motif in hiramakie on mura nashiji ground . . . . . . . . . . . . . . . . . . . . . . . . . . . . . . . . . . . . . . . $700-950

Vases (pair), 7" h., late 19th century, gilt lacquer with motif of figures and flowers Shibayama style (some inlay missing) . . . . . . . . . . . . . . . . $1,200-1,500

Box, late 19th century, black ground. (Illus.) . . . . . . . . . . . . . . . . . . . . . . . . . . . . $600-800

Box (covered), 8" dia., 20th century, negoro, carved in the form of a carp with fin forming finial . . . . . . . . . . . . . . . . . . . . . . . . . . . . . . . . . . . . . $300-400

Box, 7" h., late 19th century, gilt lacquer with inlay, Shibayama style, motif of figures and wisteria (some inlay missing) . . . . . . . . . . . . . . . . . . . . . . . . . . . . . . . . . . . . . . . . . . . . . . . . . . . . . $800-1,000

Box (covered), 4" x 2", 19th century, silver, gold, and red hiramakie on muranashiji ground . . . . . . . . . . . . . . . . . . . . . . . . . . . . . . . . . . . . . . $650-800

Box (covered cosmetic), 4¼" h., divided by gilt horizontal bands and peony scrolls with domed cover (minor chipping) . . . . . . . . . . . . . . . . . . . $350-400

Box (fan-shaped), 4" l., late 19th century, hiramakie landscape and huts, interior in nashiji . . . . . . . . . . . . . . . . . . . . . . . . . . . . . . . . . . . . . . . . . . $500-700

Boxes (pair, covered), 18" h., late 19th century, hokai, motif of leaves and leaf scrolls painted on nashiji ground, domed covers and ribbed form with four legs . . . . . . . . . . . . . . . . . . . . . . . . . . . . . $1,800-2,200

Card case (calling cards), 4⅛" h., 19th century, seascape motif in gold on gold togidashi ground featuring boats, mountains, and fisherman in takamakie . . . . . . . . . . . . . . . . . . . . . . . . . . . . . . . . . $400-600

Cabinet, 5" x 6" 4½" h, 19th century, exterior motifs of pavilion, cart, trees, hills, hinged doors, silver hardware, three drawers lacquered togidashi with brocade patterns . . . . . . . . . . . . . . . . . . . $6,000-7,000

Dish, 6½" dia., early 20th century, gold motif of vines, flowers, and trees on nashiji ground . . . . . . . . . . . . . . . . . . . . . . . . . . . . . . . . . . . . . . $75-100

Dish, 13" dia., 19th century, gold and black hiramakie on nashiji ground, water plants and riverscape with floral roundels . . . . . . . . . . . . . . . . . . . . . . . . . . . . . . . . . . . . . . . . . . . . . . . . . . . . . . . . . $500-700

*Japanese lacquer traveling box*

Hibachi, 11" dia., late 19th century, gold hiramakie,
takamakie, on kiri wood, metal liner, floral motif .............................. $500-650

Kogo (incense box), 18th century, round, hiramakie with
persimmons and branches on nashiji ground ........................... $1,500-1,750

Kogo (incense box), 19th century, red lacquer with carving of
birds and chrysanthemums .................................................... $300-350

Mask, early 20th century, red and black lacquer on
papier-mache in the form of Otoko ......................................... $275-325

*Shrine, Namban (case 11" x 16¼" x 2"), Momoyama period.
(Illus.) ...................................................................... $170,500

## Lacquer, Korean

Vases (pair), 26" h., early 20th century, black ground inlaid
with nautilus shell and mother-of-pearl to form flowering
peony branches and peacocks ............................................... $700-900


Lowestoft is a completely erroneous name attributed to a vast quantity of 18th century export china produced for the Western market bearing coats of arms, crests, monograms, etc. Although strictly Chinese in manufacture, these items appear thoroughly European.

(See: Chinese Export)

## Lowestoft
*(Chinese)*


Lung-Ch'uan is a village located in southern Chekiang province that produced celadon ware during the Sung, Yuan, and Ming dynasties. Although a wide range of celadon colors emerged from the kilns, the most famous glaze bearing the name of Lung-Ch'uan is a blue green to green shade applied on a thick, light gray body. This celadon appears in both uncrackled and crackled glazes. One particular feature of these celadons is the reddish brown tint on the unglazed portions which occurred when the exposed biscuit was subjected to the fire of the kiln. The decoration of these wares can be relief-molded, carved, or etched.

(See: Celadon)

## Lung-Ch'uan
*(Chinese)*


From 1891, wares produced in China for export to the United States were marked "China" or "Made in China." These markings or backstamps were provided in accordance with the McKinley Tariff Act, which specified that the country of origin must appear on any items imported to the United States. From 1917, paper labels or stickers were sometimes used in lieu of a backstamp and they too would designate country of origin in the manner described above. In some instances, marks or labels have been known to be deliberately removed from the porcelain in an attempt to pass the new for the old. Knowledge of style, color, and techniques introduced during the various reigns will help the collector to identify the fakes.

(See: I-Hsing Mud Figures)

## Made in China
*(Chinese)*

Bowl, 5" dia., rice pattern, blue and white decoration ........................... $10-20

Bowl, 8" dia., green interior, pastel enameled lotus,

chrysanthemum and peony blossoms on a yellow ground . . . . . . . . . . . . . . . . . . . . . $110-130

Bowl (covered), 5" dia., rice bowl of rice pattern design decorated in red and blue . . . . . . . . . . . . . . . . . . . . . . . . . . . . . . . . . . . . . . . . . $12-15

Bowl (covered), 6" h., with lotus finial on lid, Blanc de Chine porcelain with milky white glaze, modeled in form of lotus blossom . . . . . . . . . . . . . . . . . . . . . . . . . . . . . . . . . . . . . . . . . . . . . . . . . . . . $140-150

Bowls (pair), 10½" dia., turquoise glazed interior with heavily enameled "hundred antiques" motif on pale green exterior . . . . . . . . . . . . . . . . $175-220

Bowl set, consisting of 10" dia. covered bowl and four matching covered rice bowls with underplates. Millefleur design on gilt background . . . . . . . . . . . . . . . . . . . . . . . . . . . . . . . . . . . . . . . $400-550

Bulb bowl, celadon glaze with underglaze blue decoration of garden landscape . . . . . . . . . . . . . . . . . . . . . . . . . . . . . . . . . . . . . . . . . . . . $40-60

Charger, 18" dia., celadon glaze with thickly applied enamel decoration of a flower-filled vase in the center . . . . . . . . . . . . . . . . . . . . . $125-150

Cigarette set, consisting of an ashtray, match holder, and cigarette box, decorated in light blue monochrome glaze . . . . . . . . . . . . . . $25-35

Dish, 8" dia., decorated in millefleur design of pink, yellow, green, and iron red flowers on a black ground . . . . . . . . . . . . . . . . . . . . . . . $50-60

Figure, 6" h., Kuan Yin standing on rockwork . . . . . . . . . . . . . . . . . . . . . . $1,012

Figure, 12" h., Kuan Yin standing on rockwork . . . . . . . . . . . . . . . . . . . . . $40-60

Figures (pair), 18" h., phoenix birds in rose enamels perched on rockwork base . . . . . . . . . . . . . . . . . . . . . . . . . . . . . . . . . . . . . . . . . $700-800

Figures (set), 6½" h., Eight Immortals, polychrome enamels on porcelain . . . . . . . . . . . . . . . . . . . . . . . . . . . . . . . . . . . . . . . . . . . . . . . $85-100

Figures (set), 10" h., Eight Immortals, polychrome enamels on porcelain . . . . . . . . . . . . . . . . . . . . . . . . . . . . . . . . . . . . . . . . . . . . . . $100-150

Figures (set), 2¾" h., miniatures of Eight Immortals, polychrome enamel on porcelain . . . . . . . . . . . . . . . . . . . . . . . . . . . . . . $100-125

Figures (set), 12" h., Eight Immortals, bisque finish . . . . . . . . . . . . . . . . . $85-100

Figure group, 5" h. x 8" w., depicting three Chinese boys supporting a large peach . . . . . . . . . . . . . . . . . . . . . . . . . . . . . . . . . . . . $100-125

Foo dogs (pair), 8" h., on pedestals, glazed in yellow green and brown . . . . . . . . . . . . . . . . . . . . . . . . . . . . . . . . . . . . . . . . . . . . . . . $50-75

*Made in China roof ornament, 19th/20th century*          *Made in China roof ornament, 19th/20th century*

Foo dogs (pair), 32" h., male and female on pedestal base,
decorated in green, yellow, and ochre enamels ............................... $800-1,000

Garden seat, 18" h., with molded dragons and studded
borders on reticulated, barrel-shaped form, completely
covered in a streaked and mottled lavender/purple flambé
glaze ..................................................................... $500-600

Ginger jars (pair), 14" h., high shouldered form, flat lids with
orange spire finials, rooster pattern decoration on white
ground ................................................................... $145-150

*Made in China partial tea set, applied pewter decoration, marked "Made in Shanghai"*

Ginger jars (pair), 8½" h., green lily pads and pink blossoms
in relief on an aqua ground ................................................. $100-120

Ginger jars (pair), 5½" h., large floral motif outlined in black
on a white ground ......................................................... $35-50

Ginger jars (pair), 6" h., turquoise ground color with lotus
pads and blossoms molded in relief and decorated in tones of
pink and green, with one white glazed crane, also in relief ..................... $90-125

Jardinieres (pair), 12½" h., c. 1900, brightly enameled
peacocks in garden on black ground ......................................... $600-800

Jardinieres (pair), 10" h., two scenic medallions of court ladies
at table on an aqua ground ................................................. $350-400

Pillow, 15" l., nude baby on elbows and knees, white enamel
with black hair and features ................................................ $240-250

Pillow, 16½" l., child reclining on books decorated in blue,
black, and brown .......................................................... $240-250

Planter, 10" w., on four corner bracket feet, square shape,
blue glazed with pink ch'ih lung (lizard dragons) on exterior
panels .................................................................... $85-110

Planters (pair), 10" w., square shape with underplates,
alternating pink and turquoise panels with relief molded
flowers and foliage, twisted rope handles with peaches in
relief ..................................................................... $450-600

Plate, 8½" dia., white glazed with concentric bands of orange
shou symbols ............................................................. $20-22

Plate, 12" dia., millefleur design on gilt background,
simulated imperial mark of Ch'ien Lung in red on base ....................... $125-150

Plaque, 15" dia., polychrome floral design, framed for
hanging .................................................................. $140-150

Plaque, 18" dia., large polychrome pheasant on black
background, pierced for hanging ............................................ $75-100

Roof ornament, 5½" h. x 10" l., farmer astride water buffalo,
19th-20th century. (Illus.) ................................................. $275-350

151

Roof ornament, 6½" h. x 9¾" l., figure of a warrior on horseback, building cement adhering to unfinished back. (Author's note: There has been some dispute regarding 19th century production of this type of figural ornament.) (Illus.) . . . . . . . . . . . . . . . . . . . . $275-350

Serving dish, 7" w., oval shape on raised foot, turquoise glaze with yellow border, floral motif . . . . . . . . . . . . . . . . . . . . . . . . . . . . . . . . . . . . . . $20-25

Spoon, 3½" l., rice pattern, blue and white decoration . . . . . . . . . . . . . . . . . . . . . . . . . $8-10

Teacup (covered), 4" dia., with underplate, blue and iron red bats on white glaze . . . . . . . . . . . . . . . . . . . . . . . . . . . . . . . . . . . . . . . . . . . . $38-40

Teacup, 4" dia., millefleur pattern in tones of yellow/green, iron red, and green on yellow ground . . . . . . . . . . . . . . . . . . . . . . . . . . . . . . . . . . . . . $35-45

Teapot, 5" h., millefleur pattern on white background, with gilt spire finial on lid . . . . . . . . . . . . . . . . . . . . . . . . . . . . . . . . . . . . . . . . . . . . . . . . . $50-75

Tea set, consisting of covered teapot, open sugar and open creamer, decorated with butterflies on a white background . . . . . . . . . . . . . . . . . . $75-100

Tea set, consisting of a teapot, creamer, and sugar bowl, I-Hsing pottery with applied pewter decoration, signed on the pewter in Chinese and English, "Made in Shanghi, China." (Illus.) . . . . . . . . . . . . . . . . . . . . . . . . . . . . . . . . . . . . . . . . . . . . . . $250-300

Tea set, consisting of teapot, covered sugar, open creamer, six cups and saucers, millefleur design on black background . . . . . . . . . . . . . . . . . . $85-110

Tea set (child's miniature set), consisting of teapot, covered sugar, covered creamer, six cups and saucers, and six cake plates, decorated with a center floral medallion outlined in gold on a high gloss white ground . . . . . . . . . . . . . . . . . . . . . . . . . . . . . . . . . $65-85

Vase, 5" h., eggshell porcelain decorated with two pink foo lions and black border trim . . . . . . . . . . . . . . . . . . . . . . . . . . . . . . . . . . . . . . . . . $65-75

Vase, 8" h., eggshell porcelain with pastel enameled scene of woman serving mandarin at table, black border trim designs (Illus.) . . . . . . . . . . . . . . . . . . . . . . . . . . . . . . . . . . . . . . . . . . . . . . . . . . . $100-125

Vase, 14" w., square shape, celadon ground color with alternating motifs of flower-filled vases and archaic vessels painted in thick enamels . . . . . . . . . . . . . . . . . . . . . . . . . . . . . . . . . . . . . . . . $100-125

Wall vase, 6½" h., decorated with multicolored floral sprays and green leaves on pale green ground . . . . . . . . . . . . . . . . . . . . . . . . . . . . . . . $27-30

Wig stand, 11" h., multicolored transfer design of court ladies in garden . . . . . . . . . . . . . . . . . . . . . . . . . . . . . . . . . . . . . . . . . . . . . . . . . . . . $75-100

Wig stand, 11" h., blue and white peacock and floral design . . . . . . . . . . . . . . . . . . . $75-100

## Made in Japan
*(1921-1940)*

When the term "NIPPON" was no longer acceptable, wares exported from Japan to the United States were marked "Made in Japan" or "Japan." These two identifications of country of origin were either used as a backstamp or affixed to items via a paper label or sticker. The use of this identification is known as the "Made in Japan Era," and it began in 1921. During the Made in Japan Era, the markings identifying country of origin were sometimes used in conjunction with Japanese characters. Many of the items produced during this time look very much like their forerunners, be they styled after European wares, American wares, or traditional Japanese wares. Wares produced after 1921 have been considered to be of overall poor quality in the past. Such judgments are now changing. Father Time has taken his toll on such ideas and these items are now highly sought after as collectibles, with prices rising at a steady pace.

(See: Noritake)

Ashtray, cigarette holder, and match holder, donkey figural, red and green luster with small Art Deco stylized flowers ...................... $20-30

Basket, 6" dia., handled, blue and gold luster with band of Art Deco stylized flowers ................................................. $30-35

Berry set, one large and six small bowls, white porcelain with border band containing small floral sprays ..................................... $40-50

Bowl, 8¼" dia., scalloped and fluted rim, blue and gold with pink roses ............................................................. $40-45

Candleholders (pair), 2½" h., gold and blue luster with floral sprays ................................................................. $15-25

Candlesticks (pair), 8" h., orange luster with black trim ......................... $40-45

Cake set, one large and six small plates, blue luster with motif of birds in flight .................................................... $40-50

Child's tea set, blue willow, covered teapot, covered sugar, open creamer, six cups and saucers .......................................... $50-60

Child's tea set, teapot, covered sugar, open creamer, four cups and saucers, four plates (Meito China), lake scene on orange luster .............................................................. $75-85

Chocolate pot, cobalt blue and gold with red roses on white ground .................................................................. $40-50

Chocolate set, pot, six cups and saucers, pink and yellow flowers with gold handle and gold trim ..................................... $90-125

Condiment set, orange luster with blue luster band containing small floral sprays, salt and pepper, and two cruets with center handled tray ............................................. $20-30

Condiment set, covered mustard with spoon, salt and pepper and two-handled tray, blue and tan luster with band containing floral sprays ............................................... $20-25

Cookie jar, orange luster with bands of floral motifs, flat knob finial and wicker handle ............................................... $40-45

Egg cup, blue willow ...................................................... $10-12

Fish set, one large platter and seven small plates each with a leaping fish motif, gold border .......................................... $100-125

Figure, 4" h., boy with umbrella, Hummel style ................................. $15-25

Figure, 4½" h., girl with basket, Hummel style ............................... $15-25

Figures (pair), boy and girl seated on bench, Hummel style ..................... $20-30

Figure (double), 5½" h., boy and girl walking to school, Hummel style ............................................................. $35-50

Figure, 5" h., girl playing a banjo, Hummel style ............................ $15-25

Figure (double), 2½" h., bride and groom .................................... $20-25

Group, three German shepherds, with two seated, pearl luster .................................................................. $15-20

Humidor, brown pottery simulating tree bark cloisonné with floral motif in orange and gold ............................................ $60-80

Inkwell, cobalt blue and gold with red roses and green foliage ................................................................ $80-100

Jardiniere, 6½" dia., oval, deep blue with wide border band having stylized fruit ..................................................... $40-50

Kitchen set, four large covered jars, four small covered jars, one salt box, marked flour, coffee, sugar, tea, salt, nutmeg, allspice, cloves, and ginger, blue and tan luster with black sailboats ............................................................. $100-125

Plate, 6" dia., phoenix bird pattern (blue and white) ........................... $4-8

Plate, 8" dia., openwork border with scenic motif featuring house, trees, and two children at play ....................................... $35-40

Plate, 8½" dia., black and pale green stripes and swirls with white floral spray in the center ............................................ $15-20

*Japanese luster teapot. Courtesy Mrs. Florence Simon*

Shoe, 3" h., lady's pump, pearl luster with pink bow ............................ $15-25

Teapot, 5" h., blue and gold luster. (Illus.) .............................. $25-35

Tea set, blue and orange luster, lake scene at sunset, teapot,
covered sugar, open creamer, six cups and saucers .......................... $75-100

Tea set, pale blue with small yellow and pink flowers, teapot,
open sugar and creamer, five cups and saucers, five plates .................... $50-60

Tea set, tan and blue luster with sailboat motif, teapot,
covered sugar, open creamer, four cups and saucers, four
plates ....................................................... $45-65

Vase, 11" h., black pottery, painted motif of flowers overall .................... $20-30

Vases (pair), 12" h., porcelain, flared mouths, bulbous forms,
overall motif of roses and foliage on pale blue ground ......................... $75-90

Vases (pair), 8½" h., overall motif of decals featuring
portraits of Japanese women on high gloss white porcelain .................... $50-60

Vases (pair), 14" h., porcelain, gold trim, two handles, motif
of red roses on pale green ground .......................................... $65-90

# Mandarin Squares
## (Chinese)

Among the highly collected forms of textiles are Mandarin Squares. These embroidered badges were worn to show rank during the Ming and Ch'ing dynasties. If they are seamed or made in two halves, they were worn across open front robes. The five-clawed dragon is the imperial symbol. However, many dealers and collectors find these badges with symbols other than a dragon. Each of the following symbols denotes the position (rank) of the bearer.

**Civil officials:**

| | |
|---|---|
| first order | phoenix |
| second rank | a bird of gold |
| third rank | peacock |
| fourth rank | crane |
| fifth rank | pheasant |
| sixth rank | stork |
| seventh rank | mandarin duck |
| eighth rank | quail |
| ninth rank | paradise flycatcher (similar to a sparrow) |

**Military officials:**

| | |
|---|---|
| first order | kylin |
| second rank | lion |
| third rank | panther |
| fourth rank | tiger |
| fifth rank | bear |
| sixth rank | small tiger |
| seventh rank | rhinoceros |
| eighth rank | stork |
| ninth rank | seahorse |
| censor | unicorn |

Crane, 10" x 10", crane in white satin stitch above waves with
multicolored clouds and dragon with key fret border ......................... $175-210

Kylin, 11½" x 12", kylin on a rock above waves, motifs
include bats, clouds, flowers, with key fret border c. 1800 .................... $250-425

Leopard (third rank military official's wife), 12″ x 12″, yellow
and black satin stitch on black silk, leopard crouching on
rocks above gold waves, bat and key fret border ............................$175-200

Lion, 12″ x 11″, Peking knots and gold couching on gold
ground with multicolored Buddhist symbols surrounding the
lion ......................................................................................................$175-200

Mandarin duck (seventh rank civil official's wife), 10″ x 10″,
late 19th century, in satin stitch on blue ground and
landscape motif surrounded by Buddhist symbols ...........................$125-150

Paradise flycatcher, 12″ x 12″, c. 1900, blue, green, and yellow
stitching and white Peking knots on blue satin ground ........................$175-220

Peacock, 13″ x 13″, stitched in Peking knots and couching
simulating real feathers ....................................................................$185-215

Pheasant, 12″ x 12″, Kuang Hsü period, gold couching on
blue and black, with pheasant on a rock above waves and
clouds ..................................................................................................$110-140

Quail, 11″ x 12″, gold couching, quail standing on rock above
waves, with clouds and flowers ............................................................$250-200

Tiger, 12″ x 12″, late 19th century, Peking knots and satin
stitches in pale greens, blues, and pinks with gold couching ..................$110-120

Unicorn, 11″ x 11″, mid-19th century, Peking knots and satin
stitches, unicorn surrounded by waves and flowers ...........................$135-155

## Menuki
*(Japanese)*

The purpose of the menuki was to keep in place the peg that locks the hilt
and blade together. When styles changed, from the latter part of the
Kamakura period, the menuki were placed on either side of the handle,
so as to prevent one's fingers from slipping. These small ornaments have
become highly collectible, as all forms of sword furniture have become.

Menuki (pair), shakudo chased with lilies ....................................$100-200

Menuki (pair), yamagane in the form of a bull (rectangular
posts) ...............................................................................................$150-250

Menuki (pair), yamagane in the form of a Shishi (Goto style) ...................$250-450

Menuki (pair), shakudo, formed as a group of vegetables
including melons and gourds (Goto style) .......................................$400-600

Menuki (pair), gold plate and shakudo, double daikon form
(Goto style) ......................................................................................$75-150

Menuki (pair), shakudo with silver and gold wash, formed as
a peony branch (copper posts) ........................................................$150-245

Menuki (pair), shakudo, in the form of bats .................................$100-175

## Millefleur
*(Chinese)*

The millefleur design appeared late in the reign of Ch'ien Lung.
Millefleur is a French word meaning "thousand flowers." The design
consists of a variety of rose pink, blue, and yellow enameled flowers
(sometimes gilded) on a white or black background. The design is so
profuse it all but covers the background color which really serves as a
backdrop to set off the colors of the flowers. Most porcelains with this
pattern date from the late 19th and early 20th century.

(See: Cloisonné; Made in China; Nineteenth Century, Satsuma)

# Ming Dynasty
*(Chinese)*

The great Ming Dynasty ruled between the years 1368-1643. There were seventeen different emperors who reigned during this time.

| | | | |
|---|---|---|---|
| Hung Wu | 1368-1398 | Hung Chih | 1488-1505 |
| Chien Wên | 1399-1402 | Chêng Tê | 1506-1521 |
| Yung Lo | 1403-1424 | Chia Ching | 1522-1566 |
| Hung Hsi | 1425-1426 | Lung Ch'ing | 1567-1572 |
| Hsüan Tê | 1426-1435 | Wan Li | 1573-1619 |
| Chêng T'ung | 1436-1449 | T'ai Ch'ang | 1620-1621 |
| Ching T'ai | 1450-1456 | T'ien Ch'i | 1621-1627 |
| T'ien Shun | 1457-1464 | Ch'ung Chêng | 1628-1643 |
| Ch'êng Hua | 1465-1487 | | |

(See: Blue and White; Celadon; Chêng Hua; Chia Ching; Fa Hua; Hsüan-Tê; Kiangnan Ting; Kraak; Swatow; Underglaze Red; Wan Li)

Bowl, 5" dia., Cheng Tê mark, imperial yellow glaze .......................$1,500-1,800

Bowl, 5½" dia., blue and white decoration, exterior with children in a garden; interior with a medallion of four figures and rockwork ....................................$800-1,200

Bowl, 6½" dia., 15th century Hsüan-té, rare, blue-and-white decoration, the interior with lotus surrounded by camellias, tree peonies, and chrysanthemums; the exterior with lotus scroll. (Illus.) ....................................$5,000-7,000

Bowl, 7" dia., 16th century, with full, rounded sides, glazed in a pale bluish white tint ....................................$500-700

Bowl, 7½" dia., signed with Ming mark in double circles on the base, the exterior decorated in an overall floral pattern, the interior with a central floral medallion and swirls of blue, with a copper rim over the lip, one hairline crack. (Illus.) ....................................$250-300

Bowl, 7½" dia., blue and white decoration with four Koranic inscriptions in medallions meaning, "There is no God but one God and Mohammed is his prophet"; interior with a butterfly in a central medallion ....................................$2,500-3,000

Bowl, 8" dia., Chia Ching period (unmarked), decorated with peonies, chrysanthemums, and lotus in yellow and iron red ....................................$1,500-2,000

Bowl, 9½" dia., Wan Li period (unmarked), blue and white decoration, set on three mask head feet, the everted rim with Buddhist emblem decoration, the exterior with a continuous scene of figures in a garden setting ....................................$800-1,000

Bowl, 9½" dia., Wan Li six-character mark, blue and white decoration; exterior decorated with bamboo and banana palms growing from rockwork, a petal lappet border at the base; interior with chrysanthemum, camellia, and peony, the rim with ling chih scrolls ....................................$1,800-2,400

Box, 5" dia., with incised decoration of scrolls and flowers covered with blue, green and yellow, the interior with a pale blue white glaze ....................................$400-500

Box, 5¾" h., T'ien Chi period (unmarked), three-tiered, polychrome decoration of three boys in a garden, with four floral reserves on each tier, with colors of iron red, green, yellow, aubergine, and turquoise ....................................$2,500-3,000

Box, 8½" dia., Wan Li mark, with sectioned compartments around a scalloped central section, interior cover resting on the metal lip of the lower rim; exterior decoration of dragons among flower scrolls, the outer cover with five oval dragon reserves surrounded by pierced cash on a diaper pattern ....................................$3,000-4,000

Candlesticks (pair), 12", pottery molded in vase form and set on hexagonal stands molded with scrollwork, glazed in mottled turquoise, cream, and brown ....................................$900-1,000

*Ming Dynasty censer, 4½" h., pottery with thick glaze*

Censer, 4½" h., Chun style glaze, on tripod legs, the thick and glossy glaze with dark patches over buff pottery. (Illus.) .................. $800-1,000

Censer, 8½" h., supported on three feet, glazed in cobalt blue ............................................ $600-800

Dish, 5½" dia., 16th century, of hexagonal shape with wild bamboo and plum trees in underglaze blue along with overglazed green, yellow, and iron red ................................... $500-700

Dish, 6" dia., showing birds and scrolls, in colors of underglaze blue, green, yellow, red, and aubergine .......................... $400-600

Dish, 6" dia., Cheng Tê six-character mark, with an imperial yellow glaze, the base in a bluish tinted white ........................... $1,400-1,600

Dish, 9" dia., Chia Ching six-character mark, glazed in a pale imperial yellow; the base in a bluish white tint ........................... $2,200-2,500

Dish, 13¼" dia., with fluted rim, blue and white decoration, the center with a seashell surrounded by four galloping horses on a stylized wave ground; the border with a lotus scroll band ............................................ $1,500-1,800

Dish, 14" dia., incised Chia Ching mark in a double circle, with incised decoration of a dragon and a flaming pearl under an imperial yellow glaze ....................................... $6,000-7,000

Dish, 14" dia., 6" d., blue and white decoration, with a center medallion of a kylin standing on rockwork, the border with band on flowers and squirrels; exterior with five phoenix medallions .............................................. $1,200-1,500

Ewer, 7" h., blue and white decoration, with a garlic-shaped top, tall spout and long curved handle; center decoration of two winged monsters, floral sprays on neck and spout .................... $2,400-2,800

Figure, 8" h., 16th century, the seated dark brown pottery figure holding cash and leaning on a dragon head. (Illus.) ..................... $700-900

Figure, court official, 10" h., Wan Li period, polychrome enameled decoration, posed standing wearing a white robe with yellow border ......................................... $2,500-3,500

Figure, 12" h., pottery, Kuan Yin, decorated with green, ocher, aubergine, and turquoise. (Illus.) ................................... $400-600

Figure, court attendant, 13" h., pottery figure with one arm raised, the other hidden in a long-sleeved robe, wearing a peaked hat, with traces of glaze and pigment ........................... $800-1,000

Figure, 13½" h., Wan Li Buddha, blue and white, in dhyanasana wearing a loose robe belted below his naked chest with floral scroll borders, painted in underglaze blue, neck restored ............................................. $3,000-5,000

Figure, Kuan Ti, 15" h., pottery figure posed seated on a base with a serpent and a turtle at his feet, with traces of black and red pigment ............................................ $900-1,200

Figure, Vajropani, 16" h., with his right fist held above his head and the ritual thunderbolt in his left hand, with a green and yellow glazed robe .......................................... $1,200-1,500

Figure, Kuan Yin, 18" h., seated on a rock base, glazed in purple, amber, and turquoise with the feet, head, and hands left in the biscuit ............................................ $1,200-1,400

Figures (pair), 11" h., 16th century, pottery, male and female, decorated in san t'sai colors of ocher, green, and black on buff pottery. (Illus.) .......................................... $800-1,000

Jar, 6" h., provincial stoneware, hexagonal form, with molded body covered with green glaze falling short of the base, commonware ............................................ $40-60

Jar, 9" h., Chia Ching mark, blue and white decoration, the neck decorated with ju-i heads, with beaded chains and eight Buddhist emblems, the lower section with galloping horses, clouds, and waves ....................................... $2,500-3,000

*Ming Dynasty bowl, 6½" dia., rare, Hsüan-tê reign mark*

*Ming Dynasty bowl, 7½" dia., Ming mark, with copper rim*

*Ming Dynasty figure, 12" h., glazed pottery figure*

157

*Vase, Wan Li, wu tś ai decoration, 15¼" h.*

Jar, 14" h., with four loop handles at the shoulder, covered with a yellow lead glaze . . . . . . . . . . . . . . . . . . . . . . . . . . . . . . . . . . . . . . . . . . . $500-700

Jarlet, 3" h., blue and white, reticulated with quatrefoil panels with double underglaze blue line borders, the short neck having a lipped rim and two small loop handles . . . . . . . . . . . . . . . . . . . . . . . . . $500-800

Kendi, 7" h., decorated with two yellow dragons and aubergine clouds on a pale green glaze . . . . . . . . . . . . . . . . . . . . . . . . . . . . . . . . . . . $900-1,200

Kendi, 8" h., Wan Li period )unmarked), blue and white decoration painted freely with a floral motif of insects and flowers . . . . . . . . . . . . . . . . . . . . . . . . . . . . . . . . . . . . . . . . . . . . . . . . . . . . . $800-1,200

Kendi, 8" h., Wan Li period (unmarked), decorated with "precious objects" and florals, with five dots as decoration on the spout and shoulders; the flanged rim with a ju-i border . . . . . . . . . . . . . . . . . $800-1,000

Libation cup, 6" h. x 7" w., of archaic shape (chueh) with a deep bowl, two cylindrical finials and three tall splayed legs, with a thick bluish tint glaze and burnt marks on the unglazed feet . . . . . . . . . . . . . . . . . . . . . . . . . . . . . . . . . . . . . . . . . . . . . . . . . $6,500-7,500

Pilgrim flask, 7" h., 16th century, of deep, relief molded pottery, with a design of an enthroned Buddha on one side and fish and waves on the reverse, with short pierced loops at the shoulders . . . . . . . . . . . . . . . . . . . . . . . . . . . . . . . . . . . . . . . . . . . . . . . $350-400

Plate, 7½" dia., Wan Li period (unmarked), blue and white decoration, freely painted with two stylized deer in the center and border of flowers alternating with panels of horizontal lines . . . . . . . . . . . . . . . . . . . . . . . . . . . . . . . . . . . . . . . . . . . . . . . . . . . . . . $200-250

Plate, 7½" dia., Wan Li period (unmarked), blue and white decoration, freely painted central design with rim decoration of alternating flowers and emblems, with floral border on underside, copper rim, firing crack . . . . . . . . . . . . . . . . . . . . . . . . . . . . . $175-225

Plate, 11" dia., provincial ware, blue and white decoration, with sketchy curving lines in the center surrounded by an unfinished biscuit ring, the border with groups of diaper pattern alternating with curving lines. (See Color Section) . . . . . . . . . . . . . . . . . $100-150

Roof tile, warrior, 12" h., pottery figure of standing warrior; the warrior with a blue robe and turquoise helmet, the glaze degraded and flaking . . . . . . . . . . . . . . . . . . . . . . . . . . . . . . . . . . . . . . . . . $900-1,200

Roof tile, warrior, 13" h., pottery figure shown with raised arms seated on saddled, prancing horse, domed base with cloud motif scrolls, glazed in green, yellow, aubergine, chipped and flaked, mounted as a lamp . . . . . . . . . . . . . . . . . . . . . . . . . . . . . $700-900

Roof tiles (pair), 12" h., two boys seated on winged fish, glazed in chestnut and turquoise, chips and restorations . . . . . . . . . . . . . . . . . $800-1,000

Roof tile, temple guardian, 15" h., decorated in green, turquoise, yellow, and cream glazes, some chips . . . . . . . . . . . . . . . . . . . . $1,200-1,400

Saucer dish, 7" dia., Wan Li six-character mark, blue and white decoration, center showing a scene of a Buddhist paradise with Shou Lao on a crane and an immortal burning incense; border with ling chih fungus scroll interspersed with Sanskrit characters . . . . . . . . . . . . . . . . . . . . . . . . . . . . . . . . . . . . . . . . . $2,500-3,000

Stem cup, 4½" h., six-character mark of Hsüan-té, polychrome enamels, the exterior decorated with a scholar practicing the four liberal accomplishments, the interior with a figure playing the flute, in yellow, aubergine, iron red, and green . . . . . . . . . . . . . . . . . . . . . . . . . . . . . . . . . . . . . . . . . . . . . . . . . . . . . $6,000-8,000

Stem cup, 4½" h. x 6" dia., Ch'êng Hua period (unmarked), with a slightly flared lip on a tapered, hollow foot, covered with waxy white allover glaze; edge of the foot left unglazed . . . . . . . . . . . . . . . $2,000-2,600

Stem cup, 6" dia., late 15th century, with rounded sides and a lipped rim on a flared base, glazed white . . . . . . . . . . . . . . . . . . . . . . . . . . $1,500-2,000

Storage jar, 24" h., molded with dragons, butterflies, bats, and overlapping lotus petals, with four looped handles at the shoulders, twisted rope band at lip, covered with yellow/brown lead glaze . . . . . . . . . . . . . . . . . . . . . . . . . . . . . . . . . . . . . . . . . . . . . . $1,600-2,200

Storage jar, 27" h., of ovoid form with two lug handles,
glazed dark brown . . . . . . . . . . . . . . . . . . . . . . . . . . . . . . . . . . . . . . . . . . . . . . . $1,000-1,200

Vase, 8½" h., Wan Li period, double gourd shape, blue and
white, decorated with floral and scroll design, kiln grit
adhering to the base . . . . . . . . . . . . . . . . . . . . . . . . . . . . . . . . . . . . . . . . . . . $1,600-1,800

Vase, 10¼" h., 14th century, mei ping form covered with a
heavy porous glaze, running in streaks and coagulations of
white and milky blue on a background of deep brown;
pottery body with earth encrustations on the base . . . . . . . . . . . . . . . . . . . . . . . . $600-800

Vase, 11" h., Wan Li period, mei ping shaped with top, blue
and white decoration, body decorated with panels of flowers,
birds, and precious objects, neck with a ju-i border and
overlapping lotus petals . . . . . . . . . . . . . . . . . . . . . . . . . . . . . . . . . . . . . . . . . $1,600-2,000

Vase, 15¼" h., Wan Li six-character mark within rectangle on
base, of hexagonal beaker form, decorated in wu ts'ai
enamels, upper and lower body decorated with dragons and
cloud scrolls on each panel separated by a phoenix in cloud
scrolls on the bulbous center panel. (Illus.) . . . . . . . . . . . . . . . . . . . . . . . . . $45,000-65,000

Ming Dynasty figures, 11" h., faces restored, 16th century

Ming Dynasty figure, 8" h., pottery, 16th century

Mirror black (wu chin) is a lustrous black glaze which originated in the
K'ang Hsi period. It was created by using a combination of golden brown
(tzü chin) and a cobalt ferrous ore of manganese. The decoration is

## Mirror Black
*(Chinese)*

159

*Mirror black vase, 21" h., with gilt tracery, K'ang Hsi*

usually purely monochrome but it may have added gold tracery designs. On original items of the K'ang Hsi period the gold will have signs of wear and may be only faintly observable. These early examples are also recognized by their soft brown reflections in the surface, particularly at the neck rim of vases where the glaze is thin. Mirror black is still being made.

Box, 5½" dia., K'ang Hsi period (unmarked), covered box decorated with brilliant mirror black glaze fading to dark brown at the edges . . . . . . . . . . . . . . . . . . . . . . . . . . . . . . . . . . . . . . . . . . . . . $800-1,200

Brush pot, 4" h., K'ang Hsi period (unmarked), black glaze; interior and base covered with bluish tinted white glaze . . . . . . . . . . . . . . . . . . . . . $300-400

Brush pot, 5½" h., 18th century, the shape slightly flaring at the base, with traces of gilt; interior and base glazed white . . . . . . . . . . . . . . . . . $350-450

Ginger jar, 10½" h., K'ang Hsi, of tall elongated form, with cover. (See Color Section) . . . . . . . . . . . . . . . . . . . . . . . . . . . . . . . . . . . . . . . . . . $500-700

Vase, 8½" h., 19th century (commemorative six-character mark of K'ang Hsi in underglaze blue), of ovoid form, with gilt decoration of exotic birds among peony and bamboo . . . . . . . . . . . . . . . . . . . $200-250

Vase, 14" h., K'ang Hsi period (unmarked), with globular body tapering to a long slender neck, with deep black glaze that thins to greenish brown at the lip; interior and base glazed white . . . . . . . . . . . . . . . . . . . . . . . . . . . . . . . . . . . . . . . . . . . . . . . . $2,000-2,400

Vase, 14" h., late 18th/early 19th century, black glaze with the lip and interior glazed white . . . . . . . . . . . . . . . . . . . . . . . . . . . . . . . . . . . . . . . . $500-700

Vase, 17" h., 19th century, rouleau shape, decorated with gilt floral and scroll designs . . . . . . . . . . . . . . . . . . . . . . . . . . . . . . . . . . . . . . . . . . . $600-800

*Vase, 21" h., K'ang Hsi, black glazed body painted with gilt in alternating panels of prunus and bamboo within gilt reserves on a gilt chrysanthemum scroll ground; the shoulder with striding dragons on a gilt ground, the neck with long life invocations. (Illus.) . . . . . . . . . . . . . . . . . . . . . . . . . . . . . . . . . . . . . . . . . . $1,500

Vase, 22" h., K'ang Hsi, baluster form, deep rich mirror black glaze, carved wood lid. (Illus.) . . . . . . . . . . . . . . . . . . . . . . . . . . . . $1,400-1,600

Vase, 23" h., 19th century, yen yen shape, black glaze with the interior and base glazed white . . . . . . . . . . . . . . . . . . . . . . . . . . . . . . . . . . $800-1,000

## Mogul Carpets

During the time of Akbar (1556-1605) and Jahangir (1605-1628), Persian weavers were brought to India. During these reigns the Persian influence was predominant but Indian and European elements were being gradually introduced. Hindu craftsmen worked under the guidelines of Persian weavers, and the trade in these early carpets/rugs began to flourish. The early carpets are similar in style to the Herat florals. Gradually, designs took on a naturalistic flavor, and floral, plant, figure, and animal patterns evolved, along with the use of a wine (burgundy) colored ground. Indian carpets having approximately 700 to 1,250 knots per inch, are among the finest pieces. Wool and/or silk have been employed and the general rule suggests that the all silk rugs date from the reign of Jahan (1528-1658).

Carpet, 13'6" x 9'9", deep red field containing lobed blue medallion trimmed with gold and surrounded by vines and flowers with ivory floral spandrels within a deep blue border of flower heads, foliage, and vines . . . . . . . . . . . . . . . . . . . . . . . . . . . . . . . . . . . . . $3,500-5,000

Carpet, 13'10" x 11'10", burgundy field covered with flowers surrounded by an outer border containing flower heads . . . . . . . . . . . . . . . . . . . $3,000-4,500

Prayer rug, 6' x 4', silk and velvet, red ground with large
flower vase, floral motif on spandrels above; the ground
having silver threads, border containing floral panels ...................... $3,100-4,400

Saddle cloth, 32" x 42", silk, orange field, B-shaped border
with orange flowers and green stems and foliage on a silver
ground ........................................................................ $1,500-2,100

# Mogul Paintings

During the 16th to 19th centuries (Mogul period 1526-1857), the Mogul rulers introduced an art form in the style of the Persian tradition. The school of Mogul painting began in 1549 when Humayun invited two Persian painters to his court. At that same time, Emperors Akbar and Jahangir were also encouraging painting. Mogul paintings are brightly colored. They have detailed landscaping and generally depict a range of subject matter which included themes (stories) taken from legend and religion. All Mogul paintings are flat, meaning the perspective is one-dimensional. The effect of these magnificent paintings is elegant. Among the most famous Mogul painters are Mansur, Manohar, and Jahangir.

Painting, 11" x 8", mid-19th century, a woman holding a
parrot .......................................................................... $700-900

Painting, 8⅞" x 5½", mid-19th century, a young man dressed
in a green robe and black pointed hat ...................................... $400-600

Painting (portrait), 13" x 9", mid-19th century, seated man
wearing blue coat which is braided and jeweled, holding a
jeweled scabbard ............................................................ $2,300-4,500

Miniature, 7" x 6" frame size, late 17th/early 18th century,
erotica, a man and woman in intimate embrace .............................. $500-800

Miniature, framed size 8" x 7", a woman dressed in red skirt,
carrying a lamp, with birds in the foregound ................................. $250-325

Miniature, framed size 6⅞" x 4⅞", late 18th/early 19th
century, a prince watching young women who are seminude ................. $600-900

Miniature, framed size 7⅞" x 5⅛", early 19th century, a
prince dressed in mauve attire astride a white horse ........................ $325-450

*Mirror black vase, 22" h., baluster form with carved wood lid, K'ang Hsi*

# Monochrome Glazes
*(Chinese)*

The reader is advised to refer to the individual reigns and dynasties for the finest examples of monochrome glazes relating to each era.

(See: Blanc de Chine; Café au Lait; Celadon; Ch'ing Pai; Claire de Lune; Copper Red; Iron Rust; Mirror Black; Peach Bloom; Powder Blue; Robin's Egg; Sang de Boeuf; Shu Fu; Tea Dust; Ting; Ying Ching)

# Moriage
*(Japanese)*

Moriage refers to applied clay (slip) relief motifs and decorations used on certain classes of Japanese pottery and porcelain.

**Methods:**
**Handrolling and shaping** — with this method the clay is applied by hand to the biscuit, in one or more layers. The thickness and shaping of the clay is dependent upon the design and effect required.

**Tubing** — a more conventional method made use of tubing. The tubing was filled with softened clay (slip) and was trailed onto the biscuit in much the same manner as one would decorate a cake. This method is also referred to as slip trailing.

**Hakeme** — this technique requires the slip to be reduced to a liquefied state so that it may be manipulated with a brush.

Moriage designs may be applied before or after glazing and moriage motifs and decorations may be treated with color either before or after application.

Bowl, 10" dia., pre-Nippon, red roses and green foliage covered in moriage scroll ornamentation, unmarked . . . . . . . . . . . . . . . . . . . . . . . . . . . . . . . $175-200

Bowl, 11" dia., Blue Maple Leaf Nippon, two open handles, lake scene with moriage ornamentation on trees . . . . . . . . . . . . . . . . . . . . . . . . . . . . . . $125-150

Demitasse set, pot, open creamer, covered sugar, six cups and saucers, gray ground with moriage motif of house and garden executed in pastel shades, "Made in Japan" . . . . . . . . . . . . . . . . . . . . . . . $125-150

Demitasse set, pot, open creamer, covered sugar, four cups and saucers, slip-trailed dragon motif, "Made in Japan" . . . . . . . . . . . . . . . . . . . . . . . $50-65

Pitcher, 7¼" h., fluted base and rim, moriage ornamentation on flowers and border designs (unmarked) . . . . . . . . . . . . . . . . . . . . . . . . . . . . . . . $125-150

Pitcher, squat form, (unmarked), lavender and pink flowers covered with moriage ornamentation in the form of scrollwork . . . . . . . . . . . . . . . . . . . . . . . . . . . . . . . . . . . . . . . . . . . . . . . . . . . . . $150-175

Plate (club-shaped), 6½" dia., moriage motif of green gray leaves over pastel flowers . . . . . . . . . . . . . . . . . . . . . . . . . . . . . . . . . . . . . . . . . . . . $125-150

Plate (divided into three compartments), 8¼" dia., slip-trailed dragon, "Made in Japan" . . . . . . . . . . . . . . . . . . . . . . . . . . . . . . . . . . . . . . . . . . . . . . $15-25

Plate, 7½" dia., gray ground with pastel moriage motifs of house and garden (unmarked) . . . . . . . . . . . . . . . . . . . . . . . . . . . . . . . . . . . . . . . . . . . $25-30

Mug, floral and geometric moriage motifs, unmarked . . . . . . . . . . . . . . . . . . . . $125-150

Mug (pre-Nippon), gray ground with pansies and moriage latticework . . . . . . . . . . . . . . . . . . . . . . . . . . . . . . . . . . . . . . . . . . . . . . . . . . . . . . . $175-200

Mug, gray ground with red roses, gray moriage motif of scrolls overall (pre-Nippon) . . . . . . . . . . . . . . . . . . . . . . . . . . . . . . . . . . . . . . . . . . $125-150

Tea set, slip-trailed dragon motif, teapot, covered sugar, open creamer, eight cups and saucers, eight cake plates, "Made in Japan" . . . . . . . . . . . . . . . . . . . . . . . . . . . . . . . . . . . . . . . . . . . . . . . . . . . . . . . . . . . . $110-150

Tea set (child's), pot, open creamer, covered sugar, three cups and saucers, "Made in Japan," slip-trailed dragon motif on mottled ground . . . . . . . . . . . . . . . . . . . . . . . . . . . . . . . . . . . . . . . . . . . . $50-75

Tea set (child's), pot, open sugar, open creamer, six cups and saucers (pottery), pale green ground, slip-trailed dragon motif, unmarked . . . . . . . . . . . . . . . . . . . . . . . . . . . . . . . . . . . . . . . . . . . . . . . . . $75-100

Vase, tree stump contour, moriage motif of scenic design featuring house and trees, unmarked . . . . . . . . . . . . . . . . . . . . . . . . . . . . . . . . . $190-225

Vase, 6½" h., squat-form, turned-out handles, brown ground with stylized flowers and geometric patterns, unmarked . . . . . . . . . . . . . . . . . $170-195

Vase, 10" h., moriage trim on handles, rim, neck, and base with moriage white cranes flying against a background of waves . . . . . . . . . . . . . . . . . . . . . . . . . . . . . . . . . . . . . . . . . . . . . . . . . . . . . . . . . . $175-220

Vase, 6½" h., orange luster with gray and white moriage motif of bird on a tree branch, "Made in Japan" . . . . . . . . . . . . . . . . . . . . . . . . . $75-100

Vase, 4½" h., slip-trailed dragon, "Made in Japan" . . . . . . . . . . . . . . . . . . . . . . $15-20

Vase, 12" h., muted ground in shades of brown and mustard, moriage motifs of flowers in shades in turquoise and pink, fluted neck and two small looped handles . . . . . . . . . . . . . . . . . . . . . . . . . . . . . $125-150

Vase, 14¾" h., mottled gray-black and white ground with scenic motif of trees, flowers, and lake . . . . . . . . . . . . . . . . . . . . . . . . . . . . . . . . $120-145

Vase, 9¼" h., fluted neck, mottled ground, scenic motif with moriage ornamentation in the form of flying geese . . . . . . . . . . . . . . . . . . . . . . $125-150

Vase, 11" h., bulbous form with two looped handles, moriage
motif of red roses ...................................................... $175-200

One of the most sought after collectibles is Mud Figures, also known as
Mud People and Mud Men. These ceramic pieces succeeded Kwantung
figures. Dating for the most part from the 1920s to WW II, with the
exception of the minis, which date c. 1905, they generally depict Chinese
elders. Mud Figures were produced in Fat Shang (Kwantung province,
China) with the exception of the popular water carrier, which originated
in Jiwah, near Hong Kong. The smallest figures were used as backdrops
in fish tanks, and the larger figures were used in planters. Very large
pieces were sometimes made into lamp bases. The usual marking found
on these wares is an impressed mark reading "CHINA."

# Mud Figures
## (Chinese)

*Mud figure, elder wearing
sandals, 13" h*

**Animals**
Duck, 1" h. x 2" w., glazed in either blue, green, white, or
yellow ................................................................ $15-20

**Ashtray**
Boy leaning over a bowl-shaped ashtray which contains three
fish. Blue with gold trim ............................................. $65-95

Two figures standing on the rim of an ashtray, glazed in
blue, green, and yellow .............................................. $35-40

**Bowls**
Bowl, 2" dia., with family seated on base, glazes of green,
brown, and gold ..................................................... $40-50

**Bridges** (all bridges are polychrome)
1" h ................................................................. $5-10

2" h. ................................................................ $8-11

3" h. ................................................................ $10-12

4" h. ................................................................ $14-16

**Huts** (both water and land huts, with or without stilts)
1" h. ................................................................ $20-25

3" h. ................................................................ $12-15

5" h. ................................................................ $25-30

8" h. ................................................................ $45-55

**Figurines** (single, ranging from ½" to 1" high, all c. 1905)
Elderly man (seated), white robe with yellow hat and brown
beard ............................................................... $15-20

Elderly man holding a staff, blue glazed coat ...................... $12-15

Woman with pink robe and yellow fan ............................... $25-35

Woman with purse, glazed in pink, brown, and yellow .............. $25-30

**Figurines** (pairs, ranging in height from ½" to 1", all c. 1905)
Elderly man with staff and kneeling woman .......................... $25-35

Two elderly men playing a game .................................... $25-35

Two seated elderly men fanning themselves .......................... $20-25

**Figurines** (larger sizes)
Elder holding a flute, blue glazed robe, 2½" h. .................... $25-35

Elder (fisherman with pole), 3" h. ................................. $30-40

Elder seated with a book, blue glazed robe, 2½" h. ................. $25-40

Elder (fisherman with pole), 4" h. ................................. $35-50

*Mud figure, woman with
basket*

Elder (fisherman with hat on his back and pole), 6″ h. . . . . . . . . . . . . . . . . . . . . . . . . . $75-80

Elder, seated with a fish in his hand, 6″ h. . . . . . . . . . . . . . . . . . . . . . . . . . . . . . . . . . $60-65

Elder, coin carrier, green glazed robe, 5″ h. . . . . . . . . . . . . . . . . . . . . . . . . . . . . . . . . $45-50

Elder, coin carrier, dark skin, 10″ h. . . . . . . . . . . . . . . . . . . . . . . . . . . . . . . . . . . . . . $150-185

Elder, coin carrier, light skin, 10″ h. . . . . . . . . . . . . . . . . . . . . . . . . . . . . . . . . . . . . . $125-140

Elder, seated, dark brown skin, gold and blue glazed robe, crossed legs, 6″ h. . . . . . . . . . . . . . . . . . . . . . . . . . . . . . . . . . . . . . . . . . . . . . . . . . . $65-80

Elder standing, blue glazed robe, 6″ h. . . . . . . . . . . . . . . . . . . . . . . . . . . . . . . . . . . . $45-50

Elder, seated with legs crossed, 7½″ h. . . . . . . . . . . . . . . . . . . . . . . . . . . . . . . . . . . . $75-90

Elder, hat on back with yellow staff and robe, 7½″ h. . . . . . . . . . . . . . . . . . . . . . . $85-90

Elder with bundle of sticks on his back, blue robe, finely detailed . . . . . . . . . . . . . . . . . . . . . . . . . . . . . . . . . . . . . . . . . . . . . . . . . . . . . . . . . . . $115-140

Elder holding a bowl and hat, hand showing, wearing sandals, turquoise and blue robe with gold trim, 13″ h. x 4½″ w. (Illus.) . . . . . . . . . . . . . . . . . . . . . . . . . . . . . . . . . . . . . . . . . . $250-280

Woman holding a peach, green and blue robe, 2½″ h. . . . . . . . . . . . . . . . . . . . . . . $40-75

Woman standing with a book, green and blue robe, 4″ h. . . . . . . . . . . . . . . . . . . . $70-85

Woman sitting on a platform with hands extending a bowl, yellow robe, 4″ h. x 5″ w. . . . . . . . . . . . . . . . . . . . . . . . . . . . . . . . . . . . . . . . . . . $115-130

Woman water carrier, pole across her back with water buckets, glazed in brown and green, 5″ h. . . . . . . . . . . . . . . . . . . . . . . . . . . . $85-100

Woman standing with a book, robe glazed green and blue, 5″ h. . . . . . . . . . . . . . . . . . . . . . . . . . . . . . . . . . . . . . . . . . . . . . . . . . . . . . . . . . . . $65-80

Woman with teapot, both hands showing, robe glazed in blue and green, 10″ h. . . . . . . . . . . . . . . . . . . . . . . . . . . . . . . . . . . . . . . . . . . . . . . $145-160

Woman with pocketbook, blue robe, 14″ h. . . . . . . . . . . . . . . . . . . . . . . . . . . . . . $250-275

Woman with basket, pink and blue robe, 6″ h. (Illus.) . . . . . . . . . . . . . . . . . . . . . $95-115

**Figurines** (pairs, larger sizes)
Elder holding a musical instrument, turquoise and royal blue glazing. Woman holding a tray with teapot and cup. Robe in blue and green with gold sash. Both pieces are 15″ h. . . . . . . . . . . . . . . . . . . $600-700

**Pagodas** (either monochrome or polychrome)
1″ h. . . . . . . . . . . . . . . . . . . . . . . . . . . . . . . . . . . . . . . . . . . . . . . . . . . . . . . . . . . . . . . . $8-11

2″ h. . . . . . . . . . . . . . . . . . . . . . . . . . . . . . . . . . . . . . . . . . . . . . . . . . . . . . . . . . . . . . . . $9-13

3″ h. . . . . . . . . . . . . . . . . . . . . . . . . . . . . . . . . . . . . . . . . . . . . . . . . . . . . . . . . . . . . . . . $12-16

4″ h. . . . . . . . . . . . . . . . . . . . . . . . . . . . . . . . . . . . . . . . . . . . . . . . . . . . . . . . . . . . . . . . $14-18

6″ h. . . . . . . . . . . . . . . . . . . . . . . . . . . . . . . . . . . . . . . . . . . . . . . . . . . . . . . . . . . . . . . . $15-20

**Vase**
Vase with molded fish that have large black eyes . . . . . . . . . . . . . . . . . . . . . . . . . $75-90

**Wall plaque**
Wall plaque decorated with grasshoppers, glazed in blue, yellow, and brown . . . . . . . . . . . . . . . . . . . . . . . . . . . . . . . . . . . . . . . . . . . . . . . . . . . $70-80

## Nabeshima
*(Japanese)*

Prior to the Meiji restoration (1868), Nabeshima wares were not sold on the open market. Their use and ownership was limited to the daimyo (feudal lord) of Nabeshima and those to whom he presented these wares. Nabeshima wares are perhaps the finest porcelains ever produced by the Japanese. They are easily recognized by a high foot rim, upon which a comb pattern was drawn. The reverse (exterior) usually has a coin pattern, and the early pieces have a slight bluish cast. The designs are bold, naturalistic, and generally floral in form.

Dish, 5¾" dia., 18th century, three floral sprays in
underglaze blue, raised on a high foot, comb pattern in
underglaze blue . . . . . . . . . . . . . . . . . . . . . . . . . . . . . . . . . . . . . . . . . . . . . $5,000-5,500

Dish, 8¼" dia., early 20th century, two irises in underglaze
blue, high foot, comb pattern with border of cloud scrolls . . . . . . . . . . . . . . . . . . . . . $300-400

Dish, 6" dia., 19th century, high foot, polychrome motif of
narcissus . . . . . . . . . . . . . . . . . . . . . . . . . . . . . . . . . . . . . . . . . . . . . . . . . . $1,200-1,500

## Nanking Blue and White
*(Chinese)*

Nanking blue and white porcelain wares usually have a band border which is more delicate than that found on Canton blue and white. Instead of a scalloped containment, the Nanking border has a continuous containment of spears and posts. Unlike Canton blue and white, Nanking wares can be embellished with gold. The central theme generally found on Nanking blue and white is a form of the willow pattern, but unlike Canton blue and white, the Nanking pattern usually has a standing figure on a bridge holding an open umbrella.

(See: Canton Blue and White)

Bowl, 15" oval, late 18th century, with flat octagonal rim,
with elaborate rim border of ju-i lappets, flowers, and diaper
pattern . . . . . . . . . . . . . . . . . . . . . . . . . . . . . . . . . . . . . . . . . . . . . . . . . . . . . $600-700

Cup and saucer . . . . . . . . . . . . . . . . . . . . . . . . . . . . . . . . . . . . . . . . . . . . . . . . . $50-75

Cup plate, 5½" l., lozenge shape, with flat bottom and short,
straight sides . . . . . . . . . . . . . . . . . . . . . . . . . . . . . . . . . . . . . . . . . . . . . . . . . $100-125

Dish, 6" l., leaf-shaped, c. 1840 . . . . . . . . . . . . . . . . . . . . . . . . . . . . . . . . . . . . $100-140

Dish, 9" dia., petal form with scalloped rim . . . . . . . . . . . . . . . . . . . . . . . . . . . . . $150-225

Dish, 10" l., early 19th century, unusual form resembling ju-i
head . . . . . . . . . . . . . . . . . . . . . . . . . . . . . . . . . . . . . . . . . . . . . . . . . . . . . . . . $250-300

Ewer, 11" h., late 19th century, tall cylindrical shape with a
small spout at the mouth . . . . . . . . . . . . . . . . . . . . . . . . . . . . . . . . . . . . . . . . . $275-300

Ginger jar, 6" h. . . . . . . . . . . . . . . . . . . . . . . . . . . . . . . . . . . . . . . . . . . . . . . . . $125-175

Plate, 10" l., late 18th century, oval shape with reticulated
border . . . . . . . . . . . . . . . . . . . . . . . . . . . . . . . . . . . . . . . . . . . . . . . . . . . . . . . $250-300

Platter, 12" sq., late 19th century . . . . . . . . . . . . . . . . . . . . . . . . . . . . . . . . . . . . $185-225

Platter, 14" l., c. 1800 . . . . . . . . . . . . . . . . . . . . . . . . . . . . . . . . . . . . . . . . . . . . $375-425

Platter, 15" l., c. 1800 . . . . . . . . . . . . . . . . . . . . . . . . . . . . . . . . . . . . . . . . . . . . $500-550

Platter, 16" l., late 19th century . . . . . . . . . . . . . . . . . . . . . . . . . . . . . . . . . . . . . $250-325

Tureen, 9" l., with flower-shaped knop on lid surrounded by
gilt leaves, gilt rim on lid and handles . . . . . . . . . . . . . . . . . . . . . . . . . . . . . . . . $575-675

Tureen, 10" l., c. 1780, oval, with acorn knop on lid, gilt trim . . . . . . . . . . . . . . . . $550-600

Tureen, 10" l., rectangular, with acorn knop on lid . . . . . . . . . . . . . . . . . . . . . . . . $425-500

Tureen, 12" l., early 19th century, rectangular, with acorn
knop on lid . . . . . . . . . . . . . . . . . . . . . . . . . . . . . . . . . . . . . . . . . . . . . . . . . . . $450-550

Tureen, 14" l. x 12" h., late 18th century, with a foliate knop
on lid, deep blue . . . . . . . . . . . . . . . . . . . . . . . . . . . . . . . . . . . . . . . . . . . . . . . $700-900

## Netsuke
*(Japanese)*

The Japanese kimono was not equipped with pockets. This necessitated the need for a method for carrying one's personal accessories. The netsuke was used as toggle. It was attached to the end of a cord, upon which objects such as inro, money purse, seals, etc., were carried. The cord was pulled through the netsuke, thus preventing the cord and its attachments from slipping through the obi (sash). In order to secure the netsuke, two holes were drilled through it, at an angle, so that they met at the bottom. These holes are seldom the same size. When the netsuke was fitted with a ring bolt, it was intended to be hung from a chain. The average size of a netsuke is approximately 1½″, but this can vary.

## Materials and forms:

Netsuke can be found in many materials, including ivory, wood, metal, porcelain, bone, lacquer, horn, etc. Among the various forms are: katabori (animals and figures); manju, usually round, either made in one piece or two halves (slightly hollow and sometimes deeply carved); trick netsuke; and erotic netsuke.

**Bone**

A bat upon a leaf . . . . . . . . . . . . . . . . . . . . . . . . . . . . . . . . . . . . . . . . . . . . . . . $150-200

Sennin, egressing from a bamboo section . . . . . . . . . . . . . . . . . . . . . . . . . . . . . . . $100-125

**Coral**

Monkey with an abalone shell (pink coral) . . . . . . . . . . . . . . . . . . . . . . . . . . . . . . $200-250

Recumbent horse (pink coral) . . . . . . . . . . . . . . . . . . . . . . . . . . . . . . . . . . . . . . . $250-325

**Glass**

Glass netsuke in the form of a lotus pod . . . . . . . . . . . . . . . . . . . . . . . . . . . . . . . . $500-600

**Hornbill**

Boar upon a lily pad . . . . . . . . . . . . . . . . . . . . . . . . . . . . . . . . . . . . . . . . . . . . . . $400-500

Mouse scratching his ear . . . . . . . . . . . . . . . . . . . . . . . . . . . . . . . . . . . . . . . . . . $225-300

**Ivory**

Actor holding a string of beads and a fan, green and brown
stain . . . . . . . . . . . . . . . . . . . . . . . . . . . . . . . . . . . . . . . . . . . . . . . . . . . . . . . . . . $200-300

Badger dancing with one foot raised . . . . . . . . . . . . . . . . . . . . . . . . . . . . . . . . . . $400-585

Bat upon a roof tile . . . . . . . . . . . . . . . . . . . . . . . . . . . . . . . . . . . . . . . . . . . . . . . $400-600

Boy embracing a goat . . . . . . . . . . . . . . . . . . . . . . . . . . . . . . . . . . . . . . . . . . . . . $350-500

Chick hatching from an egg . . . . . . . . . . . . . . . . . . . . . . . . . . . . . . . . . . . . . . . . . $200-220

Child playing a drum . . . . . . . . . . . . . . . . . . . . . . . . . . . . . . . . . . . . . . . . . . . . . . $200-265

Daikoku in a reclining pose, dark stain . . . . . . . . . . . . . . . . . . . . . . . . . . . . . . . . . $300-500

Double gourd with motifs of chrysanthemum and paulownia
mons . . . . . . . . . . . . . . . . . . . . . . . . . . . . . . . . . . . . . . . . . . . . . . . . . . . . . . . . . . $500-600

Dragon coiled with eye of inlaid brass . . . . . . . . . . . . . . . . . . . . . . . . . . . . . . . . . $500-800

Dragon entwining the rim of a censer which has loose ring
handles and four legs, dragon having inlaid gold eyes . . . . . . . . . . . . . . . . . . . $800-1,200

Entertainer with a lion costume on his back . . . . . . . . . . . . . . . . . . . . . . . . . . . . . $250-325

European man clutching a rooster . . . . . . . . . . . . . . . . . . . . . . . . . . . . . . . . . . . . $800-950

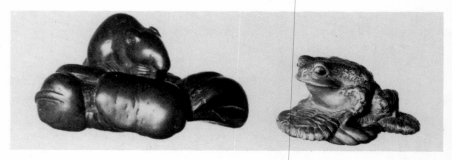

*Netsuke rat on water chestnuts (left); toad, 19th century, signed Masanao (right). Courtesy the Rosett Collection*

*Netsuke ivory rose signed Shuho (left); man calming earthquake fish (right). Courtesy the Rosett Collection*

Fisherwoman holding a knife . . . . . . . . . . . . . . . . . . . . . . . . . . . . . . . . . . . . . . . . . . $750-900

Flower basket, carved flowers and foliage in an oval box with
a pierced cover . . . . . . . . . . . . . . . . . . . . . . . . . . . . . . . . . . . . . . . . . . . . . . . . $1,200-1,600

Frog on a tree stump . . . . . . . . . . . . . . . . . . . . . . . . . . . . . . . . . . . . . . . . . . . . . . $400-500

Grazing horse, 18th century, signed Yoshi with Kahihan.
(Illus.) . . . . . . . . . . . . . . . . . . . . . . . . . . . . . . . . . . . . . . . . . . . . . . . . . . . . . . . $1,200-1,400

Hotei dancing and holding a fan . . . . . . . . . . . . . . . . . . . . . . . . . . . . . . . . . . . . . . $175-225

Kirin seated with head turned straight up . . . . . . . . . . . . . . . . . . . . . . . . . . . . . . . $500-700

Man calming earthquake fish. (Illus.) . . . . . . . . . . . . . . . . . . . . . . . . . . . . . . . . . . $1,100-1,200

*Netsuke wood bowl with wind god (left); ivory bowl, shakudo disc with Mongolian boy riding a ram (center); Noh and Kyogen masks, boxwood (right). Courtesy the Rosett Collection*

*Netsuke ivory Shishi with egg and two pups (left); ivory pups wth lacquer motif (center); ivory grazing horse, 18th century (right). Courtesy the Rosett Collection*

*Netsuke Manju (ivory) fierce tiger. Courtesy the Rosett Collection*

Man with sake bottle (vendor), Tangarai Bishu ........................... $1,200-1,400

Monkey trainer with monkey on his shoulder ........................... $500-600

No actor holding a fan and wearing a red wig ........................... $700-1,000

Okame clutching long nose (Shunga) ........................... $600-800

Oni holding a rosary and beating on a drum with a mallet ........................... $200-300

Oni inside a money box ........................... $175-250

Ox recumbent with detailed harness, large size ........................... $900-1,200

Peapods on a stalk ........................... $200-250

Puppy reclining ........................... $300-400

Rose, 20th century, signed Shuho. (Illus.) ........................... $850-950

Samurai warrior leaning on his sword ........................... $200-285

Samurai seated on the severed head of a demon ........................... $375-500

Sesshu (painted), seated with a mouse on his lap ........................... $600-800

Shoki standing on oni ........................... $200-240

Snail emerging from its shell ........................... $800-1,000

Tiger, inlaid mother-of-pearl eyes, signed Hakuryu ........................... $1,000-1,300

Two pups and Shishi, signed Hidemasa. (Illus.) ........................... $1,900-2,100

Two pups with lacquer motifs of flowers, 18th century. (Illus.) ........................... $750-800

### Ivory, groups
Bathers (nude) three women bathing with a young child washing their backs ........................... $400-600

Cluster of seashells, including clam and conch ........................... $1,200-1,500

Cluster of skulls, 19th century, snakes, and toad, stained, eyes of inlaid horn ........................... $2,300-2,700

Daikoku seated on the shoulders of Fukurujoku ........................... $250-300

Rabbits seated with paws and heads raised to form a triangular contour, eyes inlaid with carnelian ........................... $400-500

### Ivory Manju
Daikoku and a rat, Shibayama style ........................... $600-750

Pierced with depiction of tea ceremony utensils ........................... $475-655

Pierced and hollow, depicting a fox in the guise of Benten ........................... $600-800

Relief carvings of vegetables ........................... $400-500

Twelve animals of the zodiac ........................... $600-700

Warrior and tiger. (Illus.) ........................... $650-750

### Ivory, Okimono style
Boy on an ox, holding a rope tied to the ox's halter ........................... $250-300

Child nursing with a monkey and rabbit at the feet of the nursemaid ........................... $600-900

Man sitting on a bundle of sticks, holding a peach while his wife is washing clothes in a tub ........................... $300-450

Monkey looking at a monkey through a magnifying glass ........................... $300-400

Skull with a snake entwined around the top ........................... $300-375

### Lacquer
Box (kidney-shaped), gold lacquer motifs of paulownia leaves ........................... $300-400

Karako seated, 19th century (cinnabar) ........................... $400-500

Table (Chinese-style), with four curved legs and carved motif of cranes and foliage ........................... $275-375

### Metal
Shakudo disc, Mongolian boy and ram. (Illus.) ........................... $750-850

Silver-shakudo-gold, wind god (wood bowl), 19th century.

(Illus.) . . . . . . . . . . . . . . . . . . . . . . . . . . . . . . . . . . . . . . . . . . . . . . . $700-800

**Narwhal**
Narwhal tusk section, with silver flower mounts . . . . . . . . . . . . . . . . . . . . . . . . . . . $400-500

**Porcelain**
Bell (celadon/siji) with loose clapper . . . . . . . . . . . . . . . . . . . . . . . . . . . . . . . . . . $150-200

Dancer with dragon mask, 19th century . . . . . . . . . . . . . . . . . . . . . . . . . . . . . . . $400-500

Man holding a crane in his arms . . . . . . . . . . . . . . . . . . . . . . . . . . . . . . . . . . . . $250-450

Manju, sometsuke with a bamboo motif . . . . . . . . . . . . . . . . . . . . . . . . . . . . . . . $400-500

Sage dressed in blue robes, seated on a tree stump . . . . . . . . . . . . . . . . . . . . . . $200-300

Shishi head (sometsuke) . . . . . . . . . . . . . . . . . . . . . . . . . . . . . . . . . . . . . . . . . $200-265

Two fish (ying/yang), Hirado, 19th century . . . . . . . . . . . . . . . . . . . . . . . . . . . $500-700

**Shell**
Nautilus shell section lacquered red . . . . . . . . . . . . . . . . . . . . . . . . . . . . . . . . $200-410

**Staghorn**
European gentleman in complete European attire and having
a very long beard . . . . . . . . . . . . . . . . . . . . . . . . . . . . . . . . . . . . . . . . . . . . . $400-750

Fukurokoju, 18th century . . . . . . . . . . . . . . . . . . . . . . . . . . . . . . . . . . . . . . . . $200-400

Kwan Yu (a war god), holding a weapon and stroking his
beard . . . . . . . . . . . . . . . . . . . . . . . . . . . . . . . . . . . . . . . . . . . . . . . . . . . . . . $350-450

Tiger with head turned back . . . . . . . . . . . . . . . . . . . . . . . . . . . . . . . . . . . . . . $200-300

**Wood**
Chestnuts, 19th century, with ivory worm . . . . . . . . . . . . . . . . . . . . . . . . . . . . $700-900

Gama Sennin with a basket in his right hand and a dog
slung over his shoulder . . . . . . . . . . . . . . . . . . . . . . . . . . . . . . . . . . . . . . . . . $300-400

Kiyohimi, 19th century, the dragon/witch around the bell of
Dojo-ji . . . . . . . . . . . . . . . . . . . . . . . . . . . . . . . . . . . . . . . . . . . . . . . . . . . . . $300-450

Lohan, 18th century, signed Shuzan, loose robes holding
right arm upward . . . . . . . . . . . . . . . . . . . . . . . . . . . . . . . . . . . . . . . . . . . . . $700-900

Noh and Hyogen mask, 19th century. (Illus.) . . . . . . . . . . . . . . . . . . . . . . . . $900-1,100

Ox reclining, ivory and horn inlaid eyes, signed Tomotada . . . . . . . . . . . . . . . . $450-550

Rat on water chestnuts, signed Awataguchi. (Illus.) . . . . . . . . . . . . . . . . . $1,600-1,800

Sage and buffalo, 18th century . . . . . . . . . . . . . . . . . . . . . . . . . . . . . . . . . . . $600-800

Toad on upturned sandal, 19th century, signed Masanao . . . . . . . . . . . . . . $2,200-2,400

**Wood, groups**
Three turtles, pyramid form . . . . . . . . . . . . . . . . . . . . . . . . . . . . . . . . . . . . . $1,100-1,200

**Okimono style**
Four small tortoises upon a large tortoise, eyes of inlaid horn . . . . . . . . . . . . . . $900-1,200

The first emperor of the 19th century was Chia Ch'ing (1796-1820), who should not be confused with the Ming emperor of the same name. Underglaze blue vases with gilded background and rice grain patterns were a specialty of the period. Other porcelains followed in the tradition of those of Ch'ien Lung. In the reign of Tao Kuang (1821-1850) the degeneration of the artwork that began in the late Ch'ien Lung period continued. The enamels and monochromes show differences in color although their shapes are still perfect. Produced in this period are small carved porcelains executed much in the same style as cinnabar but glazed with yellow or green. Enameled celadons were also produced. There was little porcelain production in the reign of Hsien-fêng (1851-1861) since the imperial factory had burned down and was not rebuilt until 1864 during

# Nineteenth Century Porcelains
*(Chinese, Ching Dynasty)*

*Nineteenth century Chinese jardiniere, 12½" h.*

the reign of T'ung Chih (1862-1873). The manufacture of this period consisted primarily of bowls, plates, cups and saucers, and vases. Kuang Hsü reigned from 1875-1909. The quality of the porcelain at this time was very coarse, yet at the end of this reign the potters managed to reproduce some earlier wares with remarkable success. Many are marked with K'ang Hsi reign marks. The last emperor Hsüan T'ung (1909-1911) left no particular mark on the ceramic history of China, which then closed with the establishment of the Peoples Republic in 1912.

Since so much of the 19th century wares bear marks of Ming and earlier Ch'ing emperors, it becomes the task of the collector to learn to distinguish the differences between early wares and later productions. The quality of the paste can be felt on the foot rim, and 19th century wares have a decidedly coarse feel. Knowledge of the colors and types of enamels used in early periods will help to highlight the variations appearing on later items. Museum trips help to identify the various shapes and styles of early wares. A qualified and knowledgeable dealer can be helpful to the new collector by sharing his knowledge and allowing the merchandise to be handled. Numerous books are now available with a wealth of information for the interested reader.

(See: Blue and White; Chinese Export; Eggshell; Rice Pattern; Rose Canton; Rose Mandarin; Rose Medallion; Underglaze Red)

Bowl, 2" dia. x 3" d., with carved design of dragons under celadon glaze . . . . . . . . . . . . . . . . . . . . . . . . . . . . . . . . . . . . . . . . . $400-500

Bowl, 9" dia., exterior of bowl glazed in a lustrous brown; reserved with a dragon in pursuit of a flaming pearl in polychrome . . . . . . . . . . . . . . . . . . . . . . . . . . . . . . . . . . . . . . . . . $600-700

Bowl, 5" dia., Tao Kuang period, completely covered with a crackled turquoise glaze, mark and period in red seal . . . . . . . . . . . . . . . . . . $200-300

Bowl, 6" dia., shaped with rounded sides and flared rim, with motif of colored flower bouquets in three reserves . . . . . . . . . . . . . . . . $100-150

Bowl, 6" dia., Tao Kuang seal mark and period, delicately enameled in rose colors with flowers and leafy scrollwork on a yellow ground, interior glazed white . . . . . . . . . . . . . . . . . . . . . . . . . . . $600-800

Bowl, 2" dia., interior and exterior painted in flower clusters of tou-ts'ai enamels, with a blue key fret border at rim and foot . . . . . . . . . . . . . . . . . . . . . . . . . . . . . . . . . . . . . . . . . . . . $200-300

Bowl, 4⅜" h., Tao Kuang seal mark, decorated with three yellow medallions containing pink peonies and blue blossoms set on a coral ground, interior glazed white . . . . . . . . . . . . . . . . . . . . $1,000-1,200

Bowl, 5" h., Chia-Ch'ing mark and period, exterior covered with a celadon glaze, the interior painted with underglaze blue decoration of flowers of the four seasons, with iron red borders containing black enameled key fret design . . . . . . . . . . . . . . . . . $500-600

Bowl, 5½" dia., Kuang Hsü mark, decorated with "three friends" and a cloud scroll medallion in the center . . . . . . . . . . . . . . $350-450

Bowl, 8" h., with flared sides, decorated in blue and white with kylins, dragons, and a dragon in center medallion . . . . . . . . . . . . . . $200-300

Bowl, 6" h., T'ung-Chih mark in iron red, glazed white on interior, exterior glazed with ruby red color of orange peel texture . . . . . . . . . . . . . . . . . . . . . . . . . . . . . . . . . . . . . . . . . . $250-350

Bowl, 7" h., Kuang Hsü mark and period, decorated in polychrome enamels of red, green, yellow and blue, with exterior design of animals, interior containing a medallion of a winged kylin . . . . . . . . . . . . . . . . . . . . . . . . . . . . . . . . . . . . . . . . $600-800

*Bowls (pair), 8" dia., commemorative Ch'ien Lung mark, enameled in colors with four alternate reserves of mythical horned beasts and flowers in archaic vessels, all on a

*Nineteenth century Chinese bowls, 6½" dia., Tao Kwang*

millefleur and k'uei dragon studded ground; interiors with
lions, iron red clouds . . . . . . . . . . . . . . . . . . . . . . . . . . . . . . . . . . . . . . . . . . . . . . . . . . . . . . . $380

Bowls (pair), 6¼" dia., T'ung-Chih six-character mark and
period, exterior decorated in a deep heavy ruby enamel,
interior and rims glazed in white . . . . . . . . . . . . . . . . . . . . . . . . . . . . . . . . . . . . . . . . . . . $500-600

Bowls (pair), 4" dia., Tao Kuang seal mark and period, blue
and white decoration, the exterior painted with two dragons
chasing flaming pearls among cloud scrolls, interior
containing a central medallion of a dragon surrounded by
flames . . . . . . . . . . . . . . . . . . . . . . . . . . . . . . . . . . . . . . . . . . . . . . . . . . . . . . . . . . . . . . . . . . . . $600-800

Bowls, 6½" dia., Tao Kwang six-character mark in underglaze

*Nineteenth century Chinese vases, 10¼" h., Sung Dynasty style*

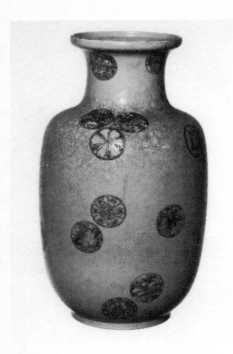

*Nineteenth century Chinese vase, 11" h., Rose Canton medallions*

blue, the exterior painted in underglaze blue and enameled in iron red, green, yellow, and aubergine with alternate green and iron red five-clawed dragons in pursuit of flaming pearls divided by flying phoenix, all below a band of Buddhist emblems; interior with dragons among cloud scrolls and flaming pearls. (Illus.) .................................... $1,600-2,000

Bowls (pair), 8½" dia., Kuang Hsü six-character mark and period, shallow bowls, heavily enameled in deep pink with orange peel texture, the bases enameled green ................................ $800-900

Bowls (pair), 6½" dia., Tao Kuang mark and period, kiln design executed in tou-ts'ai enamels in colors of green, yellow, aubergine, and red, interiors glazed white ........................... $800-1,200

Brush pot, 4" h., celadon glaze, incised scroll design ......................... $100-150

Brush pot, 5" h., shaped in pine tree form with relief-molded pine branches around a gnarled trunk, with incised bark and fungus at base, covered with a milky white glaze ................................ $275-350

Brush pot, 6" h., cylindrical, relief-molded with the figure of a man crossing a river, glazed blue ...................................... $100-150

Charger, 14" dia., commemorative Ch'ien Lung mark, millefleur pattern on gilt background .................................... $150-200

Cup, 3" w., shaped as a flower resting on a twig foot, the interior decorated with turquoise enamel, the exterior glazed white with iron red outlined petals containing yellow shading .................... $125-150

Dish, 6" dia., the underside enameled turquoise, the inside decorated in iron red with a central shou character surrounded by five bats ...................................... $100-150

Dish, 6½" dia., decorated in blue and white, depicting maidens in a garden setting ...................................... $50-75

Dish, 7" dia., Tao Kuang seal mark and period, decorated with a central medallion of a flying dragon in iron red and waves of underglaze blue, underside decorated with nine small dragons in underglaze blue ...................................... $900-1,200

*Nineteenth century Chinese vases, 10" h., blue and white decoration*

Dish, 11" dia., Kuang Hsü mark and period, polychrome enamel decoration of four winged dragons holding scrolling lotus stalks, surrounded by a gilt band, underside decorated with three floral sprays . . . . . . . . . . . . . . . . . . . . . . . . . . . . . . . . . . . . . . . . . . $300-400

Figure, Buddha, 10" h., in seated position with children, polychrome . . . . . . . . . . . . . . . . . . . . . . . . . . . . . . . . . . . . . . . . . . . . . . . . . . . . . $150-200

Fish bowl, 14" dia., decorated in famille verte colors on a pink ground, depicting wildlife scene on a lake as the interior design, exterior decorated with a mountain landscape, with diaper patterns as rim borders . . . . . . . . . . . . . . . . . . . . . . . . . . . . . . . . . . . $600-700

Foo dogs (pair), 36" h., male and female with ball and cub on rectangular pierced bases, enameled in ocher, brown, and green . . . . . . . . . . . . . . . . . . . . . . . . . . . . . . . . . . . . . . . . . . . . . . . . . . . . . . $800-1,200

Food warmer, 5¾" h., ruby-glazed exterior with two pierced knobs to attach handles, the interior and the liner glazed white, the cover with a peach form finial . . . . . . . . . . . . . . . . . . . . . . . . . . . $250-350

Garden seats (pair), 16" h., late 19th/early 20th century, of hexagonal shape, celadon glaze, with two floral panels decorated with flowers and symbols, with pierced cash symbol on top . . . . . . . . . . . . . . . . . . . . . . . . . . . . . . . . . . . . . . . . . . $1,800-2,200

Garden seats (pair), 19" h., with reserves of polychrome floral sprays and a pierced cash medallion at the top . . . . . . . . . . . . . . . . . . . . . . $1,200-1,400

Jar (covered), 12" h., late 19th century, rouleau shape, decorated in blue and white design of men praying in a garden on a celadon glaze, the lid decorated with three symbols . . . . . . . . . . . . . . . . . . . . . . . . . . . . . . . . . . . . . . . . . . . . . . . . . . $175-250

Jar, 12" h., late 19th century, the covered jar with multicolored flowers in the millefleur pattern on a gold background . . . . . . . . . . . . . . . . . . . . . . . . . . . . . . . . . . . . . . . . . . . . . . . . . . $200-250

Jardiniere, 12½" h., octagonal shape, with recessed reserves of blue and white decoration on a pale pink ground, with other reserves of calligraphy. (Illus.) . . . . . . . . . . . . . . . . . . . . . . . . . . . . $1,200-1,400

Plate, 16" dia., late 19th century, commemorative six-character mark of K'ang Hsi, painted in famille verte colors, depicting children playing in a garden in the center surrounded by bands of flowers and butterflies. (Illus.) . . . . . . . . . . . . . . . . . . . . $250-325

Saucer dish, 6" dia., decorated in blue and white in the Ming style with center medallion of children, the exterior decorated with a scene of two boys in a garden with two seated women . . . . . . . . . . . . . . . . . . . . . . . . . . . . . . . . . . . . . . . . . . . . . . . . . $150-200

Saucer dish, 7" dia., T'ung-Chih mark and period, decorated in blue and white in the Ming style with a depiction of "three friends" in the center, the underside decoration of three figures in a garden . . . . . . . . . . . . . . . . . . . . . . . . . . . . . . . . . . . . $300-400

Saucer dish, 6¾" dia., Kuang Hsü mark and period, decorated with a pale yellow ground with two incised and green glazed dragons chasing a flaming pearl among clouds, with similar decoration on the exterior . . . . . . . . . . . . . . . . . . . . . . . . . . . $400-500

Saucer dish, 6½" dia., Kuang Hsü seal mark and period, covered with a yellow glaze, the rim and base glazed white . . . . . . . . . . . . . . . . . . . $400-600

Saucer dishes (pair), 6" dia., Tao Kuang seal mark and period, the exteriors glazed in lemon yellow, the bases and interiors glazed white . . . . . . . . . . . . . . . . . . . . . . . . . . . . . . . . . . . . . . . . . . $500-700

Spoon, rice pattern, blue and white . . . . . . . . . . . . . . . . . . . . . . . . . . . . . . . . $10-15

Stem cup, 4" h., yellow and turquoise, decorated with painted emblems, interior and base with turquoise enamel . . . . . . . . . . . . . . . . . $150-200

Stem cup, 5" dia. x 4" h., Tao Kuang period (unmarked), set on a slightly splayed foot and entirely glazed in a mottled, deep pink ruby glaze . . . . . . . . . . . . . . . . . . . . . . . . . . . . . . . . . . . . . . . . . . . . $400-500

Teacup, 4½" dia., Tao Kuang seal mark, decorated with pink camellias and underglaze blue leaves . . . . . . . . . . . . . . . . . . . . . . . . . . . . . . . $100-150

Teacup (no handle), 3½" h., rice pattern ...................................... $20-25

Vase (miniature), 3" h., finely painted in the famille rose
palette, with floral decoration in the 18th century style ................ $250-400

Vase, 11" h., commemorative Ch'ien Lung mark, covered
with an opaque white glaze with delicate incised floral motif
and scattered medallions of flowers and birds in the famille
rose palette. (Illus.) ....................................................... $700-800

Vase, 12" h., pear shaped, covered with a celadon glaze and
decorated with reserved panels of birds ................................. $200-225

Vase, 12" h., Kuang Hsü mark and period, bronze form,
glazed in blue, with yellow and green enameled designs of
bronze form vessels on either side ...................................... $450-650

Vase, 24" h., flared quadrangular form narrowing to
rectangularly flared lip, decorated in blue and white on a
celadon ground depicting phoenix birds within geometric key
fret borders with ju-i lappets and wide geometric band at
base, the motif completed with birds in clouds and a series of
tall, stiff leaves on neck ................................................. $500-600

Vase, 12½" h., baluster form with mask handles, the front
and back with reserves of flowers on a yellow ground ................. $300-400

Vase, 12½" h., commemorative Ch'ien Lung mark in blue,
decorated with the millefleur pattern in tones of pale pink,
blue, and iron red, the base and interior decorated in
turquoise ................................................................. $300-400

Vase, 15" h., mid-19th century, bottle form decorated in
underglaze blue with overglaze yellow and red in a design of
leaves and flowers, the rim with a key fret border .................... $220-300

Vase, 15" h., late 19th century, pear shaped, decorated with
two birds in relief that are colored in pink and gilt ................. $300-400

Vase, 9¼" h., with imitation of Wan Li four-character mark,
late 18th/early 19th century, decorated in wu-ts'ai enamels in
the Wan Li style, elephant head handles with loose rings on
neck, possibly a Japanese copy .......................................... $600-700

Vase, 9½" h., commemorative Ch'ien Lung mark, mei ping
form, decorated with a deep rich yellow glaze, incised with
dragons, clouds, and flaming pearls above a band of waves
at the base ............................................................... $550-750

Vase, 24" h., double gourd form with blue, pink, turquoise,
yellow, and black floral decoration ..................................... $400-600

Vases (pair), 10" h., with flattened body and double lizard
handles, blue and white decoration, central medallions on
each side, one showing two frolicking deer, the reverse
showing a mountain and river scene, with flower and scroll
borders and key fret designs on the rim. (Illus.) ..................... $500-700

Vases (pair), 10¼" h., Sung style Ching pai glaze over
molded and incised decoration. (Illus.) ................................ $450-550

Vases (pair, covered), 11½" h., baluster form, decorated in
polychrome and gilt with birds perched on branches among
rockwork, all on a yellow ground, mounted on gilt bronze
bases, with gilt acorn finials on the covers ........................... $600-800

## Ninsei

Ninsei (Nonomura Seiyemon) is perhaps the most famous of all Japanese ceramists. The works attributed to him have delicate contours and are sometimes molded in animal forms. He was superb in the use of polychrome enamels over the glaze (glazing which contains minute crackles). Many works show how effective he was in the use of sprinkled gold and minute and delicate detailing. Ninsei lived from 1596 to 1666.

In compliance with the McKinley Tariff Act, implemented as of March 1, 1891, the country of origin had to be marked on items exported to or imported by the United States. Nippon was simply Japanese for "Japan" (the country of origin). The word Nippon was used until September of 1921, at which time the marking for country of origin was changed to the word Japan, because the word Nippon was no longer in compliance with U.S. regulations. Most collectors of Nippon era wares specialize in European-styled porcelains. During the Nippon era, such wares were quite abundant, especially during the years of WWI. During WWI European production was at a standstill and Japan became the supplier and filled a void in this market. Aside from European-style wares, traditional Japanese wares were produced during the Nippon era and such included Kutani, Imari, Satsuma, lacquer wares, cloisonné, etc. (see specific categories). And, aside from the production of traditional and European wares, the Japanese produced copies of American wares, including Roseville, Newcomb, and McCoy. Nippon era wares should be judged according to workmanship, method and style of decoration, size and contour, etc. Marks are the last consideration (see Marks Section).

(See: Coralene; Cloisonné, Japanese; Dolls; and Moriage)

# Nippon Era
*(Japanese)*

Ashtray, 6" x 4¾", Green M in Wreath, with Indian portrait molded in relief .................................................... $375-425

Ashtray, 4¾" l., Green M in Wreath, motif of an Indian on horseback ......................................................... $125-175

Ashtray, 5" dia., Green M in Wreath, motif of a bulldog ...................... $125-150

Basket, 8½" h., Green M in Wreath, simulating a Chinese cloisonné motif ................................................... $175-225

Basket vase, 7" h., gold ground with bright red and pink roses ........................................................... $220-250

Basket vase, 7" h., Blue Maple Leaf, cobalt blue ground with gold latticework ................................................. $220-250

Bowl, 12" dia., Blue Maple Leaf, scalloped rim heavily encrusted with gold, center motif of pink and yellow roses on a matte ground ................................................ $120-145

Bowl, 8" dia., two handles, encrusted with gold and strawberries, Green M in Wreath .............................. $55-70

Bowl, 7½" dia., Green M in Wreath, molded acorns on a matte ground in shades of brown and gold .................................. $135-160

Bowl, 8" dia., Blue Maple Leaf, slightly ruffled rim heavily encrusted with gold over a cobalt blue ground with bright pink and red roses ............................................. $170-220

Bowl, 7¾" dia., Green M in Wreath, scenic motif in shades of gold and brown ............................................. $80-95

Candlesticks (pair), 9" h., Green Maple Leaf, heavily encrusted with gold and gold beading ............................. $150-190

Candlestick, 8" h., Green M in Wreath, pink ground with white chickens and gold trim ................................... $95-145

Candlesticks (pair), 8½" h., Blue Maple Leaf, muted gray ground with yellow flowers .................................... $135-180

Chocolate pot, 11" h., Imperial Nippon, light pink roses and pale green foliage on white ground ............................... $65-85

Chocolate set, pot 10" h., four cups and saucers, Green M in Wreath, gold encrusted borders, with large dahlias against a muted ground of pink and green ................................. $250-300

Chocolate set, Green M in Wreath, pot 10" h., six cups and saucers with hexagonal contour, gold borders with lakeside scene and birds in flight on a powder blue ground ........................... $300-375

Chocolate set, Green Maple Leaf, pot 9½" h., with six cups and saucers, matte gold ground with red and pink roses .......................... $475-550

Chocolate set, Blue Maple Leaf, pot 9½" h., with six cups and saucers, cups having scalloped feet, muted tones with gold rim and outlining, gold beading with pink roses ........................... $275-350

Chocolate set, RC Nippon, pot 11" h., four cups and saucers having hexagonal contours, geometric motifs executed in silver ............................................................................ $300-385

Chocolate set, Pagoda Nippon, pot 10" h., six cups and saucers, pink and red roses with foliage .................................. $175-220

Chocolate set, Royal Kaga Nippon, pot 8½" h., four cups and saucers, featured is a Japanese beauty and child with gold diapered borders ................................................... $285-375

Cigarette box, 4½" l., Blue M in Wreath, gold encrusted with scenic reserve on lid .......................................................... $120-145

Dish, 5¼" dia., triangular with three open handles, snow scene in muted tones, Green M in Wreath ..................................... $45-55

Dish, two handled oval, 5" dia., central motif resembling an armorial pattern, gold trim, black outlining, Red M in Wreath ..................... $20-35

Ewer, 12½" h., Blue Maple Leaf, cobalt blue with gold encrusted latticework and reserves of delicate pink amaryllis ................... $275-320

Ewer, 11" h., Blue Maple Leaf brown and shaded gold ground with large white and red roses, gold handle and trim ................... $185-220

Humidor, 7" h., Green M in Wreath, Indian chief molded in relief ...................................................................... $450-550

Moustache cup and saucer, Blue Maple Leaf, gold lattice and scrollwork with stylized flowers .......................................... $60-85

Pitcher and three mugs (lemonade set), pitcher 6" h., mugs 3¾" h., desert motif with tents, camels, and riders, E-OH .................. $110-150

Plaque (pierced for hanging), 10" dia., Green M in Wreath, lake scene, autumnal hues ................................................... $150-175

Plate, 6" dia., Rising Sun, border of pastel flowers and posts with a bird handle ................................................... $50-65

Plate 8¼" dia., Chinese-style with bird of paradise and peony executed in blue, pink, green, and yellow on black ground stamped NIPPON ............................................................ $95-115

Plate, 8" dia., lake scene with beaded maroon border in pale muted tones, Green M in Wreath ...................................... $35-50

Salt and pepper, squat, bulbous form with bright red roses, Blue Maple Leaf ....................................................... $25-30

*Nippon vase (RC Noritake), 6½" h. (left); teapot, 6" h. (right). Courtesy Tom and Lynn Austern*

Sugar and creamer, portrait, encrusted gold, green Maple leaf .................. $195-225

Sugar and creamer, covered sugar, open creamer, scenic motif with lake and houses in autumnal hues, Green M in Wreath .................................................................. $50-75

Teapot, 6" h., (Illus.) .................................................... $100-125

Tea set, M. M. Hand Painted Nippon, teapot, covered sugar, covered creamer, four cups and four saucers, silver overlay dragons on an orange ground .................................... $265-300

Tea set, Blue Maple Leaf, teapot, covered sugar, open creamer, six cups and saucers, all footed, gold matte ground with red roses ............................................ $500-600

Tea set, Royal Satsuma Nippon, teapot, open creamer, covered sugar, six cups and saucers, reserves featuring two children with overall diapered motif and heavy gold outlining .................. $300-400

Tea set, Green Maple Leaf, teapot, covered sugar, open creamer, four cups and saucers, green matte ground with pink flowers and heavily encrusted gold with gold beading ..................... $400-550

Tea set, S & K Nippon, teapot, covered sugar, open creamer, four cups and saucers, gold handles and trim with pink and red roses on exterior and interior of cups ..................... $85-110

Vase, 12" h., Blue Maple Leaf, burgundy and gold encrusted latticework with gold handles and game birds in grass ......................... $275-320

Vase, 5½" h., Blue Maple Leaf, pale tones, two handles, scalloped neck and four legs, scenic motif, Art Nouveau style ................... $75-110

Vase, 9" h., Blue Maple Leaf, bottle form, muted shades of green and brown with lavender and purple water lilies and gold trim ............................................... $70-95

Vase, 6½" h. (Illus.) ..................................................... $110-125

Vase, 10" h., Green M in Wreath, matte gold ground with motifs of grapes and vines .................................... $90-125

Vase, 10" h., Green M in Wreath, matte ground with motifs of berries and roses extending from the neck down three-fourths of the way ........................................ $140-180

Vase, 9" h., Green M in Wreath, matte gold ground with large irises and leaves outlined in black, two handles and bold beading on neck and handles ............................ $100-145

Vase, 9" h., Green M in Wreath, four looping handles on rim extending to base of neck, carved open foot, motif of poppies with gold outlining ........................................ $95-135

Vase, 8½" h., Green M in Wreath, bulbous form with four legs, two handles, and fluted rim, jeweled throughout with soft pink roses .......................................... $145-180

Vases, 6½" h., two handles and footed, scenic motif in pale hues with gold trim on neck and foot, melon-ribbed, Mt. Fuji Nippon ............................................... $65-80

Vase, 6" h., pale hues with motif of flowers in pink and blue, corset form, Rising Sun (blue) .............................. $40-55

Vase, 5½" h., bulbous form, green and gold ground with motif that simulates Newcomb pottery, Royal Nishiki Nippon .................. $85-120

Vase, 7" h., Plum Blossom mark, scenic motif with boat. (Illus.) ................................................... $65-80

*Nippon era porcelain vase with Plum Blossom mark, 7" h.*

Noritake wares produced during the Nippon era have been highly collectible for many years. The collecting community is now showing great interest in the wares produced by the Noritake Company from 1921 to 1940. The Noritake Company was first registered in 1904. At that time,

# Noritake
*(Japanese)*

*Noritake ashtray, lioness motif. Courtesy Tom and Lynn Austern*

*Noritake bowl, 8" dia. Courtesy Tom and Lynn Austern*

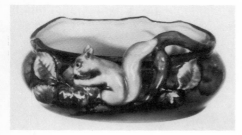

*Noritake bowl with squirrel. Courtesy Tom and Lynn Austern*

the name of the company was Nippon Toki Gomei Kaisha (meaning a family owned company). Until 1917 the word Nippon appeared on the backstamp (this differs from Nippon as used in denoting the country of origin). From 1918, "Noritake" appeared on the backstamp. The Noritake company is still operating and it has continued to use Nippon Toki and Nippon Toki Kaisha on various backstamps (these markings do not indicate the period of production as being the Nippon era). All items listed below date from 1921 to 1940.

(See: Azalea Pattern)

| | |
|---|---|
| Ashtray, 6" dia. (Illus.) | $130-160 |
| Berry set, large bowl 9" dia., open gold trim handles, finely detailed forest scene in pastel shades | $100-120 |
| Bowl, 8" dia., two open handles, scenic motif. (Illus.) | $85-110 |
| Bowl, 7" dia., squirrel motif. (Illus.) | $160-190 |
| Box, 3" dia., orange luster ground, motif of a woman holding a cigarette in a holder | $50-75 |
| Child's tea set, 15 pcs. (four place settings) orange ground with yellow, blue, and red parrot on each piece, gold trimmed handles | $120-140 |
| Child's tea set, 21 pcs. (six place settings) green band with black scalloped trim, gold traced medallion with pink flowers and small blue bird | $140-165 |
| Cigarette holder, orange luster, green trim, motif of dog's head on each side | $40-50 |
| Coffeepot, demitasse, cobalt blue and gold with two scenic medallions | $75-90 |
| Coffee set, demitasse, 21 pcs. (six place settings), covered sugar, open creamer, red/orange ground, black banded border, gold handles, Art Deco motif of bird on flowering branch, brightly colored | $100-125 |
| Cracker jar. (See Color Section) | $175-195 |
| Humidor, elk motif. (See Color Section) | $195-220 |
| Humidor, Art Deco, royal blue ground with rust, gray, green, and yellow stylized flowers and geometrics executed in black | $155-185 |
| Humidor, 6" h., beige, tan, and brown ground with motif of collie molded in relief | $275-325 |
| Mantel set, vases, 11½" h. (Illus.) | $500-550 |
| Pancake set, powdered sugar shaker, 6½" h., and syrup pitcher, 6½" h., orange and brown country scene | $75-85 |
| Plate, 8¼" dia., two open handles, wide green border, central motif of bird perched on flowering branch, Art Deco | $30-45 |
| Plate, 8½" dia., two open handles, wide blue luster band, motif of sailing ship in black on a gold luster ground | $50-60 |
| Plate, 7¾" dia., two open handles, blue luster border, scenic mountain motif in pale shades | $30-45 |
| Spoonholder, 2¼" x 8", gold and black trim on ivory ground with floral medallions | $20-25 |
| Tray, 8" x 11", orange luster ground with Art Deco stylized floral motif of pansies against black and white stripes, two open handles | $45-55 |
| Vase, 12" h. (See Color Section) | $200-220 |
| Vase, 6¼" h. (Illus.) | $75-100 |

*Noritake mantel set. Courtesy Tom and Lynn Austern*

*Noritake vase with pink and blue flowers. Courtesy Tom and Lynn Austern*

## Occupied Japan

Occupied Japan items have attained a new appreciation within the collecting community. Following WW II, Japan was occupied by a foreign country (1945-1953) for the first time in its history. It was a time of rebuilding and reestablishing industry. Articles exported from Japan to the United States during this period were marked Occupied Japan or Made in Occupied Japan, used singularly or in combination with a manufacturer's marking. Perhaps Ardalt, SKG, and Maruyama are among the marks appearing on the pieces of best quality. During this period traditional as well as European (Western) style items were produced.

Ashtray, 3″ x 5″, Imari style . . . . . . . . . . . . . . . . . . . . . . . . . . . . . . . . . . . . . . . . . $50-75

Busts (pair), 6½″ h., Ardalt. (See Color Section) . . . . . . . . . . . . . . . . . . . . . . . . . . $200-235

Candy box with cover, 5½″ dia., leaf and floral motif on interior and exterior . . . . . . . . . . . . . . . . . . . . . . . . . . . . . . . . . . . . . . . . . . . . . . . $75-110

Card box, 6¼″ x 4¼″ x 3½″, three drawers for chips, one large drawer for two decks of cards, brown lacquer with floral, and leaf, and butterfly motif . . . . . . . . . . . . . . . . . . . . . . . . . . . . . . . . . . . . . $90-115

Cherub with cart. (See Color Section) . . . . . . . . . . . . . . . . . . . . . . . . . . . . . . . . . . $145-165

Couple, court jesters. (See Color Section) . . . . . . . . . . . . . . . . . . . . . . . . . . . . . . . $250-275

Fisherman, 8½″ dia. (Illus.) . . . . . . . . . . . . . . . . . . . . . . . . . . . . . . . . . . . . . . . . . . $300-400

Group, 12″ h., man holding and kissing a woman, double bisque, outfitted in 18th century circus garb . . . . . . . . . . . . . . . . . . . . . . . . . . . . $300-350

Group, 5½″ x 5½″, man and woman, bisque, seated man and woman, man holding porcelain flowers in basket . . . . . . . . . . . . . . . . . . . . . . . $200-250

Group, 6″ h., man and woman, woman at piano with man seated, and parrot perched on piano . . . . . . . . . . . . . . . . . . . . . . . . . . . . . . . . . . . $175-225

Group, 10″ x 5½″, man and woman, both dressed in Victorian garb, man holding opera glasses, small dog jumping up at the couple . . . . . . . . . . . . . . . . . . . . . . . . . . . . . . . . . . . . . . . . . . . $250-300

Musicians, 7½″ dia. (Illus.) . . . . . . . . . . . . . . . . . . . . . . . . . . . . . . . . . . . . . . . . . . $225-250

Nodder, 7″ x 6″, celluoid, in the form of a donkey . . . . . . . . . . . . . . . . . . . . . . . $100-125

*Occupied Japan fisherman with boat. Courtesy Tom and Lynn Austern*

*Occupied Japan musician group. Courtesy Tom and Lynn Austern*

Salt and pepper set, pigs in a poke with pigpen holder ......................... $40-50

Salt and pepper set, Satsuma, motif of maple leaves ............................. $60-75

Teapot, 5" x 6", figural, bearded face, blue hat, contour of pot in form of a man's head ............................................................. $120-150

Tea set, Kutani style, covered teapot, covered sugar, open creamer, six cups and saucers, six cake plates, scenic motif with Mt. Fuji in the background ...................................... $250-300

Water carriers. (See Color Section) ....................................... $500-600

## Ojime
### *(Japanese)*

Bone ojime, Karako holding the cord ........................................ $220-310

Coral ojime in the form of a pumpkin ...................................... $75-85

Ivory ojime, ball with motif of leaves and vines ........................... $45-70

Ivory ojime, bead carved as a facsimile of Daikoku's sack ................. $70-90

Ivory ojime, boy with hands clasped ....................................... $200-300

Ivory ojime, carved with the 12 animals of the zodiac ..................... $225-350

Ivory ojime, double gourd form, painted ................................... $165-210

Ivory ojime, in the form of a shoe ........................................ $50-60

Ivory ojime, oval with high relief carving of a Lohan and dragon ......................................................................... $175-220

Ivory ojime, spherical with a dragon and tiger in relief .................. $150-185

Ivory ojime, tree stump ................................................... $130-190

Ivory ojime, turtle on a lotus leaf ....................................... $60-70

Ivory ojime, woman carrying a lantern ..................................... $175-205

Lacquer ojime, negoro (red/black) with figures and pine tree ............. $70-85

Lacquer ojime, circular motifs ............................................ $75-80

Metal ojime, brass in the form of a lotus leaf ............................ $35-45

Metal ojime, brass in the form of a lotus pod with an applied fly ......................................................................... $100-150

Metal ojime, gilded, oval, and pierced with motif of flowers ............. $100-140

Metal ojime, gilded, in the form of a clamshell .......................... $120-145

Metal ojime, silver, flattened cylindrical contour with motif of Mt. Fuji ................................................................... $160-190

(See: Inro)

Oribe is Japanese pottery which derives its name from Furuta Oribe (1543-1615), a famous tea master. Oribe wares were originally made for use in Cha no yu (the tea ceremony). Unusual contours and simple designs are attributed to Furuta Oribe. For the most part, Oribe wares are asymmetrical with bold and sketchy designs which are totally Japanese in concept. Oribe wares were among the first Japanese ceramic wares to be painted under the glaze (iron oxide/a brown rust hue). Oribe can be divided into three groups: 1. Ao Oribe (green Oribe); 2. Kuro Oribe (black Oribe); and 3. Aka Oribe (red Oribe).

All three varieties are partially covered with a dark green glaze, which has edges of blue and/or purple pink where it thins out. Aka Oribe is partially covered with a red-brown glaze. Ao and Kuro Oribe are partially covered with a gray or buff glaze.

# Oribe
*(Japanese)*

Bottle, 9" h., 19th century, motif of Mt. Fuji (AO) ............................ $300-400

Bowl, 7" dia., 19th century, Ao fluted rim, brown diapers ..................... $200-250

Bowl, 14" dia., Ao brown motifs ............................................ $300-400

Bowl, 5" h., Aka ......................................................... $250-300

Dish, 10" dia., leaf form (AO) ........................................... $300-400

Jardiniere, 7¾" h., Kuro, motifs of calligraphy ............................ $400-500

Umbrella stand, 24" h., Ao, early 20th century, two simulated
ring handles with motifs of stalks and plum blossoms ....................... $400-550

The peach bloom glaze, which was a creation of the K'ang Hsi period, varies in color from a pale red to a pinkish "liver" shade and often contains spottings of olive green. Like sang de boeuf, the color is obtained by the use of copper oxide in the glaze. The porcelain body is white and the foot rims are narrow, containing the perfectly and delicately drawn K'ang Hsi reign mark in underglaze blue. These wares may appear with incised decoration, which is faintly visible under the glaze.

# Peach Bloom
*(Chinese)*

*Peach bloom bowl, 5" h., Ch'ien Lung*

Amphora bottle, 5" h., 18th century, commemorative K'ang
Hsi mark in underglaze blue, glaze a pinkish red color with
heavy mottled green flecks .............................................. $800-1,000

Amphora bottle, 5" h., 19th century, K'ang Hsi
commemorative mark, glaze in reddish tone fading, interior
and base white glazed ................................................... $300-400

Bowl, 8" dia. x 5" h., Ch'ien Lung mark and period, the
bulbous body in pale to strong, reddish pink tone, the glaze
fading to white at the inverted rim. (Illus. here and in Color
Section) ............................................................... $1,000-1,200

Box, 4" dia., K'ang Hsi period, glaze reddish pink with green
flecks, interior and base greenish white tinted glaze .................... $600-800

Brush washer, 4½" dia., K'ang Hsi period, six-character mark
in underglaze blue, rounded sides covered with liverish pink
glaze lightly speckled with green ....................................... $5,000-6,000

Brush washer, 5½" dia., decorated with pink glaze, interior
and base green tinted white glaze ....................................... $600-800

Brush washer, 6" l., Ch'ien Lung period, seal mark in
underglaze blue, shallow oval form, exterior in mottled pink
tone, interior glazed white ............................................. $800-1,000

Brush washer, 7" dia., Ch'ien Lung period, seal mark in underglaze blue, shallow form, with mottled pink red glaze, interior and base with white glaze . . . . . . . . . . . . . . . . . . . . . . . . . . . . . . . . . . $550-700

Plate, 6" dia., six-character mark of K'ang Hsi in underglaze blue, covered with a thin mottled pink glaze . . . . . . . . . . . . . . . . . . . . . . . $1,200-1,500

Vase, 8" h., 18th century, mei ping form, with a brilliant pink-red glaze, the interior and base with a white glaze . . . . . . . . . . . . . . . . . $1,000-1,200

Vase, 10½" h., 18th century, double gourd shape, with a brilliant pink-red glaze, the base with a greenish tint . . . . . . . . . . . . . . . . . . $2,000-3,000

Water pot, 3½" h., 18th century, incised with three dragon medallions, glaze a reddish color with small green spots, interior and base with green tinted white glaze . . . . . . . . . . . . . . . . . . . . . . . $1,000-1,200

Water pot, 5" h., 19th century, commemorative six-character mark of K'ang Hsi in underglaze blue, glaze a pinkish tone with speckled green flecks all over . . . . . . . . . . . . . . . . . . . . . . . . . . . . . . . . . . $350-450

## Peking Glass
### (Chinese)

*Peking glass vase, 9½" h., unusual overlay of five colors on a yellow ground, 18th century*

Chinese glass is said to date as early as the late Chou Dynasty. The earliest objects were in the form of Pi discs and eye beads. Early Chinese glass was used as a medium for the imitation of precious materials. It was not until the late 17th century that a glass factory was established in the palace at Peking, and it was not until the Ch'ien Lung period that the production of glass finally developed to the high degree of elegance known and admired today. Objects produced during the Ch'ien Lung period included articles for personal adornment, occasional and ornamental pieces, snuff bottles, and other objets d'art. It should be noted that not all glass was made in Peking. Much of the glass called "Peking" was actually manufactured in Poshan, Shantang province. Types of glass: Carved glass made to simulate stones such as agate, jade, quartz, etc.; Ku Yüeh Hsuan, which was enameled like porcelain; opaque glass; overlay glass done in cameo style. (See: Snuff Bottles)

Bowl, 4½" dia., carved blue overlay of floral over translucent white glass . . . . . . . . . . . . . . . . . . . . . . . . . . . . . . . . . . . . . . . . . . . . . . . . . . . . . $300-350

Bowl, 6" dia., yellow overlay of translucent white glass, carved with flying birds among prunus, with yellow bands at foot rim . . . . . . . . . . . . . . . . . . . . . . . . . . . . . . . . . . . . . . . . . . . . . . . . . . . . . $150-200

Bowl, 6" dia., red overlay on transparent yellow glass, carved with chrysanthemums, with red bands at the rim and foot . . . . . . . . . . . . . . . $250-300

Bowl, 6½" dia., yellow glass carved and etched with three reserves of flowers with thick border . . . . . . . . . . . . . . . . . . . . . . . . . . . $200-250

Bowl, 7" dia., red overlay on transparent white glass, with overlay decoration of frogs and lotus on pond . . . . . . . . . . . . . . . . . . . . . . $250-350

Bowl, 7" dia., yellow translucent glass, with deeply carved rock and flower motif on the flared and scalloped rim . . . . . . . . . . . . . . . . $525-600

Bowl, 7" dia., green overlay on white glass depicting prunus branches in bloom . . . . . . . . . . . . . . . . . . . . . . . . . . . . . . . . . . . . . . . . . $150-200

Bowl, 10" dia., translucent yellow glass . . . . . . . . . . . . . . . . . . . . . . . . . $200-250

Bowl, 12" dia., blue overlay on translucent white glass, carved with birds and flowering branches of prunus and peonies . . . . . . . . . . . . . . . . . . . . . . . . . . . . . . . . . . . . . . . . . . . . . . . . . . . $600-800

Bowls (pair), 6" dia., pale purple overlay on translucent white glass, carved with four ducks in pond with lotus plants . . . . . . . . . . . . . . . $250-350

Bowls (pair), 7" dia., opaque egg yolk colored glass carved with songbird on flowering branches and rockwork . . . . . . . . . . . . . . . . $450-550

Dish, 8" dia., widely flared sides and everted rim, with a recessed center, translucent, bright green tone .............................. $75-125

Jar, 6" h., 18th century, globular form with incurved rim, ruby red glass, set on a wood stand ...................................... $1,000-1,200

Vase, 8" h., double gourd form, blue overlay on white ......................... $250-300

Vase, 8" h., blue overlay on translucent white glass showing birds on flowering prunus branch ................................. $150-200

Vase, 9½" h., 18th century, bottle form, overlay pattern of random bats in colors of blue, green, amber, turquoise, and wine on yellow glass. (Illus.) ........................................ $1,000-1,200

Vase, 9½" h., 18th century, bottle form, opaque blue glass overlay on white, motif of peach branches. (Illus.) ....................... $800-1,000

Vase, 10" h., bottle form, green overlay on white glass, carved with bands and floral reserves ................................. $400-500

Vase, 11" h., baluster form, plain translucent glass of creamy yellow color ..................................................... $600-800

Vases (pair), 9" h., gourd shape, olive green floral overlay on opaque white glass ............................................ $600-800

Vases (pair), 10" h., bottle form, opaque yellow glass carved with birds in flight and orchid plants ............................ $600-800

Vases (pair), 12" h., baluster form, carved opaque white overlay of cranes on a deep blue translucent ground ..................... $800-1,000

Vases (pair), 13¾" h., 18th century, bottle form, red overlay on white glass, the ruby glass carved in relief in peony blossom pattern with two bands of glass at the lip ...................... $1,500-2,000

Water pot (miniature), 1¾" h., multicolored overlay glass of pink, green, lavender, yellow, brown, olive, and turquoise, decoration of flowers, birds, and seals, Yang Chow school, small chip at foot rim ................................................. $300-400

Water pot, 4" h., green overlay of bird on white glass, green bands on rim and foot ............................................. $300-400

*Peking glass vase, 9½" h., blue overlay on white, 18th century*

Box, 9" l. x 5¾" w. x 4½" h., incised design of bamboo on sides and top, inner pewter tray, three-character inscription on bottom plus "Kut Hing Pewter, Swatow." A few shallow dents. Weight: 5 lbs ............................................... $200-300

Jar, 18" h., Chia Ching period, octagonal, with reserves depicting figures in landscapes and pavilion settings on shoulder, one of which shows a boy holding a tablet with inscription which translates as "made in 1562 by the Chung family"; various flowers in vases inlaid upon the splayed base; faceted neck depicting scholars, attendants, and officials; inscribed characters on the cover which has a faceted knop surmounting ground of radiating leaves and petals. Degraded and flaking ground ........................................ $2,100-2,200

Snuff bottle, 18th century, pilgrim flask shape, well hollowed, with dull textured surface ................................... $750-1,000

Tea set, probably early 20th century, six-cup teapot, bulbous, with allover design of engraved flowers, bats, etc. All pieces bear round engraved seal on side, side handles with green jade inside the handle, dog heads tops with raised, green jade decorated flower spray on lids ........................................ $250-350

Tray, 10½" dia., Ching Dynasty, circular, with incised design of woman and two children on horseback, bannermen, and terrace on the interior dark ground ................................... $350-600

Figure, 10½" h., c. 1900, design of cowherd playing a flute astride a buffalo ................................................. $160-400

# Pewter
## *(Chinese)*

# Porcelain, Miscellaneous
## (Japanese)

Figure, snake, 6" h., 19th century, wrapped around rockwork. (Illus.) ............................................................ $350-550

Plate, 7" dia., c. 1900, colors and gilt in scenic motif with birds in flight. (Illus.) ............................................. $125-150

Plate, 7" dia., c. 1900, openwork border, colors and gilt. (Illus.) .................................................................. $150-175

Vase, 8" h., late 19th century, signed Ryosai, low relief motif of morning glories, applied silver at neck and base. (See Color Section) .......................................................... $900-1,200

Vase, 9½" h., 19th century, gilt and colors, cranes and waves in relief, modified mei ping form. (Illus. here and in Color Section) .................................................................. $600-800

Vase, 12" h., late 19th century, signed Ryosai, pink ground, flowers in low relief .............................................. $700-900

Vases (pair), 9¼" h., 19th century, frogs in various poses. (Illus. here and in Color Section) ................................. $1,200-1,400

Vases (pair), 9½" h., early 20th century, same glaze shaded blue to pink. (Illus. here and in Color Section) ................ $900-1,200

*Japanese snake with rockwork. Courtesy Alan and Ina Sims*

*Japanese scenic motif plate (left); Japanese plate with openwork border (right).*

*Japanese porcelain vase with cranes and waves*

*Japanese porcelain vases with Same glaze*

*Japanese porcelain vases with frogs in poses*

Bottle (Futakawa), 9" h., bulbous with elongated neck, motif of pine trees executed in brown, green, and white ............................ $750-900

Bowl (Namban), 8" dia., yellow glaze with brown cross ........................ $500-700

Bowl (Namban), 4" dia., covered, motif of Dutch sailing ships .................. $300-350

Chair (Takatori), 3" h., 19th century, baluster form, flat shoulder, red/brown/ocher glaze, ivory cover ............................. $1,200-1,400

Chaire, Takatori, ocher glaze, ivory cover ..................................... $400-600

Chawan (teacup), 5½" dia., Shino ware, 20th century, buff with bubbled gray glaze, sgraffitto of crosshatched motif ...................... $600-700

Chawan (Mokubei style), Edo period, green, red, blue, and white ground, dragon motif .................................................... $175-225

Chawan, Akahada, 19th century, comb motif ................................. $400-500

Dish (Mingei), 10" dia., blue and white with motif of lobster ................... $500-600

Dish (Mokubei style), 10" dia., Edo period, scenic motif, red, green, and blue on white ground .................................................. $250-350

Figure (Iga), 5¾" h., c. 1900, Daruma seated and wearing a cowled robe ............................................................. $100-160

Jar (Hagi), 14" h., baluster form, in-rolled mouth, lower portions having motif of pine executed in brown, overall white gray glaze .......................................................... $600-800

Koro (Shino), 4" h., 18th century, buff and gray ............................. $500-700

Napkin holder, Edo period, signed Akahada. (Illus.) ......................... $200-300

Plate, 6" dia., with matching bowl and cover, Koyama ware, green and black motif of Mt. Fuji. (Illus.) ................................ set, $100-150

Pourer, white crackle interior, white and brown exterior glazes. (Illus.) ............................................................. $100-125

Tea tile, c. 1900, Aichi prefecture (Illus.) .................................... $50-65

Teapot, Onda ware, turquoise green splashes. (Illus.) ......................... $100-160

Teapot, c. 1890, pottery, in form of Mt. Fuji (Illus.) ......................... $125-175

Vase, bottle form, (Kiyomizu), 9½" h., buff pottery with stylized scrolling foliage and flower heads in blue and green with gilt highlights ..................................................... $1,500-1,700

Vase (Ryosai), c. 1890, floral motif molded in relief and embellished with silver (Illus.) ......................................... $200-250

Vase (Shofu), c. 1890, heron molded in relief (Illus.) ......................... $150-220

Vase (Dohachi), 4" h., cylindrical form, polychrome and gilt motif of maple leaves and clouds ........................................... $600-800

Vase, Wakayama, 19th century, lacquer ground with motif of polychrome and gilt insects. (Illus.) ..................................... $800-1,200

# Pottery, Miscellaneous
## (Japanese)

*Vase, Shofu, with heron*

*Tea tile (Aichi prefecture)*

*Teapot in form of Mt. Fuji*

Ryosai vase, floral motif molded in relief

Japanese Wakayama vase

Akahada napkin holder for Cha no yu

Japanese Onda ware teapot

Japanese Koyama plate and covered bowl

Japanese pottery pourer with crackled interior

Powder blue glazes (an adaptation of the use of cobalt blue pigment) were developed in late 17th/early 18th century at the imperial kiln of Cheng-tê-Chên. Cobalt blue in its powdered form was sprayed through a bamboo tube onto the unglazed porcelain. Transparent glaze was then applied over the pigment and the mottled blue "soufflé" effect was achieved. Oftentimes reserve panels were created and later painted in famille rose (pink family) or famille verte (green family) enamels. Powder blue was also decorated with gold tracery designs.

# Powder Blue
*(Chinese)*

*Powder blue vase, 16½" h., gold tracery, K'ang Hsi*

Bowl, 6" dia., 18th century, soufflé blue color inside and out, lip and base glazed white . . . . . . . . . . . . . . . . . . . . . . . . . . . . . . . . . . . . . . . $400-500

Dish, 10" dia., 18th century, center reserve of birds and three smaller reserves of birds and flowers decorated famille verte, all on mottled blue background . . . . . . . . . . . . . . . . . . . . . . . . . . . . . . . . $400-500

Dish, 11" dia., unmarked (K'ang Hsi period), decorated in the center with famille verte medallion with four smaller Taoist emblems on outer border . . . . . . . . . . . . . . . . . . . . . . . . . . . . . . . . . . . . . . $700-800

Dish, 14" dia., K'ang Hsi period, with barbed rim, decorated allover with powder blue, with gilt tracery designs, base glazed white, signed underneath with artemis leaf within double circles . . . . . . . . . . . . . . . . . . . . . . . . . . . . . . . . . . . . . . . . . . . . $1,000-1,300

Jardiniere, 16" h., 19th century, commemorative K'ang Hsi mark in underglaze blue, decorated with famille verte reserves of maidens and children in garden settings . . . . . . . . . . . . . . . . . . . $600-800

Mug, 5" h., 18th century, with twisted vine handles and two famille verte reserves, one of a woman and one of a mandarin, both in garden settings . . . . . . . . . . . . . . . . . . . . . . . . . . $250-300

Vase, 9" h., 18th century, the interior glazed white. (See Color Section) . . . . . . . . . . . . . . . . . . . . . . . . . . . . . . . . . . . . . . . . . . . . . $400-600

Vase, 10" h., unmarked (K'ang Hsi period), gourd shaped, with two reserves painted in famille verte of landscapes and florals, with gilt traces on powder blue ground . . . . . . . . . . . . . . . . . . $800-1,000

Vase, 14" h., 19th century, baluster form, with two large and four small reserves of figures and landscapes decorated in famille verte . . . . . . . . . . . . . . . . . . . . . . . . . . . . . . . . . . . . . . . . . . . . . $600-800

Vase, 14½" h., 18th century, (double concentric circles in underglaze blue on base), bottle shaped, with two large reserves of mountain and lake scenes and four smaller reserves, decoration in famille verte . . . . . . . . . . . . . . . . . . . . . . . . . . . $1,200-1,500

Vase, 16½" h., K'ang Hsi period, with gold tracery designs and foo dogs, the gilt worn. (Illus.) . . . . . . . . . . . . . . . . . . . . . . . . . . . $1,300-1,500

Vase, 18" h., 19th century, rouleau form with cover, decorated with gilt tracery . . . . . . . . . . . . . . . . . . . . . . . . . . . . . . . . $600-800

*Vase, 18½" h., unmarked (K'ang Hsi period), of rouleau form with four iron red carp swimming on a mottled blue ground along with other gilt carp, flowerheads and aquatic plants . . . . . . . . . . . . . . . . . . . . . . . . . . . . . . . . . . . . . . . . . . . . . . . . . . $5,100

Vase, 20" h., 18th century, with a white glazed interior, double concentric circles in underglaze blue on the base. (Illus.) . . . . . . . . . . . . . . . . . . . . . . . . . . . . . . . . . . . . . . . . . . . . . . . . . . . . $800-1,000

Wine pot, 8¼" h., unmarked (K'ang Hsi period), with famille verte reserves of branches and birds, some gold decoration on the powder blue ground . . . . . . . . . . . . . . . . . . . . . . . . . . . . . . . . $1,200-1,500

*Powder blue vase, 20" h., 18th century*

## Raku
### (Japanese)

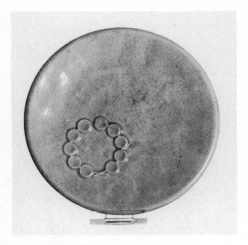

*Japanese Raku offering plate (yellow)*

Ameija (a Korean) is said to have produced a pottery ware fired at a low temperature and covered with a lead glaze. Tanaka Chojiro (his son) continued making this pottery. Sometime about 1588, Hideyoshi (military dictator of Japan) awarded this ware a gold seal, upon which was the word "Raku." The Chojiro family continued to make Raku wares and such were favored by the tea masters. The contours of Raku wares are generally thick walled, straight sided, with narrow bases and heavy glazing. The glaze can be dark brown, orange/red, straw (yellow) color, cream or green. Aside from Chawan (tea bowls) and other articles used in Cha no yu (the tea ceremony) figures, vases and other ornamental objects were produced. On occasion these objects have enameled ornamentations.

Chaire, 18th century, black with ivory cover ................................... $500-600

Chawan (teacup), 4½" h., 19th century, finger molded and covered with orange/red glaze ........................................... $400-450

Mizusashi (water jar), 8¾" h., 19th century, globular form, pinched waist, wide mouth, black glaze with red splashes, wood cover ................................................................. $400-500

Offering plate with mon, signed (yellow). (Illus.) ............................. $250-300

## Reverse Painting on Glass
### (Chinese)

The export market for reverse painting on glass was at its peak from 1750 to 1900. Unlike Verre Eglomise, the Chinese artisans were skilled in producing a painting directly on glass. Early reverse paintings on glass are a delicate interpretation of Chinese or Western subject matter, executed in pastel hues. Subjects included landscapes, portraitures, Oriental figures, copies of old masters, and of course, individually commissioned paintings. This art form was also used to ornament upper or lower portions of frames which were either in Chinese or Chinoiserie style. Toward the end of the Ch'ing Dynasty, the export product of this art form consisted basically of a lone female figure.

Reverse painting on glass, framed size 24" x 19", pavilion with attendants ............................................................. $250-300

Reverse painting on glass, framed size 15" x 20", a dignitary on horseback with attendants ......................................... $350-500

Reverse painting on glass, framed size 18" x 14", seated woman holding a single yellow flower ................................... $500-600

Reverse painting on glass, framed size 20¼" x 16", mirrored ground, a seated woman holding an open fan ......................... $300-420

Reverse painting on glass (mirror back), framed size 21" x 16", Kuan Yin riding a Ch'i-lin ........................................... $300-400

Reverse painting on glass, framed size 22" x 16", a woman holding a fan and hand mirror (mirror back) ......................... $225-295

## Reverse Painting on Glass
### (Indian)

Paintings on glass (pair), mirror backs, framed size 14" x 12", late 19th century, dancing girl wearing a red headdress .............. $300-400

Paintings on glass (pair), mirror backs, framed size 12" x 16", late 19th century, portraits of women wearing elaborate earrings and holding a rose, gilt frames ................................. $325-390

## Rice Pattern
*(Chinese)*

Rice pattern is a name associated with porcelain which has a design of rice-shaped transparent areas. The openwork decoration is accomplished by cutting through the yet unfired porcelain body. The rice-shaped cutout areas are covered when the object is glazed with a clear glaze. After firing, the cutout pattern is visibly transparent. This technique became popular in the 18th century. Most items are decorated in blue and white. Rice pattern is still being made.

(See: Nineteenth Century Porcelains)

## Robin's Egg
*(Chinese)*

By using a double glaze technique the robin's egg color was created in the early half of the 18th century. A deep blue ground color was applied first, followed by a sprayed on, pale, opaque turquoise. The result of this double glaze technique is a mottling of color which resembles the egg of a robin.

Brush pot, 6" h., 19th century, with an overall flecked glaze of turquoise and blue . . . . . . . . . . . . . . . . . . . . . . . . . . . . . . . . . . . . . . . . $400-600

Censer, 6¾" h., Yung Chêng seal mark and period in underglaze blue, supported on a short flared foot with double loop handles, covered in a turquoise flecked purple and dark blue glaze . . . . . . . . . . . . . . . . . . . . . . . . . . . . . . . . . . . . . . . $3,400-3,800

Censer (covered), 7" h., Ch'ien Lung period with impressed seal mark, of archaic bronze form, the robin's egg glaze heightened with gilding on the lid and key fret borders, lid reticulated, with a wood stand . . . . . . . . . . . . . . . . . . . . . . . . . . . . $1,800-2,400

Figure, 14" h., seated official, 18th century, official with robe and pedestal glazed in a heavy robin's egg glaze of turquoise flecked with blue and red, his face and hands having a bronze glaze, his beard enameled black, with a carved rosewood base. (See Front Cover) . . . . . . . . . . . . . . . . . . . . . . . . $5,500-6,500

Vase, 6" h., Ch'ien Lung period (unmarked), baluster form with a short rounded lip rim, covered with a brilliant mottled turquoise glaze containing purple streaks . . . . . . . . . . . . . . . . . . . . . . . . $1,500-1,800

Vase, 7" h., Ch'ien Lung period (unmarked), pear-shaped, with a deep blue and turquoise mottled glaze . . . . . . . . . . . . . . . . . . . . . . $1,400-1,800

Vase, 8¾" h., 18th century, bronze Hu form and oval section set with animal mask and loop handles, covered in a mottled blue and turquoise glaze . . . . . . . . . . . . . . . . . . . . . . . . . . . . . . . . . . . . . . $6,000-8,000

Vase, 9¼" h., incised seal mark and period of Ch'ien Lung, with a turquoise glaze speckled all over in brick red . . . . . . . . . . . . . . . . . . $10,000-12,000

Vase, 9¼" h., incised seal mark of Tao Kuang, cylindrical body with a short neck and lipped rim, covered with a turquoise glaze speckled all over with bright blue . . . . . . . . . . . . . . . . . . . . $5,000-6,000

Vase, 10" h., Ch'ien Lung incised seal mark and period, baluster form with two elephant head handles, covered in mottled tones of turquoise and blue . . . . . . . . . . . . . . . . . . . . . . . . . . . . . $1,200-1,500

Vase, 13" h., 19th century, wide archaic bronze form shape with a mottled pale blue glaze . . . . . . . . . . . . . . . . . . . . . . . . . . . . . . . . . $160-250

Vase, 14" h., 18th century, rouleau form, covered with a speckled turquoise and blue glaze . . . . . . . . . . . . . . . . . . . . . . . . . . . . . . . . $1,200-1,500

## Rose Canton
*(Chinese)*

Rose Canton is an export ware of the early 19th century similar to Rose Medallion. In Rose Canton, however, the subject matter in the medallions is flowers rather than people. Other Canton wares have designs including people but the medallion partitions are absent. Various pattern names falling into the category of Rose Canton are Black Butterfly, Rooster, Rose and Long Life, Butterfly and Cabbage. In the most general sense we can consider all rose pink decorated enamels that do not fall into the definition of Rose Medallion or Rose Mandarin as "Rose Canton."

**Note:** We reserve the title Famille Rose for all 18th century wares decorated in the then "foreign" color of pink. We have retained the following listings from our previous book. With few exceptions, the prices for Rose Canton wares have been stable for the past several years.

*Dish, butterfly and floral pattern on celadon glaze, 10½" dia.*

Basin, 14" dia., late 18th/early 19th century, with straight sides and wide flat rim, the center of the bowl decorated with reserves of children playing separated by flowers and butterflies on a green enameled ground, with four smaller similar reserves on the rim, the outside of the bowl decorated with five bats painted in iron red . . . . . . . . . . . . . . . . . . . . . . . . . . . . . $700-850

Basin, 16½" dia., c. 1820, wide rimmed bowl with decoration of court ladies in center reserves, separated by reserves of birds and flowers all on a green ground decorated with birds, flowers, and butterflies, with four bird and flower reserves on the rim, the exterior painted with three evenly spaced peony fleurets on a white ground . . . . . . . . . . . . . . . . . . . . . . . . . . . . . . $900-1,000

Bowl, 5¾" dia., Tao Kuang seal mark and period, decorated with multicolored foliate scrolls on a bright lemon yellow ground . . . . . . . . . . . . . . . . . . . . . . . . . . . . . . . . . . . . . . . . . . . $1,500-2,000

Bowl, 10" w., c. 1850, of quadrafoil shape, enameled with peonies, birds, and butterflies on the exterior, the interior in turquoise . . . . . . . . . . . . . . . . . . . . . . . . . . . . . . . . . . . . . . . . . . . $60-100

Bowl, 11½" dia., late 19th century, alternating panels of pavilions and figures, birds and butterflies all reserved on a green ground decorated with flowers and butterflies . . . . . . . . . . . . $250-300

Bowl, 16" dia., interior decoration of warriors on horseback with border designs of florals and landscapes, exterior decorated with foliage and sages in a mountain landscape . . . . . . . . . . . . . . . . $1,200-1,600

*Bowl, 18" dia., early 19th century, mounted in ormolu with a central roundel of a court scene with figures around a table, divided by floral and butterfly motifs on a millefleur ground . . . . . . . . . . . . . . . . . $800-900

Brush pot, 4¾" h., c. 1850, decorated with ladies in a pavilion, reticulated and molded in relief with gilt ornamentation . . . . . . . . . . . . . . . . . . . . . . . . . . . . . . . . . . . . . . $275-350

Brush pot, 6" h., Chia Ch'ing period, of hexagonal form with deeply molded panels depicting landscapes in rose enamels with gilt and coral red borders on each side, the base and interior glazed turquoise . . . . . . . . . . . . . . . . . . . . . . . . . . . . . . . . $400-500

Charger, 18" dia., 19th century, depicting hunters on horseback and flower sprays among rocks, rim decorated with wild geese . . . . . . . . . . . . . . . . . . . . . . . . . . . . . . . . . . . . . . $200-350

Creamer, 4" h., c. 1820, decorated with figures in pavilions in reserves, with double twisted handle, gilt trim, the floral motif molded in relief . . . . . . . . . . . . . . . . . . . . . . . . . . . . . . . $175-225

Dish, 8½" dia., late 19th century, flowers and butterflies in enamels on a celadon ground . . . . . . . . . . . . . . . . . . . . . . . . . . . . $75-100

Dish, 10½" dia., late 19th century, flowers and butterflies in enamels on a celadon ground (Illus.) . . . . . . . . . . . . . . . . . . . . . $100-150

Dish (rectangular), 14" x 7", late 19th century, figures in pavilions, floral reserves, all reserved on butterfly and gilt ground . . . . . . . . . . . . . . . . . . . . . . . . . . . . . . . . . . . . . . . . . . $375-450

Dish, 11" dia., Kuang Hsü mark in iron red, allover design of
four phoenixes and floral sprays ............................................... $150-225

Dish, 13" dia., c. 1820, with reticulated border, decorated
with figures in a landscape, the pierced border painted in
iron red ........................................................................... $400-600

Dish, 9½" sq., early 19th century, center decoration of figures
in a pavilion overlooking a stream, the rim decorated with
figures and birds within gilt scroll borders ................................. $500-600

Figure, 6½" h., 19th century, seated boy holding a
pomegranate, the figure decorated with a floral jacket in
tones of yellow, rose pink, turquoise, and blue, highlighted
with black, the pants painted iron red ..................................... $400-500

Garden seat, 18" h., 19th century, of hexagonal form, well
painted in overall design of birds, flowers, and flowering
branches, with formal borders at base and top, the top
pierced with a cash symbol and decorated with the overall
design ............................................................................... $1,500-2,000

Jardiniere, 16" h., 19th century, of square form on corner
bracket feet, each panel painted with a different design of
birds, butterflies, and various floral motifs ................................. $800-900

Jardinieres (pair), 12" h., on wood stands, late 19th century,
decorated in rose enamels with two panels of warriors and
dragons on a blue ground ..................................................... $1,000-1,200

*Rose Canton table screen, 22" h., 19th century*

Moon flask, 9" h., 19th century, decorated with rose enamels on a yellow ground, one side depicting figures and deer, the other with birds, peony and magnolia blossoms . . . . . . . . . . . . . . . . . . . . . . . . . . . . . . . . . . . $300-375

Mug, 5" h., mid-19th century, cylindrical form, depicting seated dignitaries surrounded by attendants and ladies, with a rim border of flowers and fruits within gilt bands . . . . . . . . . . . . . . . . . . . . . . . . . . . . $350-400

Plaque, 8½" h. x 11½" w., mid-19th century, decorated in the rose palette showing flying birds above clusters of lotus flowers . . . . . . . . . . . . . . . . . . . . . . . . . . . . . . . . . . . . . . . . . . . . . . . . . . . . . . . . . . . $400-600

Plate, 9" dia., 19th century, decorated with a court official and two ladies holding a child, with a reserved floral border, the back of the plate decorated with ruby pink enamel . . . . . . . . . . . . . . . . . . . . . . $400-450

Rose jar (covered), 9" h., late 19th century, enameled with large butterflies and flowering branches, ju-i head decoration on shoulder, lid topped with a gilt acorn finial . . . . . . . . . . . . . . . . . . . . . . . . . . . $100-150

Sugar bowl (covered), 4" h., c. 1820, decorated with figures in pavilions in reserves, with twisted double handles, the floral motif molded in relief, gilt trim and gilt acorn finial on cover . . . . . . . . . . . . . . . . . $175-225

Table screen, 22" h., 19th century, the floral decorated porcelain plaque set in a carved rosewood stand. (Illus.) . . . . . . . . . . . . . . . . $1,000-1,200

Tea bowl (covered), 4½" dia., six-character mark of Kuang Hsü on cover and base of bowl, delicately painted in rose enamel palette, cover and exterior with motif of butterflies and flowers, interior decorated with iron red scrolling lotus . . . . . . . . . . . . . . . . $300-400

Teapot (covered), 7" h., late 18th/early 19th century, with scenes of ladies and attendants at tea in a garden . . . . . . . . . . . . . . . . . . . . . . . . . . $500-650

Teapot (covered), 4" h., c. 1820, decorated with figures in pavilions in reserves, with twisted double handle, the floral motif molded in relief, gilt trim and gilt acorn finial on cover . . . . . . . . . . . . . . . . . $450-500

Tureen (covered), 11" w., early 19th century, lozenge shaped, enameled with figures on terraces divided by panels of ducks and insects on gilt floral ground . . . . . . . . . . . . . . . . . . . . . . . . . . . . . . . . . . . . . . $250-350

Vase, 9" h., 19th century, double gourd shape, with overall decoration of "precious objects" and Buddhist emblems, key fret border at the rim, floral border at the base . . . . . . . . . . . . . . . . . . . . . . . . . $250-300

Vase, 9" h., 19th century, commemorative Yung Chêng seal mark in overglaze blue enamel, rouleau shape with two gilt elephant mask handles on the shoulders, the decoration consisting of two reserves of flowering branches, floral sprays, and birds, with two shou medallions at the sides . . . . . . . . . . . . . . . . $600-800

Vase, 9½" h., late 19th century, with trumpet neck and splayed foot, depicting panels of figures and exotic birds divided by bands of millefleur . . . . . . . . . . . . . . . . . . . . . . . . . . . . . . . . . . . . . . . . $90-130

Vase, 9½" h., 19th century, seal of Chia Ch'ing in iron red, with a long flaring neck, allover floral design with reserves of peonies . . . . . . . . . . . . . . . . . . . . . . . . . . . . . . . . . . . . . . . . . . . . . . . . . . . . . . . $700-1,000

Vase, 10½" h., 19th century, seal mark of Chia Ch'ing in iron red, with finely detailed floral decoration on a green ground . . . . . . . . . . . . . . . . $1,300-1,600

Vase, 12¾" h., late 19th century, floral decoration on a yellow ground . . . . . . . . . . . . . . . . . . . . . . . . . . . . . . . . . . . . . . . . . . . . . . . . . . . $250-350

Vase, 16" h., 19th century, commemorative Ch'ien Lung seal mark in iron red, with allover decoration of lotus, prunus, magnolia, and hibiscus on a turquoise ground . . . . . . . . . . . . . . . . . . . . . . . . $500-700

Vase, 27½" h., c. 1860, baluster form, the neck and body decorated with numerous ladies in varied settings, with two gilt stylized dragon handles on the neck . . . . . . . . . . . . . . . . . . . . . . . . . . . . . $800-1,000

Vase (covered), 17½" h., baluster body decorated in colors and gilt with two rectangular and two oval panels showing court figures and pavilions, with a gilt Buddhistic lion finial on the cover, metal mounts on lid and neck . . . . . . . . . . . . . . . . . . . . $900-1,200

Vases (pair), 10½" h., mid-19th century, with medallions of

flowers, birds, and butterflies between floral borders . . . . . . . . . . . . . . . . . . . . . . . . . . . $750-850

Vases (pair), 25" h., c. 1820, baluster form, each large vase
with unusual, high-relief molded figures of an immortal and
a court lady, set on a diapered ground, with two panels of
Buddhistic emblems and scrolls at the sides surmounted by
two gilt mock ring handles, all with gilt highlights . . . . . . . . . . . . . . . . . . . . . . . . $4,500-5,500

Wine cups (pair), 3" h., 19th century, Kuang Hsü mark, each
cup with a warmer stand, decorated with yellow, blue, and
rose enamels in a floral motif, with a ju-i border at the rim . . . . . . . . . . . . . . . . . . . . $250-350

# Rose Mandarin
## (Chinese)

Rose Mandarin is a pattern of Chinese export porcelain decorated primarily in rose pink colors. Its span of production ranges from the late 18th century to approximately 1840. The pattern (named for a robed mandarin who is always depicted in the design) contains panels of mandarins, ladies, and children in garden settings separated by elaborate mosaic borders of flowers, birds, and butterflies executed in polychrome enamels. The pattern can be found on vases, bowls, candlesticks, and entire dinner services using Western shapes, i.e., cups with handles, flat plates, etc. The ladies always appear with gold decoration in their hair. Overdone and gaudy to the Chinese taste, these wares were exported in great quantity to the West where the pattern was in great demand. **Note:** We have retained the following listings from our previous book. With few exceptions, the prices for Rose Mandarin wares have been stable for the past several years.

(See: Rose Canton; Rose Medallion)

Bowl, 12" dia., of shallow form, with a central scene of
mandarins and women in Western dress, the border with
melons and flowers on a gold background . . . . . . . . . . . . . . . . . . . . . . . . . . . . . . . . . $450-475

Brush box, 4" l., oval shape with general mandarin design . . . . . . . . . . . . . . . . . . . . $125-150

Brush box, 6" l., decorated with mandarins and court officials
seated at a table in a garden setting, with profuse gilding . . . . . . . . . . . . . . . . . . . . $275-325

Brush pot, 5" h., showing a mandarin and court officials in a
garden setting . . . . . . . . . . . . . . . . . . . . . . . . . . . . . . . . . . . . . . . . . . . . . . . . . . . . . . . $250-300

Cup and saucer, with panels of mandarins and ladies, the
border with butterflies and flowers . . . . . . . . . . . . . . . . . . . . . . . . . . . . . . . . . . . . . . $125-150

Garden seats (pair), 19" h., 19th century, hexagonal shape,
with bird and butterfly borders and central designs of ladies
and mandarins in gardens and pavilions. (Illus.) . . . . . . . . . . . . . . . . . . . . . . . . . $3,500-4,500

Mug, 5" h., with large mandarin figures and two orange
carp, the border with a floral and bird design . . . . . . . . . . . . . . . . . . . . . . . . . . . . . $400-500

Mug, 5½" h., with mandarins and ladies in a court setting . . . . . . . . . . . . . . . . . . . $250-300

Plate, 10" dia., enameled with four panels of mandarins and
a central landscape medallion, background with gold and
green butterflies, flowers, and Chinese symbols, all on a
celadon ground . . . . . . . . . . . . . . . . . . . . . . . . . . . . . . . . . . . . . . . . . . . . . . . . . . . . . . . $300-350

Plate, 10" dia., with a central medallion of ladies and
mandarins in a garden setting, border in flowers and
butterflies . . . . . . . . . . . . . . . . . . . . . . . . . . . . . . . . . . . . . . . . . . . . . . . . . . . . . . . . . . . $175-200

Plate, 11" dia., with five mandarins in a center medallion,
butterfly border with reserves of ducks and goldfish . . . . . . . . . . . . . . . . . . . . . . . . $300-350

Plate, 12" dia., with the center of mandarins in a garden
setting, the border reserved with panels of bats . . . . . . . . . . . . . . . . . . . . . . . . . . . $250-300

Platter, 14" l., in predominantly blue and green enamels,
with a mandarin scene in the center, with a border of

butterflies and flowers with six-panel reserves of insects and flowers on a gold ground ............................................... $500-600

Punch bowl, 11" dia., 18th century, with panels of figural groups including mandarins on an orange diapered ground .................... $700-900

Punch bowl, 24" dia., c. 1820, decorated with panels of mandarins and women in court scenes, with profuse gilding ............... $2,500-3,000

Teapot, 7½" h., with mandarin panels and a background of "hundred antiques" in enamels of orange, pink, green, lavender, and yellow, with gilding .................................... $600-700

Urn, 16" h., with lid held by metal mount, with reserves of mandarins in garden settings, background of an allover floral design .................................................................. $1,500-2,000

Vegetable dish, 10" l., with a cover and scalloped edge border, with a boating scene on the lid, with panels and borders of birds, flowers, and butterflies ..................................... $500-700

Water pitcher, 8" h., eight-sided, decorated with general mandarin design .................................................... $600-800

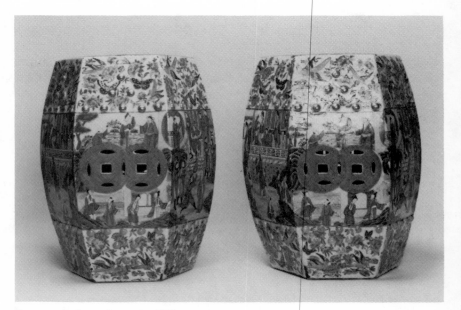

*Rose mandarin garden seats, 19th century*

## Rose Medallion
*(Chinese)*

Rose Medallion is a pattern of Chinese export porcelain featuring rose pink colors along with other polychrome enamels. The pattern is arranged with alternating reserves (panels) of flowers, birds, and/or butterflies along with reserves of Chinese figures. These reserves are usually four in number, evenly spaced around a center medallion. The areas between the panels are generally filled with rose pink peonies and green foliage (and on early pieces a gold ground as well as gold tracery in the women's hairdos). The vast majority of 19th century Rose Medallion was produced in Ching-tê Chên. However, most of these wares were decorated in Canton. The earliest pieces date from the latter part of the Chia Ch'ing period. Most of the Rose Medallion found on today's market dates from the last quarter of the 19th century to early 20th century. Complete dinner services were made for export in this pattern. An entire set would consist of 144 pieces, plus additional serving and ornamental items.

**Note:** We have retained the following listings from our previous book. With few exceptions, the prices for Rose Medallion wares have been stable for the past several years.

Basin, 15½" dia., c. 1840, gilt ground . . . . . . . . . . . . . . . . . . . . . . . . . . . . . . . . . . . . . . . . $850-1,000

Basket and underplate, 12" dia., late 19th century . . . . . . . . . . . . . . . . . . . . . . . . . . . $500-600

Bowl, 4½" dia., late 19th century . . . . . . . . . . . . . . . . . . . . . . . . . . . . . . . . . . . . . . . . . . . $20-30

Bowl, 7" dia., late 19th century . . . . . . . . . . . . . . . . . . . . . . . . . . . . . . . . . . . . . . . . . . . . $60-80

Bowl, 8" dia., late 19th century . . . . . . . . . . . . . . . . . . . . . . . . . . . . . . . . . . . . . . . . . . . . $70-80

Bowl, 8" dia., c. 1820-1840 . . . . . . . . . . . . . . . . . . . . . . . . . . . . . . . . . . . . . . . . . . . . . . $150-200

Box (covered), 3" x 6", late 19th century . . . . . . . . . . . . . . . . . . . . . . . . . . . . . . . . . . . . $60-80

Candlesticks (pair), 8" h., late 19th century . . . . . . . . . . . . . . . . . . . . . . . . . . . . . . . $400-450

Creamer (bulbous), late 19th century . . . . . . . . . . . . . . . . . . . . . . . . . . . . . . . . . . . . . . $50-60

Creamer (helmet-shaped), late 19th century . . . . . . . . . . . . . . . . . . . . . . . . . . . . . . . $80-100

Creamer (helmet-shaped), early 20th century . . . . . . . . . . . . . . . . . . . . . . . . . . . . . $175-250

Cup and saucer, late 19th century . . . . . . . . . . . . . . . . . . . . . . . . . . . . . . . . . . . . . . . . $25-35

Cup (without handles), late 19th century . . . . . . . . . . . . . . . . . . . . . . . . . . . . . . . . . . $20-30

Cup (bouillon), late 19th century . . . . . . . . . . . . . . . . . . . . . . . . . . . . . . . . . . . . . . . . . $30-40

Garden seat, 18¼" h., 19th century, barrel form, with pierced
cash medallion on top. (Illus.) . . . . . . . . . . . . . . . . . . . . . . . . . . . . . . . . . . . . $2,000-2,500

Ginger jar, 8" h., late 19th century . . . . . . . . . . . . . . . . . . . . . . . . . . . . . . . . . . . . . . $120-140

Pitcher, 7" h., late 19th century . . . . . . . . . . . . . . . . . . . . . . . . . . . . . . . . . . . . . . . . . $100-120

Pitcher, 8" h., late 19th century . . . . . . . . . . . . . . . . . . . . . . . . . . . . . . . . . . . . . . . . . $150-175

Plate, 6" dia., late 19th century . . . . . . . . . . . . . . . . . . . . . . . . . . . . . . . . . . . . . . . . . . $25-30

Plate, 7" dia., late 19th century . . . . . . . . . . . . . . . . . . . . . . . . . . . . . . . . . . . . . . . . . . $30-40

Plate, 8" dia., late 19th century . . . . . . . . . . . . . . . . . . . . . . . . . . . . . . . . . . . . . . . . . . $40-50

Plate, 9½" dia., late 19th century . . . . . . . . . . . . . . . . . . . . . . . . . . . . . . . . . . . . . . . . . $50-60

Plate, 12" dia., late 19th century . . . . . . . . . . . . . . . . . . . . . . . . . . . . . . . . . . . . . . . . . $75-100

Plate, 12" dia., c. 1820 . . . . . . . . . . . . . . . . . . . . . . . . . . . . . . . . . . . . . . . . . . . . . . . . . $250-300

Plate, 14" dia., late 19th century . . . . . . . . . . . . . . . . . . . . . . . . . . . . . . . . . . . . . . . . $150-200

Plate, 16" dia., late 19th century . . . . . . . . . . . . . . . . . . . . . . . . . . . . . . . . . . . . . . . . $200-250

Plate, 16" dia., c. 1820 . . . . . . . . . . . . . . . . . . . . . . . . . . . . . . . . . . . . . . . . . . . . . . . . . $375-450

Platter, 7" x 10", late 19th century . . . . . . . . . . . . . . . . . . . . . . . . . . . . . . . . . . . . . . . $75-100

Platter, 9" x 12", late 19th century . . . . . . . . . . . . . . . . . . . . . . . . . . . . . . . . . . . . . . $125-150

Platter, 12" x 17", late 19th century . . . . . . . . . . . . . . . . . . . . . . . . . . . . . . . . . . . . . $160-200

Platter, 14" x 17", late 19th century . . . . . . . . . . . . . . . . . . . . . . . . . . . . . . . . . . . . . $200-250

Punch bowl, 12" dia., late 19th century . . . . . . . . . . . . . . . . . . . . . . . . . . . . . . . . . . $200-250

Punch bowl, 14" dia., late 19th century . . . . . . . . . . . . . . . . . . . . . . . . . . . . . . . . . . $300-350

Punch bowl, 16" dia., late 19th century . . . . . . . . . . . . . . . . . . . . . . . . . . . . . . . . . . $500-600

Sugar bowl (covered), 6" h., late 19th century . . . . . . . . . . . . . . . . . . . . . . . . . . . . . $60-80

Teapot, 6" h., late 19th century . . . . . . . . . . . . . . . . . . . . . . . . . . . . . . . . . . . . . . . . . . $90-100

Teapot, 7" h., late 19th century . . . . . . . . . . . . . . . . . . . . . . . . . . . . . . . . . . . . . . . . . $100-125

Teapot, 7" h., early 19th century . . . . . . . . . . . . . . . . . . . . . . . . . . . . . . . . . . . . . . . . $250-300

Vase, 6" h., late 19th century . . . . . . . . . . . . . . . . . . . . . . . . . . . . . . . . . . . . . . . . . . . . $50-60

Vase, 8" h., late 19th century . . . . . . . . . . . . . . . . . . . . . . . . . . . . . . . . . . . . . . . . . . . $110-140

Vase, 10" h., late 19th century . . . . . . . . . . . . . . . . . . . . . . . . . . . . . . . . . . . . . . . . . . $150-175

Vase, 12" h., late 19th century . . . . . . . . . . . . . . . . . . . . . . . . . . . . . . . . . . . . . . . . . . $200-250

Vase, 12" h., early 19th century . . . . . . . . . . . . . . . . . . . . . . . . . . . . . . . . . . . . . . . . . $300-400

Vase, 16" h., late 19th century . . . . . . . . . . . . . . . . . . . . . . . . . . . . . . . . . . . . . . . . . . $300-375

*Rose medallion garden seat, 19th century*

Vases (pair), 11" h., mid-19th century, with lids, with flattened, pear-shaped bodies, gilt elephant mask and ring handles, and gilt foo dog finials on lids . . . . . . . . . . . . . . . . . . . . . . . . . . . . . . . . . . $600-800

Vases (pair), 15" h., late 19th century with bulbous bodies and tall ringed necks . . . . . . . . . . . . . . . . . . . . . . . . . . . . . . . . . . . . . . . . . . . . . . $900-1,100

# Sang de Boeuf
## (Chinese)

*Sang de Boeuf vase, 10" h., mei ping form, 18th century*

*Sang de Boeuf water container, 18th century*

196

The Sang de Boeuf (oxblood) glaze was first developed during the Ming Dynasty. The color ranges from cherry red to deep blood red to dull pinkish brown. It is sometimes flambé with purple splashes. The glaze may be crackled and may lighten to a pale color, cream or celadon, at the lip. Early examples had very controlled glazes which did not run. Later (18th century) examples show evidence of the glaze running over the foot rim, which was then ground down. Usually, 19th century examples have a very rough footing, showing evidence of having been chipped away from the kiln floor.

**Authors' Note:** Sang de Boeuf color range is broad enough to include the following variations: Lang Yao — a bright cherry to deep blood red; Sang de Pigeon — pigeon's blood; Sang de Poulet — chicken's blood; and the dull deep pink brown dubbed mule's liver by the Chinese. We have arbitrarily chosen to list these glazes under the topic heading of Sang de Boeuf, the justification being their mutual origins evolving from the use of copper oxide, and the characteristics of each color depending on the controlled kiln conditions under which they were fired.

(See: Copper Red; Flambé)

Bowl, 6" dia., flared rim with a deep red glaze . . . . . . . . . . . . . . . . . . . . . . . . . $400-600

Dish, 8" dia., Ch'ien Lung seal mark in underglaze blue, covered with dark mule's liver red glaze, the base glazed white . . . . . . . . . . . . . . . . . . . . . . . . . . . . . . . . . . . . . . . . . . . . . . . . . . . . . . $500-700

Dish, 8½" dia., 18th century, the liver red glaze thinning at the edge and foot rim to a pale celadon, foot with a celadon glaze . . . . . . . . . . . . . . . . . . . . . . . . . . . . . . . . . . . . . . . . . . . . . . . . . . . . . . $600-800

Jar (covered), 9½", mid-19th century, of hemispheric form with a domed wood cover and a jade finial, the glaze a streaky red fading to white at the rim and puddling at the foot . . . . . . . . . . . . . . . . . . . . . . . . . . . . . . . . . . . . . . . . . . . . . . . . . . . . . . $500-600

Jarlet, 3½" h., 18th century, with a streaky apple red glaze thinning to white at the rim, fitted with a brass well and mounted on an ormolu base for use as an inkwell . . . . . . . . . . . . . . . . . $250-300

Vase, 10" h., 18th century, mei ping shape, with flanged rim, mottled deep copper red "pigeon blood" glaze tinged with brownish black, and a white glazed rim. (Illus.) . . . . . . . . . . . . . . . . . . . . $600-800

Vase, 12" h., late 18th century, pear shaped, the red glaze fading to celadon at the rim . . . . . . . . . . . . . . . . . . . . . . . . . . . . . . . . . . $450-650

Vase, 12½" h., 18th century, pear-shaped with flaring rim, mounted on a pedestal foot, covered in deep crimson glaze, interior and base glazed white . . . . . . . . . . . . . . . . . . . . . . . . . . . . . $800-1,000

Vase, 13" h., 18th century, pear shaped, covered with a bright crackled lang yao glaze fading to cherry at the neck . . . . . . . . . . . . $1,000-1,200

Vase, 15¼" h., 18th century, baluster form with cylindrical neck and everted rim, covered with a red glaze fading to celadon at the rim . . . . . . . . . . . . . . . . . . . . . . . . . . . . . . . . . . . . . . . $900-1,000

Vase, 16" h., 19th century, of a heavy shouldered form with a waisted neck and flared rim, covered with a dark red glaze with mottling at the rim . . . . . . . . . . . . . . . . . . . . . . . . . . . . . . . . . . . $300-400

Vase, 16″ h., K'ang Hsi period (unmarked), bottle form, covered with reddish pink crackled glaze ending in a thick roll at the foot rim, base with a creamy crackled glaze .......................$3,000-4,000

Vase, 17″ h., 19th century, pear-shaped with a long neck, covered with dark red glaze with heavy accumulations at the foot, the foot with rough chips ..................................$400-600

Water pot, 4½″ h., 18th century, pale mule's liver glaze fading to a greenish tint at the edges. (Illus.) ...................$400-600

Water pot, 4½″ h., K'ang Hsi mark and period, with three phoenix head medallions incised around the body, deep red color revealing buff highlights under the glaze, the lip interior and base glazed in a blue tinted white glaze ........................$850-1,000

# Satsuma
## (Japanese)

Satsuma vase with continuous motif, 19th century

Satsuma is a Japanese faience (pottery) with a fine glaze which possesses a network of crackles, and such (if produced after 1787) will have ornamentations of varying colored enamels. Satsuma was first produced just after 1600. It was not until the Kwansei era (1787-1800) that Satsuma wares were decorated in the manner recognized today. It was during this era that the employment of enamels, including gold, was first initiated. The incorporation of human figures, processionals, demons, Lohans, etc., was not initiated until c. 1850. From 1871 on, Satsuma wares were produced in many localities throughout Japan.

Bowl, 6½″ dia., c. 1905 (signed Seikozan), 1,000 crane motif, gilt, white and colors ................................................$600-800

Bowl (covered), 8″ dia., c. 1890, cover molded in form of Mt. Fuji and two dragons, overall motif of clouds, flowers, and scrolls in colors and gilt ...........................................$2,000-2,500

Bowl, 6″ dia., millefleur (1,000 flowers motif) ...............................$220-245

Bowl (covered), 7″ h., c. 1850 (signed Ide), motif of birds and seasonal flowers in red, gosu blue, turquoise and gilt with gilt highlights and spire finial .......................................$1,800-2,500

Box (covered), 5″ dia., c. 1885 (signed Taizan), overall diapered motif in colors and gilt with panel containing a Lohan and two children, interior of lid and base with similar panels ...........................................$600-650

Box, 4″ dia., c. 1860, melon form, with gilt butterfly medallion in center of lid, motif of seasonal flowers, birds, and butterflies in colors and gilt, interior of lids and base having motif of butterflies and clouds in colors and gilt .......................$450-550

Brush pot, Taizan, 19th century. (Illus.) ..................................$200-300

Button, 1″ dia., c. 1910, scalloped rim, motif of quail and grasses in colors and gilt ......................................$135-150

Button, 1½″ dia., c. 1910, round with motif of Bijin .........................$100-150

Chaire, 3½″ h., 19th century, Taizan, kiku mon, blue and iron oxide ..................................................$500-600

Chaire, 3″ h., 18th century, buff with tea dust glaze, ivory cover ......................................................$600-800

Chamber stick, c. 1884, Kinkozan. (Illus.) ................................$100-120

Figure, 5¼″ h., Bijin, gilt, blue and red. (See Color Section) ..................$1,500-1,800

Figure, 3½″ h., seated nobleman. (See Color Section) ........................$1,500-1,800

Figures (pair), 20th century. (Illus. here and in Color Section) .............each, $160-180

Figure, 6½″ h., c. 1860, Lohan on rockwork base with crab seated in front of him, colors and gilt ...............................$1,100-1,200

Figure, 5¼″ h., Edo period, Rakan. (See Color Section) ....................$1,700-2,100

Satsuma vase, 14″ h. Courtesy Jerry King

*Taizan brush pot*

*Kinkozan chamber stick*

*Satsuma rabbit censer, 19th century*

Figure, 13½" h., c. 1930, Kannon holding a basket, red, blue, green, yellow, black robe with gilt highlights on brown ground .................................................. $150-185

Incense burner, 5" h., Edo period, signed Taizan, furo form, blue and iron oxide kiku mon .................................. $1,900-2,200

Incense burner, 20" h., c. 1885, oviform, gilt and colors with overall motif of Lohan, brocade ground, three mask feet, gilt Shishi handles and finial, crack in cover ........................ $900-1,100

Incense burner, 5" dia., c. 1811, squat form with three stub feet, center band filled with fan-shaped reserves of chrysanthemum heads, cage work silver cover, red, gosu blue, and gilt ...................................... $2,700-3,500

Incense burner, 7" h., late 19th century, signed Ryozan, elephant head handles, pierced cover .......................... $800-950

Incense burner, 4" h., c. 1840, signed Fuwa Sodo, motif of flowers in red, gilt, gosu blue, and turquoise with pierced silver cover .......................................... $2,250-2,800

Incense burner, 2½" h., c. 1900, signed Taizan, blue and gilt ground with panels featuring courtesans and children ........ $600-800

Incense burner, 3½" h., c. 1830, lappet border, two panels filled with chrysanthemum scrolls, gilt, gosu blue with red, domed, silver-pierced cover with embossed kiku mon ........ $2,200-2,600

Jar (covered), 9¾" h., c. 1850, signed Umeoka, domed cover with flower head finial, red, gosu blue, turquoise, and gilt, motif of seven gods of good luck, border bands of lappets ...... $3,500-3,800

Jar (covered), c. 1885, diamond-shaped panels filled with processionals, overall gilt diapers .......................... $500-600

Jar (covered), 3¾" dia., c. 1850, pear-shaped with floral motif in red, gosu blue, and gilt, two panels filled with Kirin, pierced silver cover .................................... $2,500-2,800

Jar (covered), 11" h., c. 1820, motif of chrysanthemums in red, turquoise, gosu blue, and gilt, border band of chrysanthemum heads and lappets, gilt jeweled clouds overall, domed silver cover with alternating kiku and maru mitsu aoi mons and kiku mon finial ...................... $8,000-10,000

Mizusashi, 6" h. (See Color Section) ........................ $2,200-2,800

Mizusashi, Meiji period, motif of white and gilt chrysanthemums ............................................ $800-1,200

Plate, 7" dia., Edo period, fine floral and diapered motifs with gilt (minor restoration on underside) ...................... $800-900

Plate, 10" dia., c. 1885, colors and gilt with four circular panels filled with Samurai in battle, diapered border, enamel heavily applied ........................................ $800-1,200

Rabbit, 19th century (censer). (Illus.) ...................... $500-650

Suiteki (water dropper), 18th century. (See Color Section) ...... $950-1,250

Teapot, Edo period, Naeshirogawa. (See Color Section) ........ $1,200-1,500

Teapot, 7½" h., c. 1790, two loop handles, cover, neck and midsection with motif of wide band of brown flowers and scrolling foliage .......................................... $1,500-1,700

Teapot, Edo period, Ryumonji, green and red motif ............ $500-600

Vase, 3¼" h., double gourd, silver overlay, signed Tanzan. (See Color Section) ...................................... $275-325

Vase (bottle), same glaze. (See Color Section) ................ $2,500-3,200

Vase, 14" h., Edo period, Lohan in colors and gilt. (Illus.) ...... $1,400-1,600

Vase, 6" h., 19th century, continuous scene, gilt and colors. (Illus.) ................................................ $1,500-1,700

Vases (pair), 10½" h., c. 1860, motif of birds and waterscape, foliate border bands, overall pale hues and gilt highlights ...... $1,700-2,000

Vase, 7¼" h., beaker form. (Illus.) .......................... $450-600

Vase, 6" h., 19th century, Shishi and vase. (Illus.) . . . . . . . . . . . . . . . . . . . . . . . . . . . . . $450-600

Vase, 46" h., c. 1915, baluster form, fishtail handles, two
panels of courtesans on river bank, overall vine and floral
ground in heavily applied shades of pink and deep green . . . . . . . . . . . . . . . . . . $1,800-2,200

Vases (pair), 15" h., c. 1900, baluster form with panels of
warriors on terraces, open square handles, colors and gilt;
one base damaged . . . . . . . . . . . . . . . . . . . . . . . . . . . . . . . . . . . . . . . . . . . . . . . . . $600-750

Vases (pair), 6½" h., c. 1920, square form, colors and gilt
with motif of Lohans and Kannon on gilt ground . . . . . . . . . . . . . . . . . . . . . . . . . . $400-500

Vase, 10" h., c. 1930, colors and gilt on brown ground, motif
of Lohans and dragon with dragon head handles . . . . . . . . . . . . . . . . . . . . . . . . . . $100-140

Vase, 6¼" h., 1,000 flowers motif (millefleur) . . . . . . . . . . . . . . . . . . . . . . . . . . . . $400-500

Vase, 6" h., c. 1890, signed Kinkozan, gourd shape (minor
hairlines). (Illus.) . . . . . . . . . . . . . . . . . . . . . . . . . . . . . . . . . . . . . . . . . . . . . . . . . . . $250-275

*Kinkozan double gourd vase, 19th century*

*Satsuma figures, 20th century*

*Satsuma beaker-form vase (left); vase and Shishi (right).*

World War I cut off the supply of European hard-paste porcelain blanks
to the United States and Canada. Japan became the new source of
supply. Aside from exporting porcelain blanks, Satsuma blanks were
exported, but not in the large quantities as the porcelain blanks.
Although not terribly old, Satsuma blanks are rarities. The American and
Canadian artists who decorated these blanks were, for the most part,
unaffiliated with wholesale or retail outlets (except for those pieces

## Satsuma Decorated Blanks
*(Japanese)*

decorated by Pickard). Decorated blanks show the Art Nouveau and Art Deco influences in both motif and style. Due to the rarity of these objects, those pieces available are fetching high prices. (See: Satsuma)

**Pickard Studios, Chicago**

Box (covered), 3″ dia., with legs, motif name Bouquet .......................... $450-600

Vase with four bracket feet, same pattern as above .............................. $600-850

**American Artists**

Box, 3½″ dia., motif of woman and basket. (Illus.) ............................... $400-500

Box, 3¼″ dia., dated 1916, Jan., four stub feet, floral motif in
pastel shades (Illus.) ................................................................ $400-465

Bowl, 8″ dia., motif of grapes and vines in blue-green and
gilt, signed M. O'Connell ........................................................... $200-225

Cachepot, unsigned, orange ground with black geometric
motif ..................................................................................... $800-900

Humidor, Art Deco geometric motif, red-orange ground with
black and gold design ................................................................ $800-1,100

Incense burner, 5″ h., undecorated, stub feet, pierced domed
cover ..................................................................................... $500-600

Nut set, c. 1915, large bowl, eight small bowls, square form,
motif of reserves filled with flowers and ribbons in pastel
shades .................................................................................... $500-625

Sugar and creamer, unsigned, motif in blue and yellow with
gilt accents. (Illus.) .................................................................. $500-675

Teapot, 4″ h., Art Deco motif, pink, blue. (Illus.) ............................... $450-550

*Sugar and creamer, unsigned*

*Satsuma decorated blanks: box with floral motif (left), box with woman holding basket (right)*

Vase, 6″ h., c. 1923, peacock. (Illus.) .......................................... $400-500

Vase, 6″ h., dated 1/27/18, two medallions filled with roses,
gold and black border trim ................................................. $800-900

Vase, 9½″ h., dated 4/17, two large open handles, and initials
F.D., motif of summer flowers against a pale green ground ..................... $800-900

Vase, 8¼″ h., dated 12/22 and initial R., red-orange ground
with black swirls and small medallions filled with pansies ................... $1,000-1,400

*Satsuma-decorated blanks: vase with peacock (left), teapot (right)*

## Satsuma, Kinkozan
*(Japanese)*

The Kagiya family produced Awata wares as far back as the latter part of the 17th century. It was not until 1756 that the Tokugawa gave the name "Kinkozan" to the third generation of the Kagiya family. The wares produced from 1870 to 1927 are the easiest to find. Most Kinkozan wares have a body tint of yellowy cream, with motifs executed in shades of green, crimson, yellow, purple, black, and white with gold outlining and fleeting, cloudlike masses of gold.

(See: Satsuma; Japanese Cloisonné Tōtai)

## Satsuma Style
*(Japanese)*

These are porcelain wares which have raised gold enameled motifs in the style of Satsuma.

Bowl, 8″ dia., c. 1930, black matte ground with motif of birds
and foliage in gilt ......................................................... $100-120

Bowl, 9½″ dia., c. 1935, brown ground with motif of three
Lohans in colors and gilt .................................................. $50-70

Box, 4″ x 3″, brown ground with two Lohan and Kannon in
colors and gilt ........................................................... $40-50

Box, 6″ dia., brown ground with dragon in colors and gilt .................... $35-45

Cup and saucer, c. 1905, eggshell porcelain, motif of Lohans ................. $120-145

Dish, 6″ dia., c. 1935, brown ground, two open handles,
motif of Kannon and child in colors and gilt ................................ $40-45

Humidor, c. 1925, brown ground, gilt Shishi finial, body
entwined with dragon ...................................................... $185-250

Figure (Hotei), 9¼″ h. x 6″ w., c. 1930, orange, green, blue,
yellow, and gilt robe ..................................................... $250-325

201

*Satsuma-style eggshell porcelain vase, 19th century*

Figure (Hotei), 6″ x 8″, c. 1955, same coloration as above ....................... $225-250

Figure (Kannon), 14″ h., same coloration as above, holding a gilt scroll ................................................................. $300-400

Figure (Benten), 14″ h., same coloration as above ...................... $200-225

Jar, cookie, 8″ h., gilt Shishi finial and handles, motif of Kannon and Lohans on brown ground ................................... $85-100

Teapot, c. 1930, elephant figural with mahoot, brown ground with colors and gilt ................................................... $50-65

Teapot, c. 1925, dragon handle, spout and finial with Kannon and Lohans on black ground ......................................... $100-125

Tea set, c. 1925, teapot, covered sugar, covered creamer, six cups and saucers, six cake plates, brown ground, motif of Lohans and Kannon, with molded dragon entwining each piece, dragon handle, spout, and finial ................................. $400-475

Vase, 6″ h., c. 1930, black matte ground with gilt motif of pavilions ................................................................. $75-100

Vase, 8″ h., c. 1925, brown ground, motif of Lohans, Kannon in colors and gilt, two elephant head handles ...................... $40-50

Vase, 10″ h., 19th century, eggshell, red, blue and gilt (minor hairline). (Illus.) ..................................... $2,800-3,200

## Seiji
### *(Japanese Celadon)*

Japanese Seiji (Celadon) has a waxy appearance and a thick opaque glaze. For the most part, Seiji is either green or green with a bluish cast. It has a glossy shine and does not have crackling. Japanese Seiji may be ornamented with motifs executed in under-the-glaze blue, white, and pastel hues. Many late 19th century and early 20th century pieces can be found that will have motifs molded in relief.

*Seiji wine pot*

Bottle, 16″ h., late 19th century, pear-shaped, motif of dragons in underglaze blue and white ................................. $320-450

Flowerpot, 11″ h., late 19th century, wide lip, four stub feet, motif of trees and foliage in black, brown, blue, and pink against a swirled, melon rib body .................................... $350-450

Flowerpot, 12″ h., late 19th/early 20th century, square form, wide lip, key fret motif within square forms under the lip, executed in white and underglaze blue, four stub feet ............. $375-400

Flowerpot, 2½″ h., early 20th century, round with wide lip, four stub feet, motif of branches and prunus blossoms in underglaze blue and white ......................................... $45-60

Planter (tray-type), 12″ x 9″, late 19th century, underglaze blue branches with pink peonies and white prunus ................. $200-250

Plate, 12″ dia., late 19th century, underglaze blue scenic motif with pagodas against a riverscape ................................. $345-400

Tea set, early 20th century, covered pot, sugar and creamer, bamboo form finials, motif of trees and flowers in greens and pink ..................................................................... $125-150

Vase, 7″ h., early 20th century, cylindrical form, flowers molded in relief .......................................................... $90-120

Vase, 10″ h., early 20th century, bulbous with elongated neck, motif of trees and foliage in shades of green and brown ...... $85-100

Vase, 6″ h., late 19th century, Korean style, mishima inlay of cranes and wave patterns in white and black ........................ $125-175

Vases (pair), 12" h., late 19th century, lozenge form, four
panels of relief motifs of birds perched on branches, and
peony, chrysanthemum and lotus blossoms, polychrome ....................... $500-600

Vases (pair), 12" h., late 19th century, trumpet neck, flared
and fluted rim, with underglaze blue motif of branches and
prunus ............................................................ $400-450

Wine pot, 8" dia., 18th century, underglaze florals. (Illus.) ................... $1,200-1,500

## Seto
*(Japanese)*

The first kiln in Seto has been linked to Kato Shirozaemon (known as Toshiro). This kiln dates back to the early 1200s, at which time a coarse, rudimentary pottery was produced. The work of this first potter, Toshiro, has been carried on through the centuries by his descendants. Yellow Seto (Ki Seto) is a term used to describe early Seto pottery, which has a yellowy glaze. Other Seto pottery includes objects made for Cha no yu (the tea ceremony) and having brown glazes, and/or incised and impressed motifs. Particularly popular with collectors are tea jars. During the last century, porcelain was produced in addition to the long admired pottery articles. Generally, Seto porcelain wares are white with underglaze blue decorations.

Bottle, 7" h., 19th century. (Illus.) ........................................... $400-500

Bottle, 16" h., 19th century, reddish brown glaze to foot, buff
gray glaze on foot ..................................................... $500-700

Bottle, 13" h., 19th century, elongated form, square mouth,
red brown glaze ....................................................... $400-500

Chaire (caddy for thick tea), 3½" h., 18th century, slightly
elevated foot, red brown glaze, ivory cover ............................... $950-1,500

Chaire, 4" h., 19th century, two handles, elongated form,
brown glaze with slight ochre curtain, ivory cover ........................ $650-800

Water dropper, 2" h., 19th century, peach form, mottled
brown glaze ........................................................... $185-225

Wine pot, 6¾" h., late 18th century. (Illus.) .............................. $1,500-1,700

*Seto sake bottle (left), handled wine pot (right)*

## Shakudō
*(Japanese)*

Shakudō is an alloy of almost pure copper, with a small amount of gold and silver (Harada states that it is 95 percent copper, 1 percent gold and 4 percent silver), which oxidizes to a bluish-black. It is often used in conjunction with other metals and with effective chiseling, graving, relief, etc. (Japanese items made from the above alloy are referred to as shakudo.)

Kozuka, 17th/18th century, Nanako, applied with a gold tachi, unmarked . . . . . . . . . . . . . . . . . . . . . . . . . . . . . . . . . . . . . . . . . . . . . . . . . . . . . $200-350

Kozuka, 19th century, Nanako (Goto style), applied in fine detail with a celestial dragon, unmarked . . . . . . . . . . . . . . . . . . . . . . . . . . . . . $300-565

Kozuka, 19th century, Nanako, applied with three gold and shakudo pigeons, Seiunsha Toho signature, with kakihan . . . . . . . . . . . . . . . . . . . $650-915

Kozuka, 18th/19th century, a lone shibuichi goose in water, molded in Nanako Yoshioka . . . . . . . . . . . . . . . . . . . . . . . . . . . . . . . . . . . . . . . . $850-985

Kozuka, late 18th/early 19th century, Nanako, applied in shakudo, copper, and gold, Chinese style halbard, unmarked . . . . . . . . . . . . . . . . . $325-455

Kozuka, 18th century, Nanako, applied with a takazogan fur-covered quiver and bow in gold and shakudo, copper blade, unsigned . . . . . . . . . . . . . . . . . . . . . . . . . . . . . . . . . . . . . . . . . . . . . . . . . . . . $200-265

Tsuba, 2⅓" dia., 19th century. Mokko tsuba (Ishime Hitotsuyanagi style), applied in gold, copper, and shakudo with a reed and ladle and Shojo mask; reverse depicts a large sake vat, kozuka-hitsu, unmarked . . . . . . . . . . . . . . . . . . . . . . . . . . . . . . . $250-385

Tsuba, 2⅓" dia., 18th century, Nanako Mokko, in brownish shakudo and gilt, depicting kiri and ho-o, unmarked . . . . . . . . . . . . . . . . . $50-115

Tsuba, 2½" dia., 18th/19th century, Nanako Mokko, with hay clover decoration on the openwork guard, with ryu-hitsu formed by two of the open lobes, unmarked . . . . . . . . . . . . . . . . . . . . . . . . . . $175-305

Tsuba, 2½" dia., 19th century, Nara style, shakudo, copper, silver, and gold applied on the oval guard with design of Samurai, kozuka-hitsu, unmarked . . . . . . . . . . . . . . . . . . . . . . . . . . . . . . . . $325-455

Tsuba, 2¾" dia., 18th century, Nanako Mino Goto style, scene of Taira no Tadamori apprehending the oil thief molded in high shakudo and gilt on the mokko guard, kozuka-hitsu, unmarked . . . . . . . . . . . . . . . . . . . . . . . . . . . . . . . . . . . . . . . . . . . . $175-305

Tsuba, 2¾" dia., 19th century, Hamano style, design of two farmers rafting across a river delicately carved and applied in gold, shakudo, and copper on the oval guard, ryu-hitsu, unmarked . . . . . . . . . . . . . . . . . . . . . . . . . . . . . . . . . . . . . . . . . . . . . . . . . . . . $400-665

Vases, pair, 10¹⁄₁₀" h., late 19th century, baluster bodies with trumpet necks and butterfly bronze handles, with design of flowering and fruiting branches in iro-e takazogan, seal mark of Yoshiyuki . . . . . . . . . . . . . . . . . . . . . . . . . . . . . . . . . . . . . . . . . . . . $2,000-3,000

## Shibayama
*(Japanese)*

Shibayama Dosho perfected the art of applying ivory and shell to lacquer. This form of decoration was also used on metalwares, screens, cabinets, boxes and plaques. Wares made with this type of decoration are referred to as Shibayama or Shibayama-style.
(See: Bronzes; Furniture; Inro; Ivory; Lacquer.)

## Shibuichi
*(Japanese)*

A gray-colored alloy of copper and silver, shibuichi is often used in conjunction with other metals and with effective chiseling, graving, relief, etc. (Japanese items made from the above alloy are referred to as shibuichi.)

Box, 4½"x 3⅗", late 19th century, rectangular, with akebi, orchid and magnolia design; iro-e takazogan; two Chinese scholars with scroll on cover; silver-lined interior, signed Katsusada . . . . . . . . . . . . . . . . . . . . . . . . . . . . . . . . . . . . . . . . . . . . $3,000-3,500

Dish, 8⅞" dia., late 19th century, circular, decorated with two standing cranes in stream in iro-e takazogan, dark, with small scratches, signed, with inlaid seal, Katsuhiro . . . . . . . . . . . . . . . . . . . . . . . $1,400-1,600

Koro, 3⅗" h., late 19th century, tripod shape with snowflakes design beneath the irregular silver shoulder in gold takazogan and hirazogan; gold finial in shape of two puppies on silver cover, signed Shomin with kao . . . . . . . . . . . . . . . . . . . . . . . . . . . . $3,200-3,400

Koro, 5⅞" h., late 19th century, tripod shape with herons and stream design in takazogan on the globular form; silver heron finial on the silver cover (finial damaged), signed Ranpo shujin Yoshiaki . . . . . . . . . . . . . . . . . . . . . . . . . . . . . . . . . . . $2,600-2,800

Kozuka, c. 1800, design of five gold and shakudo shells on the dark surface, signed Nomura Masahide, with kakihan . . . . . . . . . . . . . . . . . . . $150-300

Kozuka, 19th century, design of flying crane above waves in takabori, shakudo and gilt detail, unmarked . . . . . . . . . . . . . . . . . . . . . . . . . . . . . $130-265

Kozuka, 19th century, design of five birds perched on a hoe in gilt and silvered takazogan, signed Atari Hirosada, kao . . . . . . . . . . . . . . . . . . . . $250-380

Tray, 8⅓" x 10⅔", late 19th century, rectangular, with indented corners on the concave edge, design of farmers having tea and laying out wet cloths on banks of stream in iro-e takazogan, katakiribori, and sukidashibori, signed Ichiosai Masatoshi tsukuru, inlaid seal reading Masatoshi . . . . . . . . . . . . . . . . . . $4,000-4,100

Vessel, 10⅓" h., late 19th century, tripod shape with design of Shoki and oni in iro-e takazogan; the cover with a large oni holding a smaller one on his shoulders, wood stand, signed Ryounsai (Unno Moritoshi) . . . . . . . . . . . . . . . . . . . . . . . . . . . . . . . . . . . $22,000-22,500

Yatate, 6⅖" l., 19th century, the penholder and inkwell with relief carving and inlay of plover among waves, signed Kobayashi yoshimasa saku . . . . . . . . . . . . . . . . . . . . . . . . . . . . . . . . . . . . . . . . . $600-800

## Shino Wares
*(Japanese)*

Shino wares are predominantly articles made for use in Cha no yu (the tea ceremony). They were first produced during the late 1400s. These wares are thickly potted and the glaze (white) runs thick and thin. E-Shino are decorated wares with simple motifs executed in iron oxide. Gray Shino wares have white bodies ornamented with brown slip (liquid clay) under the glaze (sgrafitto). Shino wares are highly prized by collectors.

Dish (Shino-style), 10½" dia., underglaze blue gray motif of grasses with gray glaze edging to brown . . . . . . . . . . . . . . . . . . . . . . . . . . . . . . . . . . $750-900

## Shiragaki
*(Japanese)*

Shiragaki is known as one of the six ancient kilns. The others being Tokoname, Seto, Bizen, Tamba, and Karatsu. The earliest wares were basically storage vessels. After the tea ceremony was developed the tea masters looked favorably upon Shiragaki wares, especially for those vessels designed for holding cold water and flower containers (vases). Shiragaki has a thick, rough biscuit and the glazes are applied at the top of an object and then allowed to run down.

Storage jar, 18" h., 17th century, concave foot, baluster form, rolled lip, brown transparent glaze . . . . . . . . . . . . . . . . . . . . . . . . . . . . . . . . . $2,400-3,200

Storage jar, 12" h., 17th century, baluster form, wide mouth, rolled lip, two concentric mons impressed with flower heads on the shoulder, transparent brown glaze ........................... $2,400-3,500

Storage jar, 23" h., 19th century, Shino glaze, copper green stripe. (Illus.) ................................................ $1,800-2,400

Teapot, c. 1910, same glaze. (Illus.) ........................................... $200-250

*Shiragaki teapot, Same glaze*

*Shiragaki storage jar, Shino glaze, copper green stripe*

## Shoji Hamada
### (1894-1978)

Shoji Hamada was a ceramist and is referred to as the "greatest potter" of the 20th century. His works were a fine combination of feeling and taste. He was a potter, teacher, and worked to establish museums in the field of preservation of folk art. Most of his ceramics are unsigned.

Chawan, gray glaze .................................................... $700-900

Stoneware dish, 11¾" sq., decorated with brown slip in five squares alternating with lighter squares ............................ $1,000-1,500

Stoneware jar (covered), 8¼" h., oviform with impressed vertical bands forming a V pattern, dark brown glaze, the domed cover having a flat knob finial ..................................... $800-950

Vase. (Illus.) ...................................................... $800-1,100

*Vase attributed to Shoji Hamada*

## Shu Fu
### (Chinese)

Shu Fu wares date back to the 14th century (Yüan Dynasty). The name originates from the two Chinese characters (calligraphy) denoting "official ware," which usually appear on the object. The glaze is a thick, semi-opaque oily blue which almost obliterates any incised decoration beneath it. Molded, incised, and slip decorations were employed.

## Silver
### (Chinese)

Bowl, 6½" dia., relief of flowering tree peony, floral band, on compressed globular body with spreading foot and foliate rim .................. $395-525

Box, 1½" x 1", butterfly-shaped with filigree, gold wash over the silver, turquoise enameled bug on green leaf surmounting lid, ring attached at top ......................................... $50-75

Epergne, 13⅜" h., late 19th century, a central large trumpet surrounded by three smaller ones, decorated with relief dragons, domed foot, signed Ts'ang Chi, wood stand ......................... $650-900

Mirror, 3½" dia., T'ang Dynasty, a band of fruiting vine and outer floral scroll band with ridge divisions surrounding a central boss, traces of malachite encrustation, fitted box ..................... $800-1,065

Pendant, 1⅞" h., early 19th century, gold-washed silver, design of Lao Tzu on animal, with an attendant; detailed textile patterns evidenced ....................................... $85-150

Snuff bottle, 2⅜" h., early 19th century, gilt, design of flowering branches in vases on either side, monster mask handles with rings on sides, top carved in flower form, marked ......................................................... $175-300

Snuff bottle, early 19th century, flask form, mask and mock-ring handles on the shoulders, design of dragon medallions surrounded by leafy borders on either side, a collar of lotus petals on the foot, matching stopper .......................... $550-815

Tea service, late 19th century export, 18½" w., rectangular tray, teapot, tea kettle, sugar bowl, waste bowl, and milk jug with peony and prunus sprays cast design, imitation bamboo handles, marked Leunwo, Shanghai ......................................... $395-700

## Silver
### (Japanese)

Bottles, perfume (pair), 10" l., carp-shaped, with articulated bodies that move at the spine, turquoise-inlaid eyes, removable stopper at the carp's mouth, wood stands ......................... $300-450

Bowl, 6" dia., slightly tapered body with high spreading foot; repousse design of continuous band of lotus, matching inset, signed on base Watanabe sei. (Illus.) ......................................... $260-500

Bowl, 7" dia., compressed globular body with design of continuous coiling dragon among waves in high relief; separately cast feet in shapes of dragons; foliate everted lip, base missing, marked Masayoshi Jungin. (Illus.) ............................ $520-860

Punchbowl and ladle, 14½" dia. bowl, 17¼" l. ladle, bowl with relief design of two writhing dragons well defined on punched ground; splayed foot below steeply rounded sides. Wt. 129 oz., 17 dwts. Signed Nomura. Matching ladle signed Samurai Shokai Yokohama. Wt. 19 ozs. 5 dwts. .......................... $7,000-10,000

Box, 8¼" l., rectangular with chrysanthemums, cherry blossoms, and bamboo design applied in high relief and heightened with gold; design of cherry blossoms around sides, wood liner, incised view of Mt. Fuji, signed ......................... $450-580

Box, 10½" l., form of tortoise, the cover formed by removable shell of animal, signed Y. Konoike, Yokohama .............................. $500-650

Dish, serving, 6" dia., stylized diaper design inlaid with gold on rim; central area of the sterling depicts tea-leaf pattern inlaid in gold; footed, signed beneath ....................................... $900-1,100

Incense burner, 5¾" dia., Kiku design in relief on the rounded sides; pierced domed cover, signed Masashiya Yokohama ........................................................... $400-665

Netsuke, 19th century, shape of a Samurai helmet, a winged dragon design front-knop; the Shikoro stitched together with thread, held together by rivets; the cord attachment formed by three rings, unmarked ........................................... $1,100-1,765

Ojime, flattened cylindrical form with design of Mt. Fuji and pine trees incised, unmarked ............................................ $60-75

Table service, early 20th century, twelve each: tumblers, footed cordials, stemmed goblets, and stemmed wines, each with gilt interior and applied designs of coiled dragons on their exteriors. Stamped Arthur & Bond, Yokohama. 200 oz. .. ............... $6,000-7,000

Tea caddy, 5 1/10" h., globular body with design of chrysanthemum embossed, a band of lappets on the shoulder; similar designs on the domed cover (slightly dented); base impressed with Jungin (pure silver) ....................... $320-450

Teapot, 7" l. with handle, globular body with a high relief design of continuous dragon; ivory handle, short spout; flat cover with design of encircling dragon clutching a pearl in one claw as the finial, base marked Jungin (pure silver). (Illus.) ................................................................. $260-470

Tea service, c. 1900, six pieces: teapot, tray, covered sugar, waste bowl, tea kettle on stand, creamer, all chased in high relief on hammered ground, handles shaped as foliage and blooms. 400 oz. ...................................................... $8,000-9,000

Vases, pair, 5 1/10" h., pear-shaped, broad neck, decorated with the imperial kiku mon ............................................. $480-610

*From left:* Japanese silver items: bowl, 6" dia.; bowl, 7" dia.; teapot, 7" l.

### Silver
*(Mongolian)*

Dagger and sheath, 14½" l., repousse dragon emblems with turquoise, coral, and lapis lazuli borders on sheath .......................... $450-715

Snuff bottle, circular design medallions, lotus petal design on foot, two mask and mock ring handles ...................................... $200-265

Sword, 20" l., repousse flower panels with coral and turquoise inlays on sheath, pale green nephrite ring on one side, trefoil (Mogul style) handle ..................................... $1,000-1,700

### Silver
*(Persian)*

Bowl, c.19th century, three-footed sterling bowl with Arabic hallmark on reverse side, rope border on edge, intricate pattern on interior and border of bowl. 11½ troy oz. wt. ...................... $700-900

Dagger case, 10″ l. (scabbard and knife), c. 18th century, repousse figural and mythological designs; floral repousse silver insert on ivory handle ................................................... $600-800

## Smokers' Requisites
*(Japanese)*

When tobacco was costly, its use was limited or reserved for the upper classes. During the Edo period it was fashionable to carry pipes (with the largest measuring more than three feet in length) and tobacco pouches in much the same manner as the Inro. By the Meiji era, all classes were allowed to partake in the smoking of tobacco (except for Samurai). Various contours, materials, and styles were used. The pouch and container for the pipe were generally made of leather with magnificent motifs executed in a multitude of colors. Pipe cases were made of horn, ivory, wood, etc., having carved motifs. The pipe itself had a narrow stem, a tiny metal bowl, and a metal mouthpiece.

Pipe case, staghorn, bonsai form, carved Oni with mallet ....................... $700-800

Pipe case, embossed leather ................................................. $250-300

Pipe case, stag antler, shibayama style ...................................... $800-900

Pipe case, 19th century, ebony with silver, gold, and shakudo ornamentation on motif of cat watching a perched bird .......................................................... $300-425

Pipe, 19th century, silver tone with gold wash, applied silver ornamentation of birds and foliage ......................................... $200-300

Tobacco pouch, 19th century, embroidered motif of dragons and clouds, silver clasp with ivory manju carved with flower heads ........................................................... $200-300

Tonkotsu, briar wood, pipe case, rootwood, agate ojime. (Illus.) ............................................................ $175-250

Tonkotsu, early 20th century, wood in form of Daruma, eyes being cord holes, pipe holder in the form of a man, with bamboo pipe.......................................................... $175-225

Tonkotsu, wood trapezoid shape, lacquer lobster motif, crab lacquer ojime, snail netsuke ............................................. $550-650

Tonkotsu, kiri wood, wood ojime, leather pipe and case, c. 1885 ............................................................ $100-175

*Tonkotsu briar root. Courtesy the Rosett Collection*

# Snuff Bottles
*(Chinese)*

The custom of partaking of snuff became popular in China during the 17th century. It was likely introduced earlier, via Portuguese and Spanish traders. The small bottles used for drugs and herbs were the forerunners of the snuff bottle. By affixing a small spoon to the cap, easy access to the snuff was possible. The snuff bottle was carried in one's sleeve, as the garments worn by the Chinese had no pockets. To partake of the snuff, it was removed from the bottle with the aid of the little spoon, laid on the left hand at the lower joint of the thumb, lifted to the nose and sniffed in. Snuff bottles are generally 2″ high or under. They come in numerous materials, including:

**Porcelain** (enameled and/or molded in relief)

**Glass** (Peking): 1. opaque glass; 2. overlay glass either carved or in cameo style; 3. glass that has been painted on the interior; 4. glass carved to simulate semiprecious gemstones; 5. enameled glass (Ku Yueh Hsuan style)

**Gemstones:** agate, jade, serpentine, amber, malachite, rose quartz, smoke crystal, calcite, soapstone, coral, jet, etc.

Snuff bottles were also made of ivory, lacquer, cloisonné and other materials. They are miniature works of art and have been collected for more than two hundred years.

(See: Cloisonné)

*Snuff bottle, Peking glass with overlay motif of fish*

*Snuff bottle, amethyst, with carved prunus blossoms*

| | |
|---|---|
| Agate, translucent blue gray with beige/brown bands, well hollowed | $200-250 |
| Agate, translucent gray with dark markings, simulated mask and ring handles | $300-400 |
| Agate (carnelian), oval sections carved with shi'ih lung | $350-400 |
| Agate (carnelian), carved and undercut with peony trees and rockwork | $275-325 |
| Agate (brown), carved with two horses, well hollowed | $200-225 |
| Amber carved and pierced with pine branch, oviform | $85-110 |
| Amber flat form carved overall with immortals amid peony and rockwork | $600-850 |
| Amber carved with two dragons and cloud scrolls | $200-285 |
| Amber flat rectangular form with simulated mask and ring handles | $140-185 |
| Amethyst with amber inclusion and carved overall with prunus blossoms (Illus.) | $300-400 |
| Carnelian, flattened baluster body (plain) | $250-325 |
| Carnelian, flattened form with carvings of duck, bat, horse, and monkey | $700-900 |
| Cinnabar, cylindrical form carved with scholars and pine, willow and rockwork | $125-175 |
| Cinnabar, flattened oviform with carved foliage and rockwork | $100-125 |
| Cinnabar (pair), oviform carved in high relief with figures, pavilions, gardens | $350-450 |
| Cinnabar, inset with Canton enamel painted plaques of women in a window | $800-900 |
| Coral, flattened tapering form carved with t'ao t'ieh masks and fretwork | $450-500 |
| Coral (white), carved as a standing elephant with trunk turned downward | $250-325 |
| Coral, carved with Kuan Yin, a basket, and peony | $500-600 |

Coral, body carved with peony and prunus ................................... $275-325

Hornbill, flattened form carved on one side with three
immortals and on the reverse are carved k'uei dragons ........................ $650-750

Hornbill, flattened baluster body carved in high relief and
openwork with phoenix and dragons with cloud scrolls ..................... $500-700

Interior painted glass, with butterflies hovering above a
garden with long inscription (c. 1895) ................................... $1,700-2,000

Interior painted glass, with continuous marriage scene ...................... $900-1,100

Interior painted glass (double bottle), painted with vases of
flowers and riverscapes with trees and rockwork ........................... $1,000-1,275

Interior painted glass, with motif of goldfish swimming
around water foliage and flowering plants, insects, and
riverscape ............................................................... $375-500

Interior painted glass. (Illus.) ........................................... $300-350

Interior painted glass, with motif of a bird on a tree branch
with a spray of peony blossoms ........................................... $325-475

Interior painted glass, with continuous mountain landscape ................... $150-175

Interior painted glass (sapphire blue), with warriors on
horseback ................................................................ $175-200

Ivory, octagonal form, carved with Shou Lao and attendant
with pine tree and rockwork .............................................. $100-175

Ivory, double gourd with a boy kneeling to one side,
matching twig stopper .................................................... $175-250

Ivory, carved to simulate an ear of corn with beetles and twig
stopper .................................................................. $200-300

Ivory, elaborate carving of openwork and high relief with
figures engaged in the game "Go" ......................................... $500-700

Ivory (pair), cylindrical forms etched with figures in a
mountain landscape ....................................................... $150-185

Ivory, carved as a boy with a vase on his shoulder .......................... $275-400

Jade Fei Ts'ui, oviform with green brown mottlings, well
hollowed ................................................................. $300-500

Jade Fei Ts'ui, ovate form with green brown mottling, well
hollowed ................................................................. $350-500

Jade, gray flat flask form with rounded sides, well hollowed .................. $175-300

Jade, gray, carved with fluted vertical pattern, well hollowed ................. $175-200

Jade, onion green, flattened form, with russet inclusion ...................... $175-220

Jade, white, formed as a fruit (finger citron) ............................... $270-400

Jade, white, flattened quadrangular form carved with raised
rectangular panels ....................................................... $175-225

Jade, white, ovoid form carved with lotus blossoms and
plum blossoms ............................................................ $150-220

Jade, white and russet, flattened oviform carved with
bellflowers and a cockerel (Illus.) ........................................ $200-300

Lapis lazuli, carved on both sides with a bird on a flowering
branch ................................................................... $150-220

Lapis lazuli, carved to form a carp rising from waves ........................ $275-325

Lapis lazuli, flat form carved with cranes and pine .......................... $225-300

Malachite, flattened oviform (plain) ....................................... $250-350

Mother-of-pearl, baluster form inlaid with agate and two
white birds .............................................................. $200-225

Mother-of-pearl, carved with two ling-ch'ih and on the
reverse a bee and flowers ................................................ $200-300

Mother-of-pearl, double gourd, inlaid in mother-of-pearl,
with scrolls and foliage .................................................. $125-175

Mother-of-pearl, carved with dragon and cloud scrolls, the

*Snuff bottle, interior painted glass*

*Snuff bottle, white and russet jade*

*Snuff bottle, Peking glass with four-color overlay and motif of blossoming plants*

reverse with deer and tree ....................................................... $300-400

Peking glass, mottled yellow ..................................................... $120-140

Peking glass, green overlay on frosted glass with carved crickets on branches with pierced rockwork, silver stopper ...................... $200-275

Peking glass, with overlay of opaque blue on both sides, carved with po ku utensils and simulated ring handles, Ta Ching mark ................................................................ $200-225

Peking glass, overlay of red on cloudy bubble glass with both sides carved with ch'ih lung .......................................... $225-325

Peking glass, blue overlay on transparent glass carved with two dragons ................................................................ $185-245

Peking glass, simulating aventurine quartz ................................. $150-185

Peking glass, blue overlay on opaque white with carved vines, fruit, and foliage ............................................... $400-500

Peking glass, overlay of opaque white on transparent blue carved with pagoda and temple upon rockwork ...................... $750-1,000

Peking glass (Tao Kuang), black overlay on blue shading to white near the neck, carved with two birds and lotus blossoms ............................................................... $1,500-1,700

Peking glass, of translucent sapphire blue with sides having simulated mask and ring handles of overlay ruby red ................ $250-300

Peking glass, opaque white with baluster body, three-color overlay of red, yellow, and blue with carved fish throughout. (Illus.) ................................................................ $200-300

Peking glass, pear-shaped, clear glass with purple overlay carved with bird and antelope on one side and fox and hawk on reverse ................................................................ $400-500

Peking glass, opaque white, with four-color overlay of pink, green, turquoise, and blue with motif of blossoming plants (Illus.) ................................................................ $300-450

Peking glass, with pink, green, turquoise and royal blue overlay on opaque white body carved with lotus blossoms ........... $300-400

Peking glass, clear glass with green translucent overlay carved with ch'ih lung .......................................... $175-225

Peking glass (t'ung Chih), transparent turquoise glass with overall faceted motif .................................................. $500-650

Peking glass, amethyst, in the form of a bean ......................... $300-400

Peking glass, frosted bubble glass with red overlay carved with sages and trees upon rockwork .................................. $225-300

Peking glass, "snowflake" glass with blue overlay, simulated mask and ring handles, carved with face of clock with time reading 1:50 ................................................................ $300-475

Peking glass, cloudy bubble glass with black overlay and carving of sages and attendants, flask shape ........................ $225-350

**Porcelain, blue and white:**
Blue and white, 18th/19th century, ovoid form with 100 deer motif, bats around the shoulder, shou symbols around the neck ................................................................ $700-1,200

Blue and white, baluster form porcelain with fisherman ............... $100-150

Blue and white, baluster form porcelain with mountain scene ................... $100-125

Blue and white, porcelain, continuous motif of dragons ............... $125-175

**Porcelain, blue, white, and copper red:**
Blue, white, and copper red, with continuous scene of warriors and banners in a landscape ...................................... $250-350

Blue, white, and copper red, with continuous scene of animals in a forest ................................................................ $200-375

Blue, white, and copper red, with emperor and noblemen in a room with harlequin flooring ........................................ $450-700

Blue, white, and copper red, figures in a landscape ........................... $100-125

Blue, white, and copper red, dragons amidst clouds, slight
chipping on base ................................................. $100-125

Blue, white, and copper red, four panels with winter scenes ................... $175-200

Blue, white, and copper red, a court figure and attendant ...................... $75-100

**Porcelain, famille rose:**

Famille rose, late 19th century, scenic motif on yellow ground .................. $150-175

Famille rose, late 19th century, butterflies and blossoms on
red ground ..................................................... $200-245

Famille rose (Tao Kuang), motif on each side consisting of
circular panels of a crane, lotus, and five bats on a blue
ground ........................................................ $375-450

Famille rose, molded in relief, figural in the form of Liu Hai
holding a string of cash .......................................... $350-400

Famille rose, molded in relief, Lohans and their attributes ..................... $200-300

Famille rose, molded in relief, form of a kneeling boy ......................... $300-425

Famille rose, molded in relief, allover design of women and
children, and gardens ........................................... $220-300

Famille rose, molded in relief, Buddhist lions and balls,
pierced, Chi Ch'ing .............................................. $700-900

Famille rose, molded in relief, riverscape with men and boats .................. $240-375

Famille rose, molded in relief, men and women in various
erotic poses .................................................... $700-900

Famille rose, molded in relief, sages and attendants, with
some riding lions ................................................ $400-500

Famille rose, molded in relief, with lotus buds and leaves
(Illus.) ......................................................... $150-250

*Snuff bottle, porcelain, famille rose
molded in relief with lotus blossom
and leaves*

**Porcelain, monochrome:**

Apple green, ovoid form ......................................... $250-300

Robin's egg blue, pear-shaped on flared foot ................................. $300-400

Sang de boeuf, tapered cylindrical form ...................................... $125-160

Sang de boeuf, squat form with narrow neck ................................. $175-220

Tea dust, mei ping form .................................................. $300-450

Rock crystal (cloudy), with relief carving of celery, cabbages ................... $175-225

Rock crystal (cloudy), carved with flowers and foliage ......................... $75-100

Rock crystal (cloudy), simulated mask ring handles ........................... $75-95

Rock crystal, rectangular shape with mask and ring-simulated
handles ........................................................ $75-100

Rock crystal, carved with bamboo trees ..................................... $75-100

Rose quartz (pair), carved with bird on pine branch .......................... $200-250

Rose quartz, carved with sage upon a horse and an attendant
standing next to him ............................................. $120-150

Rose quartz, carved with peony and rockwork ................................ $125-150

Sapphire, flattened oviform carved with pavilion and prunus .................. $700-1,000

Soapstone, rectangular form in brown black with storks in
relief .......................................................... $50-75

Soapstone, carved in relief with Shou Lao on one side and
attendant, pine, and rockwork on the other .............................. $200-290

Tiger's eye, flattened baluster form carved on each side with
a k'uei dragon and cloud scrolls ..................................... $200-225

Tortoiseshell with flattened baluster body, natural markings
with deep brown clouds and pale translucent areas ........................ $250-350

Turquoise, flattened baluster form carved with man and boy .................. $500-650

Turquoise, carved and pierced in high relief with peony and phoenix .................................................. $250-300

Yi Hsing, famille rose enamels with motif of incenser, bowl, and other ornaments, Tao Kuang ................................ $400-500

Yi Hsing, molded in relief, double gourd contour, motif of fruit and foliage .................................................. $300-450

Yi Hsing, motif of branches, birds, and plum blossoms in enamels .................................................... $400-500

Yi Hsing, motif of enameled plum blossoms and branches in shades of yellow and green with white trim .................... $500-650

Yi Hsing, sgrafitto of stylized florals .................................... $500-700

## Sometsuke
### *(Japanese)*

*Sometsuke vases*

Japanese wares which are blue and white (under the glaze blue motifs) are termed Sometsuke. The earliest Japanese blue and white porcelain wares date from the first half of the 1600s. The blues can vary in tints and include blue gray, blue black, blue violet, and sapphire blue. The blue pigments were applied directly on the biscuit and then the article was glazed and fired. Many varieties of Japanese porcelains fall under the heading of Sometsuke; such include Hirado wares, Imari wares, Nabeshima wares, Arita wares, etc.

Bottle, 10½" h., 17th century, floral sprays ...................... $550-750

Bowl, 4¾" dia., c. 1910, motif depicting children at play, stencil and transfer .................................................. $50-75

Box, 4¾" x 4¾" x 3¾", c. 1900, two-tiered, square form with underglaze blue panels of houses and a riverscape .............. $150-225

Dish, 8" dia., 17th century, bird on a branch ...................... $1,000-1,200

Ewer, 5½" h., decorated with a seated figure of Buddha and attendants, with geometric diapers ............................... $250-340

Fishbowl, 20 2/3" dia., late 19th century, everted rim, motifs of birds, peonies, bamboo, and plums, interior with vines and grapes, .................................................... $1,100-1,500

Figure, Hotei, 10" h., holding a fan and bag ...................... $125-175

Figure, Kannon, 8" h., seated with legs crossed .................. $200-250

Incense burner, 10¼" h., a ferocious animal leaning against a rock covered with large peonies, body of incense burner entwined with a dragon molded in relief, panels include bamboo, pine, and plum, Shishi finial ............................. $600-750

Jar, 9½" h., spherical, dragon and clouds in underglaze blue, cover with dragon finial, and entwining the neck is a dragon molded in relief .................................................. $375-650

Jar, 34" h., slender body with two phoenixes and peony blossoms .................................................... $600-850

Jar, 28" h., baluster body with two doves and dense floral motifs, domed lid with kylin finial, chipped lid .................. $425-500

Jar, 5¾" h., motifs of carp and other fish, domed lid with spire finial .................................................... $150-220

Jardiniere, hibachi, 32¼" h., baluster body, motif of phoenix and peony .................................................... $1,800-2,200

Jardiniere, 14" h., c. 1900, continuous frieze of Shishi and peony blossoms .................................................. $750-1,000

Jardiniere, 18" dia., late 19th century, birds among garden flowers .................................................... $650-725

Jardiniere, 17" dia., continuous frieze of boats on a river, with cherry and pine trees and mountains in the distant background, molded in slight relief .............................. $400-485

Jardiniere, 17¼" dia., late 19th century, motif of tiger in a
garden, minor restoration . . . . . . . . . . . . . . . . . . . . . . . . . . . . . . . . . . . . . . . . . . . $350-400

Platter (oval), 19" l., motif of leaping dragon and rain clouds
with lightning bolts with Mt. Fuji in the distant background . . . . . . . . . . . . . . . . . . $300-375

Vase, 50" h., c. 1900, ovoid body having octagonal sections
decorated with phoenix and floral motifs . . . . . . . . . . . . . . . . . . . . . . . . . . . . . . . . . $550-625

Vase, 30" h., late 19th century, slender body and waisted
neck with motif of rooster and hens . . . . . . . . . . . . . . . . . . . . . . . . . . . . . . . . . . . . $900-1,700

Vase, 29½" h., c. 1890, slender ovoid form with motif of a
falcon on a branch with background of dense foliage . . . . . . . . . . . . . . . . . . . . . . $1,200-1,500

Vases (pair), approximately 44" h., late 19th century,
pear-shaped with flaring necks. (Illus.) . . . . . . . . . . . . . . . . . . . . . . . . . . . . . . . . . $3,000-4,000

Umbrella stand, 24" h., pierced with rectangular panels,
transfer pattern of flowers and lotus scrolls . . . . . . . . . . . . . . . . . . . . . . . . . . . . . . $300-400

Wall plate, 17" dia., transfer pattern of cranes flying over a
stream, Mt. Fuji in the distant background . . . . . . . . . . . . . . . . . . . . . . . . . . . . . . . . $200-250

# Sumida
## (Japanese)

In 1867, Inoue Ryosai, a Seto potter, moved to Tokyo (the Asakusa district
along the bank of the Sumida River) and set up a kiln. He produced fine
quality porcelain wares styled after Seto wares (porcelain). Eventually he
went into partnership with a pottery dealer named Shimada Sobei. From
c. 1895 to approximately 1970, pottery and porcelain wares, which have a
heavy curtain glaze, usually red grounds, and applied figures in relief
were produced. For many years these Sumida wares have been
mislabled, and among the erroneous terms used to categorize these
wares are: Poo ware, Banko ware, and Korean ware (and combinations
thereof). Correct classification - identification does not diminish the
collectibility of these wares.

*Sumida basket. Courtesy Gardner Pond*

Ashtray, 3" x 4½", domed shape (hear, see and speak no
evil), three wise monkeys in relief, incised mark . . . . . . . . . . . . . . . . . . . . . . . . . . . $150-200

Basket, 7" h., red ground with glazed handle, three children
in relief. (Illus.) . . . . . . . . . . . . . . . . . . . . . . . . . . . . . . . . . . . . . . . . . . . . . . . . . . . . . . $125-150

Basket, 8" h., red ground, four children in relief, cartouche . . . . . . . . . . . . . . . . . . . $125-150

Bowl, 5" dia., red ground, black glazing, children peering
over the rim, marked Made in Japan . . . . . . . . . . . . . . . . . . . . . . . . . . . . . . . . . . . . . . $150-175

Figures. (See Color Section) . . . . . . . . . . . . . . . . . . . . . . . . . . . . . . . . . . . . . . . . . . . . $900-1,100

Incense burner (koro), 3" h., red ground, black glaze, one
figure in relief, incised mark . . . . . . . . . . . . . . . . . . . . . . . . . . . . . . . . . . . . . . . . . . . . $100-150

Incense burner (koro), 5" h., three feet, figural finial, figure
on bridge catching fish, black ground, incised mark . . . . . . . . . . . . . . . . . . . . . . . . $200-225

Jar with cover, 7" h., children at play with child finial, red
ground and cartouche . . . . . . . . . . . . . . . . . . . . . . . . . . . . . . . . . . . . . . . . . . . . . . . . . . $250-350

Jar with cover, 7" h., green ground, people and birds in
slight relief, dog finial . . . . . . . . . . . . . . . . . . . . . . . . . . . . . . . . . . . . . . . . . . . . . . . . . . $300-400

Mug, elephant in relief, black ground, black and white glaze,
cartouche . . . . . . . . . . . . . . . . . . . . . . . . . . . . . . . . . . . . . . . . . . . . . . . . . . . . . . . . . . . . . . $40-65

Pilgrim bottle, 8" h., Rakan, red ground. (Illus.) . . . . . . . . . . . . . . . . . . . . . . . . . . . . $150-225

Pilgrim bottle, 8" h., flowers . . . . . . . . . . . . . . . . . . . . . . . . . . . . . . . . . . . . . . . . . . . . . $150-200

Pitcher, 7½" h., red ground, two children in relief, pinched
form cartouche . . . . . . . . . . . . . . . . . . . . . . . . . . . . . . . . . . . . . . . . . . . . . . . . . . . . . . . . . $150-225

Pitcher, 12" h., with six mugs, 5" h., each mug depicting a
different scene, overall monkeys and people. (Illus.) . . . . . . . . . . . . . . . . . . . . . . $1,200-1,600

Pitcher, 12" h., with six mugs, 4½" h., red ground, motif of
dragon upon rockwork, cartouche . . . . . . . . . . . . . . . . . . . . . . . . . . . . . . . . . . . . . . . $900-1,200

Pitcher, 12" h., with six mugs, 5" h., red ground, motif of monkeys, cartouche .................................................... $1,000-1,350

Teapot, 7" h., black ground with crackled white glaze at the base, contour of Mt. Fuji with figural finial and reed handle .................... $500-600

Teapot, 3" x 7", pancake shape, red ground, mottled black gray glaze, dragon and clouds in high relief ............................ $400-500

Vase, 9" h., bulbous, black ground, white crackled glaze, monkeys in relief, cartouche ...................................... $300-450

Vase, 5" h., four panels, red ground, Chinese waves and monkeys in slight relief ...................................... $100-125

Vase, 3" h., red ground, sage with blue glazed robe (Kwangtung style), incised mark ...................................... $75-100

Vase, 8½" h., two monkeys and frog with blue black glaze, incised mark .................................................. $150-200

Vase, 16" h., black ground, light blue crackled glaze, mother and children in relief, cartouche ...................................... $250-300

Vase, 9½" h., pinched ovoid form, black ground, light glazes, Lohan in relief ...................................... $300-400

Vase, 12" h., black ground, white and black glaze, mother-of-pearl flowers, Shibayama style ...................................... $500-700

Vase, 17" h., circle opening, black ground covered with monkeys in various scenes, one monkey flying a Curtis-Wright 1914 airplane, cartouche. (Illus.) ............................ $2,750-3,700

*Sumida pitcher and mug set. Courtesy Gardner Pond*

*Sumida pilgrim jug adorned with monkeys.*
*Courtesy Gardner Pond*

*Sumida pilgrim bottles. Courtesy Gardner Pond*

The northern Sung (960-1126 A.D.) potters were concerned with the production of stonewares. Their kilns were built on level ground and coal was employed as their fuel. The wares were then fired in the oxidizing atmosphere of the kiln. The clay was coated with a white slip, which was subsequently glazed and fired. The celadons produced at this time are different in color from those of the southern Sung. The shade is a green-brown. The decoration was incised, molded, or carved.

The southern Sung (1127-1279 A.D.) potters introduced a vitreous type of pottery and porcelain. The kilns were built on the sides of hills or mountains to insure a forced draft. The kilns employed a wood fuel and the wares were fired in a reduction atmosphere. The use of wood rather than the coal used in the northern Sung kilns produced a lighter, finer shade in the celadon glazes. The glaze was applied directly to the clay body and then fired. The celadons of this period were the color of a pale olive green. The rarest of the wares of this period are the black or purple Ting wares.

See: Celadon; Chien Yao; Chun; Ko Yao (crackle); Kuan (imperial ware); Ting; T'zu Chou; Ying Ching)

Bowl, 7" dia., Honan, decorated in tones of yellow and
brown glaze . . . . . . . . . . . . . . . . . . . . . . . . . . . . . . . . . . . . . . . . . . . . . . . . . . . . $800-900

Bowl, 8¼" dia., Honan, conical shape, covered with a deep
brown glaze . . . . . . . . . . . . . . . . . . . . . . . . . . . . . . . . . . . . . . . . . . . . . . . . $900-1,000

Box, 2½" h. x 3½" dia., unglazed molded top medallion on
lid over a deep warm brown glaze (a fine example of black
Sung wares that were exported to Southeast Asia). (Illus.) . . . . . . . . . . . . . . . . . . . . $400-600

Censer, 6" dia., iridescent green glaze of compressed circular
form on tripod legs . . . . . . . . . . . . . . . . . . . . . . . . . . . . . . . . . . . . . . . . . . $1,000-1,200

Ewer, 6" h., Honan, with a long spout and covered with
brown glaze . . . . . . . . . . . . . . . . . . . . . . . . . . . . . . . . . . . . . . . . . . . . . . . . . . . . $700-800

Ewer, 6½" h., with two loop handles and a short spout,
covered with a brown glaze . . . . . . . . . . . . . . . . . . . . . . . . . . . . . . . . . . . . . . . . $700-800

Jar, 4" h., Honan, squat form, with two small loop handles at
the neck, the thick black glaze falling short of the base,
glazed inside with a brown glaze over a buff stoneware body . . . . . . . . . . . . . . . $1,500-1,800

Jar, 4½" h., Honan, with an ovoid body, black glazed with
ferruginous brown splashes, the foot unglazed . . . . . . . . . . . . . . . . . . . . . . . . . $1,800-2,200

*Sung Dynasty box, 3½" dia., deep brown glaze with unglazed, impressed medallion*

Jar, 6" h., Honan, painted with white slip on a black glaze showing brown on the ribs, interior with a beige wash ...................... $600-800

Jar (covered), with five strap handles, covered with an iridescent green glaze ..................................... $600-800

Jar, 10" h., Honan type, molded, with a brown glaze turning to a brown black at the neck, the base drilled ................... $600-800

Tea bowl, 4" dia., Honan, with rust brown speckles on a lustrous black glaze, a countersunk foot and an unglazed rim ............... $500-600

## Swatow
### (Chinese)

Swatow is a Ming period provincial ware probably made in the Fukien province. Decoration includes incised decoration, slip decoration, blue-white ware, and polychrome colors of red, turquoise, green, and black. Oftentimes, sand remnants from the kiln are found adhered to the base of the coarse gray body.

Bowl, 5" dia., blue and white decoration, the interior with calligraphy, the exterior with floral reserves and diaper patterns .............................................. $225-325

Dish, 8" dia., polychrome decoration, center with a medallion of a chrysanthemum, outer rim with oval panels of floral decoration on a diapered ground, painted in iron red, turquoise, and green, the glaze somewhat degraded ............ $800-900

Dish, 10½" dia., blue and white decoration, center with an exotic bird in a garden, rim with a border of floral reserves on a scale diapered ground .............................. $600-800

Dish, 11" dia., blue and white decoration, center with a freely drawn scene of a deer and a bird in a garden bordered by a floral band, rim with border of floral reserves on a scale diapered ground .............................. $600-800

Dish, 12" dia., blue and white decoration, the center showing a pavilion and water scene, with four floral reserves on a diaper border .............................. $800-1,000

Dish, 12½" dia., late Ming, painted in polychrome with iron red, green, and black outline, with panels of chrysanthemums on a reserved diaper ground, a center floral medallion, the reverse undecorated, and kiln grit on the base ............ $800-1,000

Dish, 12¾" dia., polychrome decoration, the center showing a lion and foliage encircled by floral scrolls and birds, the border with floral reserves, painted in red, green, and turquoise .............................. $900-1,300

Dish, 13" dia., blue and white decoration, center with a pheasant among bamboo and flowers, with six border reserves of flowers and scrolls ........................ $700-900

Dish, 15" dia., polychrome decoration, center with two phoenixes among flowers, border with two dragons and blossoms, painted in an orange-red, green, and turquoise with black outlines .............................. $900-1,200

Dish, 15½" dia., polychrome decoration, with the center and borders showing dragons in pursuit of flaming pearls, with birds, mountains and foliage painted in turquoise and red with black outlines .............................. $1,500-2,000

Dish, 17¼" dia., blue and white decoration, freely painted with a bird in the center and a border of peonies and phoenix, with heavy kiln grit on the footing ............... $1,200-1,500

Dish, 20" dia., blue and white decoration, center with birds in a landscape setting, border with six panels of flowering branches .............................. $2,000-2,400

Jar, 10" h., polychrome enamels of iron red, green, and black outline on a creamy buff ground, with bands of decoration

Swatow jar, 10" h., 16th century polychrome enamels

above and below leaf borders, ju-i border on the shoulder,
and a motif of lions, flowers, and leaves. (Illus.) .......................... $1,500-2,000

## The Japanese Sword and Its Furniture:

1. Shozoku-Tachi or Shin no Tachi — used for court dress.
2. Tachi — a slung sword worn with cutting edge downward.
3. Wakizashi — usually 1 to 2 feet in length, worn with the cutting edge upwards. Used by the Samurai and companion sword to the Katana.
4. Katana — the fighting sword used after the Ashikaga period. It was worn with the cutting edge upward.
5. Yefu no Tachi — a sword worn by nobles and palace guards.
6. Aikuchi — a dagger without a guard
7. Tanto — a dagger (usually a foot or less in length).
8. Kaiken — a dagger used by women (it has no guard).
9. Daisho — the Katana and Wakizashi together.
10. Koto — blades made from 900 A.D. to 1530.
11. Shinto — blades made from 1530 to 1867.
12. Shin-Shinto — blades made from 1868 on.

## Parts of the Sword:

1. Bonji — the character writing on the blade.
2. Kissaki — the tip of the blade.
3. Kasaki — the sharp edge.
4. Yakiba — the tempered edge.
5. Nakago — tang.
6. Mei — an inscription.
7. Mekugiana — hole in the tang for the peg.
8. Horimono — carved motifs on the blade.

## Sword Furniture:

1. Tsuba (see Tsuba).
2. Kozuka (see Kozuka).
3. Kogai — Skewer.
4. Menuki (see Menuki).
5. Mekugi — securing peg.
6. Seppa — guard washer.
7. Kohiri — finial of the scabbard.
8. Saya — scabbard.

Aikuchi, Koto Bizen Sukesada, silver kiku mounts (Tomei),
c. 1544. (Illus.) ........................................................ $5,500-7,500

Daisho, approximately 20" l., fittings 19th century, katana
blade 17th century, wakizashi blade 17th century, gold and
silver togidashi (a lacquer surface process employed by
grinding), motifs of waves, silver fittings with motifs of
dragons in nikubori (chiseled in relief), two menuki of
gagaku dancers; katana blade honzukuri and toriizori with
tama-oi-ryu horimono; two menukigana approximately 27" l.;
wakizashi blade, honzukuri, and toriizori with bonji and
horimono; two menukigiana with black togidashi scabbards ................ $8,000-12,000

# Swords
## (Japanese)

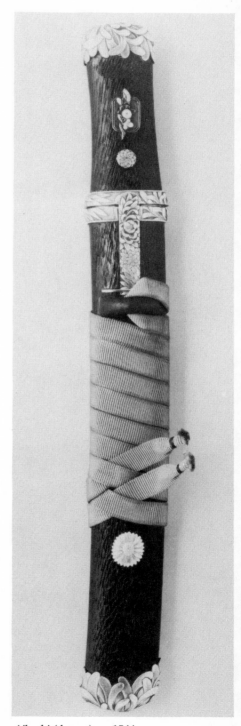

*Aikuchi (dagger), c. 1544*

219

Kaiken, approximately 11″ l., fittings 19th century, blade early 18th century, fittings include kozuka (silver with chrysanthemum in nikubori), the blade, hirazukuri with mitsumune decorated in gold, nakago with kurijiri and one mekugiana . . . . . . . . . . . . . . . . . . . . . . . . . . . . . . . . . . . . . . . . . . . . . . $2,600-3,300

Katana, approximately 25″ l., fittings late 19th century, blade early 19th century, fitting of copper with motif of figures in iro-e takazogan (inlay raised above the surface), menuki of Moso carrying bamboo and a woman and deer; the blade, honzukuri, and toriizori with bonji and horimono . . . . . . . . . . . . . . . . . . . . $8,000-10,000

Katana (Soshu-style) approximately 26″ l., fittings late 19th century, blade early 19th century, gold togidashi with Shoki's sword, shibuichi fittings in iro-e takazogan with Shoki and Oni; the blade, broad katakiri zukuri with bonji, black lacquer scabbard . . . . . . . . . . . . . . . . . . . . . . . . . . . . . . . . . . . . . . . . . . . . . . . . $5,000-7,000

### Tachi:

1. Kabuto-gane — the cap of the hilt.
2. Musubi-gane — the top of the habuto-gane, with a cord attached.
3. Tsuka-ai — similar to menuki.

Tachi, approximately 20″ l., late 19th century fittings, blade early 18th century, gold heidatsu with Kuyo mon, matching shitogi (with hoops), tsuba, one menuki; blade-honzukuri and toriizori, two mekugiana, nashiji (pear rind surface) scabbard . . . . . . . . . . . . . . . . . . . . . . . . . . . . . . . . . . . . . . . . . . . . . $3,500-4,700

Tachi, approximately 24″ l., fittings 19th century, blade 17th century, the fittings of ishime-ji (rough surface) silver, matching saya-jiri, kashira (the pommel), inlaid in gold with kiri mon, kabuto-gane (cap of the hilt) carved in the form of a phoenix; the blade — honzukuri and hoshizori with horimono; two mekugiana with Kikko Aogai scabbard . . . . . . . . . . . . . $4,200-6,000

Tachi, fitting (sectional), 19th century, ivory with relief carving of immortals, oni, dragons, and other animals, approximately 29″ long . . . . . . . . . . . . . . . . . . . . . . . . . . . . . . . . . . . $3,200-4,500

Wakizashi, approximately 16″ l., 19th century, copper kashira and menuki with motifs of turtles, oval copper tsuba with motif of foliage in gold and shakudo takazogan, plain blade, black lacquer scabbard . . . . . . . . . . . . . . . . . . . . . . . . . . . . . . . . . . . . $700-1,100

Wakizashi, 19th century fittings, blade 16th century, oval shibuichi tsuba iro-e takazogan with motif of tiger, shakudo kozuka, suriage nakago with two mekugiana and lacquered scabbard . . . . . . . . . . . . . . . . . . . . . . . . . . . . . . . . . . . . . . . . . . . . . $3,000-4,500

Wakizashi, approximately 20″ l., 19th century fittings, Koto blade, decorated in bold hiramakie motif of foliage, shakudo nanako tsuba, menuki formed as dragons in gilded bronze, with kozuka, kogai, one mekugi, gold nashiji (pear rind) scabbard . . . . . . . . . . . . . . . . . . . . . . . . . . . . . . . . . . . . . . . . . . . . . $1,700-2,300

### Tamba
(Japanese)

Bottle, 6″ h., 19th century, gourd shape, white slip calligraphy. (Illus.) . . . . . . . . . . . . . . . . . . . . . . . . . . . . . . . . . . . . . . . $185-225

Bottle, 7″ h., umbrella form. (Illus.) . . . . . . . . . . . . . . . . . . . . . . . . . . . $250-350

Chaire (caddy for thick tea), 3″ h., 19th century, barrel form, mottled brown curtain glaze near shoulder, ivory cover . . . . . . . . . . . . $250-385

Jar, 6″ h., 19th century, squat baluster form, four small loop handles, deep green glaze . . . . . . . . . . . . . . . . . . . . . . . . . . . . . . . . . $200-325

Storage jar, 18″ h., 17th century, in baluster form, rolled lip, partially glazed in green . . . . . . . . . . . . . . . . . . . . . . . . . . . . . . . . . $1,200-1,700

Storage jar, 14″ h., 17th century, partially glazed about the shoulder in deep green . . . . . . . . . . . . . . . . . . . . . . . . . . . . . . . . . $1,800-2,400

*Tamba double gourd sake bottle*          *Tamba umbrella-type sake bottle*

The years of the T'ang Dynasty extend from 618-906 A.D. Several important kiln sites of the period have been found at Hopei, Honan, and Kiangsi provinces. Unlike the earlier Han glazes, which have dark and muddy tones, the T'ang glazes were bright, applied over a white slip, and often combined three colors (san ts'ai) in splash glazes of green, brown, and yellow or cream, white, and blue. Straw-colored glazes were also popular. These glazes all reveal a minute crackle. The T'ang potters concerned themselves with the production of mortuary wares, vessels, and figures which appear either glazed or unglazed. The horse was the most popularly portrayed figure of the period.

## T'ang Dynasty
*(Chinese)*

*T'ang Dynasty horse, 13¾" h., ivory glaze with red and black pigment*

Bowl, 5½" dia., with a streaked, degraded glaze of brown
and green on buff ground . . . . . . . . . . . . . . . . . . . . . . . . . . . . . . . . . . . . . . . . . . $900-1,200

*Ewer, 6¾" h., stoneware, with an oviform, melon fluted
body and pinched loop handles, decorated with a mottled
brown glaze with a flecked Yüeh type celadon glaze . . . . . . . . . . . . . . . . . . . . . . . $1,700

Ewer, 13¾" h., stoneware amphora with double dragon
handles shaped from the shoulder to clasp the mouth of the
vase, the white slip covered with a straw colored glaze . . . . . . . . . . . . . . . . . . . . $5,000-7,000

Figure, goose, 2½" h., posed with head turned over back,
some glaze chips . . . . . . . . . . . . . . . . . . . . . . . . . . . . . . . . . . . . . . . . . . . . . . . . . . $800-1,000

221

*T'ang Dynasty lady, 8½" h., straw glaze*

Figure, rooster, 4" h., posed in standing position, the straw glaze degraded, with traces of red pigment, burial encrustation, chipped ........................................................ $600-800

Figure, ram, 4¾" h., posed in a resting position with horns curving back and legs tucked under body, flaked, chestnut glaze ................................................................. $700-1,000

Figure, dog, 4⅝" h., composed of buff clay and covered with a yellow straw glaze ........................................... $600-900

Figure, boar, 5" l., posed in resting posture, of unglazed pottery with earth encrustations ................................. $800-1,000

Figure, 10" h., boy, straw glazed with some red and black pigment remaining ........................................... $1,800-2,200

Figure, 5½" l., boar, in a reclining position, with a degraded straw glaze. (Illus. here and in Color Section) ................... $1,200-1,500

Figure, 3½" l., buffalo, on square gray pottery base ................ $900-1,200

Figure, bullock, 5" h., posed with hump and a massive neck, with his tail over his flank, covered with a deep yellow to orange glaze, restoration .......................................... $1,400-1,700

*Figure, female, posed with robe and long flowing sleeves with hands crossed, the glaze degraded ........................... $600

*Figure, 21" h., camel, splashed with green, brown and ocher glaze, some restoration. (Illus.) ................................. $14,300

Figure, 13¼" h., court lady, painted pottery, the lady having long flowing sleeves, upturned shoes and piled coif, with traces of white, blue, and green pigment. (Illus. here and in Color Section) ............................................... $8,000-10,000

Figure, 8½" h., lady, straw glaze. (Illus. here and in Color Section) .................................................... $1,200-1,500

*Figures, female (pair), 11" h., posed in pleated dresses, wearing high butterfly hats, with traces of black and red pigment, restored .............................................. $2,600

Figure, court lady, 11¾" h., posed with her hair piled into a high knot, wearing a short jacket over a long sleeved dress which conceals her hands, some traces of red and black pigment, some repairs, unglazed .................................. $700-900

Figure, earth spirit, 13" h., posed seated on his haunches, with flamelike spikes running from his tail to the top of his head, seated on a rectangular base, the pottery of buff color ....... $5,000-6,000

Figure, 12¼" h., earth spirit, seated on rockwork with two long horns and flaming mane, glazed with green, brown, and cream ................................................... $3,000-4,000

Figure, warrior, 16" h., finely detailed with armor and an animal-head mask, covered with a straw glaze, some flaking ....... $3,500-4,500

*T'ang Dynasty court lady, 13¼" h., painted pottery with some pigment remaining*

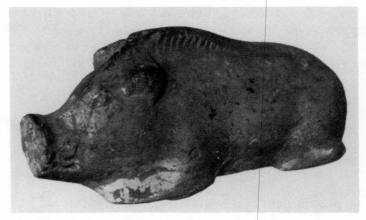

*T'ang Dynasty boar, 5½" h., straw glaze*

Figure, camel, 20" h., posed with head held high, with a splash glaze on the face and saddle cloth, repairs on the legs and hump . . . . . . . . . . . . . . . . . . . . . . . . . . . . . . . . . . . . . . . . . . . . . . . . . . . . . . . . . . . . $12,000-15,000

*Figure, 13¾" h., horse, the cropped mane and face with ivory glaze, the unglazed saddle having original red and black pigment, with replaced ears and a break across the lower legs. (Illus.) . . . . . . . . . . . . . . . . . . . . . . . . . . . . . . . . . . . . . . . . . . . . . . . . . $5,000

Figure, 10" h., Zodiac, unglazed but having some traces of white slip . . . . . . . . . . . . . . . . . . . . . . . . . . . . . . . . . . . . . . . . . . . . . . . . . . . . . . . . . . . . . . . $900-1,000

Jar, 5½" h., with white glaze falling short of the base, revealing a pale buff pottery, with some iridescence in the glaze and burial encrustations . . . . . . . . . . . . . . . . . . . . . . . . . . . . . . . . . . . . . . $1,000-1,200

Jar, 6" h., globular shape, covered with a phosphatic glaze in colors of olive green, mottled beige, and pale lavender, the glaze falling short of the base . . . . . . . . . . . . . . . . . . . . . . . . . . . . . . . . . . . $3,000-3,500

Jar, 6½" h., ovoid shape with a short neck and a lipped rim, covered in white with a translucent glaze of yellow green tint, some crackling, the base left unglazed . . . . . . . . . . . . . . . . . . . . . $3,500-4,500

Vase, 13½" h., amphora-shaped with loop handles ending in dragon heads at the rim of the slender tapered neck, with a yellow green glaze over a white slip on a gray stoneware body, the glaze degraded and flaking . . . . . . . . . . . . . . . . . . . . . . . . . . $4,500-5,500

*T'ang Dynasty camel, 21" h., splashed glaze*

# Tanka
*(Also spelled Thanka)*

Tanka means scroll painting and such generally takes on a religious theme. This type of painting on cloth or paper (paper tankas usually have a silk border) can have pictorial portrayals of deities with a central god surrounded by smaller portrayals of deities, or it may be a symbolic portrayal with a deity surrounded by scenic depictions, clouds, gardens, etc. Tankas vary in size but most are approximately 2' x 3' or slightly larger. The tanka is a highly collectible art form.

Nepalesetanka (cloth), framed size 26" x 20", seated Buddha (dhyanasana) on lotus throne, surrounded by deities, each on a nimbus cloud . . . . . . . . . . . . . . . . . . . . . . . . . . . . . . . . . . . . . . . . . . . . . . . $200-300

Nepalese tanka (cloth), framed size 16" x 10", a three-eyed god holding a scepter and riding a mythical beast, surrounded by clouds . . . . . . . . . . . . . . . . . . . . . . . . . . . . . . . . . . . . . . . . . $140-165

Nepalese tanka (cloth), framed size 27" x 18", a deity seated on a dais, surrounded by musicians and mythical animals . . . . . . . . . . . . . . . . . . . . $155-190

Nepalese tanka (cloth), framed size 27½" x 22¼", multiheaded deity before flaming mandorla surrounded by nimbus clouds . . . . . . . . . . . . . . . . . . . . . . . . . . . . . . . . . . . . . . . . . . . . . . . . $110-155

Tibetan tanka (cloth), framed size 34" x 24", deities and sages seated on clouds and lotus, clouds linked by gold-spoked wheels . . . . . . . . . . . . . . . . . . . . . . . . . . . . . . . . . . . . . . . . . . . . . . . . . . . . . $450-550

Tibetan tanka (cloth), framed size 33" x 22", bodhisattva on lotus base surrounded by scenes from the life of Buddha . . . . . . . . . . . . . . . . . . . . . $225-265

Tibetan tanka (silk), framed size 54" x 31", a many-armed shivite deity upon a mythical beast framed by fire . . . . . . . . . . . . . . . . . . . . . . . $400-600

Tibetan tanka (cloth), framed size 25" x 21", a deity surrounded by other deities and musicians, with a large tiger seated in the foreground . . . . . . . . . . . . . . . . . . . . . . . . . . . . . . . . . . . . . . . . . $200-270

Tibetan tanka (cloth), framed size 28" x 24", Syamatara on a double lotus throne holding a lotus blossom, surrounded by deities . . . . . . . . . . . . . . . . . . . . . . . . . . . . . . . . . . . . . . . . . . . . . . . . . . . . . . $450-700

Tibetan tanka (cloth), framed size 28" x 20", Simhavatra standing behind a wheel, surrounded by enshrined deities . . . . . . . . . . . . . . . . . . . $700-800

223

Tibetan tanka (cloth), framed size 30" x 20", Dharamapala
Hayagriva surrounded by deities ..................................................... $200-300

Tibetan tanka (cloth), 51" x 37", Yamantaka surrounded by
Avalokitesavara, silk border ........................................................... $900-1,400

Tibetan tanka (cloth), 20" x 15", Mahasiddha riding an
elephant and surrounded by flames and figures, with silk
border ..................................................................................... $1,100-1,500

Tibetan tanka (cloth), framed size 18" x 12", Buddhas seated
dhyanasana on lotus throne, surrounded by deities ......................... $200-250

Tibetan tanka (cloth), framed size 20" x 14", Dharmapala
Yamantaka surrounded by figures .................................................. $350-550

Tibetan tanka (cloth), framed size 30½" x 20½",
Aryavalokitesvara guarded by three figures of Hayagriva ................... $1,100-1,400

## Tea Dust
### (Chinese)

Tea dust decoration results from a double-glaze technique which was
developed in the first half of the 18th century. The porcelain was first
glazed with a yellow brown oxide, followed by a fine spray of green lead
silicate which was blown on. This combination produces a color which is
akin to that of tea leaves.

Vase, 5" h., mei ping form, 18th century, two elephant head
masks set as handles, the base with a brown wash ........................... $600-800

Vase, 10" h., 19th century Tao Kuang incised seal mark, of
double-gourd shape with long, looped handles, the waist
with a petal band in relief ............................................................. $2,800-3,200

Vase, 10" h., Ch'ien Lung period incised seal mark, bulbous
shape with a tall cylindrical neck and round lipped rim, set
on a pedestal base, the base glazed with a brown wash .................... $5,800-6,500

Vase, 10" h., early 19th century, of ovoid form with a short
neck and lipped rim, with four elephant head handles
applied below the neck ................................................................. $800-1,000

Vase, 12" h., bottle form, the base glazed with a brown wash ............ $1,200-1,400

Vase, 12" h., seal mark and period of Ch'ien Lung, a globular
body with a flared neck, and three ram heads in high relief
set at the shoulders; the uniform olive green glaze thinning
to yellow on the curved horns of the ram heads and on the
lip of the vase ........................................................................... $20,000-25,000

Vase, 14" h., 19th century, bottle form, two dragon mask
handles set at the body ................................................................ $900-1,200

Vase, 13" h., Ch'ien Lung seal mark and period, of bottle
form ......................................................................................... $3,000-4,000

Vase, 13¼" h., Hu form, mark and period of Ch'ien Lung,
the pear-shaped body molded in relief with two
peach-shaped panels, the long neck having indented corners
flanked by two handles, covered in a speckled glaze of olive
green ........................................................................................ $12,000-15,000

Vase, 14½" h., 19th century, pear shaped with a speckled
olive glaze ................................................................................ $400-500

Vase, 17" h., 19th century, Tao Kuang seal mark, rouleau
shape, with a green glaze and olive brown specks ........................... $1,000-1,200

Water dropper, Yung Chêng period (unmarked), in the form
of a toadlike animal, in imitation of an early bronze, with
finely speckled olive green color, details highlighted with gilt ........... $2,300-2,600

## Tê-hua
### (Chinese)

Tê-hua is a kiln site in Fukien province that has become famous for its
production of fine-grained blanc de chine porcelain. Figurine production

dates back to the 17th century. The designs were limited to applied relief and incised decoration. Some blue and white ware was produced there as well.

(See: Blanc de Chine)

The production of Sukhothai wares began in the 13th century in an area approximately twenty-five miles west of the present town of Sukhothai. The kilns produced a ware similar to the Tz'u-chou ware of China. The decoration consisted of iron painting on a white ground. The clay body was coarse and was coated with a white slip. Sawankhalok wares are the most numerous of the potteries produced in Thailand. There were four basic groups of glazed wares made between the 14th and 16th centuries: iron painting on a white ground, celadons, black glazed pottery, and white glazed pottery.

## Thai Ceramics
*(Thailand)*

Bowl (footed), 10¾" dia., Sawankhalok, with a clear glaze over inky blue floral decoration on interior and exterior, the footing unglazed. (See Color Section) . . . . . . . . . . . . . . . . . . . . . . . . . . . . . . . . . . . . . . . $600-800

Bowl, 10" dia., Sawankhalok, painted in the center with a flower and whorls and covered with a brown and white glaze . . . . . . . . . . . . . . . . . . . . . . . . . . . . . . . . . . . . . . . . . . . . . . . . . . . . . . . . . $400-500

Bowl, 10" dia., Sukhothai, painted with a pale grayish blue fish and a double ring . . . . . . . . . . . . . . . . . . . . . . . . . . . . . . . . . . . . . . . . . . . . . $300-400

Bowl, 10" dia., Sawankhalok, the center painted with a stylized floral design, with a broad petal border, covered with bluish green glaze . . . . . . . . . . . . . . . . . . . . . . . . . . . . . . . . . . . . . . . . . . . . . . $300-400

Bowl, 10" dia., Sukhothai, with traces of pigment on fish in center medallion, the buff slip with a degraded glaze . . . . . . . . . . . . . . . . . . . . . . . . . $200-300

*Thai pottery deer, 6" h., Sawankhalok, 14th/16th century*

*Thai Buddha, 6" h., celadon glaze, 16th century*

Bowl, 16" dia., Sawankhalok, an overall crackle glaze covering the interior motif of a center floral medallion, the exterior having four evenly spaced fleurettes, with kiln grit adhering to the footing. (See Color Section) ................................$600-800

Box, 7" h., Sawankhalok, the body painted with a blue floral design, the cover with a brown black geometric pattern, on buff stoneware ...........................................$350-400

Figure, 6" h., 16th century, the celadon glazed figure kneeling in prayer, the hollow base revealing the pinkish clay body. (Illus.) ..........................................$550-650

Figure, 6" h., Sawankhalok, deer, with a yellow brown glaze and an unglazed flat foot. (Illus.) ...........................$400-500

Figure, 4" h., Sawankhalok, female posed kneeling with a child in her arms, covered with a greenish gray glaze .........................$80-100

Figure, 9" h., Sawankhalok, male kneeling, unglazed pottery. (See Color Section) ...........................................$400-600

Oil lamp, Ban Cheng, c. 2,000-5,000 B.C., geometric design decorated in red pigment. (Illus.) ...........................$400-500

Vase, 6" h., Sawankhalok, pear-shaped, with rings around the neck and lower body, covered in a gray green glaze ......................$400-500

Vase, 15" h., Sawankhalok, covered with a thin yellow brown glaze, elaborate applied and relief slip decoration, ringed footing, applied fish figures for double handles. (See Color Section) ...........................................$1,200-1,400

*Thai pottery oil lamp, Ban Cheng ware, 1200 B.C.*

*Ting Yao bowl, 19th century copy, 8" dia.*

## Ting Yao
### (Chinese)

This northern Sung period white porcelaneous ware was made in Hopei province. It is characterized by an ivory-colored glaze and has carved, molded, or incised decorations. Noticeable on some items are the tear streaks or thickenings in the glaze where it formed in drops on the surface. Another noticeable characteristic is the bronze sheath which was sometimes added to the unglazed rim, a practical means of adorning an item that was fired upside down in the kiln. On such items the foot rims are glazed.

Bowl, 4" dia., 10th century, with a fluted rim, raised on a small foot, with some rim chips ...........................................$200-300

Bowl, 4⅝" dia., Sung Dynasty, with a flared lip, covered with a streaky white glaze, the rim unglazed ...............................$300-400

Bowl, 5" dia., raised on a small foot ...........................................$500-600

Bowl, 5½" dia., Sung Dynasty, carved with a ribbed leaf on the exterior, with a sheathed rim, unglazed base and spur marks on the interior ............................................... $1,600-2,000

Bowl, 5½" dia., Sung Dynasty, with unglazed rim ........................... $500-600

Bowl, 5½" dia., Sung Dynasty, carved with a ribbed leaf on the exterior, with a sheathed rim, unglazed base and spur marks on the interior ............................................... $1,600-2,000

Bowl, 6" dia., Sung Dynasty, with steep flared sides, the center with incised decoration, covered with a thick creamy glaze ...................................................... $3,800-4,200

Bowl, 7" dia., Sung Dynasty, with steep flared sides, the center having incised decoration, covered with a thick creamy glaze ...................................................... $3,800-4,200

Bowl, 7½" dia., Sung Dynasty, with carved floral decoration on the interior, covered with thick ivory-tinted glaze, the base unglazed, crack ...................................... $400-500

Bowl, 8" dia., 19th century copy, conical shape, interior with three molded dragons and floral scrolls, with a molded key fret border, covered with a creamy white glaze (Illus.) ........................ $400-500

Bowl, 9" dia., Sung Dynasty, lotus bowl with incised petals and six lobed rim, covered with a creamy, translucent glaze ................. $2,000-3,000

Bowl, 6" dia., northern Sung Dynasty, six lobed, incised with a large lotus spray with a leaf and numerous curly sprays, covered with a grayish white tinted glaze ................................. $800-1,000

Bowl, 9½" dia., Sung Dynasty, molded with a pair of fish in central medallion, two phoenix birds in flight and a key fret border at the rim, covered in cream-colored glaze with copper sheath at the rim ............................................... $1,200-1,500

Bowl, 9½" dia., Sung Dynasty, molded with a pair of fish in central medallion, two phoenix birds in flight and a key fret border at the rim, covered with cream-colored glaze, a copper sheath at the rim ...................................... $1,500-2,000

Dish, 4½" dia., Sung Dynasty, flower-shaped, divided into six lobes by incised lines, covered with a pale cream-colored glaze ...................................................... $2,000-2,500

Dish, 5¼" dia., Sung Dynasty, foliate form with eight petals, covered with a creamy glaze, rim chips ................................... $800-1,200

Dish, 7¼" dia., Sung Dynasty, with flared sides and short, wedge-shaped foot, carved floral motif in center, ivory tone crackle glaze, copper sheath at the rim ................................. $1,000-1,500

Saucer dish, 7" dia., Sung Dynasty, molded with dragons and phoenixes in the center, with a creamy glaze burned dark in the firing, tear streaks on the exterior .......................... $3,000-4,000

Saucer dish, 6½" dia., Sung Dynasty, a very fine molded dish with leaping dragons in the center surrounded by foliate scrolls, key fret border, with an unglazed, copper-sheathed rim, covered with a creamy glaze, with tear streaks on exterior ...................................................... $6,000-8,000

Saucer dish, 8" dia., Sung Dynasty, of shallow, six-lobed petal form, finely carved with a fungus in the center, covered with a clear milk white glaze, with tear streaks on the exterior ...................................................... $7,000-8,000

## Tokoname
### (Japanese)

Tokoname wares were originally produced for use in Cha no yu (the tea ceremony). They were unglazed stoneware (high-fired) and are found in several shades of brown. Today's collector has shown interest in the Tokoname wares of the late 19th and early 20th centuries. These later wares are terra-cotta and unglazed. Such wares usually have ornamentations molded in relief, taking on such forms as dragons and clouds. These molded motifs are usually painted black and accentuated in gilt.

*Tokoname bowl, late 19th century, 3½" dia.*

Bottle (Momoyama period), 13" h., baluster form, thick, rolled mouth, natural ash glaze . . . . . . . . . . . . . . . . . . . . . . . . . . . . . . . . . . . . . . . . . . $1,100-1,500

Bowl, 8" dia., 19th century, exterior having continuous motif of dragons against a stippled ground, interior contains three carp. (Illus.) . . . . . . . . . . . . . . . . . . . . . . . . . . . . . . . . . . . . . . . . . . . . . . . . . . . . . . $85-100

Bowl, 3½" dia., 19th century, exterior having continuous motif of dragons against stippled ground with a child leaning against edge. (Illus.) . . . . . . . . . . . . . . . . . . . . . . . . . . . . . . . . . . . . . . . . . . . . . $125-150

Humidor, 6" h., early 20th century, bamboo form finial, continuous cloud scrolls and dragons on exterior against stippled ground . . . . . . . . . . . . . . . . . . . . . . . . . . . . . . . . . . . . . . . . . . . . . . . . . $195-220

Teapot, 3½" h., late 19th century, motif executed in green, blue, red, and yellow trailed enamels . . . . . . . . . . . . . . . . . . . . . . . . . . . . . . $45-65

Teapot, reed handle, sgrafitto motifs of landscapes . . . . . . . . . . . . . . . . . . . . . . . $145-160

Vase, 8½" h., late 19th century, dragons and clouds against a stippled ground, highlighted in gilt with black accents . . . . . . . . . . . . . . . . . $145-160

Umbrella stand, 23½" h., late 19th century, continuous dragons and cloud scrolls lacquered in black and highlighted in gilt . . . . . . . . . . . . . . . . . . . . . . . . . . . . . . . . . . . . . . . . . . . . . . . . . . . . . . $245-270

*Tokoname bowl, 19th century, 8" dia.*

**Tou ts'ai**
*(Chinese)*

Tou ts'ai enamel decoration originated in the Ming Dynasty during the reign of Chêng Hua (1465-1487), using a distinctive style of underglaze blue and overglaze enamels. The literal translation of tou ts'ai means "opposed or contrasting colors." The outline and some of the details of the design were drawn on the unfired body in a soft underglaze blue. After glazing and firing, the enamels of turquoise, yellow, green, aubergine, and red were applied in transparent washes within the blue outlines. The porcelain was then refired. Tou ts'ai wares were perfected in the reign of Ch'êng-Hua and then revived in the 18th century.

(See: Ch'ien Lung; K'ang Hsi; Yung Chêng)

## Transmutation Glazes
*(Chinese)*

Transmutation glazes are characterized by color variations that occur during the firing process. The variety of color change depends on the amount of copper oxide present in the glaze. When these variations first appeared as a result of an unknown "accident" in the kiln, the Chinese potters regarded the results of their labors as an unpleasant supernatural phenomenon. Few "original" items survive since they were destroyed in an attempt to chase the "devils" from the kilns. Control and perfection of transmutation glaze techniques began in the K'ang Hsi period and resulted in the magnificent flambé glaze variations that we now regard so highly.

(See: Flambé)

## Transitional Period
*(Chinese)*

The transitional period (1620-1683) dates from the end of the Ming Dynasty (death of the Emperor Wan Li) to the beginning of the Ch'ing Dynasty (the first year of the Emperor K'ang Hsi). Imperial patronage of porcelain production was unlikely at this time due to the rapid succession of three different emperors to the throne. The export trade of the time influenced the style of the wares produced at the provincial kilns. Blue and white still flourished (the blue of the period being a bright blue violet shade). Similarity in decoration of the porcelain of this era suggests that there were certain patterns adhered to at this time. The most common theme is a landscape setting with figures, rocks, clouds, and grass. The enamels of the time, particularly the "wu ts'ai" five-color ware, suggest the influence of the Wan Li period. Although the green enamels predominate (influence of the K'ang Hsi period) the wu ts'ai underglaze blue occupied larger areas of the decoration than the wares of either the Wan Li or the K'ang Hsi reigns.

*Transitional period vase, 9" h., wu ts'ai decoration, mid-17th century*

Bowl, 9½" dia., blue and white decoration, with scene of eight immortals paying homage to Shou Lao in a wooded garden, the interior decorated with a central medallion of a figure holding a peach with the background of a river landscape, the inside rim decorated with a pine needle border, small rim chip . . . . . . . . . . . . . . . . . . . . . . . . . . . . . . . . . . . . $1,000-1,200

Brush pot, 8" h., blue and white decoration, decorated with a scene of a sage seated on some rocks and surrounded by his attendants, mountain landscape in background . . . . . . . . . . . . . . . . . . . . . . . . $1,200-1,600

Brush pot, 8½" h., underglaze blue and white, with seven sages among the trees and rocks, finely painted, small chips at the rim . . . . . . . . . . . . . . . . . . . . . . . . . . . . . . . . . . . . . . . . . . . . $2,000-3,000

Dish, 13" dia., blue and white decoration, with scene of equestrian warriors among rocks and landscape, with one warrior bearing a flag . . . . . . . . . . . . . . . . . . . . . . . . . . . . . . . . . . . . $800-1,000

Jar, 5¾" h., blue and white decoration, barrel-shaped, with scene of a general and his two soldiers standing in front of a tent . . . . . . . . . . . . . . . . . . . . . . . . . . . . . . . . . . . . . . . . . . . . . . . $600-800

Jar, 9" h., blue and white decoration, ovoid form, wood cover, with a scene of warriors marching on a mountainside . . . . . . . . . . . . . . . . . $900-1,200

Jar, 9½" h., blue and white decoration, with a scene of a kylin standing on rockwork . . . . . . . . . . . . . . . . . . . . . . . . . . . . . . . . . . . . $700-800

*Jar, 11½" h., c. 1650, wu ts'ai decoration, showing mounted and armed warriors in full gallop, with gold lacquer restoration and cracks in the neck. (Illus.) . . . . . . . . . . . . . . . . . . . . . . . . . . . . . . $1,045

Jar, 21" h., with cover, ovoid body, underglaze blue and white with a continuous scene of a scholar and his attendants

*Transitional period jar 11½" h., wu ts'ai decoration, 1650*

observing two court ladies and their attendants in a garden ................... $1,000-1,500

Vase, 7" h., baluster form, underglaze blue and white, showing a mountain landscape, with two sprays of flowers at the waisted neck ........................................... $550-700

Vase, 8" h., wu ts'ai enamel decoration, with continuous scene of a scholar and a boy with attendants in a garden setting ............................................. $800-1,000

Vase, 9" h., wu ts'ai decoration, showing a kylin and a phoenix in a garden on one side, the design continuing into leafy growth on the reverse, with stiff leaves at the neck. (Illus.) ................................................ $450-550

Vase, 13" h., wu ts'ai enamel decoration, of baluster shape, with scene of four boys and a foo lion in a fenced in setting ................. $1,200-1,600

Vase, 18" h., wu ts'ai decoration, with a scene of figures in a mountain landscape among trees and rockwork ....................... $1,600-1,800

Vase, 14⅝" h., wu ts'ai enamel decoration, transitional/K'ang Hsi period, with figure of a large kylin in a garden and a blossom design around the short wide neck .......................... $1,800-2,200

# Tsuba — Sword Guard
## (*Japanese*)

*Tsuba of bronze with twelve zodiac symbols*

The principal function of the tsuba (sword guard) was balance (to place the center of gravity properly), so that the sword was kept in the correct position. It enabled a quick grasp by keeping the hilt away from the body. The tsuba also protected one's hand from an opponent's sword. The tsuba has three openings into which are placed: 1. Kogai (skewer); 2. Kozuka (utility knife); 3. Waribashi (split chopsticks). The tsuba is usually decorated, and among the various techniques used are: zogan (inlay), sukashi (openwork), hori (chiseling or etching). Within these techniques are included: takazogan (inlay raised above the surface); chin-kin-bari (gilt or carved, or gilded lacquer); uchi-dashi (repousse work); suzi-zogan (wire inlay). Among the metals used for the tsuba are: shakudo (an alloy consisting of copper with a small percentage of gold); tetsu (iron), akagane (copper), shira-gane (silver) and ko-gane (gold).

**Shapes:**

Shin no maru-gata — round.
Naga-maru-gata — oval.
Nade-gaku-hokei — square with rounded angles.
Aoi-gata — in the form of aoi leaves.
Mokko — having two straight sides.
Hokei — square.

*Tsuba in copper and shibuichi, with Hotei*

*Tsuba, shakudo, with Chinese scholar holding a scroll in a landscape*

*Bronze tsuba, 19th century, mokko form, gilt motif of the 12
zodiac symbols, nanako ground. (Illus.) . . . . . . . . . . . . . . . . . . . . . . . . . . . . . . . . . . . . . $600

*Copper and shibuichi tsuba, 19th century, regular outline
guard with Hotei in his sack in takabori and a karako in
takazogan, gilt detail. (Illus.) . . . . . . . . . . . . . . . . . . . . . . . . . . . . . . . . . . . . . . . . . $800

Iron, 18th century, Nara School, with gold and silver inlay
motif, flying geese and bamboo leaves . . . . . . . . . . . . . . . . . . . . . . . . . . . . . . . $300-400

Iron, 19th century, inlaid with gilt and silver figure of warrior . . . . . . . . . . . . . . . . $275-350

Iron, 18th century, perforated cherry blossom motif . . . . . . . . . . . . . . . . . . . . . $185-225

Iron, 19th century, naga-maru-gata, carved and pierced with
landscapes and warriors with gilt details . . . . . . . . . . . . . . . . . . . . . . . . . . . . . . $250-400

Iron, early 19th century, naga-maru-gata, figures and dragons
in relief with silver, gold, and shakudo highlights . . . . . . . . . . . . . . . . . . . . . . . $700-850

Iron, 17th century, perforated spoke pattern . . . . . . . . . . . . . . . . . . . . . . . . . . $185-250

Shakudo, Nara style, 19th century, naga-maru-gata, applied
motif of standing Samurai in shakudo, gold, silver, and
copper . . . . . . . . . . . . . . . . . . . . . . . . . . . . . . . . . . . . . . . . . . . . . . . . . . . . . . . . . . $450-560

Shakudo, early 19th century, mokko, nanako (fish roe
ground), motif of kiri and phoenix in gilt . . . . . . . . . . . . . . . . . . . . . . . . . . . . . . $100-125

Shakudo, 19th century, naga-maru-gata, Shojo mask applied
in copper, gold, and shakudo, reverse having a carved sake
bottle . . . . . . . . . . . . . . . . . . . . . . . . . . . . . . . . . . . . . . . . . . . . . . . . . . . . . . . . . . $170-200

Shakudo, early 19th century, mokko, nanako (fish roe
ground), with openwork and motif of grasses . . . . . . . . . . . . . . . . . . . . . . . . . . $185-245

Shakudo, 19th century, naga-maru-gate, nanako (fish roe
ground), motif of two Samurai in battle with a riverscape,
details in gold and copper . . . . . . . . . . . . . . . . . . . . . . . . . . . . . . . . . . . . . . . . . $800-950

Shakudo, late 19th century, nade-gaku-hokei, applied motif
of kiku and bamboo with highlights in silver and gold . . . . . . . . . . . . . . . . . $1,200-1,400

Shakudo, 19th century, decorated in iro-e hirozogan,
takazogan, and sukidashi with Chinese scholar holding a
scroll in a landscape (Illus.) . . . . . . . . . . . . . . . . . . . . . . . . . . . . . . . . . . . . . . . . $400-600

Shibayama style, 19th century, mokko, inlaid with
mother-of-pearl, coral, ivory, and tortoiseshell on gold
lacquer with motif of man, woman, and waterfall with the
reverse depicting birds, flowers, and foliage . . . . . . . . . . . . . . . . . . . . . . . . . $3,000-3,750

Shibayama style, 19th century, mokko, inlaid with coral,
ivory, tortoiseshell, and mother-of-pearl on gold lacquer,
motif of Samurai and monkey with flowering trees . . . . . . . . . . . . . . . . . . . . $3,000-3,500

Shibayama style, 19th century, aoi-gata, ivory, horn,
mother-of-pearl on gold lacquer, motif of Bijin . . . . . . . . . . . . . . . . . . . . . . . . $2,800-3,800

## Tz'u-Chou Ware
### (Chinese)

Tz'u-chou ware is a north China, Hopei province porcelaneous stoneware emanating from the Sung Dynasty. The clay was brown or gray, to
which a whitish slip was applied. The decoration was enameled, incised,
or painted in a brownish black, red, green, or yellow. The most
numerous wares produced were often incised (sgraffito) to reveal the
white ground, or covered with a transparent, creamy tinged glaze which
was decorated with wash painting in brown.

Bowl, 6" dia., Yuan Dynasty, polychrome decoration, painted
with a red and green floral scroll over glazed white slip . . . . . . . . . . . . . . . . . . $600-700

Bowl, 8" dia., Sung Dynasty, molded into six divided petals,
glazed in white . . . . . . . . . . . . . . . . . . . . . . . . . . . . . . . . . . . . . . . . . . . . . . . . . . . $300-500

*Tz'u-chou jar, 10½" h., Ming Dynasty, painted in dark brown on a cream colored slip*

*Tz'u-chou jar, 13" h., Yuan Dynasty, painted in dark brown on a creamy gray slip*

Bowl, 8¼" dia., Yuan Dynasty, with translucent crackled glaze over creamy slip, painted with a dark brown scroll design ........................................................................ $1,500-1,800

Bowl, 9" dia., Sung Dynasty, translucent crackled glaze over creamy slip, painted with a dark brown scroll design, kiln grit adhering to the unglazed footing ............................... $2,500-2,800

Jar, 10" h., Yuan Dynasty, of wide shouldered form, painted in a dark brown floral and leaf design over a white slip, with burial stains, some chips and flaking ............................ $300-400

Jar, 10¼" h., Yuan Dynasty, painted with a large dark brown blossom and leaves on a creamy slip ground, with a floral border at the neck ................................................... $350-500

Jar, 10½" h., Ming Dynasty, painted brown in calligraphy and flowers over a creamy slip, with restorations. (Illus.) ...................... $900-1,200

Jar, 13" h., Yuan Dynasty, with brown painted decoration over creamy white slip, restorations. (Illus.) ...................... $2,500-3,000

Jar, 12" h., Ming Dynasty, massively potted with a short neck, painted in concentric wavy lines, with scroll and floral in rust over white slip, covered with a translucent glaze, chips ........................................................................ $1,500-1,700

Taper stick, 6⅞" h., Ming Dynasty, modeled in the form of a saddled horse covered with creamy glaze, the face and hooves painted in reddish and dark brown tones, small chips ................. $475-600

Figure, court official, 8" h., Ming Dynasty, depicted seated on a chair wearing his high hat, decorated in a creamy tone glaze and decorated in two tones of brown ............................. $900-1,100

Figure, court attendant, 11" h., K'ang Hsi period, standing, the buff slip colored with black and brown and covered with a translucent glaze ............................................... $600-800

Figure, 11" h., Ming Dynasty, shown seated on rockwork, covered with a creamy slip and decorated in dark brown and orange tones ...................................................... $1,200-1,400

Vase, 10" h., Yuan Dynasty, of mei ping shape, decorated in a brown glaze, incised in sgraffito design of scrolls between double lined borders on the upper body ........................ $1,200-1,500

Vase, 12" h., Ming Dynasty, polychrome decoration, bottle form with a flared mouth, the body decorated with a Kylin in a garden with clouds above on one side, the reverse with two maidens in a floral setting, the neck decorated with several borders, in colors of red, green, yellow, and black on a creamy buff slip ground .................................... $4,000-6,000

Vase, 14" h., Sung Dynasty, double gourd shape, with incised decoration of flowering tree peony on the creamy slip, separated by a dark brown wash ending at an incised double line border above the base .............................. $1,800-2,200

Wine pot, 8½" h., Sung Dynasty, with a short snout and curved handles, a dark brown floral agraffito design and solid sections of deep brown glaze ............................... $4,000-5,000

## Underglaze Red
*(Chinese)*

Underglaze red first appeared in porcelain decoration during the 14th century. It was achieved by painting copper oxide on the biscuit porcelain, which was subsequently covered with a transparent glaze. Due to the unstable firing conditions, the very early underglaze red sometimes changed to gray. It appears as a brilliant copper red during the reign of Hsüan-Tê (1426-1435). An innovation of this era was the use of underglaze red in combination with underglaze blue. (In the Chia Ching and Wan Li reigns underglaze red was replaced by an overglaze iron red which was far less costly and had the advantage of being easier to apply.) The combination of underglaze blue and red was perfected in the K'ang Hsi reign, often appearing with Hsüan-Tê reign marks; in the reign of Yung Chêng, where it sported K'ang Hsi reign marks; and in the Ch'ien Lung reign, where it copied all of the above.

(See: Copper Red)

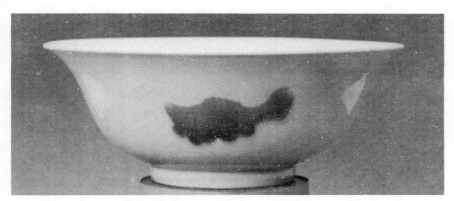

*Underglaze red bowl, 8¾" dia., Yung Chêng, with three underglaze copper red carp*

Bowl, 7½" dia., Tao Kuang mark and period, mei ping shape with molded horses in red underglaze, covered with a pale celadon glaze ................................................... $1,200-1,400

Bowl, 8½" dia., 19th century, with rounded sides and inverted rim, a band of cloud scrolls at the rim, the body with children playing under a willow, and frolicking horses, underglaze red on a white ground ........................................... $700-900

Bowl, 8¾" dia., mark and period of Yung Chêng in blue underglaze, the exterior having three carp decorated in a fine copper red glaze. (Illus.) ................................................ $7,000-9,000

Brush rest, 8" l. x 2¾" h., K'ang Hsi period, the celadon glazed basket containing a red underglazed fish. (Illus.) .................... $1,400-1,600

Censer, 8½" h., 18th century, with underglaze blue and red design of dragons chasing flaming pearls among flames and clouds ................................................. $500-700

Dish, 6" dia., K'ang Hsi mark within double circles, interior with red and blue decoration of roses, exterior with bamboo in blue ................................................. $800-1,000

Dish, 11¼" dia., 18th century, with red and blue decoration of large lotus blossoms with leaves and long stems, the floral border with reserves of fleurettes ........................................... $800-1,000

Stem cup, 4½" h., Yung Cheng six-character mark and period, exterior with three branches of peach, pomegranate, and lychee rising from a ling chih fungus, the fruits in an underglaze pinkish red, the other details and border in underglaze blue ................................................. $4,000-5,000

Vase, 6½" h., Ch'ien Lung mark and period, squat form, with elephant head handles, rich copper red underglaze decoration of fish in waves. (See Color Section) ........................... $1,200-1,500

Vase, 7" h., Yuan Dynasty, large splashes of red underglaze around the shoulders and two larger splashes of red on either side of the body, with grayish splashes of mushroom pink throughout ................................................. $20,000-40,000

Vase, 9" h., 19th century, of mei ping form, with blue and red designs of bats, a willow tree, and flying birds on a white ground ................................................. $350-400

*Underglaze red vase, 11⅛" h., Yung Chêng, mei ping form*

Vase, 11⅛" h., Yung Chêng mark and period, mei ping shape, carved on each side under a bluish white glaze with a five-clawed dragon seen almost full face leaping above waves, in bright copper red of almost peach bloom tone, all with white crested waves above two smaller dragons executed in the same technique and writhing around the lower section, incised detail. (Illus.) . . . . . . . . . . . . . . . . . . . . . . . . . . . . . . . . . . . . . . .$25,000-30,000

Vase, 14" h., 19th century, with a bulbous body and a tall cylindrical neck, with underglaze red decoration of three dragons among bats, cloud scrolls and shou medallions, the lip and base decorated with Buddhist emblems in underglaze blue . . . . . . . . . . . . . . . . . . . . . . . . . . . . . . . . . . . . . . . . . . . . . . . . . . . . . . . . . . .$400-600

Vase, 17½" h., Ch'ien Lung period (unmarked), with a bulbous body and cylindrical neck, decorated with flowers and butterflies, lotus petal borders in underglaze red and blue with bands of underglaze red in diaper patterns . . . . . . . . . . . . . . . . . . . . . .$1,800-2,200

Vase, 18" h., 19th century, with two large reserves of underglaze blue and red dragons. (Illus.) . . . . . . . . . . . . . . . . . . . . . . . . . . . . .$800-1,000

Vase, 25" h., K'ang Hsi period (unmarked), of rouleau form, with a dense underglaze blue background studded with underglaze red peonies descending from the neck and ending in long lappets onto a white background, the white area with blue and red floral medallions all around . . . . . . . . . . . . . . . . . . . . . . . .$4,500-5,500

Wine cup, 3½" dia., Yuan Dynasty, with a flared lip and a ring foot, with underglaze red in a central floral band on the exterior, a key fret band border on the interior, all in a grayish red tone on a white ground, a small crack at the rim . . . . . . . . . . . . . . . .$4,000-5,000

*Underglaze red vase, 18" h., 19th century, with underglaze blue and red decoration*

*Underglaze red brush rest, 8" l., K'ang Hsi, celadon with underglaze red fish*

234

## Wan Li
*(Chinese)*

The reign of Emperor Wan Li spans the years 1573-1629. Polychrome decoration became firmly established during this period. The technique consists of painting with enameled colors on the finished fired glaze and then refiring at a lower temperature. Popular enamel techniques include: tou-ts'ai enamels, overglaze colors applied within soft blue underglaze outlines; san ts'ai three-color scheme, a combination of green, aubergine, and yellow; wu ts'ai five-color ware, using san ts'ai colors in addition to underglaze blue and overglaze red. As in earlier and later dynasties, blue and white wares were in popular production, particularly the type named "Kraak" ware by the Dutch.

(See: Blue and White, Kraak; Ming Dynasty)

## Water Droppers
*(Suiteki)*

The small closed water container having two small holes, used to wet the inkstone, is known as a water dropper (Suiteki). Water droppers were produced in China, Korea, and Japan. They come in many shapes and are made of many materials including pottery, metal, and porcelain.

(See: various Japanese, Chinese and Korean categories)

## Wei Dynasty
*(Chinese)*

The Wei Dynasty (386-550 A.D.) was one of the six that followed the Han and preceded the T'ang. The pottery of the period resembles the Han more than the T'ang. The figures are stiff and straight, generally being made in a double mold (one for the front and one for the rear), and the pottery tends to be a grayish tone rather than the buff ones that are common in the T'ang. Although the themes for figures and animals tend to be more exotic than the Han, they still have the stubby unflowing appearance of pre-T'ang figures, the T'ang being distinguishable in style for their flowing and curvaceous lines.

> Figure, 12" h., court official, with traces of red pigment on
> the gray pottery body, covered with earth encrustations.
> (See Color Section) . . . . . . . . . . . . . . . . . . . . . . . . . . . . . . . . . . . . . . . . . . . . . . . . . . . . $1,500-2,000

## Wood Block Prints
*(Japanese)*

Wood block prints are genre pictures. The Japanese term for such prints is Ukiyo-e, which may be translated to say, "Prints of the Floating World." The wood block print was a plebeian art form. These color prints were introduced during the 17th century in Japan. Before 1765, prints were made in two colors. After 1765, the multicolor print was developed, and this is the most familiar form. A wood block print was made with the cooperation of three artists; the painter, the engraver, and the printer. A foundation picture was drawn by the artist. The engraver transferred this drawing to the blocks by carefully chiseling the picture onto wood, in relief. The printer made the color selections, although some artists did designate which colors were to be used. The printer blended the colors and applied them to the blocks with brushes. Separate blocks were used for each color. The printer transferred the lines to the paper by pressing them with a baren. Different amounts of pressure produced different degrees of color registry. The paper used was absorbent and usually a neutral color. The finish of a wood block print is beautiful and something that cannot be achieved by hand painting. (**NOTE:** Values are dependent upon condition.)

### Nomenclature:

Bijinga — prints of beautiful women.
Fukei-ga — landscape print.

*Sharaku actor portrait. Sold at Christie's, New York, for $77,000*

Kakemono-e — scroll picture.
Shibai-e — prints of actors.
Sumi-e — black ink paintings.
Sumo-e — prints of wrestlers.
Uchiwa-e — a fan painting, fan-shaped.

## Print sizes:

Aiban yoko-e — large in the length.
Chuban — medium size, approximately 10″ x 7½″.
Hashira-e — a long narrow print approximately 28¾″ x 4¾″.
Hosoban — a narrow picture approximately 13″ x 5⅝″.
Oban — literally translated to mean large size; however, it is a standard size print — approximately 15″ x 10″.
Oban tate-e — large in the width.

### Buncho (fl. ca. 1765-1792)

Chuban, yakusha-e Ichikawa Komazo holding a sambe and a lacquer cup while talking to Iwai Hanshiro IV, excellent condition . . . . . . . . . . . . . . . . . . . . . . . . . . . . . . . . . . . . . . . . . . . $9,000-15,000

Hosoban, a courtesan and her attendant, very poor condition . . . . . . . . . . . . . . . . . $260-310

Hosoban, an actor standing beneath a willow in the snow, very poor condition . . . . . . . . . . . . . . . . . . . . . . . . . . . . . . . . . . . . . . . . . . . $200-250

### Choki (late 18th/early 19th century)

Chuban, two bijin, one seated and holding a fan while the other looks on, fair condition . . . . . . . . . . . . . . . . . . . . . . . . . . . . . . . . . $1,800-2,400

Hashira, a courtesan with fancy hairdo and kimono with obi having a crane pattern, good condition . . . . . . . . . . . . . . . . . . . . . . . . . . . $1,700-2,200

Hashira, a teahouse waitress holding a fan and wearing a green kimono and black obi, good condition . . . . . . . . . . . . . . . . . . . . . . . . $1,500-2,200

Oban tate-e, Yoshitsune killing the Nuye, fair condition . . . . . . . . . . . . . . . . . $1,100-1,500

### Eisen (1790-1848)

Oban, Matsushima warming sake over charcoal fire, from the series, "Keisei Dochu Sugoroku," signed, good impression with slight damages . . . . . . . . . . . . . . . . . . . . . . . . . . . . . . . . . . . . . . . . . $600-850

Oban tate-e, a bijin powdering her nose, good condition, published by Izumiya Ichibei. (Illus.) . . . . . . . . . . . . . . . . . . . . . . . . . . . . . $1,000-1,500

### Eizan (1787-1867)

Kakemono-e, a geisha reading a hand scroll and dressed in a robe which has an overall chrysanthemum motif, fair condition . . . . . . . . . . . . . . . . . . . . . . . . . . . . . . . . . . . . . . . . . . . . . . . . . $1,200-1,500

Kakemono-e, a bijin climbing steps and looking back over her shoulder, fair condition . . . . . . . . . . . . . . . . . . . . . . . . . . . . . . . . . . . . $750-950

Oban tate-e, a courtesan with a towel, fair condition . . . . . . . . . . . . . . . . . $300-500

Oban tate-e, a courtesan and a young girl, fair condition . . . . . . . . . . . . . . $400-600

Oban tate-e, a geisha holding a toothpick with an attendant carrying a box, poor condition . . . . . . . . . . . . . . . . . . . . . . . . . . . . . . . . $400-650

### (Hashiguichi) Goyo (1880-1921)

Hashira, a woman tying her robe holding the sash in her

*Toyohiro oban tate-e*

*Jacoulet, Nuit de Neige, "Coree"*

mouth, dated 1920, excellent condition .................................... $2,700-4,000

Large yoko-e panel, "Yabakei in the Rain," dated 1918,
excellent condition ................................................... $1,500-2,100

*Oban tate-e, a woman applying beni to her lips, dated 1920.
(Illus.) ............................................................... $2,500

Oban tate-e, a woman kneeling, dated 1916, excellent
condition ............................................................ $500-900

Oban tate-e, a woman leaning on a garden railing and
contemplating, with a pale orange mica ground, dated 1916,
excellent condition ................................................... $1,800-2,500

Oban tate-e, a woman wearing a sheer kimono seated in
front of a mirror, dated 1920, good condition ........................... $2,200-2,850

Oban yoko-e, ducks with one having head bent under the
water, dated 1919 .................................................... $1,500-2,400

Sumizuri-e, a young woman applying makeup and holding a
lacquered hand mirror, dated 1918, good condition ...................... $1,400-2,000

Sumizuri-e, a woman holding an obi which has motifs of
butterflies, silver mica ground, dated 1921 excellent condition ............ $2,500-4,000

### (Suzuki) Harunobu (1724-1770)

*Chuban tate-e, margin stains, good condition. (Illus.) ................... $2,420

Chuban, flowers from "Elegant Snow, Moon, and Flowers,"
good condition ...................................................... $3,000-5,500

Chuban, a young girl cleaning her mistress's feet in the
snow, and watching them is a boy with a sake bottle, poor
condition ............................................................ $650-900

Chuban, a child by a bamboo fence, poor/fair condition ................. $900-1,400

Chuban, two women, one reading letters, the other holding
a broom, fair condition .............................................. $850-1,400

*Eisan, bijin powdering her nose*

237

Chuban, a woman sitting on a bamboo bench looking out at a river, very poor condition .......................... $600-850

Chuban, a woman holding a fan and fixing her hair, good condition ........................................ $6,000-8,000

Chuban, a woman wearing a partially closed robe and looking at a garden of irises, excellent condition .................... $19,000-25,000

Chuban, two women by the sea, one seated and the other holding a washcloth, poor condition ...................... $450-850

Chuban, a man beside a sleeping girl with another girl talking to him, poor to fair condition ..................... $1,500-2,200

Cuban yoko-e, Atsumori and Munagai at the shore, fair condition ........................................ $2,700-3,500

## (Kawase) Hasui (1883-1957)

Aiban tate-e, view of a coastal village from an edition of 200 dated 1922 .......................................... $900-1,300

Aiban tate-e, a village in the rain dated 1921, excellent condition ........................................... $1,400-1,700

Circular print on square panel from the series, "Tokyo Ju-ni kagetsu," river and houses during a snowfall, dated 1922, excellent condition ..................................... $1,500-1,800

Oban, "The Moon at Magone," dated 1930, good condition ................... $275-400

Oban, Osaka Takatsu dated 1924, good impression with fading .............................................. $250-350

Oban tate-e, a figure in a temple courtyard on a rainy day, dated 1933, poor condition ............................. $100-150

Oban tate-e, a night view of houses dated 1937, fair condition ............... $175-250

Oban tate-e, two women with parasols standing on a snow-covered terrace, dated 1931, good condition .................. $250-400

Oban tate-e, three snow-covered pine trees on a river bank, dated 1929, fair condition ............................. $175-250

Oban tate-e, "Ichikawa no Banshu," dated 1926, good condition ............................................ $300-400

Oban tate-e, night scene of a cottage with a light in the window, good condition ................................. $300-450

Oban tate-e, "Fuyu no Arashiyama," fair condition, trimmed ............... $125-175

Oban tate-e, "Seiten no Yuki," from an edition of 200, excellent condition ...................................... $1,200-1,500

Oban yoko-e, a snow scene with two farmers, excellent condition .............................................. $2,000-2,500

Oban yoko-e, a view of the torii and stone lanterns dated 1933, fair/poor condition ............................... $100-150

## Hiroshige (1797-1858)

Kakemono, Shishi and pup on a flowering ledge, signed, poor condition, trimmed wormholes ..................... $125-200

Ko-tanazaku, Mandarin duck on a snowbank beside a stream, signed, good condition ........................... $1,500-2,000

Oban, boatmen maneuvering into the harbor, from the series, "Fifty-Three Stations Along the Eastern Seaboard," poor condition ............................................ $450-700

Oban, Kakucho Shinome, visitors to the Hoshiwara going home at dawn, fair condition ........................... $475-600

Oban tate-e, boats passing through cluster of islands with Mt. Fuji in the background, from "Hundred Views of Various Provinces," poor condition, damages and trimmed .................... $165-250

*Haranobu oban tate-e*

*Utamaro, Act VII of Chushingura*

*Yoshida, Mount Rainier*

*Oban yoko-e, Mariko, good impression, margins worn,
backed. (Illus.) ................................................................ $4,400

Oban yoko-e, Kanbara from the series, "Tokaido Gojusan
tsugi no Uchi," two travelers in snow with third traveler
holding an open umbrella, signed ...................................... $3,200-4,700

Oban yoko-e, from the series, "Three Famous View Points in
Edo"; figures on a cliff with cherry trees and sailboats, titled
Gotenyama Hanami ........................................................ $900-1,250

Oban yoko-e, Kanbara, three men trudging in the snow with
mountains and a town in the distance, restored ........................... $1,900-2,300

Oban yoko-e, Descending Geese at Katada from the series,
"Omi Hakkei/Eight Views of Lake Biwa," good condition ................... $4,000-8,000

*Oban yoko-e, Shono from the series, "Tokaido Goju-san
Tsugi," centerfold, trimmed margins, fading ................................ $4,400

Same as above, publisher's mark missing from umbrella .................... $2,000-3,000

## Hiroshige II (1826-1869)

Oban, from the series, "The Province," two travelers walking
along the beach, fair condition ........................................... $260-325

Oban tate-e, evening view of tea stall on the river in Kyoto,
good condition ........................................................... $425-575

Oban tate-e, "Night Rain at Karasaki," good condition ..................... $800-1,000

Oban triptych, "Ekoin Temple Complex at Ryogaku," fair
condition ................................................................ $600-900

Oban yoko-e, from the series "Toto Meisho," men and
women picnicking among cherry and pine trees, some
damage ................................................................. $150-270

## Hokusai (1760-1849)

*Nagaban, Shonenko, series "Shika Shashinkyo." (Illus.) ..................... $12,100

*Hokusai, oban yoko-e "A View of Mt. Fuji from Surugacho"*

Oban yoko-e, from the series, "Thirty Six Views of Fuji"; two women seated on a terrace with Mt. Fuji in the distance, fair condition .................................................... $1,100-1,600

*Oban yoko-e, "A View of Mt. Fuji from Surugacho"; from the series, "Thirty-Six Views of Fuji," good impression and condition. (Illus.) .................................................. $2,900

Oban yoko-e, view of the Temma Shrine, Kameido, damages ............... $900-1,300

Oban yoko-e, from the series, "Thirty-Six Views of Fuji"; A man on horseback and a woman in a kago with Mt. Fuji in the distance, poor condition .................................... $1,400-2,100

Oban yoko-e, from "Thirty-Six Views of Fuji"; two falconers and some farmers at Shimomegure, poor condition .................. $450-580

Oban yoko-e, three kingfishers with morning glories and water lilies, fair condition .................................... $1,400-2,150

Surimono (long), from the Tokaido series; a procession of feudal lords crossing a bridge in a snow scene, fair condition ............... $700-1,500

## Paul Jacoulet (1902-1960)

*Les Perles, Mandchoukuo. (Illus.) .................................... $1,600

*Nuit de Neige "Coreê." (Illus.) ...................................... $360

Snowflakes, Penyong Korea, 2/2/48 .................................. $800-1,000

The Basket of Medlar Fruit, 5/23/50 ................................ $300-350

The Birds of Paradise, 12/25/37 ..................................... $300-450

The Bride, Seoul, Korea, 2/2/48 ..................................... $500-600

The Chinese Gambler, 6/7/41 ........................................ $300-400

The Love Letter, Mongolia, 1955 .................................... $400-500

The Miraculous Catch, Izu, Japan, 12/12/39 ........................ $200-325

The Red Lacquer Mirror, Tokyo, 2/1/58 ............................. $400-500

The Water Pipe, Chinese, 12/31/52 ................................. $350-450

Young Girl of Saipan and Hibiscus Flowers, 6/10/34 ............... $200-300

Winter Flowers, Oshima, Japan 6/55 ................................ $300-450

## Kiyochika (1847-1915)

Oban triptych, an open ferry with passengers crossing the Sumida River, dated 1894, fair/good condition ...................... $300-400

Oban yoko-e, a moonlit view across the terrace of the Kiyomizu-dera, very good condition ............................... $400-550

## Kiyonaga (1752-1815)

*Kiyonaga, oban, scene from a joruri performance*

Chuban, three bijin walking by a bamboo wall, good condition ........................................................ $1,600-2,400

Chuban, a woman with a hand lantern talking with two other women, good condition .................................... $1,300-2,000

Hashira, a woman in a black kimono on a balcony looking down at a man, poor/fair condition ............................ $700-1,200

Oban tate-e, Senzan of Choji-ya on promenade with two other courtesans and two little girls, good condition ........... $2,200-3,500

Oban tate-e, one sheet from a diptych, five women in a bathhouse, very poor condition ................................. $400-700

Oban tate-e, three women holding two open umbrellas in the rain, excellent condition .................................... $8,000-12,000

*Oban, a scene from a joruri performance with three degatari players and two actors, fine impression, faded, small wormhole. (Illus.) ................................................. $800

240

## Koryusai (fl. 1784-1788)

Chuban, a young girl with knife looking at three bonsai in a snow-covered garden while an admirer looks on, from the set of Four Seasons (Winter), excellent condition . . . . . . . . . . . . . . . . . . . . . . . . . . . $2,100-3,500

Hashira-e, a woman drawing water from a well while another woman washes, fair condition . . . . . . . . . . . . . . . . . . . . . . . . . . . . . . . . . . . . $500-800

Oban tate-e, Somenosuke resting on one knee and talking to her attendant, good condition . . . . . . . . . . . . . . . . . . . . . . . . . . . . . . . . . . $5,500-8,000

## Kunisada (1786-1864)
## (Also known as Toyokuni III)

Oban, portrait of Kataoka Gado VIII and signed, fair/poor condition . . . . . . . . . . . . . . . . . . . . . . . . . . . . . . . . . . . . . . . . . . . . . . . . . . . . . $75-150

Oban, a bijin and her attendant, poor condition . . . . . . . . . . . . . . . . . . . . . . . . . . . $75-120

Oban, a woman dancing beneath a cherry tree, poor condition . . . . . . . . . . . . . . . . . . . . . . . . . . . . . . . . . . . . . . . . . . . . . . . . . . . . . . . $60-100

Oban triptych, Prince Genji and his lover watching boats, good condition . . . . . . . . . . . . . . . . . . . . . . . . . . . . . . . . . . . . . . . . . . . . . . . $325-450

Oban triptych, a theatrical scene with three actors, good condition . . . . . . . . . . . . . . . . . . . . . . . . . . . . . . . . . . . . . . . . . . . . . . . . . . . . $375-450

Oban triptych, three bijin beneath cherry trees along the bank of the Sumida River, good impression and condition . . . . . . . . . . . . . . . . . . . . $675-900

Oban tate-e, diptych, Four Characters from Genji Monogatari, fair condition . . . . . . . . . . . . . . . . . . . . . . . . . . . . . . . . . . . . . . . . $300-500

Oban tate-e triptych, depicts actors against the backdrop, fair condition . . . . . . . . . . . . . . . . . . . . . . . . . . . . . . . . . . . . . . . . . . . . . . . $200-325

## Kuniyoshi (1787-1861)

Oban, a farmer showing a waterfall to a traveler and his attendant, from the series, "One Hundred Poems," good condition . . . . . . . . . . . . . . . . . . . . . . . . . . . . . . . . . . . . . . . . . . . . . . . $350-600

Oban harimaze-e, Otsuji seated beneath a waterfall at the top and a portrait of Yoshitusune below, from the series, "Koto Nishki Imayo Kinizukushi," fair condition . . . . . . . . . . . . . . . . . . . . . . . . $300-700

Oban tate-e, a sage with a golden cat and six children beneath a willow tree, good condition . . . . . . . . . . . . . . . . . . . . . . . . . . . . $450-600

Oban triptych, three bijin standing with a distant view of the Masaki aInari shrine with a slight view of the peak of Mt. Fuji, fine condition . . . . . . . . . . . . . . . . . . . . . . . . . . . . . . . . . . . . . . . . . $600-950

Oban triptych, a giant skeleton leaning over Mitsukini, fine condition . . . . . . . . . . . . . . . . . . . . . . . . . . . . . . . . . . . . . . . . . . . . . $4,700-7,000

Oban triptych, a group of samurai attacking a giant toad, good condition . . . . . . . . . . . . . . . . . . . . . . . . . . . . . . . . . . . . . . . . . . . $800-1,300

Oban yoko-e, the kilns at Imado, men stoking the kilns beside the Sumida River, fine condition . . . . . . . . . . . . . . . . . . . . . . . . . $2,600-4,000

O tanzaku, the seven gods of good luck on the takatabune, fair condition . . . . . . . . . . . . . . . . . . . . . . . . . . . . . . . . . . . . . . . . . . . . . . $375-500

## Masanobu (1761-1816)

Oban (double), Segawa and Matsundo and their attendant, fair condition . . . . . . . . . . . . . . . . . . . . . . . . . . . . . . . . . . . . . . . . . . . $1,200-2,000

Oban diptych, a courtesan in Heina attire writing a poem with attendants, standing around, fair condition . . . . . . . . . . . . . . . . . . $1,200-1,850

Oban yoko-e, two birds on a loquat branch eating the fruit, fair condition . . . . . . . . . . . . . . . . . . . . . . . . . . . . . . . . . . . . . . . . . . . . $800-1,000

*Shuncho, woman gazing through window*

*Ito Shinsui, oban, girl whispering to a woman*

## Koshiro Onchi (1891-1955)

*Chuban tate-e, young woman, good color/impression, unsigned. (Illus.) . . . . . . . . . . . . . . . . . . . . . . . . . . . . . . . . . . . . . . . . . . . $320

Oban yoko-e, mallards on marsh bank, dated 1877, good condition . . . . . . . . . . . . . . . . . . . . . . . . . . . . . . . . . . . . . . . . . . . . . . . . $1,500-1,900

Oban yoko-e, a low table upon which are a cluster of grapes and two pomegranates, good condition . . . . . . . . . . . . . . . . . . . . . . $700-1,700

Oban triptych, a kneeling man on a snowbank with an elder on his left, dated 1884, poor condition . . . . . . . . . . . . . . . . . . . . . . $175-300

## Sharaku

*Portrait of actor Sakata Hangoro III in the role of Fujikawa Mizuemon. (Illus.) . . . . . . . . . . . . . . . . . . . . . . . . . . . . . . . . . . . . . . . . . $77,000

## Shigemasa (1739-1820)

*Chuban, three children playing behind a screen while two others peep around it, subtitled "Night Rain at Karasaka" from the series Yatsushi Hakkei "Eight Transformed Views," signed, good impression and color. (Illus.) . . . . . . . . . . . . . . . . . . . . . $700

## (Ito) Shinsui (1896-1972)

Oban, a woman in kimono wrapping her hair in a towel, dated 1931, good condition . . . . . . . . . . . . . . . . . . . . . . . . . . . . . . . . . $650-800

*Oban, a young girl whispering to a woman, good condition. (Illus.) . . . . . . . . . . . . . . . . . . . . . . . . . . . . . . . . . . . . . . . . . . . . . . . . . . . $1,300

Oban tate-e, a woman holding a rouge pot while applying rouge to her lip, dated 1922, very good condition . . . . . . . . . . . . . . . $1,500-2,300

Oban tate-e, a woman holding a blue fan and swatting a firefly, from an edition of 250, dated 1934, very good condition . . . . . . . . . . . . . . . . . . . . . . . . . . . . . . . . . . . . . . . . . . . . . . . . . $800-1,500

Oban yoko-e, willow trees in a rainstorm, dated 1919, very good condition . . . . . . . . . . . . . . . . . . . . . . . . . . . . . . . . . . . . . . . . . . $600-950

*Oban yoko-e, an actress painting her lips, deep red background, dated Showa 3 (1928) fine impression and good condition. (Illus.) . . . . . . . . . . . . . . . . . . . . . . . . . . . . . . . . . . . . . . . . $352

## Shuncho (fl. ca. 1780-1895)

*Hashira, a woman gazing through grilled window, slightly faded. (Illus.) . . . . . . . . . . . . . . . . . . . . . . . . . . . . . . . . . . . . . . . . . . . . $715

Oban tate-e (one sheet from a triptych), three bijin and a boy walking, good condition . . . . . . . . . . . . . . . . . . . . . . . . . . . . . . . . $1,800-3,100

## Shunzan (fl. ca. 1782-1798)

Chuban diptych, a man and four women strolling, fair condition . . . . . . . . . . . . . . . . . . . . . . . . . . . . . . . . . . . . . . . . . . . . . . . . $400-600

Hashira-e, a bijin seated on a terrace after her bath, and partially clothed, her attendant at her side, fair condition . . . . . . . . . . $400-700

Oban (one sheet from a triptych), a woman watching children during a festival, good condition . . . . . . . . . . . . . . . . . . . . . . . $850-1,300

Oban tate-e (one sheet from a triptych), a bijin and eight boys entering a Shinto shrine, good condition . . . . . . . . . . . . . . . . . . $1,100-1,600

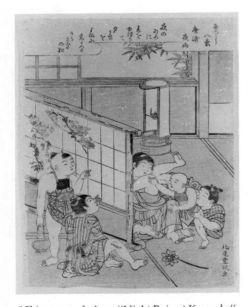

*Shigemasa, chuban, "Night Rain at Karasaka"*

*Hokusai, Shoenko*

*Toyokuni, oban, the actor Matsumoto Koshiro*

*Utamaro, oban from the Chushingura Series*

## Toyohiro (1773-1828)

Hashiro, two bijin playing with hobbyhorses, fair condition .................. $800-1,400

*Oban tate-e, one sheet (triptych). (Illus.) ........................................... $990

## Toyokuni (1769-1825)

Hosoban, two actors in scene with one in guise of a woman, good color and condition ........................................... $600-850

Hosoban, a parody on Act 11 (Chushingure), excellent condition ........................................... $1,700-2,200

*Oban, the actor Matsumoto Koshiro drawing a sword, signed, published by Ezakiya Kichibei, good condition. (Illus.) ........................................... $500

Oban, portrait of Ichikawa Yaozo holding an open fan, signed, published by Shimizu, fair condition ........................................... $280-350

Oban, portrait of Onoe Eizaburo as Kanshin drawing a sword signed, fine condition ........................................... $525-700

Oban, Sehawa Sennyo as Sakuramaru in a checkered kimono holding a sword, signed, published by Simizuya, fine condition ........................................... $600-800

Oban, portrait (head and shoulders) of Segawa Kikunojo in female role, signed, excellent condition ........................................... $13,000-15,000

Oban tate-e, Shoki holding sword over Oni, fair condition, good impression ........................................... $700-1,000

Oban triptych, princess in a kago and attendant among cherry blossoms signed, published by Soshuya Hohei, good color and impression ........................................... $775-900

Oban triptych, interior scene of a greenhouse with courtesans, fair condition, faded ........................................... $1,000-1,300

Oban yoko-e, Raiko punishing Oni, signed, good condition ........................................... $600-800

## Toyokuni II (1777-1835)

Oban, a portrait of a courtesan, signed Gasotei Toyokuni ga, published by Iseri, good condition ........................................... $250-285

Oban triptych, depicting a wrestling match, signed, good impression and color ........................................... $550-700

Oban triptych, nobleman within a villa looking out a lake, good condition ........................................... $350-450

Oban yoko-e, landscape view of Mt. Fuji with a fishing village, signed, very good condition ........................................... $750-900

## Toyonari (1886-1942)

Oban tate-e, Sonosuke depicting Umegawa on a silver mica ground, dated 1922, good condition ........................................... $600-900

Oban tate-e, Mitsugoro in the play, "Sannin Katawa," dated 1922, fair condition ........................................... $300-500

Oban tate-e, Yennosuke, on a pink mica ground, dated 1921, good condition ........................................... $750-1,000

## Utamaro (1754-1806)

Half-length portrait, of a bijin from the series Sakiwake Kotoba no Hana, signed, good condition ........................................... $4,900-7,000

Oban, seated bijin holding a mirror on her lap while an attendant cares for her hair, poor condition ........................................... $350-440

*Oban, Act VII from the Chushingura Series, good impression

*Jacoulet, Les Perles*

and good condition (Illus.) . . . . . . . . . . . . . . . . . . . . . . . . . . . . . . . . . . . . . . . . . . . . . $2,860

Oban, Yamauba handing fan to Kintaro with a bear carrying
a box, fair condition . . . . . . . . . . . . . . . . . . . . . . . . . . . . . . . . . . . . . . . . . . . . . . . . $1,900-2,300

Oban, Shoki seated with drum and holding drumsticks
looking up at Oni, who is walking a tightrope and carrying a
fan and parasol, fair condition . . . . . . . . . . . . . . . . . . . . . . . . . . . . . . . . . . . . . . . $700-900

Oban tate-e, three women gathered around a loom, fair
condition . . . . . . . . . . . . . . . . . . . . . . . . . . . . . . . . . . . . . . . . . . . . . . . . . . . . . . . . . . $850-1,100

Oban tate-e, a man in a black kimono talking to a woman
wearing a pale blue kimono, fair condition . . . . . . . . . . . . . . . . . . . . . . . . . . . $800-950

Oban tate-e, two women, one kneeling with water basin, the
other standing and cleaning her teeth, fair condition . . . . . . . . . . . . . . . . . . $3,500-5,700

Oban tate-e, portrait of the courtesan Hanaogi, poor
condition . . . . . . . . . . . . . . . . . . . . . . . . . . . . . . . . . . . . . . . . . . . . . . . . . . . . . . . . . . . $550-700

*Ito Shinsui, oban yoko-e, an actress, dated 1928*

Sheet from oban triptych, figures by the sea of man looking
at a book being shown to him by a woman, fair condition ..................... $550-800

Sheet from oban triptych, three women preparing for the
girls' festival, fair condition ............................................. 50-1,200

## Horishi Yoshida (1876-1950)

*Oban yoko-e, Mount Rainier (1923), good condition. (Illus.) ........................ $605

Oban yoko-e (on silk), Kingyo Saki, good condition ........................... $500-700

Oban yoko-e, Mitsu Kojima, very good condition ............................. $400-700

Oban yoko-e, Fujiyama, autumn, good condition, 1918 ....................... $300-400

Oban yoko-e, Sumida River/Afternoon, dated 1917, good
condition ................................................................. $350-550

Oban yoko-e, Grand Canyon, dated 1925, good condition .................... $350-500

Oban yoko-e, Lugano, dated 1925, faded ................................... $250-350

Oban tate-e, Mist, "Inland Sea series," 1926, good color,
condition. (Illus.) ....................................................... $900-1,200

Sumizuri-e (large panel), cottage and garden in the snow, fair
condition ................................................................. $275-475

Sumizuri-e (large panel), Unkai Ho o san dated 1938, very
good condition ......................................................... $2,000-2,600

Sumizuri-e (large panel), "Hodakayma after Rain," dated
1927, very good condition ............................................. $1,400-1,900

## Zeshin (1807-1891)

Chuban yoko-e, a straw hat, a bamboo staff, and a bag, good
condition ................................................................. $300-500

Chuban yoko-e, a black brush case, good condition ........................... $350-500

Chuban yoko-e, a stick of bamboo and a fishing net, good
condition ................................................................. $350-600

Chuban yoko-e, a round orange against poetry, good
condition ................................................................. $300-500

Oban yoko-e (octagonal), travelers in a country teahouse, fair
condition ................................................................. $250-375

*Goyo, oban tate-e, 1920

*Onchi (unsigned)

# Wood Carvings
## (Chinese)

*Chinese wood carving, male barge figure, 10" h., 18th century*

*Pair of Chinese wood carvings, female barge figures, 8" h., 18th century*

Our earliest records of Chinese art forms reveal wood carving as a practiced craft. The woods used include sandlewood, rosewood, ebony, redwood, and bamboo. Roots of various trees were also employed and are known today as root carvings.

Barge figure, 10" h., 18th century, modeled in posture of dance, with black, red, and gilt pigments remaining. (Illus.) . . . . . . . . . . . . . . . . . . . . . $350-450

Barge figures (pair), 8" h., 18th century, females, each holding an infant in the opposite arm, with black, red, and gold pigments remaining. (Illus.) . . . . . . . . . . . . . . . . . . . $450-550

Brush pot, 5" h., 18th century, bamboo carving, with a scene of seven sages in a bamboo grove among pine trees and rockwork with clouds above, carved in deep relief . . . . . . . . . . . . . . . . . . . . . $500-650

Brush rest, 3½" l., bamboo carving in the form of three pine trees with gnarled trunks and branches with pine needles . . . . . . . . . . . . . . . . . . . $150-200

Brush rest 4" l., bamboo carving in the form of a foo dog with a brocade ball between her paws, her head turned toward the pup on her back . . . . . . . . . . . . . . . . . . . $200-300

Figure, 8½" h., 18th century, Buddha, gilt lacquered, in a seated posture with loose robes revealing a bare chest, with surface cracks and flaking . . . . . . . . . . . . . . . . . . . $300-400

Figure, 9¾" h., gilt lacquered, Buddha, 17-18th century, seated in prayer, with a worn surface and small damages . . . . . . . . . . . . . . . . . . . $1,000-1,400

Figure, foo lion, 10" l., 19th century, with paw on a ball, with a cub climbing her shoulder . . . . . . . . . . . . . . . . . . . $200-400

Figure, Kuan Yin and child, 8" h., 17th century, shown seated holding child, with traces of red, green, black, and blue pigment, with age cracks and chipping . . . . . . . . . . . . . . . . . . . $500-700

Figure, Kuan Yin, 9" h., 18th century, posed in a seated position, with traces of red pigment and applied gilding . . . . . . . . . . . . . . . . . . . $300-400

Figure, warrior, 12" h., 18th century, standing, wearing an armored robe with traces of black and green pigment . . . . . . . . . . . . . . . . . . . $500-700

Figure, shrine group, 18" h., Ming Dynasty, the carving of a Bodhisattva seated in a yoga posture tended by two attendants, with a rockwork canopy above, the base with two figures and an official riding a dragon, traces of gilding and red pigment . . . . . . . . . . . . . . . . . . . $1,200-1,500

Figure, Amitabha, 28" h., Yuan/early Ming, the lacquered wood figure carved in a seated position, his hands resting in his lap, lacquered red with gilding . . . . . . . . . . . . . . . . . . . $3,000-3,500

Figure, 54" h., 18th century, warrior, carved standing on a rockwork base, wearing a helmet and armor, set with semiprecious stones, with traces of gilt and gesso . . . . . . . . . . . . . . . . . . . $6,000-8,000

Ju-i scepter, 14" l., carved with the eight immortals on the shaft and ju-i head, fruitwood . . . . . . . . . . . . . . . . . . . $600-800

Root carving, 10" h., of a sage seated on a rockwork base, on a freeform stand with a carved bottle . . . . . . . . . . . . . . . . . . . $125-150

Root carving, 17" h., of a blind man with both arms extended in front, set on pegged base . . . . . . . . . . . . . . . . . . . $350-400

# Wu ts'ai
## (Chinese)

The use of wu ts'ai five-color enamel decoration first appeared at the end of the Ming Dynasty and continued in popularity well into the Ching Dynasty. The finest and most varied of the wu ts'ai enamels were produced during the Wan-Li reign (1573-1619). The technique consisted of applying part of the decoration in underglaze blue and then completing the scheme in overglaze enamels of green, aubergine, yellow, and red. The overglaze enamels were outlined in black or red.

(See: Ch'ien Lung; Eighteenth Century; K'ang Hsi; Ming Dynasty; Yung Chêng)

## Yatate
*(Japanese)*

The yatate is a container for writing equipment. It was worn with netsuke and cord in the same manner as the inro. The yatate has a bowl-shaped section (inkwell) with a lid, and a long hollow stem in which the writing brush was placed.

Yatate (silver), 19th century, penholder and round inkwell, motif of incised flowers and clouds . . . . . . . . . . . . . . . . . . . . . . . . . . . . . . . . . . . . . $600-800

Yatate (shibuichi), penholder and inkwell having relief carving with inlaid plover and waves . . . . . . . . . . . . . . . . . . . . . . . . . . . . . . . . . . . . . $250-400

## Ying Ching
*(Chinese)*

Ying Ching is a modern Chinese name for the color "shadow blue," which is synonymous with the original color name of "Ching-pai." These terms refer to a white porcelain decorated with a transparent, blue tinged glaze.

(See: Ching-Pai; Nineteenth Century)

Bowl, 7" dia., Sung Dynasty, of conical form, interior incised with floral motifs, the glaze a pale blue . . . . . . . . . . . . . . . . . . . . . . . . . . . . . . . . $1,200-1,500

Box, 3¼" dia., Sung Dynasty, molded with vertical ribs, the top with two blossoms in a floral spray, the glaze ending short of the buff porcelainlike body . . . . . . . . . . . . . . . . . . . . . . . . . . . . . . . $800-1,500

Dish, 6" dia., Yuan Dynasty, with two fish molded in the center . . . . . . . . . . . . . . . . . . . . . . . . . . . . . . . . . . . . . . . . . . . . . . . . . . . . . . . . $350-450

Dish, 7½" dia., Yuan Dynasty, finely carved in the center with a floral scroll design, with a fine, translucent blue/green glaze . . . . . . . . . . . . . . . . . . . . . . . . . . . . . . . . . . . . . . . . . . . . . . . . . . . $2,000-2,500

Dish, 9" dia., Sung Dynasty, molded in the center with a floral medallion, with copper rim . . . . . . . . . . . . . . . . . . . . . . . . . . . . . . . $1,200-1,500

Dish, 9" dia., Sung Dynasty, with finely incised floral and scroll motif under pale blue transparent glaze. (Illus.) . . . . . . . . . . . . . . . . . . $1,500-2,000

Ewer, 4½" h., Yuan Dynasty, double gourd shape, with applied dragon handles and a slender, outward curving spout, covered with a pale bluish glaze . . . . . . . . . . . . . . . . . . . . . . . . . $2,000-2,500

Ewer (covered), 5" h., Yuan Dynasty, pear-shaped, decorated on both sides with molded crosses having ju-i lappets as points, with loop handle and short spout . . . . . . . . . . . . . . . . . . . . . . $800-1,000

Ewer (covered), 10" h., Sung Dynasty, with a floral medallion on each side, pale blue glaze . . . . . . . . . . . . . . . . . . . . . . . . . . . . . . . . $900-1,200

*Ewer, 13¼" h., Yuan Dynasty, modeled with a winged carp dragon loop handle, the curving spout joined to the neck by a seeded S-scroll, main body decorated on each side with a phoenix in flight, base with slip lappets filled with ju-i; neck with bands, and the cover with a crouching Buddhistic lion finial, covered with a thick and brilliant pale blue glaze, minor damage . . . . . . . . . . . . . . . . . . . . . . . . . . . . . . . . . . . . . . . . . $286,000

Funerary vase, 22" h., Sung Dynasty, slender ovoid form, with a coiled dragon and animal figures at the neck, mourning figures on the shoulders, the cover with an animal form knop, three small loop handles, the glaze a pale

*Ying Ching dish, 9" dia., Sung Dynasty, with incised floral decoration*

greenish blue ................................................. $1,400-1,800

Jar, 8" h., Sung Dynasty, ovoid form with melon ribs, the
bluish white glaze with spots of rust .............................. $1,200-1,500

Pouring vessel, 6" h., Sung Dynasty, rounded sides
decorated with molded dragon .................................. $1,000-1,200

Stem cup, 3½" h., Sung Dynasty, flower shape, divided into
six lobes and applied with beaded bands, with fleurettes in
the center of the interior, supported on a high splayed foot ........ $3,000-5,000

Vase (miniature), 4" h., Yuan Dynasty, with a flaring rim and
a pedestal foot, two bands of molded peonies around the
body and a narrow band of overlapping petals at the foot ......... $600-800

*Vase, 7½" h., late Sung Dynasty, pear-shaped with scroll
handles on the long neck, set on a pedestal base, with a
shallow relief mold of a prunus branch, the glaze with
crackle .......................................................... $3,000

# Yuan Dynasty
## (Chinese)

*Yuan Dynasty dish, 14¼" dia., celadon glaze*

The Yuan Dynasty (1260-1368) traces the history of Genghis Khan (the Mongol) and his grandson Khublai Khan. It was during the reign of Khublai that Marco Polo made his famous journey to China and the first influence of Christianity was felt. T'zu Chou wares were still being produced but now with a band of ornaments around the rims of plates and vases using floral or stylized motifs. Celadons were exported to India and the Near East. They were more elaborate than those produced during the Sung period. The molded or incised decoration was bolder and new shapes were introduced. It has not yet been proved if blue and white ware was introduced during the late Sung period. The two large vases at the Sir Percival David Foundation in London bear an inscription giving the name of the donor and the date 1351, and they are our standard for the earliest examples of blue and white. Underglaze red was also introduced at the end of the 14th century.

(See: Blue and White; Celadon; Shu Fu; Ying Ching)

Bowl, 6" dia., covered overall with a creamy white glaze,
incised with floral scrolls ........................................ $800-1,000

Cup, 3½" h., blue and white decoration, with a floral
medallion in the center and a floral band on the exterior ......... $200-250

Dish, 14¼" dia., molded in the center with dragon in pursuit
of flaming pearl, covered with a green glaze, the unglazed
foot rim burnt orange in the firing. (Illus.) ...................... $10,000-12,000

Jar, 12½" h., with wide-shouldered body, incised with floral
designs and stiff leaves rising from the base, covered with an
olive green crackled celadon glaze, with a copper rim at the
mouth ........................................................... $1,200-1,500

Jar, 13" h., the ovoid body covered with a brown glaze,
carved with a central band of ju-i heads above a band of
stylized petals, the shoulders with a key fret band, with
petals around the short neck ..................................... $5,000-6,000

Jarlet, 2½" h., blue and white decoration of a spray of lilies ..... $150-200

Vase, 9½" h., ovoid form, covered with an olive celadon
glaze with deeply etched scroll designs ........................... $2,400-3,000

Water dropper, 3" l., in shape of a three-legged toad, covered
with a grayish blue glaze with a large brown splash on the
toad's back ...................................................... $1,500-2,000

This type of "stoneware-to-porcelain" developed between the Han and Sung dynasties, a span of about 1,000 years. Leading kiln sites for these early celadons were found at Te-ch'ing, Chiu-yen, and Shang-Lin-Hu. These kilns produced, during the 9th century through the early Sung Dynasty, celadon-glazed wares that were exported throughout the Orient. The glaze became famous in the 9th and 10th centuries under the name of "Pi-sê," which meant "secret color." The typical color of the Yüeh glaze was a greenish gray. It is believed the Yüeh celadons were produced during the T'ang and Five Dynasties period and to some extent during the Sung. Production disappeared gradually in the Yüan and Ming dynasties.

## Yüeh Ware
*(Chinese)*

Bowl, 3½" dia., 10th century, with incurved sides and two small tubular handles at the shoulders, partially glazed in a pale, gray green color . . . . . . . . . . . . . . . . . . . . . . . . . . . . . . . . . . . . . . . . . . . . . . . . . . . . . . $150-200

Jar (covered), 4" h., 10th century, eight-sectioned bulbous shape, incised with herringbone notches, with four loop handles, the domed cover with a flat knop, repaired . . . . . . . . . . . . . . . . . . . . . . . . . . . . $550-650

Jar, 4" h., 10th century, squat form with rounded sides, a slender flared neck with a galleried rim, with four lug handles at the shoulders, covered with a crackled gray green glaze, with chips and glaze flaking . . . . . . . . . . . . . . . . . . . . . . . . . . . . . . . . . . . . . . $700-800

The Emperor Yung Chêng ruled during the years 1723-1735. This period of porcelain production was marked by the production of monochromes executed in the style of Sung wares, and the continued popularity of the Ming turquoise and celadon glazes. The imperial factory at Ching-tê-Chen was under the directorship of Nien Hsi Yao during the years of 1726-1736. He innovated the "claire de lune" and "soufflé red" glazes. Famille rose (a heretofore "foreign" color) appeared during this period, as did "sapphire blue," "tea dust," and "lemon yellow." The delicate eggshell porcelain also originated at this time.

(See: Eggshell; Famille Rose; Teadust; Underglaze Red)

## Yung Chêng
*(Chinese)*

*Yung Chêng bulb bowl, 9" dia., with tou-ts'ai decoration*

*Yung Chêng vase, 17" h., with underglaze blue and overglaze enamel decoration*

Bowl, 6½" h., six-character mark in blue underglaze, tou ts'ai decoration of dragons in pursuit of flaming pearls, the blue outlines filled with red, green, yellow, and aubergine ........................ $4,500-6,000

Bowl, 10" dia., six-character mark in blue underglaze, with deep rounded sides and flaring lip, covered with a green glaze and enameled with horses frolicking among waves, the interior having a center medallion of two horses ..................... $2,000-3,000

Bowl, 5¾" dia., six-character mark in underglaze blue, with a continuous scene of five gift-bearing figures in a garden, interior with a medallion of a phoenix and a dragon, with lip borders of flower sprigs, all in wu-ts'ai color scheme ................... $2,200-2,500

Bowl, 7½" dia., (commemorative mark of Cheng Hua in underglaze blue), tou-ts'ai enamels, the design of flowering branches and rockwork in soft colors outlined in underglaze blue .............................................................. $1,500-1,800

Bowl, 9½" dia., six-character mark in underglaze blue, blue and red decoration, exterior with three evenly spaced stylized phoenix emblems separated by three groups of fruit and leaf clusters, interior with a stylized lotus in the center and three groups of evenly spaced fruit and leaf clusters .................. $3,800-4,500

Bowl, 12" dia., incised four-character seal mark, quatrafoil shape, the exterior with a reddish purple streaked flambé glaze, interior with a bright milky blue glaze with greenish brown stripes on the ribs, the base with a yellow brown wash ............................................................... $1,200-1,500

Bulb bowl, 9" dia., unmarked, the exterior with a green and yellow dragon and flaming pearl motif along with calligraphy reading "10,000 times 10,000 years." (Illus. here and in Color Section) .............................................................. $3,000-3,500

Dish, 5½" dia., six-character mark in underglaze blue, monochrome, covered with a bright yellow glaze, the base glazed white ............................................................ $4,000-4,500

Dish, 6" dia., unmarked, tou-ts'ai decoration, with a scene of an immortal reading a scroll under a pine tree, his attendant mixing a potion on a small table, with a floral border, all in pale tones of green, yellow, red, and blue ..................... $1,800-2,300

Dish, 6¼" dia., six-character mark in underglaze blue, blue and white decoration, the center decorated with flying bats among peach trees with a double circle border, the rim undecorated except for a double circle border ..................... $900-1,200

Jar, 6½" h., tou-ts'ai decoration, with lotus scrolls and flowers, with pale orange, red, and yellow enamels within underglaze blue outlines ............................................. $1,000-1,300

Saucer dish, 8" dia., blue and white decoration, with a scene of children playing outside a pavilion ........................... $800-1,000

Stem cup, 3¼" h., mark and period of Yung Chêng, pale celadon glaze, molded in relief with floral design. (Illus. here and in Color Section) ................................................. $1,500-2,000

Vase, 17" h., double blue underglaze concentric circles on base, decorated in underglaze blue with overglaze enamels of pink, yellow, green, and blue, with two panels of indoor and outdoor scenes separated by floral pattern, and four smaller reserves at the neck containing blue underglaze symbols and emblems. (Illus.) ....................................................... $1,400-1,600

Vase, 5½" h., seal mark in underglaze blue, ovoid form with a short neck and pierced, domed foot, with two loops on each side for hanging, covered in a pale gray/blue celadon glaze .................................................................. $2,000-3,000

Vase, 10½" h., seal mark in underglaze blue, of archaic "hu" shape with two hollow tubular handles at the base of the neck, set on a slightly splayed foot, with raised bands at spaced intervals on the body, covered with a bluish gray Kuan-type celadon glaze ........................................ $14,000-18,000

*Yung Chêng stem cup, 3¼″ h., pale celadon glaze*

ZeZe wares were produced in Omi province. They were originated under the patronage of daimyo Ishikawa Tadatsun, c. 1640. ZeZe wares can have a reddish brown, and/or golden, and/or purplish brown glaze. They are very much like Seto wares and Takatori wares.

**ZeZe**
*(Japanese)*

Chaire, 2⅜″ h. x 1½″ w., c. 1700, shouldered, rudimentary
neck, white clay body, string cut foot, covered with iron rust
glaze stopping short of the foot . . . . . . . . . . . . . . . . . . . . . . . . . . . . . . . . . . . . . . . . . . . . . $700-900

# Marks and Identification, Chinese

## Contours

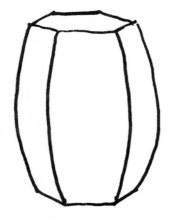

Hexagonal garden seat

Libation cup

Cup

Censer (incense burner)

Covered cup or bowl

Brush washer

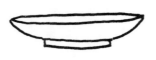

Saucer dish

*Baluster (Potiche)*

*Bronze form (Hu)*

*Kendi (with animal head spout)*

*Leys jar*

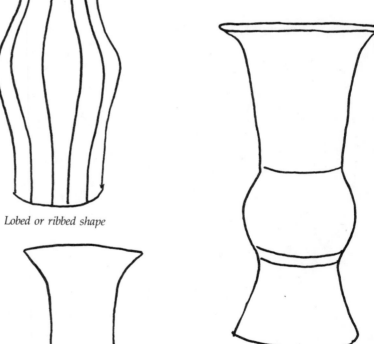

*Lobed or ribbed shape*

*Beaker vase*

*Elongated bottle form vase*

*Yen yen shape*

Pilgrim flask

Wine jar

Funerary urn

Libation cup, tripod legs

Water coup

Rouleau vase

Double gourd vase

Cylindrical brush pot

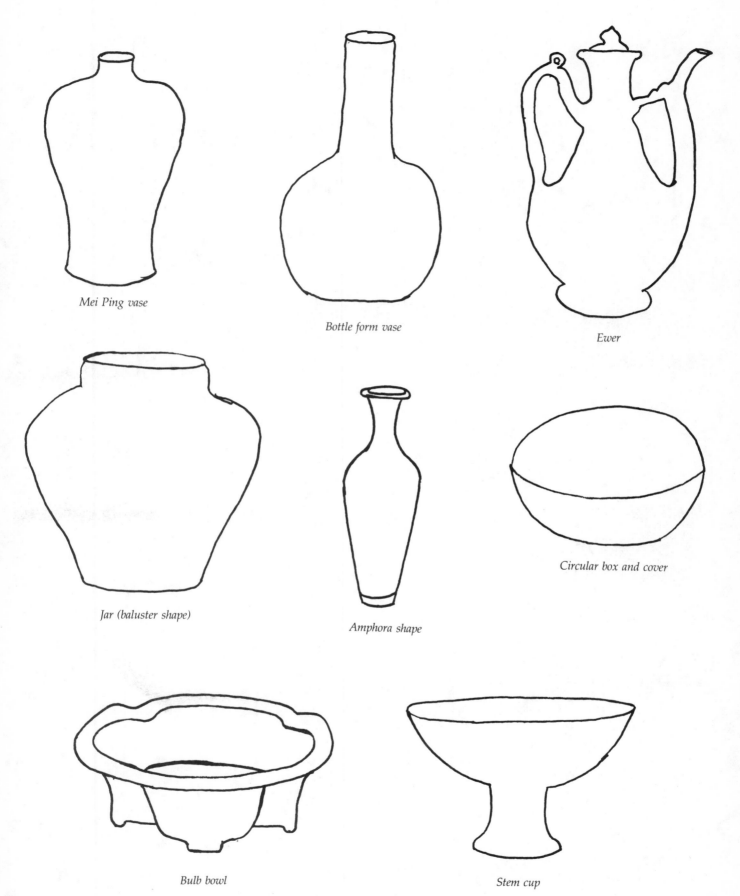

Mei Ping vase

Bottle form vase

Ewer

Jar (baluster shape)

Amphora shape

Circular box and cover

Bulb bowl

Stem cup

# Chinese Motifs

Lotus and scroll

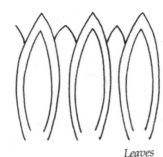

Leaves

Meander (Key)

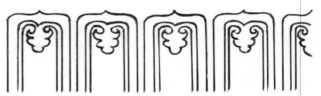

Modified coin

Waves

Plantain leaves

Waves

Triangle work

Fleur de lis

Waves

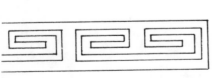

Greek key

Cord

Silkworm

Jui-i heads

Coins

Recumbent silkworm

Petals

Curl work

258

# Chronological Table of Dynasties

| | |
|---|---|
| Patriarchal Period | 3000-2205 B.C. |
| Hsia Dynasty | 2205-1766 B.C. |
| Shang and Yin Dynasty | 1766-1122 B.C. |
|   Shang era | 1766-1301 B.C. |
|   Yin era | 1301-1123 B.C. |
| Chou Dynasty | 1122- 256 B.C. |
|   Yin-Chou era | 1122-1028 B.C. |
|   Western Chou era | 1027- 771 B.C. |
|   Middle Chou era | 950- 600 B.C. |
|   Eastern Chou era | 600- 249 B.C. |
|   Spring and Autumn Annals (Ch'un Ch'iu) | 770- 481 B.C. |
|   Warring States (Chan Kuo) | 480- 256 B.C. |
| Ch'in Dynasty | 255- 206 B.C. |
| Han Dynasty | B.C. 206- 220 A.D. |
| Three States or San Tai | 220- 280 A.D. |
|   Wei kingdom | 220- 280 A.D. |
|   Shu Han or Minor Han kingdom | 221- 265 A.D. |
|   Wu kingdom | 220- 280 A.D. |
| Six Dynasties or Liu Ch'ao | 265- 589 A.D. |
|   Western Tsin | 265- 317 A.D. |
|   Eastern Tsin | 317- 420 A.D. |
|   Sung (House of Liu) | 420- 479 A.D. |
|   Ch'i | 479- 502 A.D. |
|   Liang    } Southern | 502- 557 A.D. |
|   Ch'en | 557- 589 A.D. |
|   Northern or First Wei | 386- 535 A.D. |
|   Western Wei | 535- 557 A.D. |
|   Eastern Wei    } Northern | 534- 550 A.D. |
|   Northern Ch'i | 550- 589 A.D. |
|   Northern Chou | 557- 589 A.D. |
| Sui Dynasty | 589- 618 A.D. |
| T'ang Dynasty | 618- 907 A.D. |
| Five Dynasties or Wu Tai | 907- 960 A.D. |
|   Hou (Posterior) Liang | 907- 923 A.D. |
| Hou (Posterior) T'ang | 923- 936 A.D. |
| Hou (Posterior) Tsin | 936- 947 A.D. |
| Hou (Posterior) Han | 947- 951 A.D. |
| Hou (Posterior) Chou | 951- 960 A.D. |
| Sung Dynasty | 960-1279 A.D. |
|   Northern Sung | 960-1127 A.D. |
|   Southern Sung | 1127-1279 A.D. |
| Yuan Dynasty | 1280-1367 A.D. |
| Ming Dynasty | 1368-1643 A.D. |
|   Hung-wu period | 1368-1398 A.D. |
|   Chien-wên period | 1399-1402 A.D. |
|   Yung-lo period | 1403-1424 A.D. |
|   Hung-hsi period | 1425-1426 A.D. |
|   Hsüan-tê period | 1426-1435 A.D. |
|   Chêng-t'ung period | 1436-1449 A.D. |
|   Ching-t'ai period | 1450-1456 A.D. |
|   T'ien-shun period | 1457-1464 A.D. |
|   Ch'êng-hua period | 1465-1487 A.D. |
|   Hung-chih period | 1488-1505 A.D. |
|   Chêng-tê period | 1506-1521 A.D. |
|   Chia-ching period | 1522-1566 A.D. |
|   Lung-ch'ing period | 1567-1572 A.D. |
|   Wan-li period | 1573-1619 A.D. |
|   T'ai-ch'ang period | 1620-1621 A.D. |
|   T'ien-ch'i period | 1621-1627 A.D. |
|   Ch'ung-chêng period | 1628-1643 A.D. |
| Ch'ing Dynasty | 1644-1912 A.D. |
|   Shun-Chih period | 1644-1661 A.D. |
|   K'ang Hsi period | 1662-1722 A.D. |
|   Yung Chêng period | 1723-1735 A.D. |
|   Ch'ien Lung period | 1736-1795 A.D. |
|   Chia-Ch'ing period | 1796-1820 A.D. |
|   Tao-Kuang period | 1821-1850 A.D. |
|   Hsien-fêng period | 1851-1861 A.D. |
|   T'ung-Chih period | 1862-1874 A.D. |
|   Kuang Hsü period | 1875-1908 A.D. |
|   Hsüang-t'ung period | 1909-1912 A.D. |
| Republic | 1912- |

# The Pinyin System

(Reprinted from *The Orientalia Journal*)

For the last twenty years the Pinyin system (Pinyin meaning transcription) has been used in China as a teaching aid in the study of Chinese characters. From the early part of 1979 the new official Chinese system has been used in press releases and publications which have been intended for foreigners. This in effect standardizes the romanization of Chinese names in English, Spanish, German, and other languages. The new Pinyin system, in many instances, comes closer to indicating the sound of Chinese in the Roman alphabet (based on standard Mandarin as used in Peking). Chinese names are difficult to render since the Chinese language uses characters to express meanings but such do not indicate sound. Until this time the West has used the standard Wade-Giles system, a concept developed by two Englishmen during the 19th century. The U.S. State Department and the United Nations have adopted Pinyin. In the field of antiques, the Pinyin system has been adopted by the major auction houses. The majority of reference materials used by the collecting community does not reflect Pinyin. Therefore, the following is provided as a reference tool.

**Pronunciation**

| *Initials* | *Finals* |
|---|---|
| b = p | an = en |
| p = p′ | e = o |
| d = t | i = ih |
| t = t′ | i = u (si = ssu) |
| g = k | ie = ieh |
| k = k′ | ong = ung |
| zh = ch | ue = ueh |
| j = ch | ui = uei |
| ch = ch′ | uo = o |
| c = ts′, tz′ | yi = i |
| r = j | you = yu |
| x = hs | |

**Terms**

| | |
|---|---|
| Baxian (Pa Hsien) | the Eight Immortals |
| Bailu (Po lu) | 100 deer motif |
| bagua (pa kua) | Eight triagrams |
| Budai (Pu Tai) | Mattrya (happy Buddha) |
| chilong (ch'ih lung) | lizard/dragon |
| Dehua (Te Hua) | kiln site |
| feicui (Fei ts'ui) | jadite |
| Guangdong (Kuang tung) | Canton |
| Guanyin (Kuan Yin) | God/Goddess of Mercy |
| Jingdezhen (Ching-te-Chen) | kiln site |
| Jingtailan (Ching-t'ai lan) | cloisonné |
| Lehan (Lohan) | disciples of Buddha |
| leiwen (lei wen) | thunder pattern |
| nianhoa (nien hao) | year designation |

Laozi (Lao Tzu)                      legendary founder of Daoism (Taoism)
long (lung)                          dragon
qilin (Ch'i-lin)                     kylin
ruyi (ju-i)                          scepter
sancai (san ts'ai)                   three-color ware
wucai (wu ts'ai)                     five-color ware
shizi (shih tzu)                     lion
wufu (wu fu)                         five bats

## Dynasties and Reigns

Shang                                Six Dynasties
Western Zhou (Western Chou)          Sui
Eastern Zhou (Eastern Chou)          Tang (T'ang)
Warring States                       Five Dynasties
Qin (Ch'in)                          Liao
Western Han                          Song (Sung)
Zin (Hsin)                           Jin (Chin)
Eastern Han                          Yuan (Yuan)

### Ming

Hongwu (Hung Wu)                     Hongzhi (Hung Chih)
Jianwen (Chien Wen)                  Zhengde (Cheng Te)
Yongle (Yung Lo)                     Jiajing (Chia Ching)
Xuande (Hsuan Te)                    Longquing (Lung Ch'ing)
Zhengtong (Cheng T'ung)              Wanli (Wan Li)
Jingtai (Ching T'ai)                 Taichang (T'ai Ch'ang)
Tianshun (T'ien Shun)                Tainqi (T'ien Ch'i)
Chenghua (Ch'eng Hua)                Chongzheng (Ch'ung Cheng)

### Qing (Ch'ing)

Shunzhi (Shun Chih)                  Daoguang (Tao Kuang)
Kangxi (K'ang Hsi)                   Xianfeng (Hsien Feng)
Yongzheng (Yung Cheng)               Tongzhi (T'ung Chih)
Qianlong (Ch'ien Lung)               Guangxu (Kuang Hsu)
Jiaqing (Chia Ch'ing)                Xuantong (Hsuan T'ung)
Hongxian (Hung Hsien)

# Reign and Period Marks

Chinese reign and period marks are generally written in six characters. They are read from top to bottom and from left to right. The first and second characters name the dynasty. The fifth and sixth characters translate, "period of manufacture." The third and fourth characters give the name of the reign or period. It is important to remember that marks of an earlier period can be found on wares of a later period. The use of an earlier mark on a piece of a later period (pottery and porcelain) was not intended as a forgery by the Chinese, but rather as a commemoration of an earlier period or reign. It is also important to remember that Chinese period and reign marks can be found on Japanese wares.

Note: Chinese reign and period marks can be found on Chinese cloisonné from the Ching T'ai period of the Ming Dynasty on page 265.

# Ming Dynasty

洪武年製

Hung Wu

Hung Wu (seal form)

永樂年製

Yung Lo

Yung Lo (archaic form)

大明宣德年製

Hsuan Te

Hsuan Te (seal form)

大明成化年製

Ch'eng Hua

Ch'eng Hua (seal form)

大明弘治年製

Hung Chih

大明正德年製

Ch'eng Te

大明嘉靖年製

Chia Ching

大明隆慶年製

Lung Ch'ing

大明萬曆年製

Wan Li

Wan Li (archaic form)

大明天啟年製

T'ien Ch'i

崇禎年製

Ch'ung Chen

## Ch'ing Dynasty

大清順治年製

*Shun Chih*

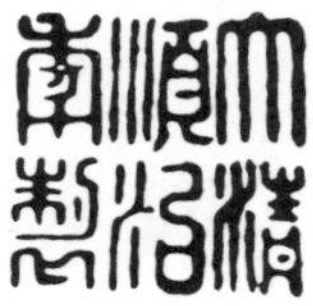

*Shun Chih (seal form)*

大清康熙年製

*K'ang Hsi*

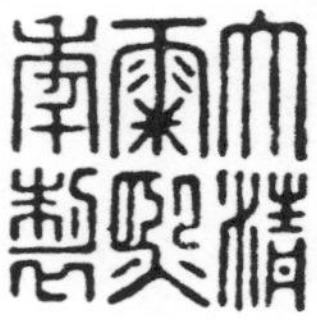

*K'ang Hsi (seal form)*

大清雍正年製

*Yung Cheng*

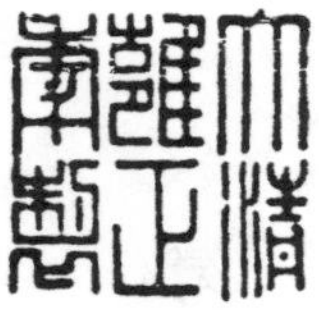

*Yung Cheng (seal form)*

大清乾隆年製

*Ch'ien Lung*

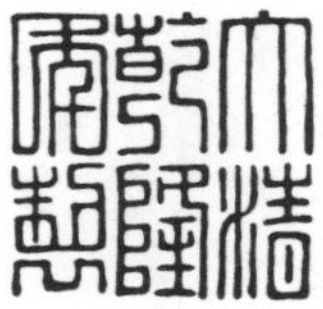

*Ch'ien Lung (seal form)*

嘉慶年製

*Chia Ch'ing*

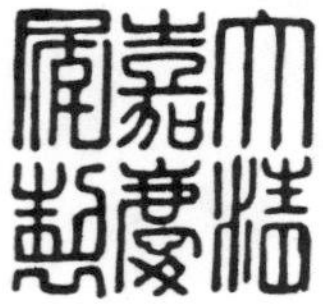

*Chia Ch'ing (seal form)*

大清道光年製

*Tao Kuang*

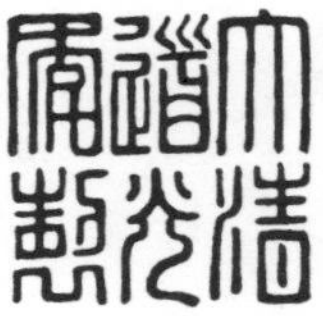

*Tao Kuang (seal form)*

大清咸豐年製

*Hsien Feng*

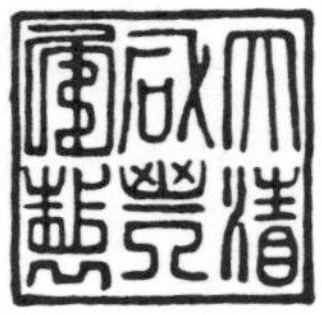

*Hsien Feng (seal form)*

大清同治年製

*T'ung Chih*

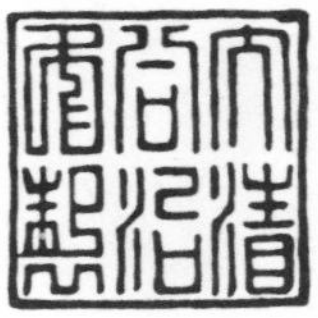

*T'ung Chih (seal form)*

大清光緒年製

*Kuang Hsu*

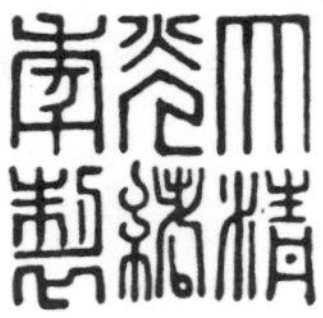

*Kuang Hsu (seal form)*

大清宣統年製

*Hsuan T'ung*

洪憲年製

*Hsuan T'ung*

# Chinese Symbols

*Artemisia leaf*

*Conch shell*

*Tripod vase*

*Lotus flower*

*Lotus flower*

*Lotus flower*

*Pair of fishes*

*Knot*

*Tripod vase*

*Tripod vase*

*Flower*

*Flower*

*Swastika*

*Knot*

*Sacred ax*

*Fungus*

*Fungus*

*Ju-i head*

*Fly*

*Gourd*

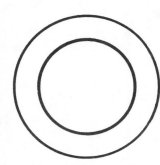

*Double concentric circles*

*Peaches and bat*

*Stork*

*Rabbit*

*Hare of the moon*

*Flute*

*Lotus*

*Flower basket*

*Bamboo tube*

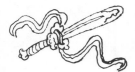

*Sword*

*Castanets*

*Fan*

*Gourd*

# Chinese Hallmarks

堂

*A hall*

軒

*A terrace*

居

*A retreat*

堂製 紫刺

*Made at the hall of the
purple thorn*

堂製 奇玉

*Made at the hall of rare jade*

*Spring in heaven and on earth
(on wares used by the Dowager
Empress)*

堂製 天昌

*Made at the hall of prosperity*

堂製 永樂

*Made at the hall of
perpetual enjoyment*

堂製 彩華

*Made at the hall of
brilliant painting*

佳器 玉堂

*Beautiful vessel of the jade hall*

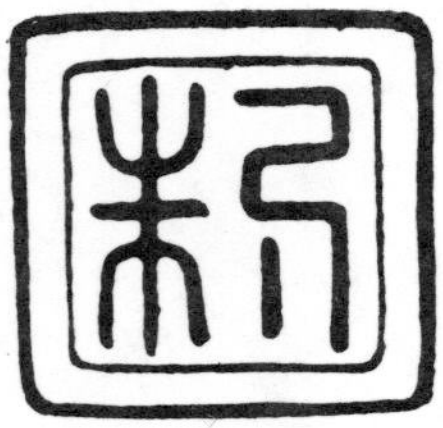

*Made to Imperial order*

堂製 彩秀

*Made at the hall of
brilliant decoration*

堂製 彩潤

*Made at the hall of
brilliant colors*

堂製 德馨

*Made for the hall of
fragrant virtue*

菉漪堂

*Hall of bamboo*

堂製 玉海

*Made at the hall of
ocean jade*

堂製 慎德

*Antique made for the hall for
cultivation of virtue*

堂製 大樹

*Made at the big tree hall*

堂製 林玉

*Made at the hall of
abundant jade*

倣古製 景濂堂

*Imitation of antiques made at the
Ching lien hall*

草堂 斯干

*Straw pavilion on the river bank*

奉先堂

*Hall for the worship of ancestors*

# Chinese Marks of Commendation

*Longevity*

*Longevity*

*Longevity*

*Spider*

*Emolument*

*Emolument*

*Long life, riches, and honor*

*Happiness and long life*

*Riches, honor, and enduring spring*

慶

*Congratulations*

珍

*A pearl*

玩

*Precious trinket*

玩

*Elegant trinket*

聖

*Imperial*

全

*Complete*

古

*Antique*

順

*Harmony*

天

*Heaven*

器用

*Vessel for use in the house*

*Vessel for public use in the generals' hall*

□

*Made to order*

囍

*Double joy*

玉

*Jade*

# Chinese Potters' Marks and Place Marks

*Yi Hsing (I Hsing) place mark*

*Mr. Wang (potter's mark)*

*Made by Wang Pu t'ing*

*Made by Chiang Ming kao*

*Made by Lin Ch'ang fa*

*Made by Ko Ming Hsiang*

*Made by Ko Yuan-hsiang*

*Li Ta-lai*
*(maker's name)*

*Yueh-ch'ang*
*(maker's name)*

*Yi Hsing (I Hsing)*
*place mark*

*Chin Yuan yu*
*(Yi Hsing ware)*

*Ch'en Ming-yuan*
*(Yi Hsing ware)*

*Hsiu Lung-te*
*(Yi Hsing ware)*

*Maker's mark, Yi Hsing ware*

*Lai Kuan*
*(potter's mark)*

*Ho Ch'ao-tsung*
*(potter's mark)*

*Made by Liang-chi*

# Chinese Cloisonné Marks

*Copy of Ming*

*Lao T'ien Li*

*Ta Ku Tsai*

*Yang T'ien Li*

# Marks and Identification, Japanese

## Contours

*Vase*      *Bottle*      *Square vase*      *Covered vase (potiche)*      *Ginger jar*

*Teapot (the larger variation
of this teapot is used to heat
the water and the smaller variation
is used for pouring the tea)*

*Double gourd bottle*

*Rounded three-tiered box
(three-tiered boxes are used
for New Year's; they are
storage boxes for snacks)*

*Tea jar (the tea jar is shaped much like
a ginger jar but has an inner lid and is
usually not more than 3½"h.)*

*Flowerpot*

*Water pot*

(Reprinted from "East Meets West," *Antique Trader Weekly*)

Rice bowl
(rice bowl lids
sit inside the bowl)

Tea bowl (used for sipping tea)

Square three-tiered box

Ewer/wine pot

Incense burner (Koro)

Food bowl
(stemmed food bowl lids
rest on the rims of the bowls)

Brush pot

Brush holder

Incense case (Kogo)

Oil jar

Tea bowl

Vase

Shoe-shaped tea bowl (Chawan)

Mei p'ing
(this vase is used
for holding one flower)

Incense case (Kogo)

Mallet-shaped vase

Melon-shaped ewer

Square saki bottle

Pear-shaped vase

Water jar
(Mizusashi — used for
holding fresh water)

Pillow or head rest

Fan-shaped cake plate

Footed wine cup

Beaker

Garden seat

# Japanese Motifs

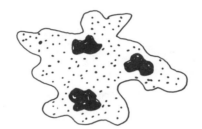

Seikainami (blue sea waves)
or Seigaiha (stylized waves)

Kumo (clouds)

Kumo (clouds)

Saya gata (a fret pattern also
termed Mani tsunagi/
Buddhist cross)

Mie dasuki (tasuki)
(triple design of crossed
swords)

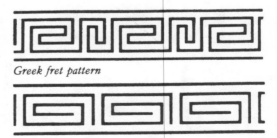

Greek fret pattern

Shippo bishi (cloisonne in a
diamond pattern)

Shippo (seven precious things,
cloisonne)

Disconnected oblong fret pattern

*Asa no ha (a leaf of hemp)*

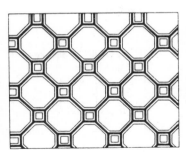
*Tortoiseshell grids (kame)*

*Rai (lightning)*

*Uroko gata (fish scales)*

*Shippo tsunagi (joined circles)*

*Komon (fine, small, repetitive patterns)*

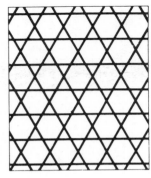
*Kogome (woven basket pattern or basket pattern)*

*Floral lozenges*

*Yotsu bishi (quadruple lozenges or Nanbu)*

*Higaki (cedar bark shingles or braided fence)*

*Peony scroll*

*Karakusa (arabesque)*

*Gentian and foliage medallion*

*Chrysanthemum medallion*

**Wave medallion**

*Tomoe (comma mon)*

*Crane medallion*

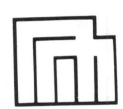
*Genji-ko*

*Wisteria medallion*

*Aisu (swastika)*

# Provinces and Prefectures

The following list gives the names of the pre-Meiji provinces (prior to 1868) and the names of the modern Japanese prefectures.

| Pre-Meiji Provinces | Modern Prefectures | Pre-Meiji Provinces | Modern Prefectures |
|---|---|---|---|
| Hiroshima | Aki | Kagoshima | Satsuma |
| Chiba | Awa (Honshu) | Hyogo, Osaka | Settsu |
| Tokushima | Awa (Shikoku) | Mie | Shima |
| Osaka | Awaji | Chiba, Ibaraki | Shimosa |
| Hiroshima | Bingo | Tochigi | Shimotsuke |
| Okayama | Bitchu | Nagano | Shinano |
| Okayama | Bizen | Yamaguchi | Suo |
| Oita | Bungo | Shizuoka | Suruga |
| Fukuoka, Oita | Buzen | Hyogo | Tajima |
| Fukuoka | Chikugo | Hyogo, Kyoto | Tamba |
| Fukuoka | Chikuzen | Kyoto | Tango |
| Niigata | Echigo | Kochi | Tosa |
| Toyama | Eichu | Shizuoka | Totomi |
| Hyogo | Harima | Nagasaki | Tsushima |
| Gifu | Hida | Akita | Ugo |
| Kumamoto | Higo | Yamagata | Uzen |
| Ibaraki | Hitachi | Fukui | Wakasa |
| Nagasaki, Saga | Hizen | Kyoto | Yamashiro |
| Tottori | Hoki | Nara | Yamato |
| Miyazaki | Hyuga | | |
| Mie | Iga | | |
| Nagasaki | Iki | | |
| Tottori | Inaba | | |
| Mie | Ise | | |
| Fukushima, Miyagi | Iwaki | | |
| Shimane | Iwami | | |
| Fukushima | Iwashiro | | |
| Ehime | Iyo | | |
| Shizuoka | Izu | | |
| Osaka | Izumi | | |
| Shimane | Izumo | | |
| Ishikawa | Kaga | | |
| Yamanashi | Kai | | |
| Osaka | Kawachi | | |
| Chiba | Kazusa | | |
| Mie, Wakayama | Kii | | |
| Gumma | Kozuke | | |
| Aichi | Mikawa | | |
| Okayama | Mimasaka | | |
| Gifu | Mino | | |
| Kanagawa, Saitama, Tokyo | Musashi | | |
| Yamaguchi | Nagato | | |
| Ishikawa | Noto | | |
| Shimane | Oki | | |
| Shiga | Omi | | |
| Kagoshima | Osumi | | |
| Aichi | Owari | | |
| Iwate | Rikuchu | | |
| Iwate, Miyagi | Rikuzen | | |
| Niigata | Sado | | |
| Kanagawa | Sagami | | |
| Kagawa | Sanuki | | |

# Year Periods (Nengo)

| Characters | Name of period | Commenced A.D. | Characters | Name of period | Commenced A.D. |
|---|---|---|---|---|---|
| 永 應 | O-ei | 1394 | 明 文 | Bunmei | 1469 |
| 長 正 | Shocho | 1428 | 享 長 | Choko | 1487 |
| 享 永 | Eikio | 1429 | 德 延 | Entoku | 1489 |
| 吉 嘉 | Kakitsu | 1441 | 應 明 | Meio | 1492 |
| 安 文 | Bun-an | 1444 | 亀 文 | Bunki | 1501 |
| 德 宝 | Hotoku | 1449 | 正 永 | Eisho | 1504 |
| 德 享 | Kotoku | 1452 | 永 大 | Daiei | 1521 |
| 正 康 | Kosho | 1455 | 禄 享 | Koroku | 1528 |
| 禄 長 | Choroku | 1457 | 文 天 | Tembun | 1532 |
| 正 寛 | Kwansho | 1460 | 治 弘 | Koji | 1555 |
| 正 文 | Bunsho | 1466 | 禄 永 | Eirko | 1558 |
| 仁 應 | Onin | 1467 | 亀 元 | Genki | 1570 |

| Characters | Name of period | Commenced A.D. | Characters | Name of period | Commenced A.D. |
|---|---|---|---|---|---|
| 正 天 | Tensho | 1573 | 和 天 | Tenna | 1681 |
| 禄 文 | Bunroku | 1592 | 享 貞 | Jokio | 1684 |
| 長 慶 | Keicho | 1596 | 禄 元 | Genroku | 1688 |
| 和 元 | Genna | 1615 | 永 宝 | Hoei | 1704 |
| 永 寛 | Kwanei | 1624 | 徳 正 | Shotoku | 1711 |
| 保 正 | Shoho | 1644 | 保 享 | Kioho | 1716 |
| 安 慶 | Keian | 1648 | 文 元 | Gembun | 1736 |
| 應 承 | Jo-o | 1652 | 保 寛 | Kwanpo | 1741 |
| 暦 明 | Meireki | 1655 | 享 延 | Enkio | 1744 |
| 治 萬 | Manji | 1658 | 延 寛 | Kwanen | 1748 |
| 文 寛 | Kwambun | 1661 | 暦 宝 | Horeki | 1751 |
| 宝 延 | Empo | 1673 | 和 明 | Meiwa | 1764 |

| Characters | Name of period | Commenced A.D. | Characters | Name of period | Commenced A.D. |
|---|---|---|---|---|---|
| 永安 | Anei | 1772 | 政安 | Ansei | 1854 |
| 明天 | Temmei | 1781 | 延萬 | Manen | 1860 |
| 政寬 | Kwansei | 1789 | 久文 | Bunkiu | 1861 |
| 和享 | Kiowa | 1801 | 治元 | Genji | 1864 |
| 化文 | Bunkwa | 1804 | 應慶 | Keio | 1865 |
| 政文 | Bunsei | 1818 | 治明 | Meiji | 1868 |
| 保天 | Tempo | 1830 | 大正 | Taisho | 1912 |
| 化弘 | Kokwa | 1844 | 昭和 | Showa | 1926 to the present |
| 永嘉 | Kaei | 1848 | | | |

277

# Family Crests (Mon)

Japanese family crests (mon) were originally used on wares made for specific families. After 1868, crests were used on export wares as well. If the family crest appears on an object or forms part of the overall design, it is considered to be an object of high quality.

KIKU — A sixteen-petaled chrysanthemum. The imperial crest of the Emperor.

KIRI — Also called the Paulownia Blossom. The imperial crest of the Empress.

The three leaf crest of the ruling family (Tokugawa) maru mitsu aoi.

Crest of the Viceroy of Kyushu (Satsuma). On early wares it appears in gosu blue.

Crest of the Prince of Kaga.

Another crest of the Prince of Kaga.

Crest of the Prince of Shendi.

Crest of the Daimyo-Harima.*

Crest of the Daimyo-Satake.

Crest of the Daimyo-Bizen.

Crest of the Prince of Hizen.

Crest of the Prince of Hikone (office of the regent, who upon occasion, ruled Japan and took over the imperial throne).

Crest of the Prince of Soma.

Crest of the House of Soma.

Crest of the Kusunoki family.

*A daimyo was a feudal landholder. After the start of the Meiji period, 1868, the feudal lords lost their privileges and the Tokugawa (imperial family) was overthrown.

# Japanese Pottery and Porcelain Marks

## Awaji (Osaka Prefecture) and Yamato (Nara Prefecture)

*Kiyen factory*

*Akahada/Kishiro maker*

*Akahada*

*Sanpei Gashu maker*

*Kashiu Mimpei maker*

*Kashiu Sampei maker*

## Bizen (Okayama Prefecture)

*Cho maker*

*Eizan maker*

*Kichi maker*

*Maker's mark*

*Yoskiage*

## Hizen (Saga, Nagasaki Prefectures)

*Good Fortune/Long Life*

*Good Fortune*

*Good Fortune*

*Hibarabayashi maker*

*Zoshuntei maker*

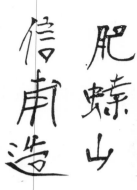

*Mori Chikara, Mikawachi
(maker and place)*

*Fukagawa maker*

*Fukagawa maker*

*Hichozan Shimpo maker*

*Hirado*

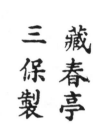

*Yamaka maker*

*Shimodo maker*

*Found on Hirado wares*

*Mikawaji*

*Zoshuntei maker*

*Happiness*

## Ise (Mie Prefecture)

*Banko
(impressed mark)*

*Banko
(impressed mark)*

*Yusetsu maker (Banko)*

*Fuyeki maker (Banko)*

*Banko  (impressed marks)*

*Banko — Tekizan maker*

*Ganto — Sanzin maker*

*Fuyeki maker*

*The Yofu factory*

*Banko ware*

## Kutani and Kaga marks (Ishikawa Prefecture)

*Kutani (place name)*

*Kutani (place name)*

*Kutani (place name)*

*Kutani (place name)*

*Kiokuzan maker*

*Yuzan maker*

*Kutani/Kayo (place name)*

*Kochoken maker*

*Tozan maker*

*Iwazo maker*

## Owari (Aichi Prefecture)

*Kawamoto Masukichi maker/Seto Japan*

*Kawamoto Hansuke maker*

*Rokubeye maker*

*Iwata, Aichi, Japan*

*Nagoya (place mark)*

*Toyosuke maker*

*Eizan maker*

*Owari (place mark)*

*Kawamoto Masukichi maker*

*Hokuhan maker*

281

## Satsuma (Kagoshima Prefecture)

 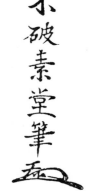    

Gyokuzan maker    Fuwa Sodo maker    Ide maker    Kai maker    Nakajima maker    Satsuma place mark

Satsuma place mark    Hoju maker    Hohei maker    Hoyei maker    Koko maker    Siekozan maker

## Tokyo, Yokahama, and Ota

      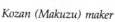

Kinko factory maker    Hiocheyen Tokyo maker    Gosaburo maker    Gozan maker    Tsuji/Tokyo Japan (maker and place mark)    Kozan (Makuzu) maker

Denka maker    Myakawa Kozan maker    Makuzu Kozan maker    Meizan maker    Kenya maker    Ryozan maker

282

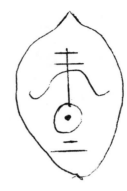

Kinsho Company Tokyo
(maker and place mark)

Inoue Ryosai

Inoue Ryosai

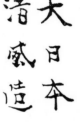

Inoue Ryosai

## Yamashiro (Kyoto Prefecture)

Kitei maker

Zoroku maker

Hichibeye maker

Sahei maker

Seifu maker

Raku

Eiraku maker

Eiraku maker

Kanzan Denshichi
maker

Makuzu Kozan
maker

Shuzan maker

Kinunken maker

Taizan maker

Taizan maker

Tanzan maker

Bizan maker

Seikozan maker

283

Shuhei maker

Kanzan maker

Hozan maker

Awata (place mark)

Ryozan

Kinkozan

Kinkozan

Dohachi

Kenzan

Ninsei

Dai Nippon
Great Japan

*Readers' note:*

When a mark is preceded by the characters Dai (Nihon), Nippon, it indicates that the mark was used after 1868.

# Japanese Cloisonné Marks

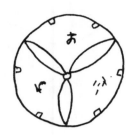

*Adachi*

*Ando*

*Gonda Hirosuke*

*Goto*

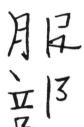

*Hattori Kodenji*

*Hayashi Kodenji*

*Hirata*

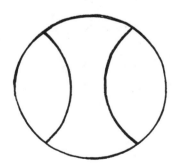

*Inaba Company*

*Inaba Nanaho*

Kata Oka

Kawade Shibataro

Kai Yo Company

Kawaguchi

Kumeno Teitaro

Miwa Tomisaburo

Namikawa Sosuke

大吉

Ota Kichisaburo

286

Namikawa Yasuyuki

Ota Tamesiro

Takahara Komajiro

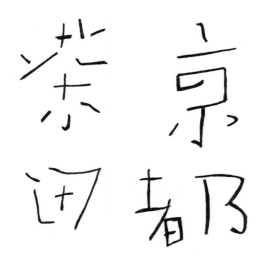

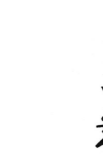

Shibata

Tamura

Yasuda

## Eight Precious Things

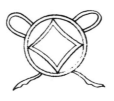

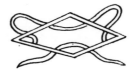

Two Books

Coin

Lozenge (also known as picture)

Dragon Pearl

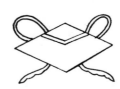

Chimes

Artemisia Leaf

Mirror (also known as open lozenge)

Rhinoceros Horns

Eight Precious Things (reprinted from "East Meets West," *Antique Trader Weekly*)

# Wood Block Print Artists' Signatures (Ukiyo-e)

Ashihiro

Banri

Eisen

Enshi

Harunobu

Hisanobu

Hokushu

Ashikiyo

Buncho

Eizan

Fusatane

Harushige

Hokkei

Hokutsui

Ashikuni

Bunro

Eishi

Gakutei

Haruji

Hokuba

Hokuei

Ashimaro

Choki

Eisho

Gokyo

Hidemaro

Hokuga

Keisai (Eisen)

Ashiyuki

Eiju

Eisui

Goshichi

Hirokage

Hoku-I

Kikumaru

Banki

Eiri

Hiroshige

Hokuju

Banki II

Eiri
(Rekisentei)

Enkyo

Hanzan

Hiroshige

Hokusai

Kiyohiro

288

清政
Kiyomasa

清倍
Kiyomasu

清峯
Kiyomine

清満
Kiyomitsu

清長
Kiyonaga

清信
Kiyonobu

清重
Kiyoshige

清忠
Kiyotada

湖龍齋
Koryusai

清經
Kiyotsune

國明
Kuniaki

國周
Kunichika

國春
Kuniharu

國房
Kunihiko

國久
Kunihisa

國員
Kunikazu

國九
Kunimaru

國政
Kunimasa

國藩
Kunimitsu

國盛
Kunimori

國長
Kuninaga

國直
Kuninao

國貞
Kunisada

國輝
Kuniteru

國富
Kunitomi

國綱
Kunitsuna

國安
Kuniyasu

國芳
Kuniyoshi

懷月堂
Kaigetsu
(Kaigetsudo)

暁斎
Kyosai

万月堂
Mangetsudo

奥村政信
Okumura
Masanobu

北尾政演
Kitao
Masanobu

政美
Masayoshi

益信
Masunobu

師宣
Moronobu

師房
Morofusa

柳谷
Ryukoku

龍雲齋
Ryu-unsai

貞房
Sadafusa

貞秀
Sadahide

貞馨
Sadahiro

貞景
Sadakage

貞信
Sadanobu

石樽
Sekiho

石上
Sekijo

泉竜
Sencho

寫樂
Sharaku

重春
Shigeharu

289

Shigemasa

Shinsai

Shunro
(later Hokusai)

Sori (Hokusai)

Toyoharu

Toyomasa

Yoshikazu

Shigenaga

Shucho

Shunsen
(Katsukawa)

Sugakudo

Toyohide

Toyonobu

Yoshikuni

Shigenobu

Shuncho

Shunsen
(Kashosai)

Sukenobu

Toyohiro

Toyoshige

Yoshimaru

Shigenobu
(Yanagawa)

Shundo

Shunsho

Taito
(Hokusai)

Toyohisa

Tsukimaro

Yoshinobu

Shigenobu
(Hiroshige II)

Shunjo

Shuntei

Terushige

Toyokuni
(also used by
Toyokuni II
(Toyoshige)
and
Toyokuni III
(Kunisada) )

Utamaro

Yoshitora

Shikimaro

Shunko

Shunei

Tominobu

Yoshichika

Shiko

Shunkyo

Shunzan

Toshinobu

Toyomaru

Yoshiharu

Shunman

Yoshitoshi

# Japanese Marks — Wood Carvings, Ivory, Lacquer, Netsuke, Metalwares, and Tsuba

Key:
N — Netsuke
I — Ivory
L — Lacquer
M — Metalwares
T — Tsuba
W — Wood Carvings

Mitsunao maker/copy of work by Tohaku Ideme (W)

Shigeyasu (N)

Mitsuhisa Ideme (W)

Ideme (N)

Tenka ichi/Magimitsu
Ideme maker (N)

Jobun maker (N)

Do maker (W)

Kou maker (W)

Shojusai (I)

Seigioku Ideme maker (I)

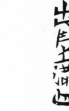

Uyemtsu Ideme (N)

Kiusaku maker (W)

Homin maker (N)

Masakuzu Ichishido maker (I)

Yuzan maker (W)

Setsusai maker (W)

Tanianaga maker (I)

Mitsuhisa maker (N)

Gyokuju maker (N & I)

Kominsai maker (N)

Hozan maker (N)

Masanobu maker (N)

291

Masahiro maker (N)

Hisanaga maker (N)

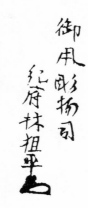

Hayashi Sohei maker (I)

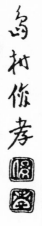

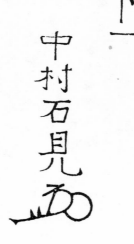

Nakamura Iwami maker (L)

Shimamura family (I)

Sakurai (W & I)

Toshitaka maker (W & I)

Ryuho maker (W & I)

Ryoen (I)

Masatami maker (I)

Rinko maker (I)

Shijui maker (I)

Harumasa maker (L)

Yuhisai (L)

Shokasai Gyokuzan maker (L)

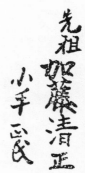

Kato Kyomasa maker (M)

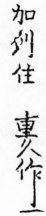

Matsuhita maker (T & M)

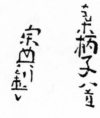

Mogarashi maker (M)

Nagaharu maker (M & T)

Shigehisa maker (T & M)

Okada Zenzayemon maker (T & M)

Komai of Kyoto maker (M)

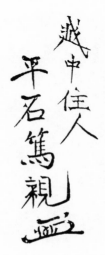

Hiraishi Atsuchika maker (M)

Fujiwara Mitsunaga maker (M)

Fujiwara Mitsushige maker (M)

Torajiro Murakami (M)

293

# Nippon Era Marks

M in Wreath (magenta, blue, green, or gold)

Maple Leaf (blue or green)

RC Nippon (green or red)

RC Noritake (green)

NORITAKE
NIPPON

Noritake Nippon (green or blue)

Double Phoenix and T (turquoise)

CHINA
E-OH
HAND PAINTED
NIPPON

E-OH (blue or green)

Transitional mark (red or blue)

HAND PAINTED

NIPPON

Torii mark (turquoise)

MADE IN
NIPPON

Made In Nippon (may be stamped or incised;
stamped marks have varied colors)

HAND PAINTED
NIPPON

Hand Painted Nippon
(may be stamped in various colors)

Tree crest

*TN in Wreath (a combination of red and green)*

*Rising Sun (blue)*

*Mt. Fuji (blue or red)*

*OAC*

*TS — Fan*

*Royal Nishiki*

*SK — Diamond*

*Royal Kaga — Plum Blossom*

*Paulownia Nippon (green or red)*

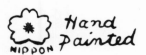

**Cherry Blossom**

**Shofu Nippon**

*Similar to Transitional mark*

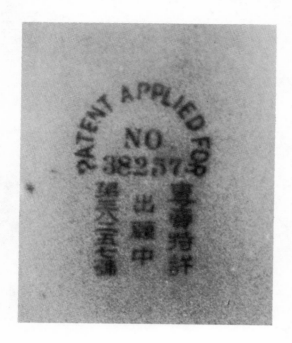

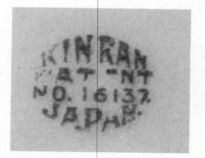

# Post-Nippon Era Marks

The marks with an asterisk* were carried over from the Nippon era.

*Meito*

*Double M*

*I. E. Co.*

*Crossed Flags\* (blue mark)*

*Noritake\**

*Noritake Tree Crest\**
*(light blue mark)*

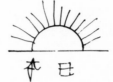

*T in Wreath*
*(black mark)*

*Rising Sun\**
*(this is an orange mark)*

*Kutani\**

*Kutani\**

*T A flower*

 KOSHIDA

*Koshida*

 SATSUMA JAPAN

*Satsuma*

*Sun & Circle*

*Princess China*

*Lefton*

*Torii\**

 JAPON

*Japon*
*(characters translate — Great Japan),*
*found on wares exported to France*

IRICE PRODUCTS

*Irice (an importer)*

NASCO

*NASCO*

FOREIGN

*FOREIGN*
*(found on wares exported to England)*

*Mt. Fuji\**

*I E O*

 R/B
 MADE IN JAPAN

*R/B*

*KOKURA*

*Paulownia in Circle*

*Paulownia*

OZEKI

OZEKI

MADE IN JAPAN
BY
TAJINI

TAJINI

*Fairyland China*

Importe de Japon

*Importe de Japon
(on wares exported to France)*

Gold Castle

O G

*Double T Diamond*

*T A in circle*

*Plum Blossom*

*A transition mark
used the first half of 1921*

*translation — JAPAN**

*translation — Great Japan**

JAPAN

*M in diamond*

MADE IN
JAPAN

*H in diamond*

*Shefford China*

*Crossed Arrows (over the glaze blue)*

AIZU
MADE IN JAPAN

*AIZU*

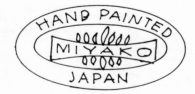

*MIYAKO*

*ACF in diamond*

*M in wreath*

# Index

299

# Meet the Authors

Sandra Andacht is the editor and publisher of "The Orientalia Journal." Her column, "East Meets West/Exploring Orientalia" is a regular feature of the *Antique Trader Weekly*. She has written numerous articles on various aspects of Orientalia for many other publications including: *Arts of Asia* Magazine, *Spinning Wheel* Magazine, *Maine Antiques Digest*, and The Oriental Art Society of Chicago *Newsletter* (an organization of which she is a member). Mrs. Andacht is also a member of Netsuke Kenkyuki, Vereniging voor Japanse Kunst (Society for Japanese Arts and Crafts), The International Chinese Snuff Bottle Society, et al. Mrs. Andacht is a lecturer specializing in various aspects of Orientalia. She is an appraiser and research consultant and is called upon in this capacity by the U.S. Customs Service among others. Sandra Andacht is the resident antiques expert for the Joe Franklin TV Show, Orientalist for the Hamilton Collection, the author of *Treasury of Satsuma* and *Satsuma: An Illustrated Guide*, and "The Orientalia Journal" column featured in numerous antiques publications, and is the editor and publisher of *The Orientalia Journal Annual of Articles Vol. I*. Residing in a suburb of New York City with her husband Carl and their two sons, Stuart and Jeffrey, Sandra has devoted many years to the researching and collecting of oriental objets d'art.

Considered by many to be a leading expert of the field of Oriental cloisonné, Mrs. Garthe traveled in many countries as an "Army brat" and lived in Germany for three years with her parents, Lt. Col. and Mrs. Charles L. Lane. Her early interest in antiques evolved into a specialization in cloisonné.

As her knowledge increased, she began to share with others. She has been invited to lecture in several states and has written for many publications such as *The Connoisseur*, The *Antique Trader Weekly*, *Hobbies Magazine*, *Spinning Wheel*, and *The Collector*. A longtime member of The Oriental Art Society of Chicago, she has served as its executive director since January 1978. A close friend of, and professional collaborator with Sandra Andacht, Mrs. Garthe is a consultant to Sandra's column in The *Antique Trader* Weekly, and is contributing editor to *The Orientalia Journal*, with a bi-monthly column, "Observations on Cloisonné." Mrs. Garthe is a Director of the International Society of Fine Arts Appraisers, Ltd., a member of the Cloisonné Collectors Club, and member of Vereniging voor Japanse Kunst (Society for Japanese Arts and Crafts). A dedicated researcher, Mrs. Garthe is frequently consulted by museum personnel, and during the course of research she and an associate translated a book and five pamphlets on cloisonné from the Japanese.

Residing with her family (husband Bill, a professor of biological sciences; sons Bill and Kevin; and their Belgian Tervuren dog, "Storm"), she gives them much credit for their patience, tolerance, and support in her many projects. Employed full-time as an Employee Relations Assistant, Mrs. Garthe is a multitalented woman, with a patent pending on a recent invention.

Robert Mascarelli and his wife Gloria are the proprietors of Accent East Gallery, 2942 Merrick Rd., Bellmore, N.Y. As both a collector and dealer, Mr. Mascarelli specializes in Chinese and Southeast Asian ceramics. He is a member of the Oriental Art Society of Chicago. Mr. Mascarelli has written numerous articles covering various aspects of Chinese pottery and porcelain. He is an appraiser, lecturer, and research consultant. Residing with his wife Gloria and their children in a suburb of New York City, Robert has spent many years pursuing his interests in oriental objets d'art.